ATLA
IN THE C

"Collins produces a tantalizing pattern of oral and written evidence that Atlantis not only existed but probably was destroyed by a comet some 13,000 years ago."

BOSTON HERALD

"Collins proves an engaging conductor of an exegetical tour of Plato's writings about a civilization in the Western Ocean that vanished when a natural catastrophe befell its homeland. His book [will] enamor imaginations sparked by the legend of lost Atlantis."

BOOKLIST

"A bold and imaginative attempt to understand the destruction of the legendary city of Atlantis, the creation of Mesoamerican civilization, and the end of the last Ice Age."

KIRKUS REVIEWS

Praise for Previous Works
by Andrew Collins

"*Göbekli Tepe: Genesis of the Gods* by Andrew Collins is a comprehensive interpretation of the oldest advanced temple complex on Earth. World-renowned for his explorations of the prehistoric Middle East, Collins weaves together archaeological, anthropological, astronomical, and spiritual aspects of Göbekli Tepe. This clear and correct interpretation of Göbekli Tepe offers even more! He draws our minds back 17,000 years to the Solutrean phase to describe human cultural development before the cultural regression. Göbekli Tepe awakens ancient memory to process deeply hidden trauma from the past because it is a faithful and accurate depiction of the Paleolithic advanced culture. A must-read for anybody who wants to know the real story before 'history' began."

BARBARA HAND CLOW,
AUTHOR OF *AWAKENING THE PLANETARY MIND:
BEYOND THE TRAUMA OF THE PAST TO A NEW ERA
OF CREATIVITY* [PREVIOUSLY RELEASED AS *CATASTROPHOBIA:
THE TRUTH BEHIND EARTH CHANGES*]

"Andrew Collins's *From the Ashes of Angels* is one of those books that comes along only once or twice a decade. Suddenly a whole new realm is opened up to us as we are invited on a hunt for our lost origins led by a voice that speaks clearly and forcefully. It is the kind of book that you can read and then read again and again and each time you will be rewarded. Andrew Collins is one of the key thinkers of a whole new generation of writers that have decided that the human past is much more interesting than we have all been led to believe."

RAND FLEM-ATH,
COAUTHOR OF *ATLANTIS BENEATH THE ICE*

"Keenly sensing the challenge of what remains to be learned, Collins does not visit old ruts. Time and time again, he reaches beyond the known and pushes the envelope of inquiry, as is seen in *Gods of Eden*. The perspectives he is developing can contribute crucially to our common task of direction-finding in the uncertain future."

JOHN LASH, ASTROLOGER, MYTHOLOGIST,
AND AUTHOR OF *QUEST FOR THE ZODIAC*

ATLANTIS
IN THE CARIBBEAN
and the Comet That Changed the World

Andrew Collins

Bear & Company
Rochester, Vermont • Toronto, Canada

Bear & Company
One Park Street
Rochester, Vermont 05767
www.BearandCompanyBooks.com

Bear & Company is a division of Inner Traditions International

Library of Congress Cataloging-in-Publication Data
Names: Collins, Andrew, 1957– author. | Collins, Andrew, 1957– author Gateway to Atlantis.
Title: Atlantis in the Caribbean : and the comet that changed the world / Andrew Collins.
Description: Rochester, Vermont : Bear & Company, [2016] | Originally published: Gateway to Atlantis. New York : Carroll & Graf Publishers, 2000. | Includes bibliographical references and index.
Identifiers: LCCN 2016005429 (print) | LCCN 2016030906 (e-book) | ISBN 9781591432654 (pbk.) | ISBN 9781591432661 (e-book)
Subjects: LCSH: Atlantis (Legendary place)
Classification: LCC GN751 .C65 2016 (print) | LCC GN751 (e-book) | DDC 398.23/4--dc23
LC record available at https://lccn.loc.gov/2016005429

Printed and bound in the United States by P. A. Hutchison Company

10 9 8 7 6 5 4 3 2 1

Text design by Priscilla Baker and layout by Debbie Glogover
This book was typeset in Garamond Premier Pro with Celestia Antiqua Std and Futura Std for display fonts

To send correspondence to the author of this book, mail a first-class letter to the author c/o Inner Traditions • Bear & Company, One Park Street, Rochester, VT 05767, and we will forward the communication, or contact the author directly at **www.andrewcollins.com**.

For Han Kloosterman,
who found undeniable proof of the cataclysm
that destroyed Atlantis,
and
Graham Phillips,
for encouraging me to go through the
gateway to Atlantis

CONTENTS

ACKNOWLEDGMENTS

Many thanks to all those who helped create this work. There are many, but those who should be mentioned in this new revised edition are Debbie Benstead-Cartwright, Karen Deeley, Bill Donato, Catherine Hale, Rodney and Joan Hale, Johan Kloosterman, Maria Smith, Graham Phillips, Brent and Joan Raynes, David Southwell, Richard Ward, Jon Graham, and all the staff at Inner Traditions. A special thanks goes out to Greg and Lora Little for their constant support and for allowing me to continue my voyage of discovery in the Bahamas and Caribbean.

PHOTO CREDITS

The author and publisher would like to thank those listed below for permission to use the following pictures included as numbered plates: 1. Stanze di Raffaello, Vatican/Scala, Florence; 4. Museo Pio Clementino, Vatican/Scala, Florence; 5. Sygma; 8. Cyrus H. Gordon; 10, 11, 12, 13, and 23. David Eccott; 15. Park and Roche Establishment Archives, Schaan; 17 and 18. Trustees of the British Museum; 19. Topkapi Museum, Istanbul; 22. Museo Nacional de Historia, Madrid; 27. Fondo de Cultura Económica from Historica Tolteca-Chichimeca; 28. Estrella Rey and Ernesto E. Tabío; 32. Essex and Suffolk Water; 35. John W. White; 36, 40, and 41. Anna Valentine;

38. Joan Zink; 39. Ava Rebikoff; 42. William M. Donato; 43. Herb Sawinski; 44. Dee Truman; 45 and 46. Lora Little.

The author would also like to thank Karen Deeley for the following line illustrations: Bimini Road, God L, and Quetzalcoatl; Rodney Hale for map texts; and Chris Ollis and Ruby for the Atlantis ground plan.

CLUE TO THE GREAT CATASTROPHE

T he date is September 29, 2014. It is beginning to rain as I cross a sparse, sandy wasteland under threat of commercial development. I am in Lommel, Belgium, close to the border with the Netherlands. With me is a TV camera crew, a local archaeologist, and an elderly gentleman in his eighties. He is wheelchair bound, partially deaf, and can barely speak due to the scars left behind by throat cancer twenty years earlier. Yet Johan (Han) Kloosterman, a Dutch geologist and mineralogist, has no intention of giving up on life any time soon. He is one of the world's acknowledged experts on what has become known as the Younger Dryas Boundary impact event, which, as we shall see, now becomes the most likely mechanism behind the destruction of Atlantis. His sheer determination to continue to learn, and deliver his findings to those who will listen, makes him one of the most inspirational people I am ever likely to meet in my life.

The Younger Dryas impact event is thought to have occurred approximately 12,800 years ago. At this time, scientists now believe, a comet appeared in the night sky, most likely entering the firmament somewhere in the vicinity of the Pleiades constellation (see chapter 20). After passing through the inner solar system this heavenly harbinger most likely entered perihelion, its close approach to the sun. All the indications are that, like Icarus in Greek mythology, it came too close to the solar orb. This caused its breakup into a freight train of fragments, some as much as a kilometer in size. These fiery projectiles, some of them hundreds of times more powerful than the largest nuclear bomb ever detonated, were sent on a collision course with the Earth.

Here, on the surface of the planet, the Upper Paleolithic populations in the American Northwest would have had a rude awakening that day, as multiple fragments of the comet entered into low orbit. Contact with the atmosphere would have caused these intensely bright fireballs to break up still further, many splitting apart and exploding as terrifying air blasts even before they reached the ground.

The result of this torrent of impacts, which carved a path of destruction across the North American continent, and beyond as far as the Atlantic Ocean and Eurasian landmass, would have triggered uncontrollable wildfires consuming everything in their path in a mass conflagration. As the fires raged, great volumes of toxic smoke and burned debris would have risen into the upper atmosphere, very rapidly creating a thick black layer, blotting out the sun and moon for an extended period of time. How long exactly, no one knows.

Some large fragments of the comet crashed into the North American ice sheets, instantly vaporizing the water locked within. This resulted in torrential rain full of toxic chemicals that would have continued for weeks on end, flooding many areas of the planet. In addition to this, torrents of water freed up from the ice sheets would have torn through the hills and valleys, consuming everything in their path and changing the face of the landscape forever. The final outpouring of this melt water into the oceans would have risen the sea level almost immediately, drowning low-lying regions of the planet in just a matter of weeks.

The total blackout of the sun and moon, combined with the sudden release of fresh water into the oceans, would have triggered a rapid plunge in global temperatures, which in just a single human generation brought about a new Ice Age that lasted for approximately 1,200 years.

This is known to scientists in Europe as the Younger Dryas event, and to those in North America as the Valders readvance.

THE USSELO HORIZON

When this book was originally published in 2000 under the title *Gateway to Atlantis,* very little scientific evidence was available on this catastrophic event, which took place in relatively recent human history. Despite this, I used what data I could find to demonstrate that the mechanism responsible for the destruction of Plato's fabled island empire was the Younger Dryas comet, which I referred to as the Carolina Bays impact. The Carolina Bays is the name given to the countless elliptical craters that litter North America's eastern Atlantic seaboard, from New Jersey all the way down to Florida. Almost certainly, they were created as a direct result of the catastrophic events of 12,800 years ago.

Among the evidence I presented was the scientific work of Han Kloosterman. He had determined that the impact left behind a distinctive, carbon-rich layer of burned debris between one and a half centimeters and thirteen centimeters in thickness. To date this has been detected in countries on six continents, including France, the Netherlands, Germany, Poland, White Russia, India, South Africa, Syria, Egypt, the United States, Canada, Mexico, Colombia, Venezuela, Australia, Great Britain, and here in Belgium, where just over the border in the Netherlands, at a place named Usselo, the significance of this ominous black layer was first recognized by Kloosterman in the 1980s.

Archaeologists originally attributed the existence of this carbon-rich layer to localized conflagrations, caused by lightning strikes, erupting volcanoes, or human deforestation. What they had not anticipated, however, was the sheer extent and uniformity of the layer, something only realized after Han's findings were announced in 1999.

Today this burned layer (known everywhere as the Usselo horizon, except in the United States, where it is referred to as the black mat) is being examined in countries all over the world. Its existence has now become the unique signature of a comet impact that very nearly destroyed the habitable world. Recently, it has been found to contain telltale microscopic impact debris, such as nanodiamonds, magnetic spherules, and tiny glass-like objects made of silica produced only at temperatures in the range of two thousand degrees centigrade.

Aside from myself, Han's extraordinary discoveries have come to the attention of other scientists in the field of catastrophism, the study of catastrophes in world history. They include Richard Firestone, a nuclear chemist at Lawrence Berkeley National Laboratory, who with his own colleagues, including geologist James P. Kennett and geological consultant Allen West, has been independently working on the idea of an impact event having taken place coincident to the Younger Dryas mini–Ice Age. It is the subject of his essential book *The Cycle of Cosmic Catastrophes,* published by Inner Traditions in 2006. In his book Firestone provides brand new evidence to suggest that the Carolina Bays are, as I propose in this book (see chapter 21), the result of massive air blasts caused by disintegrating comet fragments impacting with the Earth.

Since the publication of Firestone's book dozens of scientific papers have appeared on the subject of the Younger Dryas impact event. Even though their conclusions are fiercely contested by a group of skeptical scientists who vehemently deny that any such event ever took place, more and more evidence emerges each year to tell us very firmly that something terrible did befall the world around 12,800 years ago.

HUMAN CASUALTIES

What also seems apparent is that the effect of the impact event on human populations living at this time must have been catastrophic. In North America the Clovis people, with their highly sophisticated tool-making tradition, vanished completely during the Younger Dryas period. Advanced populations throughout the Northern Hemisphere most likely suffered similar fates. Any survivors would have been forced to migrate to warmer climes due to the sudden drop in temperature and the gradually worsening conditions of the 1,200-year mini–Ice Age.

In the Low Countries of Europe, and even in southeast England, it was the Federmesser culture that took the full force of the impact. This we know from the beautifully worked flint tools these people left behind at Lommel in Belgium. They are found with frequency in the occupational levels directly beneath the Usselo horizon, yet they disappear completely in the sandy layers immediately above it. So what happened to the Federmesser communities in the wake of the Younger Dryas impact event around 12,800 years ago? This is what I was here in Belgium to find out.

WHITE SANDS

In a huge trench cut out of the thick layers of pale yellow loess by a mechanical digger earlier that day, Han Kloosterman is desperately attempting to communicate something of importance to me. From the confines of his wheelchair he points toward a black wavy band about halfway up the 2.5-meter wall of compacted sand. This, I realize, is the Usselo horizon, the slightly unnerving signature of the Younger Dryas impact event. Removing some of the soft, black material with a trowel, I roll it around in my fingers. It feels greasy, like the oily waste left behind in the soil after an intense garden bonfire. Yet, as I knew only too well, this carbon-rich layer was laid down as much as 12,800 years ago.

Han, however, is not pointing toward the Usselo horizon. He is drawing my attention to the layer of white sand just below the wavy black line. It is about 25 centimeters in thickness and is not present above the carbon-rich layer. As I am unable to understand what Han is trying to say, the Dutch geochemist resorts to scribbling notes on scraps of paper. "A scientific analysis of the white sand," he now writes, "has shown that its chemical composition is slightly different to the sand immediately below and above it." It is a revelation that has led Han to a startling, and rather disturbing, conclusion. Either the highly toxic acid rain that fell in the wake of the impact event caused the bleaching of the sand or it is the result of a "heat flash," caused by a close proximity air blast that whitened the sandy loess in an instant.

So were the local Federmesser communities wiped out by an air blast from a disintegrating comet fragment? Or did they die as a consequence of the acid rain poisoning the local water supplies, killing flora and fauna alike? Whatever the answer, these must have been chilling times indeed.

Clearly, this would have been a horrific epoch to live in, and even if you did survive the impact and its aftereffects, there was always going to be the lingering fear that it was all going to happen again every time a comet appeared in the sky. In addition to this, there is no way that this unimaginable event was ever going to be forgotten. It will have remained at the forefront of people's minds, being preserved in catastrophe myths and legends handed down across countless generations through to the modern age.

Such legends exist all over the world, and undoubtedly they influenced Plato's account of Atlantis, destroyed, he says, in one terrible "day and night" of "earthquakes and floods." This catastrophic event, we are informed, occurred sometime around 9600 BCE, and whether Plato realized it or not, his famous account of the destruction of Atlantis was almost certainly inspired by the events that befell the world at the time of the Younger Dryas impact event.

FINDING ATLANTIS

Atlantis is a subject that has spawned a thousand books and articles. Generally they argue either that it never existed or—if it did exist—that Plato's island empire is the memory of some lost island civilization that thrived fairly recently in human history. The most popular scholarly approach, promoted even today by one of the world's largest and most influential TV channels, is that the story of Atlantis is a memory of the destruction of Minoan Crete in the wake of a massive volcanic eruption on the nearby island of Santorini (ancient Thera), sometime around the middle of the second millennium BCE.

Yet to substantiate such claims, some major fudging of the evidence is necessary. This includes the moving of Atlantis from the Atlantic Ocean to the Mediterranean and assuming that when Plato wrote solar years he in fact meant "lunar" months, reducing Atlantis's date of destruction from the stated 9600 BCE down to a more workable date around 3,500 years ago. Such research, biased toward the belief that civilization began in the Bible lands in the centuries following the Great Flood, circa 2350 BCE, has long stilted our understanding of this age-old enigma of the past.

Many other authors use the evidence of Atlantis presented by Plato to promote personal theories on the island's geographical location. The mid-Atlantic Rift, the Arctic Circle, Antarctica, the Bolivian Altiplano, Crete, Gibraltar, Spain, Morocco, and even, more recently, Indonesia, have all been proposed as the true location of lost Atlantis. It seems that every few years a new book comes along claiming to have "solved" the mystery of Atlantis. As compelling as these theories might seem many of them conveniently ignore Plato's clear statement that his lost island empire existed in the "Atlantic Sea," the whereabouts of which has never been in doubt.

THE CUBAN CONNECTION

Back in 1998, when *Gateway to Atlantis* was being written, I wanted to explore the possibility that Antarctica was the true location of Atlantis. New books from the likes of Graham Hancock and Canadian researchers Rose and Rand Flem-Ath had reignited the debate over whether this frozen continent might once have been home to a lost civilization. Yet an unexpected turn of events at the end of that year guided me on to a quite different path of discovery. It was Cuba, the largest of the Caribbean islands, I now surmised, that had been the role model for Plato's fabled "Atlantic Island," and not Antarctica. It was a conclusion reached, not only from Cuba's great similarity to the description Plato gives of Atlantis, but also from the knowledge that the indigenous peoples of the Caribbean, so horrifically annihilated by the Spanish in the wake of Columbus's "discovery" of the New World in 1492, had for countless generations preserved legends of a devastating cataclysm. This was said to have split apart and drowned a former landmass that had once united the thousands of islands and cays that today make up the Bahamian and Caribbean archipelagos.

It was information that had been conveyed to the first Spanish explorers to reach the West Indies in the late fifteenth and early sixteenth centuries. I wondered whether it was possible that similar stories had been told to more ancient voyagers, most likely Phoenician or Carthaginian traders, who had visited these islands prior to the age of Plato. Did they carry these age-old legends back to the Mediterranean, where they eventually reached the ears of philosophers like Plato? Did these stories speak of the greatest of all the Atlantic islands being destroyed in one terrible "day and night" of "earthquakes and floods"? Did Plato go on to use these stories, which came originally from indigenous peoples on the opposite side of the Atlantic Ocean, to construct his detailed account of Atlantis?

To me the answer was yes. So I embarked on a major research project to prove that maritime exploration and even highly secretive trade routes extended all the way from the Mediterranean to the Caribbean islands, then known as the Hesperides, prior to the age of Plato. I also sought out a suitable scientific mechanism to explain the stories told by the indigenous peoples of the Bahamas and Caribbean regarding the breaking up of a former landmass that left behind the thousands of islands and cays seen today. This led me eventually to the slowly mounting evidence for the Younger Dryas impact event, which took place close to the time frame offered by Plato for the destruction of Atlantis, that is, 9600 BCE.

It was confirmation of this catastrophic event that I was now witnessing here in Lommel, Belgium, in the company of Han Kloosterman, one of the pioneers in this field. We were here to do some filming for *Ancient Aliens,* the ever-popular TV show on ancient mysteries that had also come to realize the importance of these catastrophic events on popular myth and legend, including the Bible's account of the Great Flood.

The Younger Dryas impact would have devastated the Bahamian and Caribbean archipelagos. Any existing populations that inhabited these island groups would have been decimated. Although no obvious trace of their forgotten world remains on land, it could very well exist beneath the shallow waters of the Bahamas. Ever since the 1950s strange architectural features, as well as rock mounds, cave art, and human burials located in submerged caves, have been found off the coasts of several Bahamian islands. Clearly, the archipelago was occupied long before the Lucayans, the first recognized inhabitants of the Bahamas, arrived by boat from Cuba and Hispaniola, circa 600–700 CE.

How long ago the Bahamian archipelago was first settled remains unclear. Yet enough tantalizing evidence exists to demonstrate that a human population existed both in the Caribbean and on the former Bahamian landmass when fragments of the Younger Dryas comet are suspected to have struck the western Atlantic basin some 12,800 years ago. If so, then it is the survivors of this impact event that are to be credited with the inception of the Atlantis myth, their stories being passed down by word of mouth until they were told to the first Phoenician and Carthaginian traders to reach the Bahamian and Caribbean islands in the centuries before Plato wrote his famous dialogues, circa 350 BCE.

This was the bold theory outlined in *Gateway to Atlantis.* Its writing involved an extraordinary quest of discovery that had led me, early in my investigations, to explore a painted cave located on a remote island off the southwest coast of Cuba. What I discovered here provided the first clues regarding the ultimate fate of Atlantis and the symbolic manner in which knowledge of its destruction had been passed down across countless generations. It is a story introduced in the book's prologue and resumed in chapter 19.

The myth of Atlantis is like the conundrum of Schrödinger's

nebulous cat. We can speculate, argue, or present our case, but ultimately there are no real answers—no box we can open or sign we can read that will tell us exactly where Atlantis was located. And perhaps—like the eternal quest for the Holy Grail—we are not supposed to know all the answers. Yet this should not stop us searching for lost Atlantis, and presented in this book is one of the most comprehensive reviews of all the evidence left to the world since Plato wrote his famous account some 2,350 years ago. Read it and make up your own minds. When you have done this why not pick up the gauntlet yourself and continue the quest for Atlantis in the manner that, as we shall see in the epilogue, others have done, making some quite extraordinary discoveries in the process.

These new discoveries tell us very clearly that Plato was not wrong. Moreover, that the destruction of Atlantis was brutal in every manner, the evidence of which is being uncovered now in every part of the world. It is even here at Lommel in Belgium, close to my own home in Essex, southeast England. It exists as a constant reminder of the terrible fate that befell the world during an epoch that we can be thankful we never lived through ourselves.

THE QUEST BEGINS

THE ISLE OF YOUTH, CUBA

Thursday, September 2, 1998. It had taken me nearly twenty years of research to get this far. Having reached this mosquito-infested isle, following a nail-biting flight as the sun rose slowly above the eastern horizon, I now found myself amid a crowd of well-meaning local people. Each one seemed intent on offering advice and services.

In pidgin Spanish my traveling companion and I were able to convey to them the purpose for our visit, which was to reach the Punta del Este caves located in the southwest corner of this subtropical island. We had hoped to persuade a taxi driver to take us the forty or so kilometers to our destination, but this appeared to be out of the question. Not one was willing to drive us that far. It was clear that our only option was to hire a vehicle in nearby Nueva Gerona, the only town, which we reached quickly in a bashed-up taxi that would have been illegal on the streets of Europe.

With some idea of the complexity of the road journey ahead, we decided to secure the services of not only a four-wheel-drive vehicle with driver, but also an archaeologist from the local museum. Johnny Rodriguez, a stocky, ponytailed man in his twenties, could speak almost no English but was familiar at least with the caves in question.

1

Where we were going, no tourist ever ventured. This military-controlled zone contained some remarkable archaeological sites, but access was denied to anyone not in possession of the correct papers. Unfortunately, our guidebooks had neglected to mention this fact, so the whole success of the visit now rested in the hands of Johnny and the driver, who insisted that they could get us past the armed guards at the checkpoint. They said there would be no problem, and they were right. After just a brief conversation with the two cigar-smoking soldiers, the barrier was raised and we were through. From here on in it was a single unmade track across hostile terrain notorious for its crocodiles and poisonous flora.

It was one of the bumpiest, most nerve-racking journeys I have ever experienced. Yet eventually, after several kilometers of hard driving, we quite literally reached the end of the road.

With the harsh late-morning sun now beating down on our exposed skin, and black-and-white vultures gliding ominously overhead, the party left the vehicle on the edge of the tangled swamp. In front of us was a group of abandoned concrete buildings, erected during the cold war as a telecommunications center. Despite their dilapidated state, one building still appeared to be home to a small contingent of men who may or may not have been soldiers, for they wore no uniforms. Why these individuals should have had to remain in this unbearable climate was not made clear. Yet by default they had become the guardians of Punta del Este's sacred caves, and without their consent we would be going nowhere. So we offered bottled water and cigarettes as Johnny and the driver, whom they seemed to know, laughed and joked with them.

I had been told that this was the worst spot in the entire country for insects, and so there was no way on Earth I was going to spend even one night in this godforsaken place. We needed to be back at the local airport by dusk to catch the plane out, and no other option would be considered.

Yet for so many months I had yearned to be here. I had even visited the caves in my dreams. I almost felt as if some unseen *genius loci* was calling me to its lair. However, my reasons for coming to this place were based on sound historical and archaeological fact, which had led me to conclude that the answer to one of the world's greatest mysteries might lie inside one of the caves.

Very little was known about the cavern in question. Even though various Hispanic archaeologists had visited the site, very few articles had ever been written on the subject. Despite this lack of background information, I knew instinctively it was important. The cave's walls and ceilings were covered with strange petroglyphs, which perhaps expressed the indigenous people's myths and legends concerning the emergence of humanity at the beginning of time. I needed to see them and understand their meaning.

We kept to the narrow path, which was infested by large sand crabs that did not seem pleased by our intrusion into their territory. The uneasy nature of the place made me question my motives for coming here, but there was no turning back now.

Finally we entered a clearing, and in front of us lay the gaping mouth of a large open cave. A metal plaque on the wall announced that we had reached the goal of our quest—Punta del Este's Cueva #1 (Cave no. 1). Unexpectedly, my stomach churned. What if I was wrong and there was nothing here of any significance?

No supernatural guardian stood before us as we passed into the cave's unwelcoming interior, home only to bats and countless mosquitoes.

Instantly we were confronted by the sight of faded red-and-black petroglyphs, composed in the main of whole series of rings and other geometric forms. Overhead were two roughly circular skylights cut out of the soft rock by ancient hands, allowing sunlight to penetrate inside the cave. On the ground I could see broken pieces of conch shell discarded hundreds of years ago by American Indian occupants.

In Spanish, Johnny explained that beneath the skylight there would originally have been a stone dais, around which tribal ceremonies would perhaps have taken place. In its place today was a crude concrete copy, which ably allowed us to visualize what the setting might have been like in prehistoric times. He also told us that the rear skylight, now obscured by a small mountain of earth, was thought by some archaeologists to have been used to mark the transit of the planet Venus. However, he shook his head when we asked him if any academic paper had been written on the subject.

Johnny drew our attention now to the central feature of the cave, a huge multifaceted petroglyph consisting of a series of concentric rings, some sets overlapping each other, giving the impression of falling raindrops making ever-widening ripples on a surface of water. Piercing its target-like rings was the drawing of a long arrow-like dart.

While trying to translate Johnny's views on the symbolic meaning of the cave art, I carefully examined individual petroglyphs. Some seemed very familiar indeed. They were like the megalithic art found carved at certain Neolithic and early Bronze Age sites in Brittany and the British Isles, and curiously enough these examples are thought to date from a very similar time period. It was also difficult not to see them in terms of either the orbit of planets or the revolution of stars.

Once I became accustomed to the low light and persistent mosquitoes, I began to realize something important. Preserved on the walls and ceilings of this prehistoric Sistine Chapel was what appeared to be a symbolic language conveyed in abstract picture form. It seemed to tell of archaic events that had occurred in the Western Hemisphere before the dawn of history. More than this, I began to realize that here might be the key to understanding the final fate of lost Atlantis. Yet before sharing the excitement and exhilaration I experienced in the wake of my visit to Punta del Este on Cuba's Isle of Youth, we must go back to the beginning—to ancient Athens, where the legend of Atlantis was born around 2,350 years ago.

Part One
DISCOVERY

1

THE OLD PRIEST SPEAKS

Sometime around the year 355 BCE, the celebrated Athenian philosopher Plato (429–347 BCE) evoked the inspiration of the Muses before writing what is arguably one of classical literature's most enigmatic works. Already he had completed a book titled *The Republic,* which set out his vision of Athens as an ideal state. This was based to some degree on the philosophical teachings of Pythagoras (born circa 570 BCE), who was a major influence on Plato's life. His new work would be called *Timaeus,* and, like its predecessor, it would take the form of a drama, or dialogue, enacted by four historical figures in the year 421 BCE, when Plato would have been just eight years old. The participants, the same as those who featured in *The Republic,* were Socrates, Plato's great mentor and friend, who died of poison by his own hand as ordered by a jury circa 399 BCE; Timaeus, an astronomer of Locri in Italy; Hermocrates, an exiled Syracusan general; and Critias, who was either Plato's great-grandfather or his maternal uncle (see chapter 3).

This style of writing, common in Plato's day, was intended to establish, in an informative and readable manner, the principal themes of the book. In this new dialogue, which was meant as a sequel to *The Republic,* matters to be discussed included the mechanics of the universe and the nature of the physical world. Yet instead of Socrates assuming the role of chairman as he had done in *The Republic* this honor would go to Critias.

It is almost at the beginning of the *Timaeus* that Plato introduces the world to the subject of Atlantis. Critias (styled "the Younger") relates to Socrates and those present how, when only a child, his elderly grandfather, also named Critias (styled "the Elder"), had told him a fascinating story. This he had gained from Dropides, his father, who in turn had learned it from a friend and relative named Solon. Like the participants in the dialogue, Solon (ca. 638–558 BCE) is also a historical character—a celebrated Athenian legislator spoken of by Plato as one of Athens's seven great sages.

HOARY WITH AGE

The *Timaeus* informs us that Solon obtained what he knew of the story while at Sais, "the city [in Egypt] from which King Amasis came." This Amasis, who is more correctly identified as Aahmes II, ruled Egypt from his seat at Sais from circa 570 BCE onward for a duration of forty-four years.[1] Although Solon was alive at this time, the text does not specify that Solon was in Egypt during his reign. Indeed, Plato's pupil, the philosopher Aristotle (384–322 BCE), tells us that Solon visited Egypt at the beginning of a ten-year sojourn overseas, following his time as the archon, or chief magistrate, of Athens. Since this is believed to have occurred circa 594–593 BCE, some twenty-two or twenty-three years before Amasis's reign, there is a possible discrepancy here. Yet we know that Solon did indeed visit Egypt around this time because the Greek historian Herodotus (484–408 BCE) in his *History* informs us, "It was this king Amasis who established the law that every Egyptian should appear once a year before the governor of his canton, and show his means of living. . . . Solon the Athenian borrowed this law from the Egyptians and imposed it on his countrymen, who have observed it ever since."[2]

It implies therefore that Solon must have visited Egypt toward the end of his life and thus after Amasis had become pharaoh, circa 570 BCE (see also chapter 2).

Critias tells us that upon entering the temple dedicated to the worship of Minerva (the Greek name for Neith, the patron goddess of Sais), Solon engaged in conversation one of the priests, who was said to have been "a very old man."[3] He spoke about the destruction of the human race in former ages, a matter the Athenian statesman felt he knew something about from his own education in these subjects. Yet in response the priestly elder chastised Solon for knowing so little about the true history of mankind, saying, "You Greeks are always children; in Greece there is no such thing as an old man. . . . You are all young in your minds . . . which hold no store of old belief based on long tradition, no knowledge hoary with age."[4]

After enlightening Solon in respect to the "many and divers destructions of mankind, the greatest by fire and water,"[5] the priest went on to explain the nature of those catastrophes that destroy everything memorable of the past. These traditions were, he said, preserved only in the registers belonging to the temple, for they "are the oldest on record."[6]

Solon is told that the history and genealogies of Athens, which he has recited, "are little better than nursery tales."[7] It is also explained how "your people [i.e., the Athenians of Solon's age] remember only one deluge [of the Greek flood hero Deucalian], though there were many earlier; and moreover you do not know that the bravest and noblest race in the world once lived in your country." It was apparently from this race that the Athenians of Plato's day were descended.[8]

The elderly priest—identified by the Greek biographer Plutarch (50–120 CE) as "Senchis the Saite"[9]—then spoke of how before the "greatest of all destructions by water," the citizens of Athens were the "most valiant in war," their exploits and government being the "noblest under heaven."[10]

Solon is informed that the "great exploits" of the noble race of Athens are recorded in the temple's sacred registers and that perhaps they should reconvene to "go through the whole story in detail another time at our leisure, with the records before us."[11] Yet one great exploit that Solon does learn from his conversations with the old man is how the Athenian nation "once brought to an end" an almighty power that "insolently advanced against all Europe and Asia, *starting from the Atlantic ocean outside.*"[12] (current author's emphasis)

Needless to say, it is at this juncture in the dialogue that the priest of Sais reveals to Solon the story lying behind the destruction of Atlantis, the homeland of this almighty power. In most English translations of the *Timaeus* this all-important textual account takes up about fifty lines. However, each one is loaded with compelling facts regarding this sunken kingdom. Plato goes on to recount further details of his Atlantean nation in the unfinished sequel to the *Timaeus* titled the *Critias*. We must, however, never forget that although the *Timaeus* actually contains a wealth of astronomical and scientific knowledge, more or less unparalleled in its day, the whole thing was written as a fictional narrative, a kind of *X-Files* of its day.

AN ALMIGHTY LANDMASS

The priest of Sais relates next how the great force that rose up to oppose the mighty nation of Athens came from an "island" situated in front of—in other words, beyond—the Pillars of Hercules.[13] This was the name given in antiquity to the pillarlike rocks that stood on either side of the Strait of Gibraltar and marked the entrance to the Atlantic Ocean. The old man justifies the placement of this "island" in the Atlantic by revealing that "in those days" the "ocean could be *crossed*."[14] (current author's emphasis)

What might Plato have meant by "crossed"? It implies that the Atlantic "island" from which this aggressor stemmed was not only accessible in past ages, but that it was also visited by ocean-going vessels able to cross the Atlantic Ocean.

So where did Plato have in mind when he first considered the idea of an Atlantic "island" on which lived a warlike race that opposed the might of earliest Athens? Could it have been based on early maritime knowledge of the Madeiras? One of the Canary Islands perhaps, or even the Azores? All these island groups are located on the eastern Atlantic seaboard and were unquestionably known to ancient mariners during the first millennium BCE (see chapter 5).

Yet Plato does not seem to be referring specifically to any of these islands, for the old priest informs Solon that the Atlantic "island" was larger than "Libya and Asia put together."[15] This is a quite fantastic statement. In Plato's day, Libya was seen as the entire North African continent west of Egypt—a landmass comparable in size to Europe today. Asia, on the other hand, was considered to stretch between Egypt in the west, the Caucasus Mountains of southern Russia in the north, Arabia in the south, and India in the east. The Asia of Plato's day might be compared in size with North America. This therefore suggested the former existence of an almighty landmass of gigantic proportions, too big even to fit in the North Atlantic Ocean!

Since an island continent of the extent implied by Plato in his *Timaeus* could not possibly have existed in the manner he describes, scholars understandably dismiss Plato's account of his colossal island as mere fiction. Most Atlantologists—those who seek answers to the Atlantis mystery—are very much aware of this problem and often attempt to shrink down the size of Plato's Atlantic island by proposing that by Asia the author in fact meant only Asia Minor, that is, Asiatic Turkey. Yet there is no reason to make this assumption based on Plato's existing text. He does not imply this in any way. Indeed, it would appear that in comparing the size of Atlantis with that of Libya and Asia when placed together, he was simply attempting to convey the immense size of Atlantis in the absence of any true geographical knowledge.

Other scholars have assumed that if Plato really was alluding to a landmass of the size suggested in the *Timaeus,* then he must have been referring to the North or South American continents. The Americas do match the proportions of his Atlantic "island." Indeed, the idea that either North or South America could be Atlantis was first proposed by

Spanish explorers and scholars, such as Francesco Lopez de Gomara, shortly after the discovery of the New World.[16]

If Atlantis did once exist, and it really was of the immense size proposed in the *Timaeus,* there is no better solution. So when referring to his Atlantic island, had Plato been alluding to the American mainland—an opinion that has received considerable attention again in recent years?[17]

In actuality, this solution has a significant drawback, for after relating the size of the Atlantic island, the old priest of Sais tells Solon that "from it [i.e., Atlantis] the voyagers of those days could reach the other islands, *and from these islands the whole of the opposite continent.*"[18] (current author's emphasis)

This last statement should be seen in the context of the age in which it was written. To put it bluntly, there was no "opposite continent" in the classical age! According to the official history of the world, the North American mainland was not "discovered" until Christopher Columbus's third voyage to the New World in 1498. This is, of course, if we ignore the Viking settlements established in Newfoundland around the year 1000 CE, or indeed the indigenous peoples that have inhabited the continent for the past twenty thousand years (see fig. 1.1).

Yet Plato seems, quite clearly, to be referring to the Americas, suggesting that he was somehow aware of the existence of these continents on the other side of the Western Ocean. Oddly enough, there is evidence that by 300 BCE other classical writers were also aware of a separate landmass beyond Oceanus, the ocean river once thought to encircle the ancient world. A work titled *De Mundo,* written around 300 BCE and falsely attributed to the philosopher Aristotle, talks about the known world as being a "single island round which the sea that is called Atlantic flows."[19] The text's author—who was very possibly a pupil of Aristotle[20]—goes on to speculate in the following, quite revealing manner: "But it is probable that there are many other continents separated from ours by a sea that we must cross to reach them, some larger and others smaller than it, but all, save our own, invisible to us."[21]

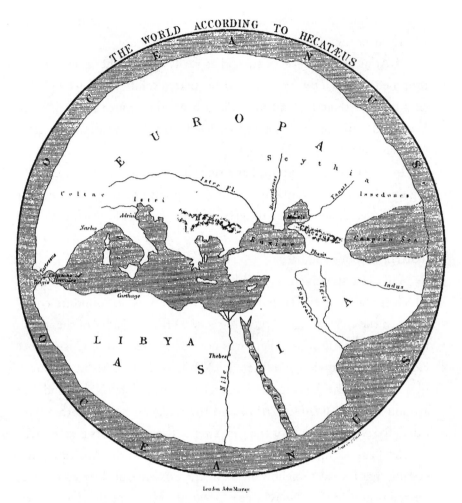

Figure 1.1. The ancient world according to Hecataeus of Miletus, circa 500 BCE. Notice the absence of any "opposite continent" beyond Oceanus, the Ocean River—a topic that became the subject of rumor and speculation in the age of Plato and Aristotle.

Pseudo-Aristotle ends his musings by stating poetically, "As our islands are in relation to our seas [i.e., the Mediterranean], so is the inhabited world in relation to the Atlantic, and so are many other continents in relation to the whole sea; for they are as it were immense islands surrounded by immense seas."[22]

LAND OF THE MEROPES

Further evidence in support of the view that early classical writers were very much aware of the American continent comes from the writings of a younger contemporary of Plato named Theopompus of Chios—a Greek historian born around 378 BCE. Only fragments of his writings survive today, and these are found in a work titled *Various Anecdotes*, written by a second-century Roman naturalist and historian named Aelian.

Theopompus relates how during one fateful journey through Phrygia, a country of Asia Minor (modern Turkey), Silenus, a satyr and teacher of the god Bacchus, became drunk and fell asleep in the rose gardens belonging to the legendary King Midas. Upon waking he found himself under the charge of the king's gardeners, who promptly marched him off to the royal palace. Having been placed under guard, Silenus was given his freedom only after suitably amusing his host with various anecdotes.

One of the tales told by Silenus is of particular interest, for he informs the king that "surrounding the outside of this world" is a "continent" that is "infinitely big."[23] Here you could find "men twice the size of those who live here. Their lives are not the same length as ours, but in fact twice as long," and they possess "various styles of life."[24] There are also "two very big cities"; one called Machimus, or "Warlike," and the other Eusebes, or "Pious."[25] In addition to those who lived in these cities, Silenus tells Midas that on the continent is a race called Meropes, "who live among them in numerous large cities."[26] At the edge of their territories is "a place named Point of No Return [Anostus], which looks like a chasm [gulf] and is filled neither by light nor darkness, but is overlaid by a haze of a murky red colour,"[27] It is said that "two rivers run past this locality, one named Pleasure and the other Grief. Along the banks of both stand trees the size of a large plane."[28]

According to Theopompus, the peoples of the distant continent once planned a voyage to "these islands of ours." No fewer than ten million of them are said to have sailed the ocean (thus supposing that they had seafaring capabilities), and they came upon Hyperborea, an unknown island usually identified as the British Isles (see chapter 7). Upon coming ashore, the visitors from another continent felt that the Hyperboreans were "inferior beings of lowly fortunes, and for that reason dismissed the idea of travelling further."[29]

LUCKY GUESSES

In addition to the accounts presented above, the Greek geographer Strabo (60 BCE–20 CE) makes reference to an unknown continent that can only have been the Americas. It comes during a discussion on the opinions of a Greek geometer and astronomer named Eratosthenes (276–196 BCE), who claimed that "if the immensity of the Atlantic Sea did not prevent, we could sail from Iberia [ancient Spain] to India along one and the same parallel."[30] In response to this statement, Strabo voiced the opinion that "we call 'inhabited' the world which we inhabit and know; though it may be that in this same temperate zone there are actually two inhabited worlds, or even more, and particularly in the proximity of the parallel through Athens that is drawn across the Atlantic Sea."[31]

It would be easy to dismiss these apparent references to the American continents as either misconceptions on the part of authors like myself or lucky guesses on the part of well-informed classical figures such as Plato, Pseudo-Aristotle, Theopompus, and Strabo. Yet if we can accept that knowledge of the existence of an "opposite" continent was available to a select few during Plato's age, might this information have been deliberately withheld from the outside world? Perhaps there were stories and rumors circulating in Greece and/or Egypt regarding the existence far beyond the Pillars of Hercules of another continent. Yet beyond maritime circles no one was aware of the full picture, leading to the sort of speculations voiced by Plato in his *Timaeus*.

It seems certain that Plato was somehow aware of either North or South America, the so-called opposite continent, and so incorporated this idea into a dialogue on the nature of the universe. Where exactly this knowledge might have come from need not detain us here. What seems more important is that this theory is strengthened considerably if we now consider Plato's assertion in the *Timaeus* that from the Atlantic island, that is, Atlantis, "the voyagers of those days could reach the other islands, and from these islands the whole of the opposite continent."[32]

ATLANTIC VOYAGERS

This all-important statement should be read again and again until it sinks in as to what Plato is implying. He is suggesting that Atlantis was located in front of, or before, "other islands" that acted like stepping-stones for maritime voyagers wishing to reach the "opposite continent," which we will take to be the Americas.

Does this information make sense in geographical terms? From the time of Columbus's first landing on the island of San Salvador in 1492, the Bahamian and Caribbean archipelagos have been used in precisely this manner—as stepping-stones for seagoing vessels journeying to the American mainland, either via the coast of Florida or the Gulf of Mexico. Moreover, the chain of islands known as the Lesser Antilles that connect Puerto Rico—the most easterly of the three main Caribbean islands—with the northern coast of South America might also be viewed in a similar manner.

Was it this island-hopping process to and from the American mainland that Plato is alluding to in his account of the Atlantic island? It seems as good a solution as any put forward by Atlantologists and scholars alike. Yet how might a Greek philosopher like Plato have come across such precious nautical information, which was supposedly unavailable during his own day? Plato himself seems to supply us with the answer, for his account suggests that this knowledge was derived from Atlantic "voyagers," who in ancient times "crossed" the Atlantic Ocean and visited these islands en route to the American continent.

In itself this is a startling revelation—one that has often been overlooked by scholars simply because it is considered inconceivable that mariners might have reached the Americas prior to the age of Columbus. So if Plato really had become aware of journeys made by transatlantic "voyagers" before his own time, how might this information affect our understanding of Atlantis? Did it really exist as an Atlantic island, and if so where exactly might it have been located?

Although the *Timaeus* does not say exactly where Atlantis was to be found, there seems little doubt that the island lay in the outer ocean. Repeatedly we find references in classical literature to similar island paradises under a variety of names, the most important being the islands of the Hesperides (see chapter 6). Almost without exception they are said to have lain either in or beyond the Western Ocean, the domain of the hero-god Atlas, and so this is where we must start our own search for Plato's Atlantic island.

Turning back to the account given in the *Timaeus,* the old priest tells Solon, "Now on this Atlantic island there had grown up an extraordinary power under kings who ruled not only the whole island but many of the other islands and parts of the [opposite] continent."[33]

There seems to be no vagueness in this statement. Atlantis, we are told, was ruled by a monarchy that Plato insisted held dominion over "other islands," seemingly those placed in front of the "opposite continent." These kings would also seem to have held sway over "parts of the [opposite] continent" itself. What sort of kingdom might we be dealing with here? Was the Atlantean nation really an island-based culture with seafaring capabilities that enabled it to control not only vast areas of the Western Ocean but also parts of the American continents?

More difficult to understand is Plato's next assertion that these same Atlantean kings held sway "within the straits," in other words, inside the Mediterranean basin.[34] He informs us that they were "lords of Libya [i.e., North Africa] so far as to Egypt, and of Europe to the borders of Tyrrhenia [modern Tuscany in Italy]," and "attempted at one swoop to enslave your country and ours and all the region within the strait."[35] There are no easy explanations for this statement, and it might seem easier to dismiss Plato's words as mere fiction. An Atlantic culture of the description given to us by Plato controlling towns and ports in both Europe and Libya seems nonsensical.

SACRED REGISTERS

This brings us perhaps to what is arguably the most controversial aspect of Plato's Atlantis narrative: the dates given for these supposed events in the Atlantic Ocean. A little earlier in the text, the old priest of Sais has informed Solon that the city of Athens was founded a full one thousand years before the "institution" of Egypt's sacred registers.[36] Since these are said to contain a record of events spanning a period of 8,000 years, and Solon visited Egypt circa 570 BCE, it implies that Athens was founded circa 9570 BCE. Almost in unison, classical historians will inform us that in 9570 BCE civilization had not yet begun and that Athens was not even a twinkle in the eye of its founding goddess Athena.

We know that humanity's transformation from nomadic hunter-gatherer to settled Neolithic farmer did not occur in the Near East until sometime after the cessation of the last Ice Age. In the opinion of archaeologists, there was nothing whatsoever happening in the vicinity of Athens in 9570 BCE. Indeed, it is only with the arrival of the first settlers from Asia Minor and the Levant circa 1500 BCE that a city was established there. So it seems that Plato got it wrong.

Yet if we examine his words a little more closely we can determine how he arrived at these dates, and in so doing understand their meaning in the context of what he has to say in the *Timaeus*.

THE MYTH OF DATES

The old priest of Sais informs Solon that "the age of our institutions is given in the sacred records as eight thousand years."[37] This might seem a fantastic statement, which, if we presume that he visited Sais circa 570 BCE, implied that Egyptian civilization began circa 8570 BCE.

Quite naturally, historians suggest that Plato must have been mistaken in this respect or that the time frame he provides in the *Timaeus* is meaningless. Yet in Plato's final work, *The Laws,* one of the characters, known only as the Athenian, attempts to explain the establishment of Egypt's legislation. During this speech he refers to the arts of the Egyptians in the following manner: "If you examine their art on the spot you will find that ten thousand years ago (and I'm not speaking loosely: I mean literally ten thousand), paintings and reliefs were produced that are no better and no worse than those of today."[38]

Even though there is a two-thousand-year difference between the figure given in the *Timaeus* and the one cited in *The Laws,* it is apparent that Plato fully believed that these dates related to real time. Such enormous time spans are considered mythical by Egyptologists. However, they appear with frequency in king-lists such as the fragmentary Royal Canon of Turin, which dates to the Nineteenth Dynasty of Egyptian history, circa 1308–1194 BCE. This tells us how a semidivine race known as the Shemsu-hor, the Followers of Horus, reigned for a period of 13,420 years before the rise of the first pharaoh circa 3100 BCE.[39] The Royal Canon also gives a total of either 33,200 or 23,200 years for the various dynasties of divine or semidivine beings.[40] Other similar canons contain equally extravagant time periods, leaving us to conclude that both the eight thousand years quoted in the *Timaeus* and the ten thousand years given in *The Laws* derive most probably from now-lost Egyptian king-lists.*

It becomes clear therefore that by suggesting the Athenians are one thousand years older than their Egyptian rivals, Plato is merely attempting to define the even-greater antiquity of his own race. Certainly there

---

*Manetho, a priest of the city of Heliopolis who lived in the third century BCE, spoke of a period of 36,525 years before the ascent of Menes, the first dynastic king (Manetho, *Aegyptiaca,* as quoted in Iamblichus, *De Mysteriis Aegyptiorum,* section 8, chapter 1, in Cory, *Cory's Ancient Fragments,* 95 fn), while the Greek historian named Herodotus (484–408 BCE) observed that 11,340 years had elapsed since the rule of the first pharaoh (Herodotus, "Canon of the Kings of Egypt," in Cory, *Cory's Ancient Fragments,* 171).

is no historical precedent to suggest that this was in fact the case. Indeed, there is overwhelming evidence to show that some of the greatest wisdom and philosophy taught at the Athenian schools was derived from the mystery schools of Egypt. The Greek philosopher Pythagoras, for instance, was educated in Egypt, where, according to Ammianus Marcellinus (fl. 353–390 CE), the fourth-century Latin grammarian and author of a history of the Roman world, the priests "taught him to worship the gods in secret."[41] Solon is also said to have visited Egypt so that he might become acquainted with the wisdom of the ancients (as did Plato himself—see chapter 2).[42] Perhaps Plato saw the fact that Egypt had a much more ancient heritage as a national embarrassment, and so in the *Timaeus* he attempted to redress the balance by bolstering up the antiquity of the Athenians, who were presumably his intended readership.

Having established a date of around 9570 BCE for the foundation of Athens, Plato has the old priest of Sais explain to Solon that it was following this time that the Atlantic nation rose up against his country. For he states, "Many great exploits of your city [i.e., Athens] are here recorded for the admiration of all; but one surpasses the rest in greatness and valour."[43] Indeed, since the kings of Atlantis are said to have risen up against Egypt also, the clear inference is that the war with Athens occurred sometime after the Egyptian sacred records were begun circa 8570 BCE. As we shall see, this is a statement blatantly contradicted in the text of the *Critias*.

With this in mind, we are informed next that thereafter the Atlantic kingdom attempted "at one swoop to enslave your country [i.e., Athens] and ours [Egypt] and all the regions within the strait [of Gibraltar]."[44] According to the *Timaeus,* the Athenians were then "forced by the defection of the rest" of the Mediterranean nations to move against the aggressor.[45] Furthermore, since the Athenian fleet was deemed to be the "foremost of all in courage and in the arts of war," it vanquished "the invaders" and freed "all the rest of us," including Egypt, from the threat of bondage and slavery.[46]

Crucially, the text of the *Timaeus* then reveals, "*Afterwards* ['*At a later time*' in the translation by H. Rackham as a part of the Loeb series published by Harvard University Press in 1938,] there was a time of inordinate earthquakes and floods; there came one terrible day and night, in which all your men of war were swallowed bodily by the earth, and the island of Atlantis also sank beneath the sea and vanished."[47] (current author's emphasis)

This is a loaded statement, and one that appears incredible. It is alleged that both the Atlantic island and the Athenian "men of war" were lost during an almighty cataclysm involving "earthquakes and floods" that can only have occurred post 8570 BCE by Plato's reckoning of dates. So what are we to make of this stupendous event, clearly unrecorded in conventional history? Did it really happen, and what can it tell us about the true location of lost Atlantis?

2

EGYPTIAN
HERITAGE

Some four hundred years after Plato wrote his Atlantis dialogues, the Greek biographer and moralist Plutarch referred to Solon's visit to Egypt, stating that his account of the Atlantic island as given by Plato had been gained during philosophical conversations with "Psenophis the Heliopolitan and Senchis the Saite, the most learned of the Egyptian priests."[1] He also spoke of Solon's assumed role in bringing the story to light, for according to him:

> Solon moreover attempted, in verse, a large description or rather fabulous account of the Atlantic Island, which he had learned from the wise men of Sais, and which particularly concerned the Athenians; but by reason of his age, not want of leisure (as Plato would have it), he was apprehensive the work would be too much for him, and therefore did not go through with it. . . . Plato, ambitious to cultivate and adorn the subject of the Atlantic Island, as a delightful spot in some fair field unoccupied, to which also he had some claim by his being related to Solon, laid out magnificent courts and enclosures, and erected a grand entrance to it, such as no other story, fable, or poem ever had.[2]

Despite this testimony, no other classical source before the age of Plutarch seems to recognize that Solon was responsible for the core material behind Plato's Atlantis account. All we can say for certain is that, following his time as Athens's archon, or chief magistrate, Solon left Greece and spent part of his ten-year absence in Egypt.[3]

Plutarch goes on to say that, because the elderly statesman was unable to do the story justice during the remaining years of his life (he died circa 558 BCE, a minimum of twelve years after his visit to Sais), it was taken up by Plato, who transformed it into the fabulous story presented in his dialogues.

Once again there is no independent evidence to confirm this was ever the case.

If it were not for Plutarch's account of Solon's meeting with the Saite priest, it could be argued that Plato merely used the historical memory of Solon's visit to Egypt in order to lend weight and credibility to his narrative. It is even possible that Plato borrowed his Saite setting for Solon's meeting with the old priest from the works of the fifth-century-BCE Greek historian Herodotus, who provides the reader with a vivid description of the Egyptian temple in a section of his *History* on the reign of King Amasis.[4] More damning still is that Solon's borrowing of the sacred laws of Amasis for use in his own country is noted by Herodotus in the very next paragraph after his account of the Saite temple.[5] It seems certain that Plato would have been very much aware of Herodotus's work when he came to write the *Timaeus*. In this knowledge, Plato's account of Solon's meeting with the old priest of Sais is, at best, suspect. Only the correlations between the chronology of the Egyptian king-lists and the dates supposedly preserved in the sacred registers of the Saite temple prevent us from completely abandoning any connection whatsoever between Plato's story of Atlantis and Solon's celebrated visit to Egypt.

What is more, there is an equally plausible source for Plato's knowledge of Egypt's mythical chronology. It is known that he himself spent time in Egypt visiting its mystery schools and ancient temples. Plutarch, in another of his works titled *Isis and Osiris,* tells us that like the "wisest of the Greeks," who apparently included Solon, Thales, Eudoxus, and Pythagoras, Plato "came to Egypt and consorted with the priests."[6] Here, too, he is said to have "acquired his glorious wisdom," according to Ammianus Marcellinus, the fourth-century Latin grammarian and author of a history of the Roman world.[7]

It is conceivable therefore that Plato learned of the Atlantis story—or at least found confirmation of it—during his own stay in Egypt. If true, he might then have used it as the basis for his famous dialogues. Yet how much of his narrative might be seen as fact, and how much of it is merely fiction? What have scholars said about the texts of the *Timaeus,* and where have others sought a historical Atlantis?

THE AEGEAN ANSWER

One solution is to assume that Plato was alluding to historical events that took place in an entirely different time frame from the one suggested by the fabulous dates presented in his Atlantis account. For instance, it has been proposed that when citing extremely long periods of time Plato was not referring to solar years but to lunar months of twenty-eight days.[8] If this was indeed the case, it would mean that instead of nine thousand years having elapsed since the foundation of Athens, the true time period was just 690 years, providing a date in the region of circa 1260 BCE. Historically speaking, this takes us into a more comfortable time frame, since it was during this age that the eastern Mediterranean began to suffer repeated attacks by a mixed-race, seaborne confederacy remembered as the "Peoples of the Sea."[9] Their ships terrorized Egyptian, Palestinian, and Syrian ports before being repelled by the forces of the Pharaoh Merenptah circa 1219 BCE and defeated finally by the army of Rameses III circa 1170 BCE.

Who exactly this confederacy might have been is still a matter of conjecture. There is, however, mounting evidence to suggest that their crews were led by displaced peoples originating from the coastal and island cultures that inhabited the Aegean-Anatolian world in the aftermath of the volcanic eruption that completely devastated the island of Thera (modern Santorini) in the Aegean, either circa 1628 BCE, circa 1450 BCE, or possibly even circa 1380 BCE, depending on the source consulted.[10]

This catastrophic event undoubtedly influenced the entire history of the Aegean world. So great was the final explosion that an estimated 114 cubic kilometers of debris was ejected outward to leave a water-filled crater with an area of fifty-one square kilometers.[11] Indeed, it has been suggested that the magnitude of the blast was the equivalent of six thousand nuclear warheads.[12]

By far the most important empire to suffer from this almighty cataclysm was that of the Minoans, whose cities and ports were to be found on Thera and, more important, on the island of Crete, which lay ninety-six kilometers south of the blast's epicenter. It is suggested that the huge eruption created enormous tidal waves, which advanced southward and obliterated not only the Minoan fleet, stationed on the northern coast of Crete, but also the towns and cities that lay in the same vicinity.[13] These enormous waves, as much as one hundred meters high, reached the eastern Mediterranean coast and struck coastal towns more than 1,120 kilometers from Thera.

How the total annihilation of Thera might have affected the coasts of Greece, Asia Minor, and Egypt is still a subject of fierce debate. Whatever the answer, such a catastrophic event would unquestionably have been remembered during the classical age. As a consequence, there seems little doubt that Plato's Atlantis account could have been influenced not only by the destruction of Thera but also by the subsequent tidal waves that resulted in the decimation of the Minoan fleet and the devastation of Crete's coastal towns and cities. Moreover, in 426 BCE a severe earthquake had shaken Greece, causing an almighty tidal wave, which devastated the town of Orobia on the Aegean island of Euboea (modern Negropont) and wrecked ships in the neighborhood of the island of Atalante, near Opuntian Locris. Such a natural catastrophe must equally have affected Plato's account of Atlantis's destruction by earthquakes and floods.

In addition to this, the memory of Rameses III's defeat of the Peoples of the Sea might additionally have influenced the contents of Plato's Atlantis story. This great battle is commemorated on the exterior walls of the temple at Medinet Habu in southern Egypt, and it has been pointed out that these relief carvings could have been viewed by Solon during his visit to the country circa 570 BCE.[14]

Conclusions such as these have led some scholars to champion what has become arguably the most academically accepted solution to the Atlantis mystery, and this is the view that either Crete or Thera was the Atlantic isle spoken of by Plato. Since the theory was first proposed in an anonymous article published in the *Times* newspaper in London on February 19, 1909, and subsequently found to have been written by a young Belfast scholar named K. T. Frost, several popular books have been published expounding these ideas. All of them have attempted to compare our knowledge of the Minoan civilization of either Crete or Akrotiri, a Minoan town excavated on Santorini, with the description of Atlantis as given in the *Critias*.[15] Yet all attempts to confirm this view have led its supporters, many of them academic writers, to adopt and accept a number of fundamental misconceptions about Plato's Atlantis narrative.

For example, it was suggested, initially by Greek geologist A. G. Galanopoulos, that the dates and dimensions given in the *Timaeus* and *Critias* are wrong, due to a mistranslation of the assumed Egyptian texts shown to Solon by the old priest of Sais.[16] In the process, the Greek statesman somehow managed to confuse the hieroglyph that denotes the number 100 with the character that represents a figurative value of 1,000.[17] If this were so, it would change the date implied for the foundation of Athens from nine thousand years before Solon's visit to just nine hundred years, providing a revised date of circa 1470 BCE, close to then accepted date of circa 1450 BCE for the Thera eruption. At first this might appear to offer a neat and logical solution to both the problem posed by the very early time frame suggested for the destruction of Atlantis and the unimaginable dimensions of Atlantis's city and plain as outlined in the *Critias* (see chapters 3 and 4).

The Aegean answer to Atlantis is, however, seriously flawed, for according to those Egyptologists who have taken time to examine the problem, no such confusion can have occurred. The hieroglyphs used to denote the numerical values of 100 and 1,000 are visually quite different. Solon—or anyone else for that matter—could not have made such a mistake. This is made clear in an important essay on the links between Egypt and Atlantis by J. Gwyn Griffiths, who points out, "If we assume a hieroglyphic form of the prototype, there seems to be very scanty ground for the proposal, since the normal forms for 100 and 1,000 are so sharply distinguished."[18]

So the idea that Solon, or indeed Plato, could have misread what was shown to him in Egypt is unfounded. Since it is also totally untenable that lunar cycles were meant instead of solar years, there seems to be no viable reason for altering the time frame connected with the events featured in Plato's Atlantis account.

MOVABLE PILLARS

Another gross misconception assumed by the Cretan-Atlantis theorists is that Plato's sunken kingdom lay *within* the Pillars of Hercules, something that neither the *Timaeus* nor the *Critias* implies in any way. Surely Plato would not have referred to Atlantis as an Atlantic island if he had meant it to be located anywhere else but in the Atlantic Ocean. Clear statements such as the Atlantic fleet "insolently advanced against all Europe and Asia, *starting from the Atlantic ocean outside*"[19] (current author's emphasis) should be enough to convince anyone that Plato's Atlantis was not located in the Mediterranean Sea. As writer James Guy Bramwell, the author of *Lost Atlantis,* so eloquently put it in 1937, "Either Atlantis is an island in the Atlantic ocean or it is not 'Atlantis' at all."[20]

In addition to changing the dates and location of Atlantis, those scholars who have supported a Mediterranean solution to the problem attempt to prove that the Pillars of Hercules referred to by Plato were nowhere near the Strait of Gibraltar. For instance, A. G. Galanopoulos and Edward Bacon, in their 1969 book *Atlantis: The Truth behind the Legend,* proposed that since some of Hercules' famous twelve labors were set in the Peloponnese region of southern Greece, his so-called Pillars might have been originally the eastern and western promontories marking the waterway between the Gulf of Lakonia and the Mediterranean Sea.[21]

With respect to Hercules labors, perhaps Galanopoulos and Bacon should have considered Hercules' tenth and eleventh labors, which were performed, respectively, at Gades in southwest Spain and Mount Atlas on the Atlantic coast of Africa. Indeed, the last mentioned labor involved him having to journey to the Atlantic isles known as the Hesperides in order that he might steal Hera's golden apples (see chapter 6). Not only are all of these locations situated beyond the Strait of Gibraltar, but it was because of Hercules' association with the Atlantic realm that the waterway between the Mediterranean Sea and the outer ocean became known as the Pillars of Hercules.

An even wilder idea proposed in 1992 by professional geoarchaeologist Eberhard Zangger is that there were originally two locations known as the "Pillars of Hercules." One pair he placed at the entrance to the Atlantic and the other at the entrance to the narrow straits of the Dardanelles that connect the Mediterranean Sea with the Black Sea. He came to this conclusion after reading a single, rather debatable, line in Servius's commentary on Virgil's *Aeneid,* which reads, "Columnas Herculis legimus et in Ponto et in Hispania" ("We pass through the Pillars of Hercules in the Black Sea as well as in Spain").[22] Having established this fact, Zangger went on to decide that Plato had been alluding to the Pillars of Hercules at the entrance to the Black Sea, and not those standing on either side of the Strait of Gibraltar. This allowed Zangger to identify Plato's Atlantis with the legendary city of Troy in southwest Turkey.[23]

All these ideas seem quite fantastic, especially as every classical historian and geographer who mentions the Pillars of Hercules places them first and foremost at the entrance to the Atlantic Ocean. Even if the Pillars of Hercules also stood at the entrance to the Black Sea, why should Plato have wanted to allude to these instead of to those that marked the exit to the ancient world, beyond which lay his Atlantic island?

As we can see, connecting Atlantis with Crete, Thera, or indeed Troy is very misleading indeed. Moreover, it misrepresents the evidence presented to us by Plato. This same sentiment is shared by at least some scholars of ancient history. For instance, in 1978 a blistering attack was launched against the persisting Cretan-Atlantis theory by American historian J. Rufus Fears of Oklahoma University in a prestigious work titled *Atlantis: Fact or Fiction*, edited by Edwin S. Ramage and published by Indiana University Press. In his view, "It is disturbing that, in the last quarter of the twentieth century, serious scholarship is still called upon to debate the possibility that Plato's Atlantis is a remembrance of Minoan Crete. Even at a superficial glance, the equation of Atlantis with Minoan Crete is revealed as a tissuework of fabrications, a flimsy house of cards, constructed by piling dubious hypothesis upon pure speculation, cementing them together with false and misleading statements and with specious reasoning."[24]

So even though there is every likelihood that much later historical events and places may well have influenced the development of Plato's Atlantis account, there is no reason whatsoever to suppose that his sunken kingdom lay anywhere else but beyond the Pillars of Hercules in the Atlantic Ocean.

THE SHALLOW SEA

As we have determined already, the *Timaeus* seems to preserve an archaic memory of ancient voyages both to and from the Americas, Plato's "opposite continent." His account also seems to allude to the

Bahamas, the Caribbean, and the Lesser Antilles, the "other islands" said to have lain beyond Atlantis. With these thoughts in mind, we find that the apparent location of the sunken Atlantic isle is given in the sentence following the reference to the island's destruction by "earthquakes and floods": "Hence to this day that outer ocean [i.e., the Atlantic] cannot be crossed or explored, the way being blocked by mud, just below the surface, left by the settling down of the island."[25]

This is a truly remarkable statement. To begin with, it contains elements of the type of misinformation that was spread by the Carthaginians of North Africa in an attempt both to throw a smokescreen over their own voyages beyond the Pillars of Hercules and to prevent any unauthorized exploration of the outer ocean by rival nations. These stories suggested that the seas beyond the Pillars of Hercules were impassable due to otherworldly hazards such as clouds of darkness, dangerous shoals, deathly mists, and great monsters.[26]

It is, however, Plato's reference to the Atlantic Ocean being "blocked by mud, just below the surface" that is most revealing, for this same idea is repeated in the works of other writers from this era. For example, an author named Scylax, who was in fact an imposter of Scylax of Caryanda, a famous Greek geographer of the fourth century BCE, states in his work the *Periplus* that at a distance of twelve days' sail "from the Pillars of Hercules" was the Phoenician island settlement of Cerne.[27] He asserts also, "The parts beyond the isle of Cerne are no longer navigable because of shoals, mud, and sea-weed. This sea-weed has the width of a palm, and is sharp towards the points, so as to prick."[28]

More significantly, Aristotle records in his work the *Meteorologica* that "the water outside the Pillars of Hercules is shallow because of the mud but calm."[29]

What exactly might these three notable authors of the classical age have been alluding to by these enigmatic statements? What was this region of the outer ocean renowned for its shoals, its mud, its seaweed, and its "calm"? Any knowledge they might have had regarding what lay beyond the Pillars of Hercules would have been second-, third-, or even fourthhand, and very likely it was derived from Carthaginian sources. This conclusion can be determined from a secondary account of the Atlantic voyages of a Carthaginian navigator of the fifth century BCE named Himilco, preserved in the *Ora Maritima* of Rufus Festus Avienus, a Latin historian of the fourth century CE. According to Avienus, "The inhabitants of Carthage and the people living between the columns of Hercules used to approach these waters [i.e., those beyond the Pillars of Hercules] which the Carthaginian Himilco asserts can barely be crossed in four months, as he reported himself to have proved the matter sailing, so widely no breezes propel the ship, so sluggish the liquid of the lazy sea stagnates."

And Avienus adds this: "Among the shoals much seaweed sticks up and often in the manner of a thicket holds back the ship. He says moreover that here the back of the sea does not go down deep, and the [ocean] floor is barely covered over by a small amount of water. The wild creatures of the sea are always appearing here and there, and among the slow ships languidly creeping along, sea monsters swim."[30]

He also wrote, "For the most part, beyond extends a shallow road-stead, so that it barely conceals the underlying sands. Frequent seaweed projects above the shoals, and here the tide is impeded by the swamp. A power of sea monsters swims through the whole sea, and a great terror of wild creatures inhabits the narrows. Long ago Himilco the Carthaginian reported that he himself had seen and proved these things upon the ocean. We have set down for you at great length these things derived from the deepest annals of the Carthaginians."[31]

Historians can only guess at the location of this shallow sea of weed, which, according to Himilco, could "barely be crossed in four months." Where exactly this accomplished Carthaginian navigator might have reached on his own celebrated voyage, or voyages, remains a mystery. It is known that on one occasion he left his home port of Carthage on the Mediterranean coast of North Africa and then sailed out through the Pillars of Hercules. After that it is anybody's guess. What does seem clear, however, is that Avienus's report of Himilco's maritime experiences preserve a somewhat better picture of the shallow sea alluded to by Plato, Aristotle, and Pseudo-Scylax a century later. So can we determine the location of this impassable sea of mud, shoals, seaweed and calm, where Plato believed that Atlantis had sunk beneath the waves?

There seems to be little question that what all these writers allude to, knowingly or otherwise, is the Sargasso Sea. This Atlantic region, marked by a vast expanse of free-flowing seaweed roughly the size of Europe, stretches between the Azores and the Bahamas. The exact origin of this seaweed—called gulfweed, sea holly, or, more correctly, *Sargassum bacciferum*—is still a matter of conjecture. It was once believed that it breaks away from the coast of North America and gathers in the calm and silent waters that fall between the various transatlantic currents and trade winds that encircle the North Atlantic Ocean. Yet today marine biologists accept that the seaweed is indigenous to the region and reproduces without any connection with the mainland coastline.[32]

It was Christopher Columbus who first officially discovered the Sargasso Sea on his initial voyage to the New World in 1492. An account of the journey recorded by his son Ferdinand states that on Sunday, September 16—twenty-seven days prior to his celebrated landing in the Bahamas—the surface of the water became "covered with a great mass of yellowish green weed, which seemed to have been torn away from some island or reef."[33] The next day they continued to encounter these "mats of weed," which were said to resemble "star grass, save that it had long stalks and shoots, and was loaded with fruit like the mastic tree."[34] The existence of this peculiar sea caused Columbus to believe that his vessels were nearing land, for he saw within the seaweed a live crab and noted also that the water was "less salty by half than before."[35]

Scholars find it impossible to accept that Himilco could have been alluding to the Sargasso Sea.[36] However, the description he gives of the languid sea that "can barely be crossed in four months" is almost perfect—a mass of seaweed, deathly calm, and the rich aquatic life viewed as "wild creatures of the sea" or even "sea monsters." Columbus himself apparently encountered large fish here that included huge tuna, which "swam about the ships, coming so near that the Nina's people [the crew of one of the boats] killed one with a harpoon."[37]

There are, of course, no shoals or mud banks lurking beneath the surface of the Sargasso Sea. However, the fact that ancient mariners readily accepted that there were is extremely important to our understanding of Plato's statement regarding the former site of Atlantis. If he was not simply basing his story on the misconceived ancient association between the Sargasso Sea and shallow waters, it is intriguing that his words also describe very well the shoals and shallows that *do* exist in the vicinity of the Bahamas. These stretch for several hundred kilometers between Great Bahama in the north and Cay de Sal in the south. Indeed, the Bahamas are not only notorious for their shallow banks, but they also take their name from the Spanish *baja mar,* meaning "shallow sea."[38] Is it possible that in addition to the Sargasso Sea, some knowledge of the Bahamas' shoals and shallows was being alluded to by early classical writers such as Plato, Aristotle, Pseudo-Scylax, and even Himilco?

Suggesting that Plato might have been referring to actual geographical locations on the western Atlantic seaboard might seem difficult to comprehend, especially as the Cretan-Atlantis theory remains the most widely accepted solution to the mystery. Yet these conclusions are on offer to anyone making an in-depth study of Plato's works, and the current author would certainly not be the first to draw such a conclusion. As early as 1875, L. M. Hosea, in a remarkable article titled "Atlantis: A Statement of the 'Atlantic' Theory Respecting Aboriginal Civilization," which appeared in the scholarly *Cincinnati Quarterly Journal of Science,* made the following statement: "Without presuming to determine whether in fact the Sargasso sea or shoal is a subsided island or an eddy of the ocean, it is sufficient for the purposes at hand to observe that in the spot designated by the Atlantic tradition [of Plato], there exists and has existed for an indefinite period an impediment to navigation which may by fair intendment relieve the ancient Egyptians and Greeks of the geographical ignorance imputed to them."[39]

We shall meet again with Hosea's writings on Atlantis. Yet in accepting the supposition that Plato was alluding in the *Timaeus* to the Sargasso Sea, and perhaps even the Bahamas, we are left with one inescapable conclusion. Whether by accident or design, Plato believed his sunken "island" was located somewhere on the western Atlantic seaboard.

So is it possible that Atlantis was once situated in the region of the ocean now occupied by the Sargasso Sea? Unfortunately not, for hydrographic surveys have revealed that the watery depths beneath this region of the North Atlantic Ocean vary between 1,500 meters and seven thousand meters.[40] No lost island continent awaits discovery at this location; it was simply never there in the first place.

It seems more likely that in singling out the Sargasso Sea as the position of the Atlantic island, Plato was merely drawing his readers' attention to the approximate area once occupied by the sunken land-mass. His reference in the *Timaeus* to "other islands" placed beyond the Atlantic island, which enabled ancient "voyagers" to reach the "opposite continent," is perhaps the greatest clue. As already suggested, Plato seems to be describing the manner in which the island chains of the Bahamas, the Caribbean Islands, and the Lesser Antilles were used like stepping stones by ancient sailing vessels attempting to reach the American continents. If this were truly the case, we must look for Atlantis in this part of the Atlantic Ocean, for it is clear that Plato believed it lay within easy reach of these "other islands."

Curiously enough, in 1130 a writer named Honorius of Autun wrote that the "curdled sea"—seemingly another reference to the Sargasso Sea—"adjoins the Hesperides and covers the site of lost Atlantis, which lay west from Gibraltar."[41] The Hesperides are legendary isles thought to have been located in the Western Ocean and, as we shall see, are very much linked with the West Indies, the name given to the Bahamas and Caribbean during the age of discovery.

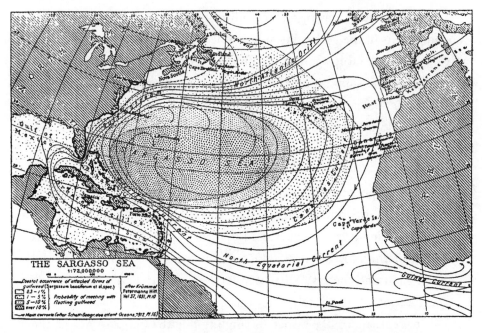

Figure 2.1. Stories circulating Plato's world concerning the
existence of the Sargasso Sea helped perpetuate the idea of
an impassable expanse of mud shoals and shallows that existed
beyond the Pillars of Hercules.

Whether Honorius simply read Plato and realized that the "curdled
sea" was one and the same as the impassable sea "blocked by mud, just
below the surface, left by the settling down of the island"[42] cannot now
be determined. However, since Honorius asserted that further mythical islands lay in the same vicinity, there is every reason to believe that
these were synonymous with the "other islands" Plato said lay in front
of the "opposite continent" (see fig. 2.1).

BEYOND BRITAIN

Quite recently, it has been proposed that Atlantis was once located in
the proximity of the British Isles, which possess rich legends of lost lands
that lay beyond their western coastlines.[43] Should this be so, it would

imply that Plato's "other islands" were those encountered by ancient mariners who used the so-called Northwest Passage to reach New England.[44] If a vessel were to leave, say, the northern coast of Ireland or Scotland, it could very easily make a transatlantic crossing via the Faeroe Isles, Iceland, the southern coast of Greenland, Newfoundland, and finally Nova Scotia. It was then just a short sea crossing to Cape Cod, Massachusetts.

There is ample evidence that fishing vessels from England and the Basque country of Spain were secretly using the Northwest Passage to exploit the abundant cod grounds off Labrador, Newfoundland, and New England long before the age of Columbus. It is a case convincingly argued in an intriguing book titled *Cod: A Biography of the Fish That Changed the World* by American writer and journalist Mark Kurlansky. He has pointed out that when in 1534 the Frenchman Jacques Cartier "discovered" the mouth of the St. Lawrence River, west of Newfoundland, he was confounded by "the presence of 1,000 Basque fishing vessels."[45]

One scholar who has attempted to demonstrate that Atlantis lay off the west coast of Britain is Russian scientist Viatscheslav Koudriavtsev of the Institute of Metahistory in Moscow.[46] He is convinced that evidence of the island's former existence will be found on the shallow banks that lie beyond Cornwall's Isles of Scilly, traditionally the site of lost Lyonesse. The main problem with this theory is that the Sargasso Sea is literally thousands of kilometers southwest of Britain. Moreover, there is no similar oceanic debris off the British Isles that might account for the impassable sea alluded to, not just by Plato but also by Aristotle, Pseudo-Scylax, and, most important of all, Himilco.

ARTIFACTS OF NEW ENGLAND

It is also a fact that a large number of Old World artifacts have turned up at various locations in New England. These have included Roman and Carthaginian coins, and Iberian and Carthaginian amphorae, as well as an assortment of inscribed stones in various Old World languages.

There are countless instances of Roman coins being found in New England, and one of the most compelling cases concerns the alleged discovery of Roman relics on a beach at Plum Island, Massachusetts. Two young men, Al Locke and Sheldon Lane, were out metal-detecting after a particularly violent storm when they came across a large piece of waterlogged wood, which they presumed had been dislodged from the sea bottom. Unexpectedly, it gave a positive reading. Upon inspection the men found that a partially worn bronze coin, the size of a silver dollar, was embedded in the wood. They found that the wood also contained two ship spikes some fifteen centimeters long and cast from bronze. Later it was determined that the coin bore the head of the emperor Severus Alexander, who was murdered in 235 CE.[47] The discovery attracted local publicity, and subsequently it transpired that a local coin dealer named Peter Pratt had found a similar bronze Roman coin of the third century while metal-detecting in the same area of Plum Island.[48]

In addition to Roman coins, a number of terracotta amphorae, either of Iberian or Carthaginian origin, have been found at various locations in New England. For instance, two intact examples were pulled out of the waters of Castine Bay, Maine, by scuba diver Norwood Bakeman. At first he was unsure of the significance of the discovery, although upon being examined by American epigrapher and prehistorian James P. Whittall, the objects were formally identified as "Spanish olive jars."[49] He found that they showed "wear from constant chafing, caused by the rolling of the vessel on long journeys at sea while the jars were secured by lines to the deck or in the hold."[50] More Iberian amphorae were dredged up from a depth of thirty-six meters by the nets of a fishing vessel out of Newburyport, Massachusetts, in 1991.[51] Other examples have also been found at Boston, Massachusetts, and Jonesboro, Maine.[52]

Evidence of an Iberic-Phoenician and Carthaginian presence in

Massachusetts has come with the discovery of coins, oil lamps, and sword blades of various dates (see chapter 10).

In addition to the discovery of various out-of-place artifacts, there exists a whole range of inscribed stones that are considered to be evidence of pre-Columbian contact with North America. One such stone was found as early as 1658 being used as a stepping-stone into an American Indian church on a reservation at Bourne, near Cape Cod, Massachusetts.[53] In size it is one and a half meters in length and four and a half meters wide, while its underside bears a curious inscription. For hundreds of years no one could interpret it, but then it came to the notice of Barry Fell. He determined that its strange characters were Iberian, a language developed by the Phoenician colonists of southwest Spain. After carefully translating the stone's short inscription, Fell concluded that the message read, "A proclamation of annexation. Do not deface. By this Hanno takes possession."[54]

Academics were not entirely convinced by Fell's findings, since it was assumed that the Hanno in question was the Carthaginian general and navigator who attempted to circumnavigate Africa with a fleet of sixty ships and thirty thousand men around 425 BCE (see chapter 5). Yet there is no reason to make this conclusion. The inscription does not say which Hanno was responsible for its carving. Furthermore, we know that Hanno was a common name in Carthage, for at least two others are recorded—both Carthaginian commanders who lived in the second half of the third century BCE.

Many other inscribed stones have been unearthed across the United States. There are simply too many to list individually, but some are incontestable and imply that foreign visitors from different cultures traveled to the Americas and left their mark in a number of different ways.[55]

If these finds are to be seen as genuine, it implies ancient contact with North America up to 1,800 years before the arrival in Newfoundland of Norse seafarers around the beginning of the eleventh century. Did some knowledge of these early oceanic crossings filter through to the Mediterranean world in Plato's day?

IN THE AZORES

Another, slightly more plausible solution to the Atlantis mystery is that Plato's Atlantic island was located in the vicinity of the island group known as the Azores in the mid-Atlantic. As we have seen, Honorius of Autun wrote that the islands of the Hesperides were adjoined to the "curdled sea" that covers the site of lost Atlantis. Since the Sargasso Sea lies to the west of the Azores, and the Hesperides have occasionally been identified with this island group,[56] Atlantologists argue that the sunken landmass must have been situated in this part of the ocean.

The cluster of nine main islands that make up the Azores are located amid a chain of underwater mountains that rise to heights in excess of nine thousand meters. They form part of the Mid-Atlantic Ridge that defines the division between tectonic plates, running roughly north–south beneath the ocean floor for a distance of around 17,600 kilometers. It is the tips of the very highest of these subterranean mountains that protrude from the ocean floor as the principal islands of the Azores that are themselves endowed with sizeable mountains that soar to a height in excess of 2,100 meters.

One of the first writers to suggest that the Azores are the remnants of an Atlantean island continent was Ignatius Donnelly, author of the seminal classic *Atlantis: The Antediluvian World,* first published in 1882. This American congressman set down the foundations for the thousands of books and articles that have been written on this subject over the past 130 years or so. Although Donnelly's book has seen countless reprints and is still available today, much of what he had to say about Atlantis being an antediluvian motherland for the diffusion of civilization on both sides of the Atlantic has since been proved incorrect. However, Donnelly's original thesis of a central Atlantean landmass has been perpetuated by a number of well-respected scholars of the Atlantis mystery.

Perhaps the most authoritative writer to develop the theory of a sunken continent in the vicinity of the Mid-Atlantic Ridge was the

Russian academic Nikolai Zhirov. During the 1960s he wrote a series of papers on the subject, as well as a definitive book titled *Atlantis—Atlantology: Basic Problems,* first published in English in 1970. Like Donnelly, he argued that the former Atlantean landmass lay in the vicinity of the Azores and that, before it sank without trace, it acted as a land bridge for the migration of flora and fauna between Africa and the Americas.[57]

Christian O'Brien, a retired industrial geologist, archaeologist, and historical writer, also tackled the concept of a mid-Atlantic continent having once existed in the vicinity of the Azores. In his 1997 book *The Shining Ones*—coauthored with his wife Barbara Joy—he proposed that a former Azorean landmass suffered immense cataclysms and eventually sank into the Earth's liquid magma, leaving only the Azores as hard evidence of its former existence.[58] The discovery of six fields of hot springs in the vicinity of the Azores was cited as firm evidence of this hypothesis. They might be seen as typical of the effects caused by cold seawater that percolates down through the lava before being forced upward to the ocean floor by rising heat.[59] During explorations off the island of São Miguel, the largest island in the Azores group, in 1971 Christian and Barbara O'Brien found clear evidence of an underwater riverbed filled with water-worn boulders.[60] By applying detailed contouring methods to hydrographic charts, the O'Briens discerned that rivers draining off the southern slopes of São Miguel once converged together in a huge valley, now situated some sixty-four kilometers out from the present coastline.[61] Other islands in the Azores group have yielded similar hydrographic anomalies, and in one case the O'Briens even traced a series of river valleys that extended for a distance of 288 kilometers before converging together in a much larger river basin.[62]

Using this knowledge of ancient river systems, the O'Briens were able to reconstruct a land profile that revealed an Azorean landmass "about the size and shape of Spain," with high mountain ranges rising more than 3,655 meters above sea level, as well as impressive rivers that run "in curving valley systems." They further pointed out, "In the southeast, a feature which we have called 'The Great Plain' covered an area in excess of 3,500 square miles [9,065 square kilometers], and was watered by a river comparable in size to the River Thames in England. It has, as we shall see, points in common with a great plain described by Plato in his Critias, as being a feature of the island of Atlantis."[63]

The conclusion drawn from these findings is that the Azores once formed part of a much greater landmass. This sank, finally, beneath the waves and is now situated "many thousands of feet" below the current sea level.[64] To obtain a more substantial insight into this fascinating subject, the O'Briens suggested that a scientific team extract a series of core samples from their proposed river channels. They confidently predicted that these would show evidence not only of ancient riverbeds, but also of freshwater flora and fauna that once thrived on the former Azorean landmass.[65]

In this theory we are presented with another attractive role model for sunken Atlantis, supported in this case by the knowledge that on the island of São Miguel a local legend tells of seven cities now submerged beneath two volcanic lakes, one of blue water and the other of green (see chapter 13).[66] Unfortunately, there are fundamental problems in accepting the former existence of an Azorean landmass. It is now known, for instance, that the volcanic mountains that constitute the Mid-Atlantic Ridge are of relatively recent composition. In many ways they can be seen as enormous geological scars on a gaping wound that never properly heals. The north-south-orientated tectonic plates produce an upward flow of magma that constantly creates new underwater mountain systems that could never have formed part of a geological landmass in the manner described.

In addition to these problems, we must also acknowledge that there is now wide-scale acceptance of the so-called continental drift theory, first proposed in 1915 by the German meteorologist Arthur Wegener. In simple terms, this asserts that many millions of years ago the American and African landmasses were joined together, yet ever since they have been slowly moving apart. Just by making paper cutouts of the different continents and slotting them together we can see they fit snugly, suggesting that the continental drift theory is correct. Furthermore, the fact that the American and African continents were once joined together explains much of the flora and fauna they have in common.

More damning still for the O'Briens' theory is that when the first Portuguese navigators reached the Azorean islands in 1427, they found them completely devoid not only of human life but also of any animals. Even though some evidence has emerged to suggest that sometime in the third century BCE Carthaginian vessels from North Africa reached Corvo, the westernmost of the Azorean islands (see chapter 5), no archaeology has come to light to suggest that the archipelago ever supported an indigenous culture.

Even if the O'Briens' proposals regarding prehistoric riverbeds located off the coast of São Miguel do prove to be correct it seems unlikely that Plato's Atlantis is based on a memory of a high culture that once thrived on any proposed Azorean landmass. Admittedly, if we look again at our global jigsaw made of paper cutouts, we can see that there are slight gaps. However, these fall not in the vicinity of the Azores but around the Gulf of Mexico and the Caribbean Sea. Could it be possible that Atlantis awaits discovery somewhere in this region of the globe?

Everything points toward Atlantis having once existed somewhere off the east coast of the American continent, plausibly in the vicinity of the Bahamas and Caribbean. Yet it is also clear that there are major problems with this theory, not least of all in respect to the supposed size of Plato's Atlantic island, which would hardly fit in the gaps of our global jigsaw. How might we justify these curious anomalies? A more careful examination of the *Critias,* the second of Plato's dialogues on the mysteries of Atlantis, will provide some useful answers.

3

THE ATLANTICUS

Plato sat down to write his second and final version of the Atlantis legend some five years after the completion of the *Timaeus*. How exactly the original story of a sunken Atlantic isle was received among his contemporaries is unclear (although see Aristotle's comment on the matter in chapter 4). Whether they applauded it, condemned it, or were merely indifferent to it remains a matter of speculation. What we do know is that some peculiar stories began to circulate in Greece within a century or so of Plato's death. One rumor put about by Timon the Pyrrhonist (ca. 279 BCE) suggested that the *Timaeus* was based on primary material borrowed by Plato from earlier authors.[1] Another accused him of having stolen the book from a rival, while still another spoke of Plato paying someone for an existing manuscript that he later claimed as his own![2] None of these allegations are likely to have any basis in truth, and no similar accusations were leveled against the *Critias*.

This clearly unfinished second text, which features the Atlantis theme exclusively, was either Plato's penultimate work (the last of his dialogues being *The Laws*), or even the final literary offering he wrote before his death in around 347 BCE. It is possible that since he knew he was nearing the end of his life (he was around seventy-nine in 350 BCE), he had nothing to lose by committing to writing all that he knew about the fabled Atlantean empire.

As in Plato's earlier works, *The Republic* and the *Timaeus,* the *Critias* features the same assembly of four: Socrates, Timaeus, Hermocrates, and Critias, after whom it is titled. Curiously, there is evidence to suggest that the work also possessed a rather intriguing second title. Proclus Daidochus (412–485 CE), a philosopher, poet, and scientist, in his *Commentaries of Proclus on the* Timaeus *of Plato,* written circa 432–440 CE,[3] refers specifically to the *Critias* as the *Atlanticus.* For instance, at one point he states, "Hence in the Atlanticus, Critias having assembled the Gods, as consulting about the punishment of the Atlantics, he says, 'Jupiter thus addressed them.'"[4] Proclus is here describing the last lines of the *Critias,* showing that he is alluding to it under this title. Later in the text, Proclus discusses the chronological order of the dialogues: "Conformably to this congruity, the Republic has an arrangement prior to the Timaeus; and the Timaeus to the Atlanticus,"[5] confirming that he is referring to the *Critias.* Whether Proclus himself named it the *Atlanticus* or whether it was a title already in existence may never be known.

THE DIALOGUE RECOMMENCES

Following an introduction to set the scene in which Hermocrates invites the presence of the god Paean, the goddess Memory, and the Muses, Critias provides the reader with a brief recap of the Atlantis story told so far. The participants of the dialogue are first reminded that "it is in all nine thousand years since a general war . . . between those who dwelt without and those who dwelt within the pillars of Heracles."[6]

Instantly a gross inconsistency has crept into the account, for although Critias affirms that Athens's aggressor came from "without" the Pillars of Hercules, the actual war is here said to have taken place "nine thousand years" before the date of the dialogue, circa 421 BCE. This implies a date in the region of 9421 BCE, which is not what was stated in the *Timaeus.* Here nine thousand years is the time that has elapsed between the foundation of Athens and Solon's visit to Sais circa 570 BCE. Since Egypt was said to have been founded a full thousand years later, and the "aggressor" rose up against both Athens and Egypt, it provides a date post–8570 BCE. These widely differing dates leave us with a glaring anomaly that defies explanation. The only obvious solution is to assume a certain amount of sloppiness on Plato's part when compiling the text.

Of equal concern is the modern belief that Plato offered a date of circa 9600 BCE for the destruction of Atlantis. This surmise comes from a wrongful reading of the *Timeus,* where it says that the Athenian nation was a full one thousand years older than Plato's proposed foundation date for the Egyptian civilization, circa 8570 BCE. However, as we have seen, nowhere in the *Timaeus,* or indeed in the *Critias,* does Plato state that the foundation date of the Athenian nation coincided with the destruction of Atlantis. If anything the date of the destruction, as taken from the *Critias,* should be post circa 9421 BCE, and after circa 8570 BCE if taken from the *Timaeus.* The bigger problem is that so many books, articles, and even academic papers use 9600 BCE as the destruction date for Atlantis that it becomes impossible to ignore. Even the present author has had no option but to resort to using it on several occasions in this book.

Back to the text and we find that those who came from beyond the Pillars of Hercules are confirmed as the "kings of the island of Atlantis," which "as you will recollect, was once . . . an island larger than Libya and Asia together."[7] The assembly is also reminded that the landmass was "engulfed by earthquakes [there is no mention of floods] and is the source of the impassable mud which prevents navigators from this quarter from advancing through the straits into the open Ocean."[8] There is no mention in the *Critias* of the "opposite continent," although Plato does affirm the belief that the Atlantic Ocean was once accessible to "voyagers" from his own world, adding that in his day this passage was impossible due to the presence of the shallow sea.

The *Critias* then proceeds with a brief review of the origins, past deeds, and deluges of the Athenian nation as recounted in the *Timaeus.* Finally, Critias turns his attention to the defeated Atlantean aggressor, saying, "As for the condition and early history of their [i.e., the Athenians'] antagonists, if my memories of the tale I heard as a boy do not play me false, I will now impart the story freely to you as friends."[9]

Using Critias the Younger as the dialogue's storyteller enables Plato to insinuate, quite cryptically, that he, too, is merely recalling a story passed on to him when just a boy by this same Critias. He is identified as either Plato's uncle or great-grandfather, depending on the genealogy consulted. Both are claimed to have had grandfathers called Critias and great-grandfathers called Dropides. Which one is being alluded to in the text is of no special relevance. All we need to presume is that Critias the Younger is suggesting that the account was inherited from his own great-grandfather, Dropides, who acquired it originally from Solon, a friend and relative.

Critias then explains why, in the narrative he is about to relate, the Atlantic "barbarians" bear Greek names. He tells us, "Solon had a fancy to turn the tale to account in his own poetry; so he asked questions about the significance of the names and discovered that the original Egyptian authors of the narrative had translated them into their own speech. In his turn, as he learned the sense of a name, he translated it back again, *in his manuscript,* into our own language. His actual papers were once in my father's hands, and are in my own, to this day, and I studied them thoroughly in my boyhood."[10] (current author's emphasis)

There is much of interest in these statements. First, it is suggested that, as the biographer Plutarch was later to repeat, Solon had intended to publish the Atlantis story, but never got around to doing it, even though he had already completed "his manuscript" on the subject. This remained in the family until eventually it came into the possession of Critias the Younger. Second, the reader is told that the names that feature in the *Critias* were first changed from their native language by the Egyptian priests before being transferred into Greek by Solon for poetic purposes: hence the next line of the text, which reads, "So if you hear names like those of our own countrymen, you must not be surprised."[11]

These few facts alone hint at the former existence of an original

Atlanticus—one that was authored by Solon and passed on in some form or another through successive generations of Plato's family. If correct, might this have been the original source material behind Plato's own knowledge of the subject? The problem here is that there is no contemporary evidence to suggest that Solon ever wrote such a manuscript. We have only Plato's own fictional account of the supposed events that led him to gain knowledge of the story, and, as we have discovered already, there are grounds to treat these claims with some suspicion.

GODS OF THE OUTER OCEAN

Returning to the text of the *Critias,* the reader learns next that the "long story" of Atlantis "began much in this fashion."[12] When the gods of old divided up the Earth, Poseidon (the Greek form of Neptune) received as his lot "the isle of Atlantis."[13] It goes on: "By the sea, in the center of the island, there was a plain, said to have been the most beauteous of all such plains and very fertile, and, again, near the center of this plain, at a distance of some fifty furlongs [10 kilometers], a mountain which was nowhere of any great altitude."[14]

"In this mountain [i.e., within a cave]," the reader is told, there lived a mortal being named Euenor and his wife Leucippe. She bore a daughter named Clito, who, following the death of her parents, was desired by Poseidon. To possess her the sea-god built a fortified "fence of alternative rings of sea and land, smaller and greater, one within another."[15] Two of these "wheels" were of earth and three were of water, making the center island inaccessible to "man," for "there were as yet no ships and no seafaring."[16]

From these words we can view these events as having taken place during the age of the gods, a time when humanity still inhabited caves and civilization had not yet begun.

Critias tells us that two fountains were to be found on the main island—one warm and the other cold. Furthermore, the soil thereabouts produced an abundance of "food-plants of all kinds."[17]

Poseidon and Clito went on to produce ten children, described as "five twin births of male offspring." Atlantis was then divided into ten portions to accommodate each of the ten sons.[18] The firstborn, Atlas, was granted the land in the middle of the island, where his mother was born, as well as the "lot of land surrounding it."[19] Through his birthright, Atlas was also appointed to be the first king of Atlantis.[20] The rest of the princes were granted sovereignty over "a large population and the lordship of wide lands."[21]

Atlas, of course, is a name integrally linked with both the antediluvian island kingdom named by Plato and the ocean in which it was located. The names Atlas, Atlantis, and Atlantic are considered by language scholars to derive their origin from the Greek word *tlâo,* meaning "to endure" or "to bear," recalling Atlas's role as bearer of the vault of heaven. The name Atlantis has a female determinative and is generally rendered "daughter of Atlas."

As one of the Titans, Atlas was said to have married either Pleione, a daughter of Oceanus, or Hesperis, by whom he produced seven daughters known as the Atlantides, or the Hesperides in some accounts. He was also a legendary king of Mauritania, an ancient kingdom of Libya, which originally embraced Morocco, Algeria, and the Western Sahara. The Greek hero Perseus, fresh from his pursuit of the Gorgons, was said to have turned Atlas into a mountain using the head of Medusa.

Today the Atlas Mountains of North Africa are considered to be the location of Atlas's petrification. Forming a crescent on the north side of the Algerian Sahara, they stretch right across to the northwest coast of Africa. There is even a Mount Atlas, the appearance of which gave rise to the belief that it is in fact a stone giant supporting the vault of heaven on his shoulders (and plausibly the origin behind the myth of Atlas—see chapter 14).

Traditionally, Atlas's connection with Libya and the Western Ocean came about because, to the Hellenic Greeks, his kingdom was seen as the most westerly point of the known world. Beyond Mauritania was an uncharted region that even accomplished mariners would not dare to navigate unless they first gained the blessings of its patron, Atlas, who presided over the depths of the sea. This, then, is why Plato's Atlantic isle, Atlantis, became the exclusive dominion of Atlas, whom Plato makes a half-mortal son of Poseidon.

In Greek mythology, Poseidon was the son of Cronus, the Greek form of Saturn, who was said to have devoured his son immediately after birth. Yet Poseidon was then restored to life by means of a magic potion provided by Metis, one of the Oceanides. On the death of his father, Poseidon divided up the world with his brothers and received for himself dominion over all waters. These included the seas, rivers, fountains, springs, and, of course, the outer ocean. He was also said to have been able to "cause earthquakes at his pleasure, and [to] raise islands from the bottom of the sea with a blow of his trident."[22] As in the case of Atlas, the veneration of Poseidon was especially strong among the peoples of Libya, who saw him as the first of all gods.[23]

These, then, are the key Greek gods in Plato's Atlantis narrative. Their role here is perhaps apt, yet their preexisting myths are expanded in the text almost beyond recognition. Poseidon is made to desire a mortal woman, Clito, who bears him five sets of male twins, the first being mighty Atlas. Although this paternal link between the two gods is unknown outside of the *Critias,* it does not necessarily invalidate Plato's story. Myths and legends are merely vehicles for the conveyance of ancestral memories of age-old events across countless generations. Plato simply exploited this same literary vehicle for his own purposes.

PRINCES OF NUMEROUS ISLANDS

Next in the *Critias* we find that, whereas Atlas becomes Atlantis's first king and so gains control over the central position of the island, his twin brother is bestowed "the extremity of the island off the pillars of Heracles, fronting the region now known as Gadira."[24] His name in Greek is Eumelus, "but in the language of his own country [it is] Gadirus, and no doubt his name was the origin of that of the district."[25]

Plato was no geographer. Neither was he a historian, or a navigator. However, as we have already established, there is every reason to assume that he did have access to garbled maritime knowledge concerning supposedly unknown Atlantic islands, and in particular their proximity to the "opposite continent" and the Sargasso Sea. It is therefore with some interest that he makes reference to a region fronting Atlantis called Gadira.

There can be little doubt that the reference to Gadira alludes to the ancient Phoenician city-port of this name situated on the Atlantic coast of southwest Spain, in ancient Iberia. In Plato's day it thrived under the control of the Carthaginians, even though it still acted independent from their main city-port of Carthage on the Mediterranean coast of Tunisia. In later Roman times the Iberian port became known as Gades, from which the modern Cadiz takes its name (although it is not located on the same spot). In the style of many other Phoenician and Carthaginian city-ports, Gades grew up around an offshore island. Here stood a temple dedicated to the Phoenician god Melqart, who in Greek tradition was identified with Hercules.

Gades was said to have been located just forty kilometers beyond the Pillars of Hercules,[26] yet in the *Critias* Plato implies that one of the princes of Atlantis, the twin of Atlas, held dominion over the portion of the Atlantic island that lay closest to this city-port. It is difficult to determine exactly what he might have meant by this statement. If, however, Plato truly believed that Atlantis was the size of Libya and Asia combined, it is conceivable he saw its eastern extremities as extending so far across the outer ocean they almost reached the coast of Spain. On the other hand, his inclusion of Gades in the Atlantis story has led some authors to conclude that either the Atlantic island lay off the Spanish coast, or that Gades (or more precisely the neighboring city-port of Tartessos) was itself Atlantis.[27] Such ideas make little sense of Atlantis's geographical placement as defined in the *Timaeus*, and, as we shall see, Gades may have played a quite different, yet equally important, role in the construction of the Atlantis myth (see chapter 12).

The *Critias* provides the reader with the names of the other four sets of male twins born to Clito, before adding that "all these and their descendants for many generations reigned as princes of numerous islands of the ocean *besides* their own, and were also . . . suzerains of the population of the hither or inner side of the straits, as far as Egypt and Tyrrhenia.[28] (current author's emphasis)

There is further confirmation here that Atlantis lay somewhere in the Western Ocean and that the Atlantic empire consisted of a series of islands ruled over by the princes of the main island. This is a statement found originally in the *Timaeus,* which also says that the kings of Atlantis held dominion over "other islands and parts of the [opposite] continent."[29]

Very possibly, these are the same islands that Plato informs us were used by ancient voyagers to reach "the opposite continent," that is, the American mainland. What is more, the suggestion that Atlantis also gained control of lands within the Pillars of Hercules clearly implies that the empire established itself in both Europe and Libya. All this would indicate some kind of connection between the supposed Atlanteans of the Western Ocean and the "voyagers" from within the Mediterranean, whom Plato tells us were able to reach "the opposite continent" via a series of "other islands," prior to the final destruction of Atlantis.[30]

MARVELS OF ATLANTIS

The *Critias* then informs the reader that the descendants of Atlas were able to retain the throne of Atlantis for many generations, creating a city on the main island that possessed immense natural resources.[31] Mining is said to have taken place, and one of the most precious metals "excavated in various parts of the island" was "orichalc," or "orichalcum."[32] Plato tells us that it "gleamed like fire"[33] and was second only in value to gold.[34] Various attempts have been made to identify orichalc. The name itself appears in other classical writings and seems to translate as "mountain copper," or even "mountain brass." Russian Atlantis scholar Nikolai Zhirov argued convincingly that orichalc was a bronze-zinc alloy produced in ancient times and known also as "tombaca." Since it contained 18 percent or less of zinc, it appeared red in color and lent "itself to cold forging, flattening, and drawing."[35]

In addition to the mining of metals, stone was quarried in Atlantis and timbers felled for use in the construction of buildings. Wild and domesticated animals were found in abundance; "even elephants," we are told, "were plentiful.[36] This last statement has often been used by skeptics to demonstrate the incredible nature of Plato's account. No evidence that elephants ever roamed any Atlantic island has ever come to light. Furthermore, no elephants were found when the first conquistadors penetrated the tropical heartland of the American continent.

What we can say is that various species of mammoth and mastodon inhabited the North American continent prior to the cessation of the last Ice Age, circa 9600 BCE. Conceivably, such enormous beasts could have been construed as elephants, invoking the possibility that they might have existed on Plato's Atlantic island. In support of this theory Atlantologists cite the fact that mammoth and mastodon bones have been trawled up from the sea bottom by vessels fishing off the Atlantic shelf, close to the Mid-Atlantic Ridge.[37] Despite such inexplicable curiosities, there is no hard evidence whatsoever to lend credibility to the idea of elephants in Atlantis.

Yet is it elephants that Plato refers to in the *Critias*. What might have caused him to introduce this noble beast into the Atlantis account? Elephants were obviously known to traders and navigators of the ancient world, particularly those who traveled through Libya, where a now extinct species once thrived. Furthermore, ancient Egyptian kings, such as Thutmosis III (ca. 1490–1436 BCE), embarked on hunting expeditions in pursuit of the elephant,[38] while the now extinct Syrian elephant, with its characteristic small ear, is depicted on an ostracon located in the tomb of Rameses III (1182–1151 BCE).[39] Since we know that both Solon and Plato visited Egypt to gain instruction in philosophy and wisdom, it is possible they learned of the existence of elephants when in this country. Both men also traveled widely throughout the

Mediterranean world and might have chanced on stories that spoke of elephants living in lands beyond the Pillars of Hercules (plausibly along the West African coast; see the account of the sea voyage of Hanno, a Carthaginian general, in chapter 5). On this basis alone, either Solon or Plato could thus have added this unusual element to the Atlantis story.

STRANGE FRUIT

After recalling the beasts present on Atlantis, the *Critias* goes on to describe the various fruits of the earth grown and cultivated on the main island, one of which makes very interesting reading indeed.

> The soil bore all aromatic substances still to be found on earth, roots, stalks, canes, gums exuded by flowers and fruits, and they throve on it. Then, as for cultivated fruits, the dry sort which is meant to be our food supply and those others we use as solid nutriment—we call the various kinds pulse [e.g., peas and beans]—as well as the woodland kind which gives us meat and drink and oil together, the fruit of trees that ministers to our pleasure and merriment and is so hard to preserve, and that we serve as welcome dessert to a jaded man to charm away his satiety.[40]

Something very significant is made clear here; the cultivated product used as "solid nutriment" that is said to give "meat and drink and oil together" has a familiar ring to it. It is surely the coconut, which does indeed contain a nutritious "drink" as well as fleshy white "meat" from which is extracted a highly prized "oil." So can Plato have been alluding to the coconut, an exotic fruit so obviously tropical in origin?

Everywhere from Florida to the Bahamas, the Caribbean, and the Lesser Antilles, coconuts grow in abundance. Yet before the discovery of the New World, it is not known exactly how widespread the distribution of the coconut palm might have been in the Western Hemisphere. In the opinion of nearly all botanists the coconut genus originated on the islands of Melanesia in the western Pacific and spread gradually westward until it entered Southeast Asia and eastward until it reached the Pacific coast of the Americas.[41] Good evidence exists to show that it was to be found from Panama right down to Colombia and Ecuador on the Pacific coast of South America before the time of Conquest.[42]

In theory coconuts were unknown on the western Atlantic seaboard until after the discovery of the West Indies in 1492, which, if so, would make nonsense of Plato's statement to this effect. This is not, however, the full story.

The great sea adventurer and historian Thor Heyerdahl made a special study of the coconut and proposed that the official attitude toward its worldwide distribution derives from biased preconceptions concerning the presumed isolation of the Americas before the time of "discovery." He ably demonstrated that the coconut palm, *Cocas nucifera,* evolved not in Asia or in the western Pacific but in the Americas, where various members of its subfamily (*Cocoinae*) occur naturally. Only in its hybrid form does it exist in Asia.[43] Heyerdahl goes on to say that the old belief in ripe green coconuts falling onto beaches and being transported by the tide to distant lands, where they then germinate, is fraught with problems. Experiments carried out in 1941 in Hawaii demonstrated conclusively that during long sea journeys "fouling organisms" enter through the eyes of the fruit and destroy its ability to germinate properly.[44] Thus there is no way that the coconut could have spread across the Pacific in such a casual fashion. More likely is that the fruit was carried across the ocean not by the actions of water but onboard vessels making transpacific journeys. Compelling evidence to suggest that contact between cultures in Southeast Asia and the Americas occurred with frequency in pre-Columbian times is presented in chapter 9.

So if the coconut genus originated in the Americas, is there any evidence to suggest that it was present either in the Bahamas or Caribbean before the age of Columbus?

No early Spanish chronicler who visited the Caribbean ever makes mention of a tree or fruit that matches the description of the coconut, certainly not until enough time had elapsed for it to have been introduced to the western Atlantic seaboard by colonial settlers. Yet the enormous distribution of the coconut throughout the entire Caribbean world makes it a little difficult to accept this solution. Furthermore, deluge stories connected with "the natives of Haiti," and the Caribbean in general, claim that "the earth was repopulated by a lone survivor who threw coconuts into the air which came down as men and women."[45] If this account originated among the indigenous tribes, it would suggest that coconuts really were present in the archipelago during the prehistoric age.

A MARVEL OF CIVILIZATION

After describing food production in Atlantis, the text of the *Critias* explains that "the kings employed all these gifts of the soil to construct and beautify their temples, royal residence, harbours, dock, and domain in general on the following plan."[46] What follows is a highly conceptualized description of Atlantis's mighty city at the height of its power. Having already been informed that Poseidon constructed a series of three water-filled rings around the foundation point of the Atlantean royal dynasty, the reader is then told that a road was built across these furrows to the central islet. Here was constructed a palace, as well as a great temple dedicated to the island's gods and great ancestors. Each new king added to these buildings until they were a marvel to behold.

Other construction projects included the cutting of a roofed canal that began at the sea and broke through each of the rings of land until it reached the innermost ring of water that surrounded the all-important central islet. In all, the canal was said to have been in length fifty furlongs (ten kilometers), in breadth three hundred feet (91.5 meters), and in depth one hundred feet (thirty meters). Towers and gates were erected on the bridges at either end of the canal to ensure the safe passage of the great seagoing vessels that continually navigated this covered waterway.[47]

Stones in three colors were employed individually or together in patterns to enhance the beauty of the Atlantean citadel. These were quarried either from beneath the central islet or from the construction sites of the various circular canals. In addition to this, the walls of the buildings are said to have been coated each with a different colored metal. Those of the outer land ring were covered in copper, those in the inner land ring were coated in "melted tin," while the walls of the buildings on the central islet were lined with orichalc, "which gleamed like fire."[48]

Surrounded by golden railings in the heart of the great temple was an untrodden inner sanctum sacred to the memory of Poseidon and his spouse Clito. It thus symbolized "the very place where the race of the ten princes had been first conceived and begotten."[49] This enormous building is said to have had a roof of ivory, ornamented with gold, silver, and orichalc, and walls lined with silver.[50] On pediments were statues covered in gold, including one of Poseidon on a chariot drawn by six winged horses and accompanied by a hundred Nereids riding dolphins. So large were these figures that their heads virtually touched the ceiling. All were focused around an altar of gigantic proportions.[51]

Outside the temple were to be found statues in gold of all the wives of the ten founding princes of Atlantis, as well as many other grand statues commissioned by both kings and private individuals. There were also dual springs (the same as the two fountains mentioned earlier?)— one hot and the other cold—the virtues of which are described as truly remarkable.[52] Around these were buildings and basins into which the waters were channeled. These provided warm baths in winter, and after their use the waters flowed into the Grove of Poseidon, where there were also trees of every kind.[53] Here, too, were temples, dedicated to other gods, as well as gardens and a gymnasium.[54] On the other island rings were more buildings, including stables for horses. The largest ring contained a racecourse that completely circumnavigated its interior. Barracks for bodyguards and dockyards full of seagoing vessels also occupied the island rings.[55]

Some fifty furlongs (ten kilometers) distant from the outer ring of water was built a great wall. It began by the sea at the mouth of the canal and surrounded the entire city.[56] Within its boundaries were a multitude of houses, while into the canal came "merchant-vessels and their passengers arriving from all quarters, whose vast numbers occasioned incessant shouting, clamor, and general uproar, day and night."[57]

This is the vivid picture of Atlantis's fabulous city painted for us by Plato some 2,350 years ago. Such a marvel of civilization exists nowhere in our memory of humanity's great achievements in the prehistoric age. Never has the spade of an archaeologist, or the explorations of a diver, ever uncovered any shred of evidence to support the popularly held belief that this fabled city once existed. This is not to say that the description offered by Plato does not bear similarities to known cities of both the ancient world and the Americas, only that at the present time we have nothing whatsoever to compare it with directly (see fig. 3.1). Should Plato's description of the Atlantean city therefore be dimissed as mere fiction conceived of by his rich and fertile imagination?

Figure 3.1. Fantastic conception of Plato's Atlantean city, complete with step pyramids (after Russian academic Nikolai Zhirov and R. Avotin). Why has the archaeological world failed to discover ruins that might confirm the former existence of this utopian realm?

At this point in many of the more popular books on the Atlantis mystery, the author will refer the reader to the discovery in 1872 of ancient Troy by German scholar Heinrich Schliemann. They will say that prior to his age this legendary city was thought by historians and classicists alike to be just a fable conjured to life in the pages of Homer's *Iliad*. Yet Schliemann thought otherwise. After following up certain clues regarding the possible location of Troy, he began excavating an occupational mound at Hissarlik on Turkey's Aegean coast, and very soon turned myth into reality.

The moral of the story is that some legends *are* based on truths and that we should never dismiss out of hand Plato's account of Atlantis. His fabulous city might await discovery somewhere in the depths, or indeed shallows, of the Atlantic Ocean. Let us hope that, one day, a city of the description provided by Plato is found; it would be the greatest archaeological discovery of modern times. For the moment, however, it is essential to stick wholly with the available evidence and look not for a city of fable but the historical source material behind the Greek philosopher's conception of the Atlantic island. Only then can we begin to piece together all the various strands of evidence that seem clearly to indicate the existence in the outer ocean of a forgotten world that thrived long before the classical age. It is in this spirit that we must now move on to examine Plato's proposed geography for his lost island paradise.

4

THE VIEW
OVER ATLANTIS

I have now given you a pretty faithful report of what I once learned
of the town and the old palace, and must do my best to recall the
general character of the territory and its organisation.[1]

With these words Plato, through the voice of *Critias,* concludes
his account of the Atlantic island's fabulous citadel before
going on to describe the more "general character" of the island and its
inhabitants.* Just how much of what he says really is a "pretty faithful report" of historical information will be up to the reader to decide.
Only after we have examined the final section of the *Critias* can we
go on to gain a more reliable picture of what was truly thought to lie
beyond the Western Ocean.

Returning to the narrative we find Critias explaining the island's
geography and terrain, about which he informs us:

---

*The English translation of the *Critias* quoted in this book, that of A. E. Taylor from
his *Plato: Timaeus and Critias,* gives the relevant measurements in furlongs, whereas
the original Greek text provides them in stadia. To confirm the original measurements
I consulted the edition of the *Critias* translated into English by Henry Davis in 1849.

The district [of Atlantis] as a whole, so I have heard, was of great elevation and its coast precipitous, but all round the city was a plain, enclosing it and itself enclosed in turn by mountain ranges which came right down to the sea. The plain itself was smooth, level, and of a generally oblong shape; it stretched for three thousand stadia [552 kilometers] in one direction, and, at its center [i.e., a line drawn north–south through the center of the plain—see below], for two thousand [368 kilometers] inland from the coast. All through the island this level district faced the south and was thus screened from the cold northerly winds.[2]

We are told that the "oblong" plain was sheltered from the "cold northerly winds" by "mountain ranges which came right down to the sea." For this to have been possible, the plain must have been orientated east–west, and not north–south as some writers have assumed. The citadel was itself situated on the plain, just fifty furlongs (ten kilometers) from the shoreline, implying that it was most probably located on the southern coast. It could not have been situated on its northern shoreline, as this was occupied by the "mountain ranges" that purportedly offered protection from the northerly winds (see fig. 4.1).

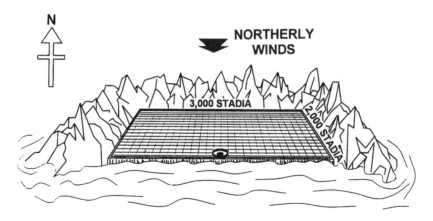

Figure 4.1. The Atlantean world according to the description given in Plato's *Critias*, circa 350 BCE. This view is not found in his earlier Atlantis dialogue, the *Timaeus*.

Thus affirmed, we are informed that the "mountains contained numerous villages with a wealthy population, besides rivers, lakes, and meadows that provided plentiful sustenance for all sorts of animals, wild or domestic, and timber of different kinds in quantities amply sufficient for manufactures of every type."[3] The rain that fell on the northern mountain range was directed down into an enormous "fosse," or trench, constructed around the entire plain. This was said to have had a perimeter of ten thousand stadia (1,840 kilometers) and a width of two thousand stadia (368 kilometers). The enormous channel was itself crisscrossed by a series of irrigation channels, perhaps like a chessboard, which allowed the plain to be well nourished with any excess water being discharged into the ocean.[4] Next in the *Critias* is a detailed account of the lands allotted to the peoples that inhabited the various districts and villages that made up the Atlantic island. The ruling princes of the various territories (and individual islands) would come together to carry out and obey the commands of Poseidon as prescribed of old on "a column of orichalc preserved in the sanctuary of Poseidon in the center of the island."[5]

At this ancient column the princes were accustomed to assemble alternately every four or five years. On such occasions they discussed common affairs and judged whether any of their number had transgressed the holy laws.[6] These periodic rites of sovereignty involved the capture of one of the sacrificial bulls allowed to roam freely in the sanctuary of Poseidon. This ritualistic act was conducted using "wooden clubs and cords only but no implement of iron," and afterward the victim was brought to the pillar of orichalc and there slaughtered, the blood being allowed to run down the pillar's inscription.[7]

The bull's "members" were then "devoted" to the god, while drops of blood—one for each prince—were mixed in a bowl of wine. One by one the princes would scoop out a cupful using a gold beaker, and, after a libation had been made onto the fire, each would swear an oath to exact judgment in the manner prescribed on the pillar.[8] The mixture would be consumed, and all would then retire to join a great banquet.[9]

After dark, when the bonfires had died down, the princes, dressed in blue robes, would return to the place of sacrifice to give and receive judgment until daybreak.[10]

CULT OF THE BULL

This idealized conception of sacrificial rites, used in conjunction with the swearing of oaths and laws, has often been used by scholars as evidence for the Aegean answer to the Atlantis mystery. In this respect they cite the legend of Minos, Crete's legendary king, whom the Athenian general and historian Thucydides (471–402 BCE) credits with having created the first navy.[11] He is said to have asked Poseidon to provide a white bull so that he might sacrifice it in his honor. A beast was duly provided, but because the king liked it so much he sought out a substitute animal and sacrificed that one instead. As punishment for his disobedience, Poseidon caused Minos's wife, Pasiphae, to fall in love with the white bull. Her unnatural desires were fulfilled through the help of Daedalus, and as a result she gave birth to a beast, half man and half bull. Known as the Minotaur, it was confined to an underground realm built by Minos and known as the Labyrinth. It was decreed that the defeated Athenian nation should offer as a yearly tribute seven boys and seven girls in order that the beast's sanguine appetite might be satisfied. This barbarity continued until the Minotaur was finally slain by the hero Theseus.

The above story is only a fable. Yet after Sir Arthur Evans began his famous excavations on Crete in 1895, it quickly became clear that by far the greatest cult practiced by its Minoan inhabitants 3,500 years ago was that of the bull. In the royal palace at Knossos he discovered walls adorned with enormous frescoes that depicted in vivid detail young men and women performing the dangerous act of bull leaping, while elsewhere bull motifs and symbols were found in profusion.[12]

To some archaeologists and historians this alone was enough to convince them that Plato's statements concerning bull sacrifices in

Atlantis were based on a memory of the Cretan bull cult. Moreover, tapered stone pillars, discovered among the Minoan ruins of Akrotiri on the remaining fragments of Thera, were likewise seen as evidence of the former existence of columns like the inscribed pillar of orichalc at which the chosen bull was sacrificed during the covenants attended by the princes of Atlantis.[13]

Is it possible that Minoan bull ceremonies on the island of Crete really did influence the development of the Atlantis legend? Strangely enough, there is every possibility that this might have been the case, yet not for the reasons suggested by the Cretan-Atlantis supporters. Ancient writers tell us that bulls were sacrificed regularly in honor of the sea-god Poseidon. The gall, or bile, of the victims was especially favored as an altar offering since its taste was considered to resemble "the bitterness of the sea water."[14] It is therefore conceivable that Plato introduced the idea of bull sacrifices on Atlantis simply because the animal was sacred to Poseidon. There seems no reason to link these taurine ceremonies with Minoan Crete purely on the basis that its young men and women performed the act of bull leaping and bull motifs litter its ruins.

One respected Atlantis author who made a serious study of the bull worship in Plato's *Critias* was L. Sprague de Camp. In his essential work *Lost Continents: The Atlantis Theme in History, Science, and Literature*, published in 1954, he found the connection with Cretan bull ceremonies "suggestive." He added, "Perhaps they entered the Atlantis story as fragments which Plato picked up and which his subconscious wove into his Atlantean fiction."[15] Yet having admitted this much, Camp also pointed out the total implausibility of the Cretan-Atlantis hypothesis by adding that "the Egyptians [as the presumed creators of the myth] are unlikely in a matter of 600 years or so to have moved Crete clear out of the Mediterranean, enlarged it a hundred-fold, and predated it by 8,000 years."[16] It is easier therefore to assume that the link between Crete and Atlantis was not a common origin to their bull ceremonies but a shared sea-god in Poseidon, who presided over the waters that encircled such islands.

END TIMES

After reviewing the sacred rites and holy laws adhered to by the princes of Atlantis, Critias turns his attention to the civil liberties and legal requirements adhered to by the Atlantic island's inhabitants. These are outlined in some detail before we are at last told the plight of the kingdom prior to the island's final destruction. It is said that the Atlanteans' love of material wealth, combined with their loss of spirituality, was the true cause of their downfall. Thus corrupted, they "began to behave themselves unseemly." Furthermore:

> To the seeing eye they now began to seem foul, for they were losing the fairest bloom from their most precious treasure, but to such as could not see the true happy life, to appear at last fair and blest indeed, now that they were taking the infection of wicked covet and pride of power. Zeus, the god of gods, who governs his kingdom by law, having the eye by which such things are seen, beheld their goodly house in its grievous plight and was minded to lay a judgement on them that the discipline might bring them back to tune. So he gathered all the gods in his most honourable residence, even that stands at the world's center and overlooks all that has part in becoming, and when he had gathered them there, he said.[17]

Here the text simply cuts off in midstream, leaving the reader to assume that Zeus, having gathered together the gods in council, made the decision to allow Athens to rise up against this mighty aggressor from the outer ocean. Once the Atlantean fleet had been defeated, "earthquakes and floods" would then have been unleashed in an attempt to wipe out the wickedness that had spread throughout the island.

Why Plato left the text unfinished has been a matter of speculation for hundreds, if not thousands, of years. Is some part of the book missing? Did Plato lose interest in the Atlantis legend just prior to the commencement of his final work, *The Laws,* apparently written just years before his death circa 347 BCE? Or could it be that this was the ending that Plato had always intended? Perhaps he wanted to leave the whole story on a cliffhanger so that he could expand the plot in some later work, perhaps a third and final volume of his Atlantean saga.

The fact remains that the sudden termination of the *Critias,* without even so much as a return to the dialogue in progress, deprives us of any further information regarding the true nature and locality of the Atlantic island. However, in some ways this might be a good thing, for it is quite clear that the writing style of the *Critias* differs greatly from that of its predecessor, the *Timaeus.* It seems to paint an entirely different picture of the Atlantic island, tinged clearly with flawed idealistic principles of a utopian world, while the two dialogues are also contradictory in respect to the pseudo-history they each present.

It is as if, in creating the Atlantis story as presented in the *Critias,* Plato has in mind somewhere else—somewhere known to him very well, which he saw as stagnating and falling into a state of decay during his own age. Might it be that he merely used the existing Atlantis legend as a warning of what could happen to a country or state if it does not adhere to the political and legislative laws outlined in his *Republic?*

PLATO'S WARNING

So what place might Plato have had in mind when he created his vision of an idealistic island kingdom that finally fell from grace? Some writers have proposed that he based the Atlantean empire on his home city of Athens. A century and a half before Plato wrote his dialogues, the Greek nations had come together to oppose the might of the Persian Empire at the same time that they were also at war with the Carthaginians. These twin conflicts came to an end in 480 BCE, when the mainland Greeks defeated the Persians in a decisive naval battle near the island of Salamis and the Sicilian Greeks defeated the Carthaginians in a land battle at Himera.

The virtues of the Greek confederacy, led by Athens, can be compared with the role played in Plato's dialogues by the Athenians in their decisive war against the might of Atlantis. Yet although in the fifty or so years that followed the defeat of the Persians and Carthaginians, Athens experienced a golden age of growth and expansion, this same period saw its decline into a state of decadence, reminiscent of that which befell the Atlantean nation.

Athens began to increase its wealth and power by invading neighboring states and islands that had previously been under autonomous control. The Greek nations viewed this tyranny with great disdain, and so accused Athens's ruling authority of being little better than their great enemies, the Persians, who had carved out their own empire in a similar manner. These events led eventually to the Peloponnesian War (431–404 BCE), in which a Greek confederacy, headed by Athens, was finally defeated by Peloponnesian forces during a decisive naval battle that once again reminds us of the war waged between Athens and the Atlantean aggressor.

Following Athens's surrender, its harbor was seized by the Peloponnesian forces, who then took control of the city, ironically on the day that the Athenians annually celebrated the defeat of the Persian navy off the coast of Salamis some seventy-six years earlier. Quite understandably, the Athenians were left totally demoralized by this humiliation. Athens's defeat marked the end of its dominion over the other Greek nations, leaving it to plunge into a long period of civil strife, political unrest, and economic decay.

Whereas Athens was once seen as the greatest and most influential Greek nation, the ineptitude and barbarity of its political leaders now became a subject that Plato strived to highlight and rectify with a heartfelt passion. Moreover, Plato had a far more personal reason to despise and loathe its ruling authority. In 399 BCE it sentenced to death his close friend and mentor Socrates, who was later to play the leading role in Plato's philosophical dialogues. A terrible incident such as this must have left a lingering emotional scar—one that Plato unquestionably bore for the rest of his life.

Plato's warning to Athens's ruling authority was therefore quite clear: either dispense with your wicked ways and return to the ideals that made you a great nation in the first place or suffer the wrath of Zeus and the gods of Olympus, the consequences of which would be ultimate destruction.

As the great American geographer and historical writer William H. Babcock concluded in respect to Plato's Atlantis narrative, "Atlantis may fairly be set down as a figment of dignified philosophic romance, owing its birth partly to various legendary hints and reports of seismic and volcanic action but much more to the glorious achievements of Athens in the Persian War and the apparent need of explaining a supposed shallow part of the Atlantic known to be obstructed and now named the Sargasso Sea."[18]

These surmises are realistic, and any scenarios introduced into the Atlantis narrative by Plato simply for political purposes will need to be stripped away before we can go on to assess the real source material behind the Atlantis legend.

SOURCES OF INSPIRATION

Other authors have attempted to demonstrate that Plato based his conception of Atlantis on Sicily, and in particular its celebrated city of Syracuse. Following the death of Socrates in 399 BCE, Plato traveled abroad, visiting Egypt, mainland Greece, and finally reaching Megara in Syracuse in 388 BCE. On his return to Athens in 386 BCE, Plato founded the school of philosophy known simply as the Academy, which occupied his time for the next twenty years. In 367 BCE he returned to Syracuse as a personal adviser of the ruler Dionysius II. Yet he became embroiled in political wrangles and power struggles, forcing him to leave once more for his native Athens. His third and final visit to Syracuse was in 361–360 BCE.

There is little question that the city-plan of Syracuse provided one or two ideas for his description of the Atlantean city as presented in the *Critias*.[19]

In addition to these facts, the Sicilians' celebrated repulsion of the Athenian naval fleet during the Peloponnesian War might also be compared with Plato's account of the Atlantean aggressor's defeat at the hands of the Athenian navy.[20] This comparison is strengthened in the knowledge that it was the historical Hermocrates, a general of Syracuse and one of the four participants in Plato's philosophical dialogues, who had helped the city repel the Athenian fleet during an all-important sea battle in 415 BCE.[21] This avenue of investigation is convincingly argued by Phyllis Young Forsyth in her book *Atlantis: The Making of Myth*.[22] Yet Sicily is an island inside the Pillars of Hercules so, like Crete, cannot have been the original inspiration behind Plato's concept of an Atlantic island.

Comparisons have also been drawn between Plato's Atlantis and other major cities of the ancient world that flourished during the classical age. These include Carthage,[23] Babylon,[24] and Ecbatana, modern Hamadan, the ancient capital of the Medians in western Iran. According to the much-traveled Greek historian Herodotus, Ecbatana was built on a hill and surrounded by a series of concentric walls, seven in number, each represented by a different color.[25] Did this knowledge influence Plato to ascribe each of Atlantis's ringed islands with different colored metals? It is certainly possible.

No one can deny these clear comparisons between Plato's Atlantean realm and the ancient world in which he lived. Yet in attempting to find contemporary explanations for the Atlantis legend it is all too easy to lose sight of the fact that his famous dialogues are supposed to be fiction. He had every right to expand on any existing knowledge he might have possessed regarding some unknown island that lay beyond the Pillars of Hercules.

Plato meant his works to be read by statesmen, politicians, and aristocrats, as well as by philosophers, in the hope that they would take heed of his warnings and build a sound future for their citizens or subjects. It is an explanation shared by many classical scholars. Yet as I have outlined in earlier chapters, the knowledge contained in both Atlantis dialogues points overwhelmingly to one conclusion. It is that Plato drew his initial inspiration for the Atlantis legend from secondary maritime sources available to him at the time. Thus it would appear that, stripped of its political and fantastic overtones, Plato's Atlantis narrative preserves a knowledge of an island kingdom or empire that:

1. Thrived in the Atlantic Ocean thousands of years before recorded history;
2. Was linked via a series of "other" islands to an "opposite continent," identified tentatively as the Americas;
3. Was accessible to ancient "voyagers" who were once able to cross the outer ocean (and thus may have been responsible for introducing knowledge of the Atlantic realm to the ancient world);
4. Was destroyed by a natural cataclysm involving "earthquakes and floods," and, finally;
5. Had an "impassable sea" of mud and shoals (identified either as the Sargasso Sea or the shallow waters of the Bahamas, or both) occupying the former position of the sunken island, preventing any further navigation to the "opposite continent."

All these facts were gleaned initially from the *Timaeus,* the first of Plato's two accounts of the Atlantis legend, suggesting therefore that it is this work, and not the *Critias,* that contains most of the original inspiration for the story. This does not mean that we now relegate the *Critias* to a position unworthy of consideration, only that the *Timaeus* appears to contain more historical data than its unfinished successor.

THE DIMENSIONS OF ATLANTIS

What, then, can we say about Plato's description of the Atlantic island as outlined in both the *Timaeus* and the *Critias?* Is it purely symbolic, the creation of the author's own mind, or does it hold important clues to our overall understanding of the real Atlantic island? Let us look again at the passages of the *Critias* containing a detailed description of the island's geography. Plato speaks clearly of a vast irrigated plain that "stretched for three thousand furlongs [603 kilometers] in one direction, and at its center, for two thousand [402 kilometers] inland from the coast."[26] In the original Greek text the great plain's measurements are specified as three thousand by two thousand stadia (552 by 368 kilometers).

Beyond the plain to the north was an extensive mountain range "which came right down to the sea," creating a "precipitous" coastline that sheltered the city "from the cold northerly winds."[27] The citadel itself was said to have been situated on the edge of the plain, apparently on the site of the "mountain which was nowhere of any great altitude," where Euenor, the mortal ancestor of the kings of Atlantis, had previously lived in a cave with his wife and daughter.[28] Rivers and streams that began in the mountains were said to have flowed down into a fosse or trench that helped irrigate the fertile plain. At a distance of 50 furlongs (10 kilometers), or 50 stadia (9.2 kilometers) in the original account, from the outer edge of the final ring of water was a great circular wall that started and finished at the mouth of the deep canal that emptied into the sea.[29]

It does not take a genius to work out that these simple facts and figures convey the idea of a much smaller island than Plato would have us believe. Only the northerly placed mountains appear to divide Atlantis' rich fertile plain from its precipitous northern shoreline. No mention is made of the extent of this mountain range, although surely this cannot have covered an area of land equal to that proposed by Plato when he tells us that the island was the size of Libya and Asia combined. Even the mighty Himalayas of central Asia, although around 2,400 kilometers in length, are only between 160 and 240 kilometers in width. Atlantis' northerly placed mountain range cannot have been any wider than the Himalayas, implying that at its greatest extent the island was no more than six hundred kilometers from north to south, and probably even smaller still. So whatever the true width of Atlantis's mountain range, Plato's account implies that his Atlantic island cannot have been any more than four hundred or so kilometers from coast to coast, which is a lot less than his original statement in the *Timaeus* implying that this island continent was the size of Libya and Asia combined.

Can Plato have been so negligent as to include two entirely different sets of reference in respect to the Atlantic island's overall size? I feel that we cannot ascribe such incompetence to arguably one of Athens' most celebrated writers, even if there are still discrepancies in the dates provided for the war between Athens and the Atlantean aggressor. So how are we able to reconcile these blatant contradictions in his Atlantis dialogues?

We are, it seems, left with four possible options:

1. Plato's Atlantis dialogues have been altered or changed, either accidentally or deliberately, by later copyists and translators of his works.
2. Plato inadvertently created confusion in his texts by featuring age-old lore that related not simply to one single island but to two or more inhabited Atlantic islands either visited by or known to ancient mariners. These he haphazardly blended together to create the memory of one key island referred to by him under the name of Atlantis.
3. The description and dimensions of Atlantis as cited by Plato in the *Critias* are basically correct, and his statement alluding to the island being as large as Libya and Asia combined is somehow wrong.
4. The entire Atlantis account is pure fiction and in creating his imperfect Atlantean kingdom Plato did not intend its dimensions to be seen as anything other than meaningful symbolism.

The final solution cannot be dismissed, yet it still implies that Plato was an incompetent writer who included facts and fancies in his dialogues without any care for consistency. The other three proposed solutions look far more promising and perhaps should be reviewed not individually but together.

KINGS OF THE ISLANDS OF ATLANTIS

It was the American author Ignatius Donnelly, the great nineteenth-century pioneer of Atlantean research, who first questioned the validity of Plato's statement about Atlantis being the size of Libya and Asia together. His version of the *Critias,* included for reference purposes at the beginning of *Atlantis: The Antediluvian World,* departs from the usual translation of the text when it comes to the size of the Atlantic island. In this we find the passage quoted as follows: "The combatants on the other side [of the war with Athens] were led by the kings of the islands of Atlantis, which, as I was saying, once had an *extent* greater than that of Libya and Asia; and, when afterward sunk by an earthquake, became an impassable barrier of mud to voyagers sailing from hence to the ocean."[30] (current author's emphasis)

Realizing the obvious significance of this statement, attempts were made to track down the English translation of Plato's dialogues used by Donnelly for his own purposes. To this end the current author consulted Canadian Atlantis scholar Rand Flemath, coauthor, with his wife Rose, of the 1995 book *When the Sky Fell: In Search of Atlantis.* He made enquiries but was unable to identify the translation quoted by Donnelly. Thus it was concluded that since it was popular in the nineteenth century for writers to make their own copies of classical texts, it is likely that Donnelly composed his English translation from an authentic Greek text available to him at the time.

Whether Donnelly's translation of the *Critias* is accurate remains to be seen. However, this new variation of the well-known quotation concerning Atlantis's immense size throws a completely new light on what Plato might have meant to convey by these words. Is it possible that he was attempting to tell us that the rulers of the Atlantic island, and indeed its "other" islands, held sway over an *area* of the ocean *equal in size* to that of Libya and Asia? Certainly, it makes perfect sense of Donnelly's reference to the "kings *of the islands* of Atlantis" (current author's emphasis), for it confirms once again that the supposed Atlantean empire was not a single landmass but a series of islands.

Central to the whole story was one great island, orientated east–west, several hundred kilometers in length and dominated by a northerly mountain range that shielded an open plain to the south. Somewhere close to its southern shoreline was its hypothetical "city," constructed on a raised plateau and symbolizing the emergence point of the Atlantean dynasty. This island was the jewel of Atlantis.

Such a location is easy to imagine. It could fit the description of any one of a number of Atlantic islands. Yet did the Atlantis of Plato really exist, or was it simply a composite creation born out of the memory of two or more unknown islands situated in the Western Ocean? If it did exist, was it really home to a powerful maritime empire that was either destroyed by earthquakes and floods or forced to abandon its homeland following a series of terrible cataclysms?

5

ISLES OF THE BLEST

The story of the rise, fall, and ultimate destruction of Atlantis appears only in the dialogues of Plato, and as we shall see shortly there seems to be no other ancient source that describes this same island empire. It is an unfortunate situation frequently highlighted by detractors of the Atlantis legend, and since the very beginning they have been in good company, for it was Aristotle, Plato's own rational-thinking pupil, who first derided the story for its obvious absurdity. In his opinion, "Its inventor caused it to disappear."[1] In other words, it was inconceivable that Plato could ever have believed that his readership would be fooled by such ludicrous fiction.

In addition to this rather disconcerting situation, we know that the subject of Atlantis was openly debated during the third century CE among the philosophers in the Platonic Academy attached to the famous library and university at Alexandria. This fact is recorded in the writings of Proclus (412–485 CE), a Greek Neoplatonic scholar and commentator on Plato's *Timaeus*.[2] As Russian scholar Nikolai Zhirov was forced to admit, "The Academy did not have [at its disposal] the pertinent documents" to resolve the matter one way or another.[3]

Before its tragic destruction by fire at the hands of, initially, Julius Caesar in 48 BCE and then later by mobs loyal to the Christian fanatic Bishop Cyril in 391 CE, the library at Alexandria was estimated to have housed some 490,000 individual items.* Among these must have been many thousands of manuscripts that are now lost to the world. Yet to consider that it contained nothing whatsoever that might have validated Plato's story is worrying to say the least. If he were the only source for this tradition, we would be on uneasy ground supporting the case for a historical Atlantis.

To take the matter further it will be necessary to review what other classical writers have had to say about legendary islands of the Western Ocean. Although none of these early sources ever uses the name Atlantis in the same manner as Plato employs it, they do offer a glimpse of very similar island paradises, some of which may well have links with Plato's own Atlantic island.

HANNO'S JOURNEY

We begin our investigations by examining a maritime journey made down the west coast of Africa by a Carthaginian general and navigator named Hanno, circa 425 BCE. An account of this voyage was said to have been recorded in the temple of Saturn (actually that of Baal-Hamman) at his home port of Carthage.[4] Although the original work is now lost, a version of the text was mercifully preserved in Greek.[†]

With a reported fleet of sixty ships, called "penteconters," loaded with "30,000" crewmen, Hanno began exploring the northwest coast of Africa. Almost immediately he founded a temple to "Poseidon" on a "Libyan promontory covered with trees."[5] Afterward, he is said to have encountered a great lake full of "tall reeds, where elephants and many other wild animals fed."[6] This makes us recall Plato's words regarding

---

*This figure is probably derived from the Pinakes, the catalog compiled by the librarian Callimachus of Cyrene (ca. 310/305–240 BCE) (Green, *Alexander to Actium,* 88, n. 46, 666–67).

†Our earliest manuscript version of Hanno's journey, the Codex Heidelbergensis 398, dates only to the tenth century CE (Harden, "Phoenicians on the West Coast of Africa," 142).

the elephants supposedly found on Atlantis. Hanno's fleet sailed on, founding a total of five cities before it came to a river named Lixos, generally taken to be the river Draa, which borders the region between Morocco and the Western, or Spanish, Sahara.[7] Here a race called the Lixitae "pastured their flocks."[8] Scholars identify these peoples with the so-called Berber tribes that inhabit the region even to this day.[9]

Hanno hired interpreters from among the Lixitae, who were, it seems, already familiar with the topographical features witnessed by Hanno on his long voyage. Moreover, they could also communicate with other tribes encountered along the way, strongly hinting that the Lixitae were themselves mariners, or that they were employed regularly as pilots and interpreters by Phoenician and Carthaginian sea captains.

Hanno explored inland and there encountered "inhospitable Ethiopians [i.e., native Africans] in a land ridden with wild beasts and hemmed in by great mountains."[10] Among these mountains sprang the source of the Lixos, and here, we are informed, lived a race of troglodytes "of strange appearance," whom the Lixitae said were able to "run more swiftly than horses."[11] It is clear that they were in fact exploring the western extremities of what are today the Atlas Mountains, which formed part of the ancient kingdom of Mauritania.

Leaving behind this region, they sailed south for two days and then eastward for another day. It was at this point that they came upon a small island at the "farther end of a gulf," said to have had a circumference of just five stadia (920 meters).[12] Here they established a settlement, which they called Cerne (as noted in chapter 2, the Phoenicians and Carthaginians made a point of founding ports on small offshore islands). All Hanno tells us about this island is that it lay "directly opposite Carthage, for a voyage from Carthage to the Pillars and from there to Cerne seemed alike."[13] Here the Carthaginian general is said to have taken an exploratory party "up a big river called Chretes," until it reached a lake "in which were three islands bigger than Cerne."[14] After exploring another great river (seemingly located beyond the lake), "teeming with crocodiles and hippopotamuses," they returned to

Cerne, before continuing the journey southward for another fourteen days and entering "an immense gulf."[15] Here they encountered further islands, smoking volcanoes, lava flows, scorching heat, and primitive peoples,[16] before the fleet eventually turned for home after exhausting its supplies.[17]

Piecing together Hanno's exact journey is beyond the scope of this book. Some scholars have suggested that he reached as far as Sierra Leone.[18] Others say he entered the Gulf of Guinea and traveled eastward as far as the Cameroons, or even Gabon.[19] Nobody really knows. The only island location mentioned in Hanno's account that historians have attempted to pinpoint with any degree of accuracy is the settlement of Cerne. Donald Harden, who has made a special study of Phoenician and Carthaginian voyages beyond the Pillars of Hercules,[20] felt Cerne must be "an island, not exactly identified, near the Senegal delta."[21]

Other scholars have placed Cerne farther north, identifying it with either Herne Island, which lies on the southern edge of the Western Sahara, or Arguin Island, located about 320 kilometers farther south.[22] Hanno himself said that Cerne was located at the same distance from the Pillars of Hercules as the Pillars themselves were from Carthage.[23] If this distance is loosely projected out from the Strait of Gibraltar, it brings us not to Senegal but to somewhere in the vicinity of the Western Sahara, which suggests that Herne Island was the original settlement of Cerne. Yet as Harden conceded in proposing the mouth of the Senegal as the true location of Cerne, "It looks as if we must abandon Hanno's distances."[24] Support for this theory comes from the writings of Pseudo-Scylax, which date to the mid-fourth century BCE. At Cerne, he recorded, "The traders here are Phoenicians. When they arrive at the island of Cerne, they anchor their cargo-boats, and pitch tents for themselves on Cerne. Then they unload and ferry their merchandise in small boats to the mainland. They are Ethiopians on the mainland; and it is with these Ethiopians that they trade. . . . They have also a great city, to which the Phoenician merchants sail."[25]

We must also not forget that Pseudo-Scylax spoke of Cerne island as lying at a distance of twelve days' sail from the Pillars of Hercules.[26] He further recorded that the "parts beyond the isle of Cerne are no longer navigable because of shoals, mud, and seaweed,"[27] a tentative reference to the Sargasso Sea. Since we know that this same shallow sea was said to have marked the site of lost Atlantis, might Cerne have been confused with the memory of Plato's Atlantic island? Is it possible that stories concerning the existence of Cerne as a prosperous island settlement that lay beyond the Pillars of Hercules could have reached the Mediterranean world and influenced Plato's composition of the Atlantis account? It is a matter dealt with in chapter 12.

PSEUDO-ARISTOTLE

We move on now to the writings left to us by Pseudo-Aristotle. This imposter of the famous Greek philosopher, who is thought to have been one of his own pupils, wrote a work titled *On Marvellous Things Heard,* circa 300 BCE. His text is important in that it speaks of a "desert island" situated "in the sea outside the Pillars of Heracles." It is said to have been discovered by Carthaginians who "frequented it often owing to its prosperity"[28] and spoke of it as just "a few days" voyage away."[29] Some Carthaginians are "even [said to have] lived there," for here was "wood of all kinds" as well as "*navigable* rivers" and "all other kinds of fruits."[30] (current author's emphasis) Any non-Carthaginian who ventured within sight of this island was caught and put to death. Moreover, its inhabitants were likewise massacred so that they "might not tell the story, and that a crowd might not resort to the island . . . and take away the prosperity of the Carthaginians."[31]

No idea of the island's location is given in the account, although it would appear to have been within easy reach of the Pillars of Hercules. Most probably it was Madeira, the larger of the two main islands that make up the Madeiras (even though they were found to be uninhabited when discovered by the Portuguese in 1427). This island group is certainly mountainous and rich in vegetation and forests and was known about in ancient times. Pliny the Elder (23–79 CE), the celebrated Roman naturalist, seems to refer to them as the Purpurariae, the Purple Isles, after the processing plant for purple dyes said to have been established there by King Juba II (died circa 18 CE) of Mauritania.[32]

Due also to its mild climate, Madeira produces a variety of different fruits that are especially prized in the European spring market. The only thing that prevents us from properly identifying Madeira as Pseudo-Aristotle's "desert island" is its lack of navigable rivers. Indeed, if it were not for its extensive system of post-Conquest irrigation channels, which enable highland water to flow down into the valleys below, Madeira would be a virtual desert.

I would not be the first person to pick up on this glaring anomaly in Pseudo-Aristotle's account. The American historian Cyrus H. Gordon similarly reviewed the evidence of Carthaginian contact with this Atlantic island and concluded, "The element of navigable rivers is significant because west of Africa there are no navigable rivers until Haiti [a country forming part of the island of Hispaniola], Cuba, and the American mainland."[33]

Could it be possible that, rather than the island of Madeira, the author of the work was alluding to another Atlantic island, plausibly one that really did possess navigable rivers and a native population? Yet in accepting this proposition we have to conclude that Pseudo-Aristotle was recalling one of the islands in the West Indies, perhaps Cuba or Hispaniola, both of which possess navigable rivers.

Pseudo-Aristotle goes on to speak of an Atlantic journey made by Iberic-Phoenician sailors from Gades.[34] They are said to have traveled for four days with an east wind behind them until they reached "desert" islands full of "brushes and seaweed."[35] Here they were able to catch "a quantity of tuna of incredible size and weight."[36] Upon being brought ashore, the fish were pickled and jarred and taken to Carthage, where they were consumed by the inhabitants and not exported to other countries.[37] Once again, this appears to be a reference to Madeira, where tuna were found in great abundance until comparatively recent times.

DIODORUS SICULUS

One of the best known of the Greek historians is Diodorus Siculus, or Diodorus of Sicily (ca. 8 BCE). He was the author of an extensive and partially extant work known as *Bibliotheca Historica* (Library of History). Originally it consisted of some forty books, although today only fifteen of these survive, some merely as fragments. Their pages feature the legendary history of many countries of the ancient world, including Libya, Egypt, Persia, Syria, Media, Greece, Rome, and Carthage. Diodorus was unquestionably a very learned man, familiar with many other classical writings—a fact that might well have influenced his apparent knowledge of Atlantic islands that lay beyond the Pillars of Hercules.

Beginning with book III of his *Library,* we find Diodorus writing about a race of fierce women known as Amazons. They are said to have been warlike and to have lived at the very edge of the inhabited world, somewhere "in the western parts of Libya."[38] Accordingly, their homeland was an island called Hespera that lay in the "marsh Tritonis," identified as an ancient salt lake connected with the Lesser Syrtis, modern Sebkha-el Faroun, in what is today the Northern Sahara. Marsh, or Lake, Tritonis is said to have gained its name from "a certain river Triton which emptied into it."[39] The island itself was apparently of "great size" with "fruit-bearing trees of every kind."[40]

Having subdued the peoples that inhabited the country around Marsh Tritonis, the Amazons moved against other nations, the first of whom were the Atlantioi, who were said to have been the "most civilized men among the inhabitants of those regions."[41] They "dealt in a prosperous country and possessed great cities," among which "mythology places the birth of the gods."[42] These Atlantioi were said to inhabit "the regions which lie along the shore of the ocean."[43]

The Atlantioi appear to be synonymous with another race known as the Atlantes, the people of Atlas, who were referred to four centuries earlier by Herodotus in his *History*.[44] He claimed that they lived in the Western Sahara, did not eat any living thing, and never experienced dreams.[45] Clearly the Atlantioi of Diodorus were likewise the indigenous peoples of this same region. Yet now, some four hundred years later, these sons of Atlas were seen as the "most civilized men among the inhabitants of those regions."[46]

Myrina, the queen of the Amazons, then gathered together thirty-thousand foot soldiers and three thousand cavalry and marched into the city of Cerne, where, in a pitched battle, she defeated the Atlantioi.[47] In order that they might continue their existence, the fallen race offered to do anything for Myrina.[48] The Amazon leader acted honorably, and on the site of the former city of Cerne she built another that bore her name. The peoples of Cerne lived on, yet from time to time their territories were invaded by a terrible race known as the Gorgons that resided on the borders of their lands (presumably the mythical Atlantic islands known as the Gorgades; see chapter 6). Myrina was asked to intervene on behalf of the Atlantioi to rid them of this enemy. This she did, going against the Gorgons and quickly "gaining the upper hand."[49] Myrina and her fellow warriors promptly seized three thousand prisoners and tried to burn out the rest.[50] Yet in this pursuit ultimately she failed and was forced to retreat. The Gorgons were defeated eventually by the hero Perseus, a son of Zeus, during his own travels through the kingdom of Mauritania.[51]

Diodorus also informs us that Marsh Tritonis "disappeared from sight in the course of an earthquake, when those parts of it which lay towards the ocean were torn asunder."[52] Afterward, he mentions once again the Atlantioi and suggests that "it will not be inappropriate in this place to recount what their myths relate about the genesis of the gods."[53]

This is the second time that Diodorus alludes to the genesis of the gods in connection with the Atlantioi, for in an earlier passage he tells us they possessed "great cities," among which "mythology places the birth of the gods."[54] Remember, he is including in this list the Carthaginian settlement of Cerne. Furthermore, why should he place the birth of the gods in the Far West—on the very edge of the known world? Does this hint at the former existence of a much earlier civilization somewhere in the vicinity of the ancient kingdom of Mauritania, where localized forms of the god Poseidon, his son Triton, the goddess Athena, and the hero-god Atlas were venerated long before the advent of the classical age? More important, might the Atlantioi, or the Atlantes, and their city of Cerne have some bearing on Plato's Atlantis narrative?

THE ATLANTIDES

Diodorus goes on to present us with an account of the history of the gods. He says that following the death of Hyperion, one of the mythical Titans, the world was divided into portions and shared among the sons of Ouranus. Of these, the most renowned were Cronus and Atlas, who received the regions bordering the ocean. It was in his memory that the inhabitants of this country were known as the Atlantioi and Mount Atlas bore his name.[55] He tells us also that Atlas was gifted in the art of "astrology and was the first to present to mankind the doctrine of the sphere," for which reason he is said to have supported the vault of heaven on his shoulders. (In some accounts this was his punishment for the part he played in the wars between the Titans and the gods of Olympus.)[56]

Diodorus also provides the reader with an account of the Atlantides, the seven daughters fathered by Atlas. They are said to have lain with the most renowned gods and heroes, because of which they became the first ancestors of the "larger part" of the human race, by whom they achieved "immortal honour" and "were enthroned in the heavens and endowed with the appellation of Pleiades."[57]

The story of the seven Atlantides is also found in the writings of a much earlier Greek historian named Hellanicus of Lesbos (died circa 411 BCE). He composed a work intriguingly titled *Atlantis,* which sets out the genealogy of the Atlantides. Despite its compelling title, this Atlantis had nothing whatsoever to do with the Atlantis of Plato's dialogues. Here it denoted only the "daughters of Atlas." Hellanicus's work records that the mother of the seven daughters fathered by Atlas was Pleione, one of the Oceanides (Diodorus gives her name as Hesperis; see chapter 6). Poseidon, the god of the sea, mated with two of them. One of them, named Celaeno, gave birth to a son named Lycus, whom the sea-god made to live in the "Isles of the Blest."[58]

Even though Diodorus tells us that the Atlantides were born at Cyllene in Arcadia, their associations with both the star constellation of the Pleiades and the "Isles of the Blest" is our first indication that their story might hold significance beyond that implied by these basic mythological concepts. We know, for instance, that the name Pleiades is derived from a Greek word meaning "to sail," because "that constellation shows the time most favourable to navigators, which is in the spring."[59] Add to this Diodorus's assertion that Atlas was the first "to present to mankind the doctrine of the sphere" and it would appear that we might well be dealing with some kind of arcane maritime knowledge preserved in mythological form.

Identifying the true location of the Isles of the Blest, or the Fortunate Isles, is a tricky business, as there are no hard-and-fast answers. They were thought to be a group of otherworldly islands that lay in the Far West.[60] The concept of a blessed isle, or indeed isles, situated on the edge of the known world, where the dead are received in the afterlife, is ages old. It is found in Egyptian myth, it is also present in Sumerian myth, and it formed part of the religion of the Minoan peoples of Crete, after whom some believe the Greeks adopted the idea.[61] Before it became widely known that islands lay outside the Pillars of Hercules, most Mediterranean cultures were happy to place their blessed isles merely beyond the western horizon. For instance, Diodorus asserted that the island of Lesbos was "blessed,"[62] while Pliny the Elder stated that Crete was likewise an "Island of the Blest."[63]

On his discovery of the Canary Islands at the end of the first century BCE, the Mauritanian king Juba II believed that he had at last found the true Isles of the Blest.[64] His announcement to this effect caught the popular imagination of the classical world, and thereafter these legendary islands became associated with the Canaries.

BOOK V

These are thought-provoking considerations as we move from book III to book V of Diodorus's *Library,* in which he informs the reader that what he is now about to deliver is "an account of those [islands] *which are in the ocean,*" (current author's emphasis) implying that those mentioned previously were still considered to be part of the ancient world.[65] He begins by noting the existence of a "fruitful" island of "considerable" size that lay "a number of days" sail to the west of Libya. It was mountainous and possessed a "plain of surpassing beauty" as well as "navigable rivers" that were used for irrigation. Here were to be found "parks planted with trees of every variety and gardens in great multitudes," traversed by "streams of sweet water."[66] Here, too, were "private villas," along with "banqueting houses" in settings of flowers as well as excellent hunting for "beast and wild animal."[67] The climate on the island was mild all the year round, enabling it to produce an abundance of fruit—a virtue that made it seem like a "dwelling-place of a race of gods and not of men."[68]

In this description of a mountainous Atlantic isle with a fertile plain and a sophisticated ancient society, we are nearing Plato's description of lost Atlantis. Yet it really does seem as if Diodorus borrowed at least part of this account from Pseudo-Aristotle. As we have seen, in his work *On Marvellous Things Heard,* Pseudo-Aristotle spoke of a "desert" island colonized by Carthaginians that lay just a "few days' voyage" beyond the Pillars of Hercules. It was said to possess "wood of all kinds," "navigable rivers," and "all other kinds of fruits."[69]

Diodorus next recounts the story of how Phoenician mariners, while sailing along the shores of Africa, were driven off course by strong winds "a great distance out into the ocean." After being "storm-tossed for many days," they were put ashore on "the island we mentioned above,"[70] that is, the one with "navigable rivers" already described. As a consequence of the island's "felicity and nature," the "Phoenicians [of Gades] . . . caused it to be known to all men."[71] This great announcement apparently prompted the Tyrrhenians, the people of Etruria, or Tuscany, as masters of the sea, to dispatch ships to colonize the island. However, the "Carthaginians" called a halt to this plan since they did not wish to have an exodus of their people to this island due to its excellence and because they saw its potential as a refuge should a disaster ever befall Carthage (it should be recalled that the Iberic Phoenicians and Carthaginians were related to each other).[72]

Since the Iberic-Phoenician sailors of this story were journeying along the West African coast when they were blown off course, it really does seem that the island alluded to in both accounts preserved by Diodorus is Madeira, a conclusion also drawn by Donald Harden.[73] Yet still we have the problem of "navigable" rivers. None are to be found on any island between Africa and the Caribbean, suggesting that, like Pseudo-Aristotle before him, Diodorus combined together traditions concerning two or more Atlantic islands. One of these was, very possibly, Madeira. The other one, with "navigable" rivers, if it existed independently, can only have been one of the islands of the West Indies.

THE LIVES OF PLUTARCH

We move on now to Plutarch (50–120 CE), the noted Greek moralist and biographer. Among the wealth of material in his monumental work titled *Lives* is an intriguing story, the "Life of Sertorius," concerning a Roman general who, while governor of Iberia between 80 and 72 BCE, learned of the accidental discovery of two Atlantic islands. This information came from two Iberic-Phoenician sailors who had just returned to Gades. Apparently, their vessel had been blown off course by northerly and easterly winds until finally they had come across the islands.*

The two islands, seen as the Fortunate Isles, were "separated only by a narrow channel."[74] Furthermore, "rain seldom falls there, and when it does, it falls moderately: but they [the islands] generally have soft breezes, which scatter such rich dews."[75] In addition to this, Plutarch asserts "that the soil is not only good for sowing and planting, but spontaneously produces the most excellent fruits, and those in such abundance, that the inhabitants have nothing more to do than to indulge themselves in the enjoyment of ease."[76]

The seasonal changes are described as an "insensible transition into each other." More curiously, Plutarch also states, "It is generally believed, even among the barbarians, that these are the Elysian Fields, and the seats of the blessed, which Homer has described in the charms of verse."[77]

The islands' mild climate and abundant fruit seems to be the hallmark of so many of the Atlantic paradises discovered either by Phoenician or Carthaginian mariners. Yet this time we have a quite specific distance connected with the story, for the islands mentioned by Plutarch are said to have lain four hundred leagues (1,920 kilometers) from the African coast.[78] If we assume that the Phoenician vessel began its journey from Gades, it might be proposed that the islands discovered were members of the Azores group, rediscovered by the Portuguese in 1427. This theory is strengthened in the knowledge that these islands are located approximately 1,850 kilometers to the west of Spain, just slightly less than the distance provided by Plutarch. Certainly, the Azores have a mild climate, and evidence of a Carthaginian presence on the islands came with the discovery on Corvo in 1749 of a broken black

*The discovery of two Atlantic islands in the manner described by Plutarch in his "Life of Sertorius" is a theme that earlier appears in a relatively unknown work by Sallust, a Latin historian of the first century BCE (see Keyser, "From Myth to Map," 157).

clay vase containing a caked mass of coins, minted either in Carthage or in the Greek North African colony of Cyrene during the fourth and third centuries BCE.[79]

Whatever the identity of the two islands in the "Life of Sertorius," we find that, in addition to being designated the Isles of the Blest, they were also equated with the so-called Elysian Fields, otherwise known as Elysium. In classical tradition, this otherworldly realm was said to have been an island that lay in the Far West. Tradition asserts that it was covered with never-ending green bowers, as well as "delightful meadows with pleasant streams."[80] Here, too, the air was always "wholesome, serene and temperate," while "the birds continually warbled in the groves, and the inhabitants were blessed with another sun and other stars."[81] According to some classical writers, Elysium was also considered to be one of the Fortunate Isles.[82] As with the other paradisaical isles of the Atlantic, traditions surrounding the Elysian Fields seem to be of Phoenician origin. Although Greek historians have long considered that Elysium means "coming," as in a place to which the pious come, the name is now thought to derive from a Semitic root meaning "field of El," with El being the principal god of the Phoenicians.[83]

So far we have found that several writers of the classical age refer specifically to ancient contact, usually by Iberic-Phoenician and Carthaginian sailors, with Atlantic island groups that lay within relatively easy reach of the Pillars of Hercules. By including names such as Cerne, Elysium, the Fortunate Isles, and the Isles of the Blest, these accounts point to a basic knowledge of the Madeiras, the Canaries, and even the Azores.

We can also say that certain elements among the many tales of Atlantic islands preserved by the classical writers so far cited do not conform with the geography, topography, and location of the various archipelagos on the eastern Atlantic seaboard. This is especially so of the Atlantic islands with "navigable rivers" mentioned by Pseudo-

Aristotle and Diodorus Siculus, making us recall Cyrus H. Gordon's statement that "west of Africa there are no navigable rivers until Haiti, Cuba, and the American mainland."[84]

Could it be possible that both accounts preserve a knowledge gained from Atlantic voyagers of one or more of the principal islands of the West Indies? In the next chapter we shall see that a memory of ancient voyages to islands on the western Atlantic seaboard would also appear to have been preserved by key geographical writers of the Roman period.

6

FORTY DAYS' SAIL

Gaius Plinius Secundus was a noted Roman naturalist of the first century CE, better remembered under the name Pliny the Elder. In a thirty-seven-volume work titled *Natural History,* he includes sections on everything from the stars, the heavens, and the winds, to all manner of other aspects of nature such as rain, hail, minerals, trees, flowers, and plants. In addition to this wealth of material, his books contain a detailed knowledge of ancient geography. Moreover, like Diodorus Siculus before him, Pliny the Elder has much to say about legendary islands of the Western Ocean. We also know that he was fully acquainted with Plato's Atlantis narrative, for he accepted without question that "cases of land [were] entirely stolen away by the [sea]," including "(if we accept Plato's story) the vast area covered by the Atlantic."[1]

"Opposite to Celtiberia [Spain] are a number of islands called by the Greeks the Tin Islands [Cassiterides] in consequence of their abundance of that metal."[2] This was unquestionably a reference to either the Isles of Scilly off Cornwall, or the British Isles as a whole, which were exploited by the Phoenicians and Carthaginians for their rich resources of tin.

Pliny spoke also of "six Islands of the Gods ["facing Cape Finisterre," a rocky peninsula on Spain's west coast], which some people have designated the Isles of Bliss [*Insulae . . . Fortunatas*]."[3] According to other ancient writers, these lay west of Mauritania and are unquestionably to be identified with the Canary Islands.[4] Juba II himself managed to discover only six out of seven of the islands, so this became the standard figure connected with the archipelago.

Pliny also informs us that aside from the Fortunate Isles, there is another island "off Mount Atlas." Its name, he says, is "Atlantis."[5]

Yes, Atlantis. He gives no details whatsoever about it, and states simply:

> From which [i.e., Atlantis] a two days' voyage along the coast reaches the desert district in the neighbourhood of the Western Ethiopians [*Aethiopas Hesperio*] and the cape mentioned above named the Horn of the West [*Hesperu Ceras*], the point at which the coastline begins to curve westward in the direction of the Atlantic. Opposite this cape also there are reported to be some islands, the Gorgades, which were formerly the habitation of the Gorgons, and which according to the account of Xenophon of Lampsacus are at a distance of two days' sail from the mainland. The islands were reached by the Carthaginian general Hanno. . . . Outside the Gorgades there are also said to be two Islands of the Ladies of the West [*duae Hesperidum insulae*, i.e., the islands of the Hesperides].[6]

As can be determined from any detailed map of Africa, the only islands that lie in the vicinity of the Atlas Mountains are the Canaries group, which seem to be synonymous with the "Isles of Bliss." Yet Pliny now informs us that one island "off Mount Atlas" is actually named Atlantis. So exactly where was Pliny's Atlantis?

Unfortunately there is not enough information for us to draw any clear conclusions. Pliny fails to tell us how large it is, how far the island is from the shore, or whether it is part of an island group. The only slight clue is his statement that from it a "two days" voyage along the coast reaches the desert district in the neighborhood of the Western Ethiopians and the promontory Hesperu Ceras. Since the journey

Pliny describes is clearly an anticlockwise circumnavigation of the West African coast, in the manner of Hanno, it is likely he is alluding to one of the small coastal islands already described. This includes Harden's Cerne island in the mouth of the Senegal River, or perhaps Herne Island or Arguin Island, which have also been proposed as sites for the Phoenician or Carthaginian settlement of Cerne.

ISLANDS OF THE GORGONS

Attempting to identify the other locations referred to in the above passage quoted from Pliny's *Natural History* will now lead us into a minefield of possibilities. He says that somewhere in the vicinity of the desert are the "Western Ethiopians" and beyond that a place known as Hesperu Ceras, generally translated as "Horn of the West." Pliny specifically refers to it as a "cape," even though the term *horn* was anciently taken to mean a gulf. This fact has led geographers to assume that the Horn of the West was a large bay in the vicinity of either Gambia or Sierra Leone. Yet bays are not capes, and, as we shall see, Hesperu Ceras is almost certainly to be identified with the jutting headland named Cape Verde, near Dakar, in Senegal. If a mariner voyages south along the West African coast he passes Mount Atlas on his port side. After this there are few landmarks until the shoreline begins to curve out toward Cape Verde, the westernmost tip of Africa, which obviously made it an important point of reference for ancient navigators.

Pliny states that "opposite" Hesperu Ceras were the Gorgades, the islands of the Gorgons. Paul T. Keyser, a classical historian at the University of Alberta, tentatively identified the Gorgades as either the Bissagos Islands, south of the Gambia River, or the Sherbro Isles, in Sierra Leone.[7] Yet in my opinion they are more likely to have been the Cape Verde Islands, which are located some 640 kilometers west-northwest of Cape Verde. Even though there is no evidence of contact with this island group before its rediscovery in 1460, this solution is by no means new. In 1563 the Portuguese historian António Galvão wrote in his *The Discoveries of the World from their First Originall unto the Yeere of our Lord 1555* that the Cape Verde Islands were anciently known as the Dorcades, Hesperides, and the Gorgades.[8] Dorcades is probably just a corruption of Gorgades, while the reference to the Hesperides is, as we shall see shortly, completely erroneous.

In 1587 the English geographer and writer Richard Hakluyt produced a map that illustrated the work of the early Spanish chronicler Peter Martyr d'Anghiera, who wrote at the beginning of the sixteenth century. On this chart the Cape Verdes are marked both as the "Gorgades vel Medusiae" and, once again, the Hesperides.[9] Since the words of Pliny the Elder make it extremely unlikely that the Cape Verdes are the Hesperides, Galvão and Hakluyt's identification of this island group as the Gorgades is very important, as the so-called Mecia de Viladestes map of 1413 shows, lying off the coast of Africa at a latitude consistent with Cape Verde, a pair of elongated islands marked with the legend "*les jles de gades se oseiruen asi p salario hi p ysidolu*" (the islands of Gades are observed here according to Salario and Isidore [of Seville]).[10] The name Gades is so similar to Gor*gades* that this cannot be coincidence, showing that the island group was anciently thought to have been located at a position corresponding to the Cape Verdes. This connection between the "jles de gades" and the Cape Verdes was noted also by the cartographical scholar Armando Cortésao in 1954.[11]

The Salario mentioned in the inscription on the Mecia de Viladestes map is the lesser-known Roman grammarian, historian, and geographer Caius Julius Solinus,[12] who lived in the first century CE. His works are said to have had a great influence on Isidore of Seville, or Isidorus Hispalensis, a Spanish bishop of Seville who died in 636 CE. He was the author of several books on worldly matters, including an encyclopedia of the arts and sciences titled *Origines*. What all of this implies is that knowledge of the "jles de gades," in other words the Gorgades and very possibly the Cape Verdes, came via an interpretation of Solinus's works by Isidore of Seville in the seventh century.

GARDEN OF DELIGHT

Yet if Pliny really was alluding to the Cape Verde Islands when he spoke of the Gorgades, why should he go on to state that beyond these "are also said to be two Islands of the Lady of the West [*duae Hesperidum insulae,* i.e., the two Hesperides]"? The origin of the Hesperides as islands is very important and needs to be examined in some detail. They take their name from the Greek word *hesper,* or *vesper,* meaning "evening," in other words the time of the "setting sun," indicating very clearly the direction in which the Hesperides were thought to lie.[13] The islands were seen as the residence of celebrated nymphs (three, four, or even seven in number) of this name whom Diodorus saw as synonymous with the seven Atlantides, through their mother Hesperis.[14] According to legend, the Hesperides were appointed to guard the beautiful golden apples that Hera entrusted into the care of Zeus. These were kept in a garden of delight that abounded in the most wonderful fruits of every kind, but which was guarded by a fearsome dragon that never slept. It was the Greek hero Hercules who was finally able to steal these golden apples as the penultimate of his twelve labors.

In one version of the story, Hercules went to Africa and demanded from Atlas three of the golden apples. Accepting the challenge, the giant unloaded on to Hercules his burden of supporting the heavens on his shoulders. Atlas then set off for the Hesperides and returned with the divine fruit. Hercules then tricked the giant into taking back the burden and promptly stole the golden apples, which had been cast to the ground. In another version, Hercules himself goes in search of the golden apples. On arriving in the Hesperides, he mortally wounds the dragon and steals away the precious fruit. Since the only place in which they could be preserved was the Hesperides, the goddess Athena returned the fruit to the garden.

The story of the golden apples is a myth integrally linked with both the western limits of the known world and the outer ocean. It brings together Hercules, whose name is attached to the entrance to the Atlantic; Atlas, whose petrified form was seen as the mountain that bears his name in Mauritania; and the Hesperides themselves, which were both nymphs of great distinction and islands situated in the Atlantic Ocean. The image of abundant fruits and a verdant paradisaical garden located on the Hesperides brings to mind the verdant islands described in a similar manner by classical writers such as Pseudo-Aristotle and Diodorus Siculus. Were these Greek legends based on ancient memories of distant islands reached in antiquity?

Curiously enough, Hercules's tenth labor—the one prior to stealing the golden apples—had been to kill the monster Geryon, king of Gades, and steal his precious cattle. Gades, as we know, was a Phoenician city-port in southwest Spain, from which Iberic-Phoenician vessels sailed on their voyages of discovery to unknown Atlantic islands.

Did this show some kind of connection between Gades, Mount Atlas, Atlantic islands, and Phoenician mariners? Might these mariners have been responsible for introducing these stories to the Mediterranean world?

That the islands of the Hesperides lay in the Atlantic Ocean does not seem to have been in doubt. The Greek poet Hesiod, who lived in the eighth century BCE, spoke of the "clear-voiced Hesperides" that lay "beyond the famous ocean,"[15] while Apollodorus, the Athenian grammarian of the second century BCE, saw them as located in the proximity of the Atlas Mountains of Mauritania.[16] As we also saw in chapter 2, in the twelfth century Honorius of Autun wrote that the "curdled sea," apparently a reference to the Sargasso Sea, "adjoins the Hesperides and covers the site of lost Atlantis, which lay west from Gibraltar."[17]

SECRET RECESSES OF THE SEA

Returning to Pliny, we learn that the two islands of the Hesperides lay even farther out in the ocean than the Gorgades. Yet beyond the Cape Verde Islands is only open sea and the pull of the North Equatorial

Current, which will carry a vessel directly to the West Indies. Since we know that the Hesperides take their name from the linguistic root *hesper*, or *vesper*, meaning "evening," or "setting sun," we can be sure they were thought to be located in the Far West, beyond the ocean river itself.

Others also have realized the significance of the Gorgades and their geographical relationship to the islands of the Hesperides. In his 1962 book *Land to the West: St. Brendan's Voyage to America,* historical writer Geoffrey Ashe noted:

> Martianus Capella, who practised law at Carthage in the fifth century, was the author of a philosophical work in which—besides affirming the Earth to be round [like Plato before him]—he repeated Pliny's statements about the three groups of Atlantic islands, but with the unexpected addition that the Hesperides lie beyond the Gorgades "in the most secret recesses of the sea." This rearrangement of Pliny's island-groups into a chain stretching away from Africa—to Madeira? to the Azores?—becomes still more explicit in Dicuil [Irish monk and writer, circa 800 CE], who says that the Gorgades are farther out than the Canaries and . . . the Hesperides are farther out than the Gorgades.[18]

The Azores are located directly in the path of the Gulf Stream, some 1,850 kilometers west of the Portuguese coast. This powerful ocean current comes in from the west, then passes around the island group on an easterly course before heading off in the direction of first the Madeiras and then the Canary Islands. The Azores seem a most unlikely candidate for the Gorgades, and in this knowledge it seems justifiable identifying them with the Cape Verde Islands. Yet where, then, were these "most secret recesses of the sea," where Martianus Capella says the Hesperides could be found? Were they on the other side of the Atlantic Ocean, among the West Indies perhaps? I would not be the first to draw this conclusion, not by a long way.

THE AUTHORITY OF STATIUS SEBOSUS

Statius Sebosus, a Roman geographical writer who lived circa 50 BCE, was a contemporary of Diodorus Siculus. He composed a book called *Periplus,* which is no longer extant, as well as another work titled *The Wonders of India.* According to Ferdinand Columbus, the son and biographer of Christopher Columbus, Sebosus stated, "Certain islands called the Hesperides were *forty days' sail* west of the Gorgonas Islands."[19] (current author's emphasis) Columbus points out this fact in order to show the "tall tales" that the Spanish traveler and historian Gonzalo Fernándaz de Oviedo y Valdez (1478–1557) "spins" in his work *Historia general y natural de las Indias* of 1535. It seems certain that this important statement regarding the sailing time between the Gorgades and the Hesperides was derived from the writings of Pliny, who quotes Sebosus as an authority on Atlantic geography. The passage in question appears in book VI of his *Natural History,* and in fact follows directly after the reference to the two islands of the Hesperides, which are said to lie beyond the Gorgades, information that was also supplied by Sebosus. According to the English translation of Pliny made by H. Rackham, it reads, " . . . and the whole of the geography of this neighbourhood is so uncertain that Statius Sebosus has given the voyage along the coast from the Gorgons' Islands past Mount Atlas to the Isles of the Ladies of the West [i.e., the Hesperides] as forty days' sail and from those islands to the Horn of the West as one day's sail."[20]

If the Hesperides are to be identified as the islands of the Caribbean, and the Gorgades as the Cape Verde Islands, this passage makes very little sense. A mariner could not possibly have passed Mount Atlas on his way from the Cape Verdes to the West Indies, while the journey time between the Hesperides and the "Horn of the West," most probably Cape Verde in Senegal, would not have been one day's sail. Something had to be wrong, especially as Oviedo clearly believed that the Hesperides lay forty days' sail "west" of the Gorgades and were synonymous with the islands of the West Indies.

Another summary of Oviedo's assessment of Sebosus's Atlantic sailing times is to be found in António Galvão's *The Discoveries of the World,* first published in 1563. Here it states, "In the 650th yeare after the flood there was a king in Spaine named Hesperus, who in his time as it is reported went and discovered as far as Cape Verde, and the Island of S. Thomas, whereof he was prince: And Gonsalao Fernandes of Oviedo the Chronicler of Antiquities affirmeth, that in his time the Islands of the West Indies were discovered, and called somewhat after his name Hesperides: and he alleageth many reasons to prove it, reporting particularly that in 40 daies they sailed from Cape Verde unto those Islands."[21]

The legend concerning the Spanish king named Hesperus has no precedent and seems to be an Iberian variation of the Greek myth surrounding Hesperus, the father of Hesperis, who married Atlas and was the mother of the Atlantides or Hesperides. Confusingly, Galvão goes on to assert that Oviedo reported that between the Hesperides and "Cape Verde" it was forty days' sail. This does not appear to have been what Sebosus, Pliny, or Oviedo actually stated, showing an error on the part of Galvão. What the Portuguese writer does appear to confirm, however, is that Pliny's Hesperu Ceras, the Horn of the West, was indeed Cape Verde—and moreover that its supposed connection with King Hesperus derives from the name Hesperu Ceras, which can also be translated as the "Horn of Hesperus."

To determine exactly what Pliny *did* say on the matter, we must examine the original Latin text of his *Natural History.* Here he states: "ultra has etiamnum duae Hesperidum insulae narrantur; adeoque omnia circa hoc incerta sunt ut Statius Sebosus a Gorgonum insulis praenavigatione Atlantis dierum XL ad Hesperidum insulas cursum prodiderit, ab his ad Hesperu Ceras unius."

For anyone with even a basic knowledge of Latin it is clear that the original text differs slightly from the English translation cited above. So with the invaluable help of Ann Deagon, professor emerita of classical languages at Guildford College in Greensboro, North Carolina, a new translation of the vital passages was obtained. This reads, "The two islands of the Hesperides are said (to be) even beyond these [i.e., the Gorgades]. And all things surrounding this are so uncertain that Statius Sebosus has stated the voyage from the islands of the Gorgons by sailing past Atlas to the islands of the Hesperides (to be) of 40 days, from these to the Horn of Hesperus of one (day)."[22]

From this new translation it is clear that Pliny obviously accepted that an ancient voyager would pass "Atlas," that is, Mount Atlas—Atlantis in the original Latin text—on a journey between the islands of the Gorgons and the Hesperides. This really makes no sense, as Pliny himself has only just told us that the Hesperides lie "outside" the Gorgades, which were themselves beyond the Horn of the West, that is, Cape Verde in Senegal. Since it also seems certain that the Cape Verde Islands are the Gorgades, we can surmise only that Pliny mistakenly confused this mythical island group with the Phoenician island settlement and city-port of Gades in southwest Spain. This theory is strengthened if we consider that early sources, such as Isidore of Seville and the Mecia de Viladestes map of 1413, allude to the Cape Verde Islands as the "jles de gades," the islands of Gades. As previously noted, Gorgades and Gades are similar-sounding names and may even stem from the same linguistic root.

This confusion, the current author believes, led some medieval scholars to assume wrongly that Sebosus, through Pliny's words, was referring to a maritime journey from Gades in Spain past Mount Atlas to the Cape Verdes. This included António Galvão and Richard Hakluyt, who both confusingly named this island group as the Gorgades and the Hesperides—a sheer impossibility!

Yet none of this seems to have been what Sebosus originally intended to say. Plus Pliny himself added confusion to the matter by assuming that a vessel would have to pass Mount Atlas on a voyage between the Cape Verde Islands and the West Indies. If this assumption proves to be correct, it also brings into question the statement found in the Loeb translation of Pliny's passage to the effect that the Hesperides lay just one day's sail from the Horn of the West, that is, Cape Verde. How might we rectify this additional discrepancy?

The answer appears to lie in our understanding of Pliny's use of other people's geographical views. We know, for instance, that immediately before Pliny cites Sebosus's claims, he informs us, "Opposite this cape [i.e., the Horn of the West] also there are reported to be some islands, the Gorgades . . . [and] according to the account of Xenophon of Lampsacus [they] are at a distance of two days' sail from the mainland."[23] When Pliny makes such statements, he is merely quoting the opinions of others whom he considers to be authorities on these subjects. Xenophon of Lampsacus recorded the journey time between the Gorgades and the "cape" as two days' sail. Does it not then make sense to conclude that what Pliny was trying to say is that in the opinion of Sebosus it was one day's sail from the Gorgades (i.e., the Cape Verde Islands) back to the Horn of the West (i.e., Cape Verde)? If we look again at the more direct rendering of the original Latin passage by Professor Ann Deagon we can see that this solution is totally plausible.

Whether Sebosus's sailing times are correct, and where exactly he might have come by this information, remains unclear. Yet if we are correct in our identification of the geographical locations to which he alludes, this is a very important discovery indeed. This can be seen from the fact that the words of Sebosus, as Oviedo obviously realized in the sixteenth century, appear to confirm that transatlantic journeys had formerly taken place between Cape Verde on the African coast and the West Indies. Evidence that this is indeed the case comes from the forty days' sailing time Sebosus gives for the voyage between the Gorgades and the Hesperides.

On his epic journey to the New World, Christopher Columbus departed from the island of Gomera in the Canaries group on September 6, 1492, "which day may be taken to mark the beginning of the enterprise and the ocean crossing."[24] In order to reach the Bahamas, Columbus is considered to have picked up the Canary Current, which, with a little help from the northeasterly trade winds, will carry a vessel southwestward toward the Cape Verde Islands. Only after having passed a point coincident to this archipelago could his ships have gone on to pick up the North Equatorial Current, which would have carried them on to the northern limits of the Caribbean. Yet on his celebrated journey, Columbus somehow managed to miss the Caribbean altogether and instead made first landfall on the island of San Salvador in the Bahamas on October 12, 1492. This means that it took his three vessels thirty-seven days to travel from Gomera to the Bahamas.

Assuming that the sailing time between Gomera and the Cape Verdes was two to three days, this would have left him with thirty-four or thirty-five days to journey on to the West Indies. This figure makes Sebosus's purported forty days' sail for a voyage between the Cape Verdes and the West Indies uncannily accurate. Moreover, on Columbus's second journey to the New World in 1493, he left Gomera on October 7 and finally reached Espanola (Hispaniola), after brief stopovers in the Lesser Antilles, on November 22, a period of forty-six days.[25] If we subtract two or three days for the fleet to pass a position due north of the Cape Verdes, it provides us with a sailing time of forty-three to forty-four days. We must therefore conclude that Sebosus's sailing times appear to be based on a genuine knowledge of transatlantic journeys that must have taken place either during or prior to his own age. More important, it strongly supports the view that the Hesperides were the key islands of the West Indies, suggesting perhaps that some knowledge of their existence circulated the Roman world.

PLINY'S APE

Yet why end here, for we have even further confirmation that not only is the above interpretation of Statius Sebosus's statements correct, but also that the West Indies are indeed the Hesperides. As we have seen already, the writings of Caius Julius Solinus greatly influenced the seventh-century Spanish bishop and writer Isidore of Seville. It was from him that the anonymous compiler of the Italian nautical chart of 1413 apparently learned of the Roman geographical writer's knowledge of the "jles de gades," the islands of Gades, which appear to be synonymous with both the Gorgades and the Cape Verde Islands.

Solinus is the author of a work titled *Polyhistor: De memoralibus mundi,* which highlights the most celebrated places of the ancient world, very much in the style of Pliny. Indeed, Solinus has been called "Pliny's ape," since his work is generally looked on as a mere copy of Pliny's *Natural History.*[26] Unfortunately, this little-known classical work has only rarely appeared in printed form, the last time being a limited edition published in Venice during 1498. One person who would appear to have consulted a copy is the great explorer and navigator Sebastian Cabot (1476–1557). He was the son of the Venetian explorer and navigator Giovanni Caboto (1455–1498/9), who as "John Cabot" sailed under the English flag during the reign of King Henry VII. In June 1497 he rediscovered the Northwest Passage to Newfoundland—the first person to do so in the wake of Columbus's more famous landfall in the West Indies just five years earlier. His son Sebastian accompanied him on this celebrated journey.

We know of Sebastian Cabot's interest in Solinus's work from official documents relating to the claims and representations made in a Seville courtroom between 1535 and 1537 by the descendants of Christopher Columbus. These were in respect to "offices and awards due to them as heirs of the 'Discoverer of America.'" Cabot had been summoned as a witness by the Spanish Crown due to his maritime experience as an explorer and navigator of the New World.

According to court proceedings dated December 31, 1536, Sebastian Cabot "declared that Solinus, an historical cosmographer, states that from the 'Fortunate Isles,' now called the Canary Isles, journeying or sailing westwards in the ocean for the space of thirty days, are the Islands named the 'Hesperides'; and that these islands, the witness presumes, are the islands which were discovered in the time of the Catholic kings of Glorious Memory; which he [Cabot] had heard said by several people, in this city of Sevilla, had been discovered by the said Cristobal Colón [i.e., Christopher Columbus]."[27]

If we accept the authenticity of this statement—and I see no reason to doubt the translation of the case documents or the word of Cabot—we have here yet another allusion to the anciently known journey time between the eastern Atlantic seaboard and the West Indies. Admittedly, Solinus's thirty days' sail between the Fortunate Isles (unquestionably the Canaries) and the Hesperides is somewhat shorter than Sebosus's proposed sailing time between the Gorgades and the Hesperides, but this does not matter. A vessel leaving the Canary Islands might pick up the northeasterly trade winds and be blown east-southeast until it reaches the westerly flowing North Equatorial Current, which would then carry it directly toward the West Indies. In this way it would avoid the Canary Current, reducing the overall sailing time by many days.

There is a problem, however. The present author was able to read a copy of the 1498 edition of Solinus's work in the Whipple Library, Cambridge, and subsequently had the chapter on the Fortunate Isles, the Gorgades, and the Hesperides translated by Professor Ann Deagon. Nowhere does it state that the sailing time between the Fortunate Isles and the Hesperides is thirty days. So whether Cabot either misinterpreted Solinus or was privy to writings by the Roman author that are no longer extant may never be known. All we can say is that Cabot quite obviously believed that, for whatever reason, the Hesperides lay thirty days' sail west of the Canary Islands. What also seems clear is that he understood the West Indies to be synonymous with the islands of the Hesperides. Since Cabot was an accomplished explorer and navigator of great renown, his statements made, presumably under oath, in a Spanish courtroom should not be taken lightly.

What Solinus does repeat in his work is Sebosus's assertion that the Hesperides lay forty days' sail beyond the Gorgades. His exact words are, "Beyond the Gorgodes [sic] are the islands of the Hesperides. Sebosus affirms that they went back into the innermost limits of the sea by a voyage of 40 days."[28] The significance here is that there is no mention whatsoever of having to pass Mount Atlas on the journey from the "Gorgodes" to the Hesperides, which seems to affirm that Pliny's statement to this effect is erroneous.

All this is good news, as we can now feel justified in identifying the Hesperides with the West Indies. Moreover, we can affirm that a sketchy knowledge of this island group's existence persisted into Roman times. It was information such as this that writers including Pliny, Sebosus, and Solinus would seem to have picked up on and used as geographical anecdotes in their respective works. In turn, much later writers such as Isidore of Seville, Dicuil, and Honorius of Autun included this information in their own works, which were much later consulted by medieval cartographers prior to the age of discovery. In this way ancient maritime lore, perhaps thousands of years old, came into the possession of European explorers and chroniclers in the wake of Columbus's first voyage to the New World. Historians such as Oviedo and navigators such as Cabot realized correctly that the islands of the West Indies had been anciently known as the Hesperides, a magnificent insight that was as controversial then as it remains today. Yet was this information available also in Plato's time, and if so how might it have affected his composition of the Atlantis story? It is these questions that we must answer next.

7

CLUES TO
CATASTROPHE

I n the fifth century CE, the Neoplatonist, poet, and scientist named
Proclus took it upon himself to write a commentary on the *Timaeus*
of Plato. History tells us that he was one of the last teachers of the
Academy before the subject of philosophy was outlawed in an edict
passed by the Emperor Justinian in 529 CE. In addition to the extraordinary achievements he made in philosophy and science, Proclus practiced religious universalism. This was his belief that a true philosopher
could attain enlightenment by paying homage equally to the gods of all
faiths, and not just those of his own country.

Even though Proclus was writing some eight hundred years after
Plato described his sunken kingdom (a time frame of 432–440 CE is
suggested for the construction of Proclus's work[1]), his commentary cites
much earlier sources to create an open forum for the philosophers of
Alexandria to give their own comments on the historical validity of the
Atlantis story. These primary sources include the testimony of a student of Plato named Crantor (ca. 340–275 BCE), styled the "first interpreter of Plato," who is supposed to have visited Egypt and confirmed
the authenticity of the "history about the Athenians and Atlantics [i.e.,
those of the Atlantic island]."[2] This he apparently achieved by speaking

with "the prophets of the Egyptians, who assert that these particulars [i.e., those narrated by Plato] are written on pillars which are still preserved."[3] Unfortunately, this is all Proclus has to say about Crantor's alleged visit to Egypt, other than to mention these same pillars again later in the text: "But the history [obtained by Solon from Sais] is from pillars, in which things paradoxical and worthy of admiration, whether in actions or inventions, are inscribed."[4]

Modern supporters of the Atlantis legend have consistently cited Proclus's statement regarding the inscribed pillars to confirm that Solon could indeed have gained his account of the Atlantic island and its war with the Athenian nation from the old priest of Sais. Yet Proclus does not make clear who exactly went to Egypt in order to confirm Solon's testimony. The only published English translation of Proclus's *Commentaries of Proclus on the* Timaeus *of Plato* is the one produced by classical scholar Thomas Taylor in 1820. In his edition the crucial paragraph reads as follows:

> With respect to the whole of this narration about the Atlantics, some say, that it is a mere history, which was the opinion of Crantor, the first interpreter of Plato, who says, that Plato was derided by those of his time as not being the inventor of the *Republic,* but transcribing what the Egyptians had written on this subject; and that he so far regards what is said by these deriders as to refer to the Egyptians this history about the Athenians and Atlantics, and to believe that the Athenians once lived conformably to this policy. Crantor adds, that this is testified by the prophets of the Egyptians, who assert that these particulars are written on pillars which are still preserved.[5]

Yet as classical scholar Alan Cameron and Atlantis author Peter James have been at pains to point out, this is not how it reads in the original Greek text.[6] Taylor made an error in his translation, for Proclus said only, "He adds that this is testified to by the prophets of the Egyptians," implying that the author was in fact referring not to Crantor but to Plato, who is the subject of the sentences immediately preceding this all-important statement. Read the whole paragraph again and decide for yourself. In the opinion of the present author, the passage can be read either way. Yet whether it was Plato or Crantor who visited Egypt, what seems more important is the supposed presence in that country of "pillars" on which the "particulars" of the Atlantis legend are said to have been "still preserved." Did they really exist, or were they merely hearsay? The honest answer is that no one really knows. No evidence of their existence has ever been unearthed, either at Sais or indeed anywhere else in Egypt. No reference to these pillars, or to the Atlantis account, is found in any Egyptian text, and no other classical writer seems to mention them. All we can say with any certainty is that Proclus obviously believed in the existence of these inscribed pillars, otherwise he would not have included them in his *Commentaries*.

In reference to the Atlantis story, Proclus goes on to say, "Some refer to the analysis to the fixed stars and planets: so that they assume the Athenians as analogous to the fixed stars, but the Atlantics to the planets."[7] In support of his case, Proclus cites the opinion of the "illustrious Amelius," an obscure third-century Platonist and follower of the Alexandrian philosopher Plotinus (205–270 CE). We are told that Amelius "vehemently contends that this must be the case, because it is clearly said in the *Critias,* that the Atlantic Island was divided into seven circles. But I do not know of any other who is of the same opinion."[8]

This is a curious statement, for nowhere in the *Critias* does it suggest that the Atlantic island was divided into "seven circles." We can assume only that the "illustrious Amelius" must have been referring to the divisions of the city, which according to Plato consisted of a central islet surrounded by three circular waterways, two ringed portions of land, and beyond that the plain itself, making seven parts in total. Are we to believe that Plato intended these seven divisions to signify the seven planets of Pythagorean philosophy, that is, the sun, moon,

Mercury, Venus, Mars, Saturn, and Jupiter? All we know is that Plato possessed a brilliant knowledge of ancient astronomy, unquestionably gained from his exposure to the teachings of Pythagoras. Not only was he aware of the correct order of all the known planets, but he also knew their approximate distance from the Earth and the fact that they rotated in their own orbits.[9] He was also seemingly aware that the Earth itself was a globe that hung suspended in space.[10] These are remarkable achievements for 350 BCE, yet even with such a profound knowledge of the solar system, there seems to be no independent evidence to link the concept of the seven planets with the design of the Atlantean city, so why should the "illustrious Amelius" have made such a bold assertion? Did the number 7 have some hitherto unrealized significance in the development of the Atlantis legend? Was this knowledge still dimly preserved among the Neoplatonists of Amelius's day, and, most important of all, did it relate to the concept of the seven planets, or to something else perhaps? It is a matter we shall return to in due course.

After relating the opinions of various other scholars for and against the former existence of Atlantis, Proclus at last draws his readership's attention to the writings of one Marcellus. That Proclus unwittingly preserved for posterity this precious piece of evidence is itself a miracle, for it might just provide us with an accurate fix not only on the true location of lost Atlantis but also the whereabouts of the seven Atlantides.

ISLANDS AFAR

Not very much is known about Marcellus. He would appear to have been a geographer of the Roman world who lived circa 100 BCE.[11] He was the author of a now-lost work titled *Ethiopic History,* and it is this that Proclus paraphrases to lend support to the view first proposed by Plato to the effect that "so great an island [as Atlantis] once existed." For this is evidenced, he says:

by certain historians respecting what pertains to the external sea. For according to them, there were seven islands in that sea, in their times, sacred to Proserpine, and also three others of an immense extent, one of which was sacred to Pluto, another to Ammon, and the middle of these to Neptune [the Roman name for Poseidon], the magnitude of which was a thousand stadia [184 kilometers]. They also add, that the inhabitants of it preserved the remembrance from their ancestors, of the Atlantic island which existed there, and was truly prodigiously great; which for many periods had dominion over all the islands in the Atlantic Sea, and was itself likewise sacred to Neptune. These things, therefore, Marcellus writes in his *Ethiopic History*.[12]

This passage is like a puzzle waiting to be unraveled. What are we to make of these statements based on the knowledge of Atlantic islands already in our possession? Where exactly were these "seven islands in that sea"? Can we identify them with a known island group? The only clue we have is that "in their times" they were sacred to the goddess Proserpine, or Persephone, the daughter of Jupiter (or Zeus) and Ceres. When Pluto (or Hades), the god of the underworld, abducted Proserpine, her mother was so distraught that she asked Jupiter to intervene, and after much persuasion he consented to allow Proserpine to live one third of the year on Earth and the remaining part in the underworld as Pluto's wife. The importance of this familiar legend is that the underworld over which she ruled as queen was synonymous with the otherworldly realm known as Elysium, or the Elysian Fields. We have seen already how Plutarch in his *Lives* linked this mysterious place with two Atlantic islands discovered by Phoenician merchants and thought to have been members of the Azores group.

Before we can go on to determine the location of the seven islands sacred to Proserpine, we must first identify Marcellus's three islands of "immense extent," dedicated to Pluto, Neptune, and Ammon (the Greek form of Amun, the Egyptian ram-headed god).[13] Only the central island, sacred to Neptune, is elaborated on in any way. It is said to have had a magnitude of one thousand stadia (184 kilometers), and, if we take this to mean its size (and not its circumference), this would suggest that it was this distance from coast to coast. Such a measurement hardly seems fitting with the statement that all three of the islands were of "immense extent," even by classical standards. Despite this fact, the reported size of Marcellus's island sacred to Neptune makes it three times larger than any individual island in the Azores, Canaries, Madeiras, or Cape Verdes.

On the eastern Atlantic seaboard only the British Isles are this large, and they can be construed as just two principal islands—Ireland and the landmass that includes England, Scotland, and Wales. Yet there are no traditions that link the British Isles with Pluto, Neptune, or Ammon. Indeed, it would seem that in classical times the British Isles were seen as sacred to the sun-god Apollo. Hecataeus of Abdera, a Greek writer of fiction who lived in the fourth century BCE, is quoted by Diodorus Siculus as having said that the race known as the Hyperboreans (the inhabitants of Hyperborea, or Britain) worshipped Apollo "above all other gods" and were classed "as priests of Apollo" because his mother, Leto, "was born on this island."[14] Furthermore, he says that on this same "island" was "both a magnificent sacred precinct of Apollo and a notable temple which is adorned with many votive offerings and is spherical in shape."[15] It has long been considered that this temple, "spherical in shape," might in fact be Stonehenge, Britain's most famous megalithic site, or indeed some other sacred monument of these isles. If this is correct, it confirms both Britain's identification as the "island" of Hyperborea and its much-celebrated connection with the sun-god Apollo.

A further complication is that Marcellus, through Proclus's words, tells us that those who inhabited the central island "preserved the remembrance from their ancestors, of the Atlantic Island which existed there." Although this sentence, as well as the ones that follow, clearly suggests that Marcellus was drawing on Plato's Atlantis account, his words are extremely important. They suggest that the central island's inhabitants believed that in the vicinity there had once existed an all-encompassing landmass—sacred to Poseidon, their own patron god—which had disappeared in the manner Plato described. Moreover, Proclus implies that this former landmass actually was Atlantis, which, as our own enquiries have determined, "for many periods had dominion over all the islands in the Atlantic Sea," that is, over local or more widespread island groups.[16]

If the historical knowledge taken by Proclus from Marcellus's *Ethiopic History* is in any way representative of the original text, it would suggest that these three islands were connected geographically with Plato's Atlantic island. If this is correct, then the discovery of these key islands could provide us with an actual location for lost Atlantis.

So how might we go about identifying these three great islands? Having decided that they are not members of any of the more obvious island groups to be found on the eastern Atlantic seaboard, we must continue our search on the other side of the ocean, in the same vicinity as the Hesperides.

THE ISLAND OF CRONUS

There is one classical reference that might well aid us in identifying Marcellus's three islands of "immense extent." It is found in a work titled *The Face of the Moon* by Plutarch, the much-celebrated biographical writer. It features a lively discourse on astronomical matters, including a debate between Plutarch's grandfather Lamprias and a Carthaginian named Sextius Sulla on whether men exist on the moon.

The Carthaginian relates a story concerning the moon and the destiny of the soul that he had gained from a stranger in Carthage. He, in turn, had learned of it during a visit to a mysterious Western isle. On being pressed as to its location, Sulla speaks only of pilgrims who periodically made long journeys to this unknown island. Eventually, he asks that in order to explain himself he might be permitted to quote from the *Odyssey,* written by the Greek poet Homer, who flourished in the ninth century BCE. On being given permission to do so, he recounts the following line: "An isle, Ogygia, which lies far off in the sea."[17]

Sulla then goes on to state:

[The island is] a run of five days off from Britain as you sail west-ward; and three other islands equally distant from it and from one another lie out from it in the general direction of the summer sun-set. In one of these, according to the tale told by the natives, Cronus is confined by Zeus, and the antique (Briareus), holding watch and ward over those islands and the sea [gulf] that they call the Cronian main, has been settled close beside him. The great mainland [conti-nent], by which the great ocean is encircled, while not so far from the other islands, is about five thousand stades from Ogygia, the voyage being made by oar, for the main is slow to traverse and muddy as a result of the multitude of streams.[18]

In this key passage Plutarch speaks of an Atlantic isle named Ogygia, alluded to in the *Odyssey* and said to be located five thousand stadia (920 kilometers) west of the British Isles. At an equal distance beyond this island, in the direction of the "summer sunset" (i.e., west-northwest), are three more islands. These are said to be situated "not so far" from the "great mainland," or continent, that encircled the ocean, the ocean river, a theme already familiar to us from Plato's Atlantis dialogues, where his "opposite" continent is also imagined as having encircled the known world. In fact, it has been suggested that Plutarch borrowed the idea directly from Plato in an attempt to raise discussion on the concept of a sunken Atlantean landmass.[19] This theory is further implied, say scholars, by Plutarch's reference to the ocean being "slow to traverse and muddy," echoing Plato's shallow sea that he saw as having resulted from the submergence of Atlantis. Yet this idea, as we have seen, was mentioned by various classical writers, such as Aristotle, Pseudo-Scylax, and Rufus Festus Avienus in respect to Himilco's voyages in the outer ocean. Moreover, we may safely conclude that these references are very probably distorted recollections of both the Sargasso Sea and the shallows that thwart shipping in the Bahamas (see chapter 2).

The geography described by Plutarch, who was hardly a navigator, is virtually meaningless. There are no obvious islands situated five thousand stadia (920 kilometers) west of Britain, and no group of three islands is to be found at an additional distance of five thousand stadia. In view of his reference to the British Isles, the easiest solution would be to propose that Plutarch had gained some knowledge of the Northwest Passage. If this was the case, were the three islands located in the vicinity of either Hudson Bay or Labrador?[20] It is just possible. However, this theory fails to identify the three islands. They could be any of a whole range of large islands in this cold, remote region of the North American continent.

What does seem likely is that Plutarch possessed some knowledge of the Northwest Passage. Did he confuse this vague geographical knowledge with tales he had heard, perhaps from Carthaginian sources, regarding what lay on the other side of the ocean river? Looking again at Sextius Sulla's words, Pliny has him say that on one of the three islands the "natives" assert that Cronus, the Greek god of time (synonymous with the Roman Saturn), had been confined for all eternity by Zeus. Here, too, the "antique" Briareus was said to watch and ward over the islands and the "sea," or gulf, "that they call the Cronian main."[21] Classical scholars usually identify the Cronian "main" with the Adriatic Sea,[22] while the "great mainland" (the Greek actually translates as "continent") is generally dismissed as the lands beyond the Caspian Sea, which was once believed to be a gulf that joined the outer ocean. Even Plutarch himself adds confusion by speaking of a "gulf" that "lies roughly on the same parallel as the mouth of the Caspian Sea."[23]

Yet there can be no mistake concerning Ogygia's placement in the Atlantic Ocean. It supposedly lay west-northwest of the British Isles, while the three islands were said to be located "not so far" from the "great" continent. Moreover, the imprisonment of Cronus by Zeus, following their paternal wars, was intimately connected with the Western Ocean. Prior to their association with Hercules, the Pillars of Hercules are said to have borne the name of Cronus's guard, Briareus, and even of Cronus himself.[24]

So what are the identities of the three islands alluded to by Plutarch? If they are not to be found either in the vicinity of Hudson Bay or Labrador, might they be the three islands of "immense extent" referred to by Marcellus? If so, then it makes more sense to search for them not in Newfoundland but farther south, in the direction of the Caribbean, where the islands of the Hesperides would appear to have lain in the "secret recesses of the sea."

Such a conclusion might at first seem premature. However, it is important to remember that from Cape Cod, Massachusetts, along the Atlantic coast to Florida, there is a single, relatively uninterrupted shoreline with southerly flowing waters placed conveniently between the beach and the more powerful, northerly flowing Gulf Stream. This would have allowed any vessel a relatively easy passage to the Bahamas and Caribbean, while on the homeward journey a ship could have picked up the Gulf Stream to sail north back to Cape Cod. Before this clockwise-flowing ocean current veers eastward toward the most westerly isles of the Azores, it is said to have a width of around sixty-four kilometers.[25]

If we are to look toward the West Indies for a solution to this problem, Plutarch's somewhat confusing geography now makes better sense. Trying to comprehend the placement of Caribbean islands in the context of an extremely baffling long-distance transoceanic journey to the "great" continent without the aid of a world map would have been virtually impossible. Yet this seems to be exactly what Plutarch managed to achieve—an account that contained knowledge of the existence not only of the Northwest Passage but also the shallows of the Bahamas and three islands in the proximity of the West Indies.

Even if Plutarch really was alluding to the West Indies, could we go on to identify these three islands, perhaps synonymous with those spoken of by Marcellus? At first this seems like an impossible task, but then I found that somebody else had beaten me to it in a most convincing manner.

THE REAL ATLANTIS

Geoffrey Ashe is a much-respected historical writer of several books on subjects that have included King Arthur, Glastonbury, sacred wisdom, and ancient cosmology. In 1962 he produced a thought-provoking work on the voyages of St. Brendan the Navigator, a legendary Irish monk of the sixth century who, tradition asserts, discovered various islands in the Western Ocean. Titled *Land to the West: St. Brendan's Voyage to America,* Ashe's book also deals with the problem of Atlantis.

Even though many hundreds of books and publications on the subject of Atlantis had preceded his own, Ashe made a careful examination of the facts and evidence at hand and provided the reader with a unique insight into this age-old mystery. He, too, saw as significant Marcellus's paraphrased material on the ten Atlantic islands, as quoted in Proclus's *Commentaries of Proclus on the* Timaeus *of Plato,* and, after due consideration, had felt inspired to write, "If only we could admit that his islands were the Antilles [i.e., the Caribbean], the main chain of the West Indies. Seven is a fair round number for the principal Lesser Antilles: the islands intended could be Guadeloupe, Dominica, Martinique, St. Lucia, Barbados, St. Vincent, and Grenada. The three greater members of the chain are Cuba, Haiti, and Porto Rico, all big by Mediterranean standards; Haiti, the middle one, is approximately a thousand stadia—i.e., a hundred miles [160 kilometers] or a little over—from side to side."[26]

Cuba, Hispaniola, and Puerto Rico. Could these really be the three islands of "immense extent" alluded to by Marcellus in his now lost work the *Ethiopic History* and by Plutarch in *The Face of the Moon*? Had Geoffrey Ashe been the first person to recognize the true location of Atlantis? Was he justified in assessing the available evidence in such an unorthodox manner? In an attempt to quantify his bold assertions, Ashe goes on to cite instances of catastrophe legends found among the indigenous peoples of the Caribbean.

> The Spanish discoverers of the Indies learned that the natives of this area had an unusual Deluge legend. Instead of saying, like most nations, that the floodwater subsided, they said it stayed where it was, in possession of the ground it had swallowed. Many of the Antilles in fact had formerly been joined into a single mass, but a disaster in ancient times had split it into fragments with sea between. Such a tradition was recorded among the Caribs and among the tribes of Haiti itself, the very island to which Proclus's assertion would seem to point.[27]

These are quite extraordinary statements. Proclus, with a little help from Marcellus, had somehow managed to provide a key to unlocking the mysteries of Atlantis. Geoffrey Ashe had then used this key to open the door. No other author in the field of Atlantology had ever picked up on these same ideas, first proposed by Ashe in 1962, especially as he has gone on to cite the same interpretation of Marcellus's paraphrased statements in two further books.[28]

Everything pointed toward the fact that Marcellus had knowingly recorded that three Caribbean islands, tentatively identified as Cuba, Hispaniola, and Puerto Rico, stood in the proximity of Plato's former Atlantic island and were thus perhaps surviving portions of its renowned island empire. Moreover, Plutarch had associated these same islands with a tradition suggesting that Cronus had been imprisoned on one of them.

Intrigued by Ashe's assertions regarding an ancient cataclysm that had split apart the Caribbean, I checked out his primary sources for these references. One of them was taken from a book titled *Histoire de la découverte de l'Amérique,* written in 1892 by French historian Paul Gaffarel, a professor of the Faculty of Letters at the University of

Dijon. He states that on arrival in the Lesser Antilles, the first Spanish explorers were told by the native Caribs that "the Antilles had at one time formed a single continent, but they were suddenly separated by the actions of the waters."[29] Gaffarel also recorded that a legend found among the indigenous population of Haiti spoke of the islands of the Antilles being created during a sudden flood.[30]

Ashe's other reference source came from a volume of *Folk-lore in the Old Testament,* written by twentieth-century mythologist Sir James Frazer. He recorded, "The Caribs of the Antilles had a tradition that the Master of Spirits, being angry with their forefathers for not presenting to him the offerings which were his due, caused such a heavy rain to fall for several days that all the people were drowned: only a few contrived to save their lives by escaping in canoes to a solitary mountain. It was this deluge, they say, which separated their islands from the mainland and formed the hills and pointed rocks or sugar-loaf mountains of their country."[31]

The stories presented by both Gaffarel and Frazer were taken from even earlier works by Spanish explorers and chroniclers who had visited the West Indies shortly after the time of the Conquest. Yet the brief accounts provided by these two historians will suffice to demonstrate how the indigenous peoples of the West Indies appear to have preserved rich myths and legends concerning catastrophic events that had apparently befallen the Caribbean before the dawn of history. Moreover, since these stories were obviously told to the first Spanish explorers who reached these islands, it was conceivable that similar tales had been transmitted to transatlantic voyagers who visited the Caribbean prior to Plato's age. If correct, then did these ancient mariners return to the Mediterranean world not simply with accounts of strange tropical islands that lay beyond the Western Ocean, but also with stories and rumors concerning a sunken landmass that had formerly existed in the same vicinity as these islands? Was this the information that came to the attention of Plato, and as a consequence was utilized by him in his Atlantis narrative? This now becomes a very real possibility indeed.

That Plato's Atlantis might have been located in the area of the Caribbean islands is an intriguing possibility. As we know, in the *Timaeus* he tells us that the Atlantic island was situated within easy reach of "other islands" that acted like stepping-stones for ancient voyagers wishing to reach the "opposite continent," in other words the American mainland. Such terminology could not describe the island chains of the Caribbean more accurately. Archaeologists Jose M. Cruxent and Irving Rouse, who spent many years examining the migration routes of early cultures arriving in the Caribbean, spoke of the islands, banks, reefs, and cays that stretch from Central America toward the Greater Antilles in the following manner: "When the sea level was lower a few thousand years ago, the chain formed a nearly continuous series of stepping-stones leading to the Greater Antilles."[32] Similarly, they describe the Bahamas as providing "the best stepping-stone route between the mainland to the north and eastern Cuba and Hispaniola to the south."[33]

What we can also say is that up until around five thousand years ago a great many of the Bahamian islands formed part of two enormous landmasses known as the Great and Little Bahama Banks, which were gradually submerged as the sea level rose following the melting of the ice fields at the end of the Ice Age (see chapter 22).[34] Hydrographic surveys of the largest of these underwater platforms, the Great Bahama Bank, have indicated that this inundation process began as early as circa 8000 BCE and continued until circa 3000 BCE.[35] Very slowly this whole landmass was flooded by the rising sea level to leave the many thousands of islands and cays that today make up the Bahamian archipelago.[36] Similar processes resulted in the drowning of other low-lying regions in the Caribbean, some much quicker than others. For instance, marine geologists consider that Cay Sal Bank, located between Cuba and Andros, the largest of the Bahamian islands, was flooded relatively rapidly, between circa 10,000–8000 BCE and circa 6000 BCE.[37]

Do the Caribbean catastrophe myths unearthed by Ashe suggest that these former landmasses were submerged during more violent cataclysms involving a devastating flood of the sort hinted at both by

Marcellus and Plato? Is it possible that these landmasses once supported not just indigenous flora and fauna, but also human life?

If so, could the cessation of this human occupation have gone on to influence the legends found among the native peoples of the Caribbean, which in turn influenced the construction of Plato's Atlantis narrative?

MR. CLARKE'S COMMENT

These are tantalizing possibilities concerning the origins of the Atlantis legend, and they will be fully explored in due course. Yet as revelatory as they might seem, I can take no credit for locating Atlantis in the region of the Bahamas and Caribbean, nor can I award this prize to Geoffrey Ashe. Leaving aside the claims by Atlantologists, such as nineteenth-century Mayan scholars Augustus le Plongeon and the Abbé Brasseur de Bourbourg as well as the celebrated Scottish mythologist Lewis Spence, who all saw the Antilles as surviving remnants of an enormous Atlantean continent, we must applaud American historian Hyde Clarke for making this same connection. In a ground-breaking paper titled "Examination of the Legend of Atlantis in Reference to the Protohistoric Communication with America," delivered to the Royal Historical Society in June 1885, he speculated on the seven Atlantides, or Pleiades, being individual Atlantic islands.[38] This was an insight in itself, yet he went on to comment on Plato's assertion in the *Timaeus* that the kings of Atlantis had subdued the Atlantic island "together with many others [in that vicinity], and parts also of the [opposite] continent."[39] Clarke's address to the assembled audience continued as follows: "My comment on this is that the head seat of the great king [of Atlantis] was possibly in the Caribbean Sea; it may be in St. Domingo [i.e., Hispaniola]. It is to be noted, however, that at the Spanish invasion this island was under the Caribs, whose language is traced there. Consequently the relics of the former civilization in this and other islands were lost."[40]

These are extremely perceptive observations that at the time could not have been fully appreciated due to the publication three years earlier of Ignatius Donnelly's *Atlantis: The Antediluvian World.* As mentioned in chapter 2, this book proposed the former existence of an enormous Atlantic landmass in the vicinity of the Mid-Atlantic Ridge. Nobody wanted to consider the possibility that, in creating his Atlantic island, Plato might in fact have been alluding to a much smaller landmass that once existed in the vicinity of the West Indies—one that was linked via a series of island chains to the American mainland. For this reason Hyde Clarke's important paper was lost to the academic world until, mercifully, it was discovered during the preparation of this book. As we shall see, this same theory has now been independently resurrected by, among others, Emilio Spedicato, the professor of Operations Research at Italy's Bergamo University, who has written a well-argued paper suggesting that Hispaniola matches the description of Plato's Atlantic isle (see chapter 18).[41]

All of this quite disparate evidence suggests that we should take very seriously the possibility that, in Ashe's words, when Marcellus proposed that the three islands of "immense extent" occupied the approximate position of the former Atlantean landmass he was "on the right track."[42] Yet before exploring the matter further, we must first take to task Ashe's view that the seven other islands mentioned by Marcellus, and said to be sacred to Proserpine, were actually members of the Lesser Antilles. Even though this is a wholly original idea, is there any reason to assume it is correct? Their number, and the fact that they seem to be linked with traditions concerning Elysium, suggests an association with a more accessible island group, plausibly the Canaries or the Azores. Moreover, Proclus, in his *Commentaries of Proclus on the* Timaeus *of Plato,* makes further reference to Marcellus's *Ethiopic History* in which he provides details of "the Atlantic mountain," that is, Mount Atlas, which is located fairly close to the Canary Islands.[43]

At face value there seems to be no reason to conclude that Marcellus's seven islands were situated on the opposite side of the Atlantic Ocean. Only the three islands of "immense extent" appear synonymous with Caribbean islands. It was a matter I put to Geoffrey Ashe after tracking him down for a brief conversation at his home in Glastonbury, Somerset, England, on New Year's Day 1999. Having listened to my queries he reemphasized that there are seven notable islands in the Lesser Antilles. So if Marcellus really had been alluding to the three main islands of the Greater Antilles, why should we assume that he was referring to the Canaries or the Azores? If we take Marcellus's three islands of immense extent to be Cuba, Hispaniola, and Puerto Rico, surely it makes better sense to identify his seven islands, sacred to Proserpine, with principal members of the Lesser Antilles (see fig. 7.1).

The mention here of a group of seven islands also brings to mind the idea, first proposed by Hyde Clarke, that the seven Atlantides, or

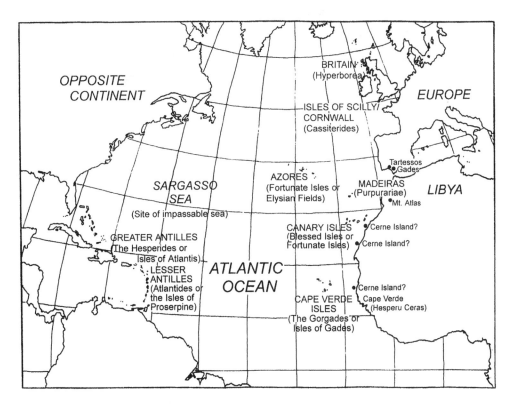

Figure 7.1. Suggested locations for the various legendary islands of the Western Ocean. The Roman geographer Statius Sebosus spoke of the Hesperides as lying forty days' sail from the African coast.

daughters of Atlas, were mythical islands, each connected with one of the seven stars of the Pleiades. Theopompus, a younger contemporary of Plato, wrote that the inhabitants of the opposite continent were known as the Meropes.[44] In the knowledge that Merope was one of the Atlantides, or Pleiades, could this name have been attached either to one of the islands of the Lesser Antilles or to the American mainland itself?

Everything points toward the conclusion that the seven Atlantides, or Pleiades, were synonymous in some way with Marcellus's seven islands, sacred to Proserpine and tentatively identified as the Lesser Antilles. Quite obviously, these astonishing revelations create fresh questions and extraordinary implications that might well provide us with important clues that will help unravel the mystery behind the supposed destruction of Atlantis. Yet before jumping ahead too far, we must first determine whether there could have existed a line of transmission between the pre-Columbian American Indians of the Caribbean and the people of Mediterranean world in which Plato lived some 2,350 years ago. Our greatest lead comes not from any evidence in the Americas but from the contents of Egyptian mummies.

Part Two
CONTACT

8

DEALING IN DRUGS

On September 26, 1976, under the full gaze of the international media, the body of the Egyptian King Rameses II, styled "the Great," was shipped from the Cairo Museum to Paris for a seven-month "state visit." Its purpose was to determine why deterioration had been noticed in the skin and around the neck of the dead pharaoh. Some twenty of France's leading scientists had offered their services in an attempt to find out what might have occurred (the problem was found to be beetle invasion).

One of these scientists was Michelle Lescot of the National History Museum in Paris. She used an electron microscope to determine whether any form of bacteria or virus was present in the wrappings, and was stunned to find herself staring through the lens at tiny samples of the tobacco plant. Confident of her findings, Lescot went public and was immediately attacked and ridiculed by her fellow academics. In their opinion, there was absolutely no way that tobacco could be present in the wrappings, unless through contamination. It was suggested that the Egyptologists who in 1881 had found the mummy among the so-called royal cache in a tomb at Deir el-Bahri in southern Egypt must have been smoking pipes at the time. If so, they could have inadvertently dropped some tobacco, which managed somehow to find its way into the wrappings.

In an attempt to counter these claims, Lescot was allowed to conduct further tests using samples taken from deep inside the body. Once again the microscopic examinations produced exactly the same results. Tiny traces of tobacco were found to be present in these samples, completely dispelling the initial belief that its presence was due to tobacco falling from a pipe.

These new results made it even more likely that tobacco had been introduced to the wrappings during the funerary procedures that followed the death of the king, who ruled for an incredible sixty-six years, circa 1290–1224 BCE. Even more tests revealed that where the internal organs of the body had been removed for placement in canopic jars, there was a stuffing of vegetable matter that, aside from plantain, stinging nettles, flax, black pepper seeds, chamomile, and wheat, included chopped tobacco leaves. Since this mixture was introduced into the mummy in order to help preserve its body tissue, it has been speculated that the tobacco was used in the embalming process as both an insecticide and to prevent putrefaction.[1]

The presence of tobacco in Rameses' mummy wrappings and body interior came as a complete surprise to Egyptologists and botanists alike for one basic reason: the plant was not known in the ancient world. It made no sense whatsoever, and although the chance find has been mentioned in a few popular books on strange mysteries of the past, no mainstream Egyptologist has been willing to embrace or explain this intrusion into an otherwise well-attested Egyptian history. The much greater problem that the tobacco plant is considered to be indigenous only to the Americas has been quietly swept aside by all.

THE COCAINE MUMMIES

There the matter rested until 1992 when a German doctor of toxicology named Svetlana Balabanova, working with the Institute of Forensic Medicine at Ulm, began conducting a series of unique tests on samples taken from Egyptian mummified remains preserved at the Munich

Museum. They came from one complete body, one incomplete body, and seven detached heads of unknown provenance.² The preserved body was that of Henuttawy, a priestess and singer in the temple of Amun at Thebes, circa 1000 BCE. Her tomb had been uncovered in a necropolis set aside for those of priestly rank at Deir el-Bahri, close to modern Luxor in southern Egypt. The early history of her mummy remains uncertain. Records show that in 1845 an English traveler named Dodwell sold Henuttawy's mummy to Ludwig I, the king of Bavaria. He and his family built up a large collection of antiquities, and these subsequently formed the basis of the museum's own collection, housed today in the old royal palace.³

From the mummified remains examined at the Institute of Anthropology and Human Genetics at Munich University, Balabanova took bone and skin tissue, as well as samples of head and abdominal muscle. The results she produced were extraordinary—so extraordinary that she felt it necessary to send similar samples to three other laboratories, which quickly confirmed her original findings. What all the tests appeared to show was that the mummified remains contained large quantities of drugs. In all nine cases hashish was present, although this was not so much of a surprise since scholars accept that it was freely available to the pharaonic Egyptians in the form of hemp. Adding still further to the mystery was the presence in eight of the nine bodies of nicotine, the narcotic ingredient of the tobacco plant. What really stunned the scientists, however, was the presence, in each and every one of the bodies, of cocaine, a psychoactive alkaloid present in the leaf of the coca plant.⁴

Balabanova knew instantly the implications of her findings. Tobacco was difficult enough to explain, but cocaine was quite another matter for it was produced for the first time only in 1859 and did not circulate among the high society circles of Europe until the late nineteenth century. Its origins are exclusively South American. In the years following the conquest of Peru by Pizarro in 1532, Spanish travelers in the Andes of Peru and Bolivia recorded that the native population seemed to be constantly chewing dried leaves called coca. This they rolled into a ball and placed in their mouth with a little ash or lime (caustic earth), a process that unlocked the cocaine content. For instance, in 1563, Galvão wrote, "Also there groweth in these fields, notwithstanding the great heate of the land, good maiz, and potatos, and an herbe which they name Coca, which they carrie continually in their mouthes . . . which also (they say) satisfieth both hunger and thirst."[5] In addition to relieving hunger and thirst, coca was also used as a mild stimulant to ease fatigue, which induced euphoria and anesthesia, factors that eventually led to its use and abuse in the Western world. During the Civil War cocaine was taken by injured soldiers to relieve pain.

Partially digested remains of coca leaves have been retrieved from rubbish dumps of ancient Peruvian cultures that go back as far as 2500 BCE, while the extended cheeks of the coca chewer appear on stone idols from Colombia that date to circa 1500 BCE.[6] Indeed, much evidence of this habit was revealed during the excavation of a number of graves in Peru that contained the bodies of mummified individuals dating to between 200 BCE and 1500 CE.[7] When subjected to tests similar to those conducted by Balabanova and her colleagues on the Munich mummies, these, too, proved positive for cocaine.[8] Furthermore, many of these Peruvian bodies were found buried with bunches of coca leaves still in their cheeks, presumably in the belief that the deceased would benefit from their effects in the afterlife.[9]

VALIDITY OF RESULTS

Balabanova is no maverick. She is a forensic toxicologist who has been frequently called on by the police to test suspect bodies for evidence of the presence of drugs or poisons. The results obtained from such tests are acceptable as legal evidence in court, so any serious doubts about her techniques, methodology, or findings must bring into question the whole subject of toxicological evidence. Furthermore, while conducting her tests on the mummies, she ensured against rogue readings by backing up her findings with chromatography. This is a process that reveals the individual signatures and metabolites (biochemical breakdown products produced by the body) present in the chemicals isolated from individual samples.[10]

Balabanova subjected the mummified remains to the so-called hair shaft test, based on the knowledge that if a person uses or has been subjected to drugs or poisons before his or her death, tiny traces are absorbed into the hair protein. These remain in a living person for some months before gradually dissipating away. It is this same procedure that allows employees, athletes, or members of the military services to be checked for possible drug abuse. These separate tests also produced positive results.

Since the original trials were conducted on the samples taken from the mummified bodies at the Munich Museum, Balabanova and her colleagues have conducted up to three thousand similar tests on other preserved bodies from countries such as Germany, China, Sudan, and Egypt.[11] A high level of these samples has also shown the presence of nicotine and/or cocaine. Date-wise, these specimens have ranged between eight hundred and seven thousand years, making some of them even older than the original samples taken from the Munich mummies. There seems very little chance that either the procedures or the equipment used by Balabanova were flawed in any way.[12]

DISAVOWING FAKERY

Another criticism leveled at Balabanova and her results is that the mummified bodies preserved in the Munich Museum, and used in the initial tests, were in fact forgeries purchased from Arab racketeers by European travelers eager to obtain genuine antiquities. Since carbon-14 testing of the organic materials relating to such remains can produce spurious and contradictory results, scientists are always eager to determine the provenance of artifacts used for testing. In the case of the mummies housed at the Munich Museum, some were, as we have seen, simply detached heads. However, other samples were taken from one whole body, that of Henuttawy, and the partial remains of another. These same mummies were examined by Rosalie David, an Egyptologist from the Manchester Museum in England, who was asked to verify Balabanova's claims by the makers of a Channel 4 *Equinox* documentary that featured the cocaine mummies. She found evidence of complex embalming methods having been employed in their preservation, along with packages of viscera, amulet inscriptions, and wax images bearing impressions of the Egyptians gods.[13] As a consequence, it seemed unlikely that these mummies were modern forgeries.

David had initially been skeptical of Balabanova's results, but during the preparation of the documentary, screened in Britain for the first time in 1996, she agreed to check for evidence of drugs on a number of mummies preserved at the Manchester Museum. The results astounded her. Three of the bodies examined contained substantial traces of nicotine. None, however, proved positive for cocaine.[14]

One final criticism of Balabanova's findings in respect to the mummified remains examined is that there is no archaeological, historical, or pictorial precedent to suggest that the ancient Egyptians were familiar with drugs such as cocaine and nicotine for either recreational or medical purposes. Certainly it is true that no wall relief, tomb painting, or ancient text alludes to the use of such substances. However, many of the herbs and plants referred to in such medical texts remain unidentified, while there is substantial evidence to show that the ancient Egyptians were habitual drug users. Furthermore, there is the clear presence of tobacco leaves inside the mummy wrappings and body of Rameses the Great. In addition to this, Balabanova's findings strongly suggest that the ancient Egyptians somehow absorbed nicotine into their bodies, either through smoking, chewing, or injecting tobacco in some manner currently unknown to us. Even though Egyptologists have found no evidence of smoke inhalation in Egypt before Arab times, there is tantalizing evidence of this practice in a Middle Eastern country that had very close ties with the pharaonic world.

INCENSE IN SYRIA

In 1930 Near Eastern scholar Stefan Przeworski wrote a useful article for the scholarly journal *Syria* about the discovery at various archaeological sites in northern Syria of a number of curious objects that might well turn out to be smoking pipes.[15] He cataloged ten in all that have been tentatively dated to between circa 1200 and circa 850 BCE.[16] Each one takes the form of a bowl carved from hard stone, usually blue-green steatite. They have a short stem, centrally perforated through to the bowl itself and tapered at the end so that it can be inserted into a hollow tube, probably made of wood or metal.[17]

The bowls themselves are modeled into distinctive forms, such as reclining lions[18] or hands that clasp their convex exteriors.[19] Often the undersides have additional decorative patterns, such as stylized lotus flowers.[20] Sizes vary between 8.1 and 13.5 centimeters in length, 5.2 and 7.7 centimeters in diameter, and 2.1 and 6 centimeters in height.[21]

The purpose of these curious, and little understood, stone bowls has been largely ignored by Near Eastern scholars. Sir Leonard Woolley, the famous English archaeologist who discovered the treasures of the city of Ur in southern Iraq during the 1920s, was inclined to label them as "libation bowls" due to their general appearance.[22] Przeworski, on the other hand, admitted that their "purpose remains quite obscure."[23] He dismissed Woolley's view that they were libation bowls and instead favored the idea that they might be a unique form of incense burner. In Przeworski's opinion, "The Syrian tube was not only used to handle the incense burner, it was also used as a pipe, through which one blew into the bowl, via the small communicating hole. Thus making it easy to maintain the glowing embers, and release the perfume."[24]

Przeworski illustrated the point by reproducing the outline of a Syrian relief that shows a male priest with a long pipe to his lips, smoke emerging from its bowl (see fig. 8.1).[25] If this carved relief were to be found on the wall of a temple in Mexico there would be little doubt as to what it represented. Yet the same image in northern Syria is inter-

Figure 8.1. Syrian priest with smoking pipe, circa 1000 BCE. Did the Phoenicians learn the art of smoking during trading expeditions beyond the Pillars of Hercules?

preted quite differently. Since oral smoking is not attested to in western Asia until the Arab period, scholars can only conclude that the figure must be exhaling instead of inhaling smoke!

That these curious objects from northern Syria are not incense burners but smoking pipes is an intriguing possibility, and one that was proposed originally by American prehistorian Cyrus H. Gordon in his 1971 book *Before Columbus*.[26] He pointed out that, following the publication of Przeworski's article in 1930, more of these bowls had come to light during excavations. One specimen was found in 1932 at a Judean archaeological site named Tell Beit Mirsim, where Gordon was present as a member of the field staff.[27] In his opinion, they bore all the hallmarks of smoking pipes and could be compared with the decorated stone pipes used by native American Indians, many of which also have "animal heads on the bowl" and "a hand (with all five fingers) carved in relief on the bottom of the bowl."[28] He added, "The heads indicate that the bowls were personified, while the hands not only suggest that the fragrant smoke was being offered, but also that the whole cultic object was called a 'hand' (*kaf*, 'hand,' is the name of such an object in Hebrew). Since smoking bowls appear during Old Testament times in the Near East, it is possible that the American peace pipes are an adaptation of Near East pipes."[29]

There is no clear indication of exactly what kind of substance the Syrians might have used in the pipes. It could have been opium or hemp. However, the presence of such pipes between circa 1200 and circa 850 BCE is strange in itself, particularly as this time frame coincides exactly with the rise of the Phoenicians, the undisputed merchants of the high seas whose city-states were to be found on the Lebanese and Syrian coasts (see chapter 10).

Curiously enough, Przeworski proposed that the Syrian pipes developed, via a now lost intermediary, from more conventional incense burners used in Egypt during the second millennium BCE.[30] It is an interesting idea, although there exists no hard evidence to support this theory, other than a basic comparison in styles between the reclining lions some of the bowls resemble and the sphinxlike leonine form so familiar to Egyptian art. It seems far more likely that Phoenician seafarers adopted the idea of inhaling smoke, as opposed to exhaling incense fumes, from one of the many diverse cultures they encountered on the fringes of the ancient world. Yet where exactly and from whom? And what might the connection be between the Syrian smoking pipes and the presence in ancient Egypt of tobacco and cocaine?

ON THE CASE OF TOBACCO

In America the two oldest attested smoking pipes date from circa 1500 BCE. One comes from Marajo Island, situated at the mouth of the Amazon in Brazil, while the other was found at Poverty Point, Louisiana.[31] Central American cultures, such as the Maya of the Yucatán, the Aztecs of central Mexico, and the islanders of the Caribbean, are also known to have used pipes to smoke tobacco. Yet these examples were little more than conical tubes, made out of silver, stone, or wood, into which they would place tobacco and rolled-up pieces of grass. These acted as filters to prevent fragments of leaf going into the mouth. In the Caribbean, the first Spanish explorers came across *caciques,* or tribal leaders, using a form of Y-shaped pipe made of reed that was inserted up both nostrils in order to inhale smoke. Pipes, however, were only for the elite. Less important members of the community would have to make do with rolling up the leaves and smoking them as a cigar.

The virtues of tobacco smoke were seen as manifold. It was used in America as a cure against asthma, nasal congestion, headaches, snakebite, boils, toothache, and complications during childbirth.[32] For more priestly or shamanistic purposes, nicotine could be ingested by first extracting a resin from the tobacco and then using it as an enema. The absorption of such high concentrations meant that the user would quickly experience an altered state of consciousness. In other cases, it could be rolled into a ball and chewed, something that, similar to coca chewing, was done to stave off hunger. What we know as recreational smoking bears very little resemblance to the use of tobacco among Mesoamerican cultures.

It is a common belief that there was no tobacco in the ancient world until after it was introduced from the Americas during the age of discovery. This, however, is a complete misconception, for there is ample evidence to show that a form of wild tobacco, called *Nicotiana rustica,* as opposed to the New World variant *Nicotiana tabacum*, was widely known in parts of Africa, including the western Sudan, long before Columbus.[33] It is thought to have been used as an Arab smoke medicine,[34] while black African cultures ingested tobacco fumes to attain meditational states and "tranquillising pleasure."[35] The act of smoking was known as *tubbaq,* and it was under this name that it filtered into a number of African dialects as variations such as *taba, tawa,* and *tama*.[36]

In order to use tobacco as a medicine, Afro-Arabians would first cure or dry fresh leaves, which would then be pressed together to make compact bricks.[37] Afterward, the resulting compound would be applied to the body in some manner, or it would be mixed with other substances, such as charcoal, so that it could be burned to produce smoke. This is in contrast to the Americans, who first dried and then crushed their tobacco leaves.[38] The leaves could then be administered as a powder, a juice, or a leaf poultice, or rolled into a ball and chewed, a method of ingestion that might possibly have been used in Egypt.[39]

The African tobacco plant is also mentioned in a medical treatise written by a medieval Arab physician named Ibn al-Baitar. He referred to it as "a species of tree growing upon the mountains of Mekkah, having long, slender, green leaves, which slip between the fingers when squeezed."[40] Apparently, "it attains the size of a man . . . lives in groups . . . one never finds one alone."[41] Furthermore, we are told, "It is beneficial as an antidote against poisons, taken internally or applied as a dressing, and as a remedy for the mange or scab, and the itch, and fevers of long continuance, and colic, and jaundice, and obstructions of the liver."[42]

Additional evidence that tobacco was not only present in Africa prior to the age of Columbus but was also used as a smoke medicine by the Arabs comes from the writings of the nineteenth-century explorer Captain G. Binger. He found it being used in Africa as money, and said, "The inhabitants of the Darfur [in Sudan] call it in their language *taba* . . . in Fezzan and at Tripoli in Barbary it is called *tabgha*. I have read a kasidah or poem, composed by a Bakride or descendant of the Khalif Abu Bakr, to prove that smoking is no sin. These verses, I think, date back to the ninth century of the hegirah."[43]

This suggests a date of 1450 CE, more than forty years before Columbus's celebrated journey. Furthermore, the use of the terms *tubbaq, taba,* and *tabgha* for smoking leads us to question the origin of the word *tobacco,* employed by the pre-Columbian peoples of the Caribbean to denote both the act of smoking and the instrument used in the smoking process.[44] That Afro-Arabian variants of the word existed before the age of Columbus seems too much of a coincidence. Could it be that there are common origins for these word variations that all denote the same thing—smoking tobacco?

The similarities between these root words for tobacco smoking only deepen the mystery and strongly suggest that either the tobacco plant was introduced into Africa via transatlantic contact before the age of Columbus or it was taken to the Americas by visitors from the African continent. If this is possible, it could mean that tobacco was present on both sides of the Atlantic as early as circa 1500 BCE, the date attributed to the earliest known smoking pipes found in the Americas.

Since we know that a species of the tobacco plant was present in Sudan before the age of Columbus, and samples taken from mummified remains in western Sudan also reveal high quantities of nicotine, it is possible that tobacco entered Egypt via Nubia. Yet when can we say this might have taken place? It could have occurred as early as pharaonic times or as late as the mid-fifteenth century. However, knowledge that cocaine has also been detected in Egyptian mummified remains suggests that the picture is a little more complicated. Even though we might attempt to explain the presence of tobacco in ancient Egypt in terms of an indigenous African variety, we cannot do this with cocaine. As we have seen, the coca leaf, and coca chewing, is native only to the Americas.*

As fantastic as this proposal might seem, the only realistic solution to explain the discovery of cocaine in Egyptian mummies is to suggest trading contact between the two continents. Furthermore, if the coca leaf was really being exported in this manner, there has to be a possibility

---

*Skeptics of the cocaine mummies theory have pointed out that a species of *Erythroxylon*, the genus of the coca plant, is found on the island of Mauritius in the Indian Ocean, suggesting that coca chewing might once have been practiced in the Old World. Yet when European sailors reached that island in the sixteenth century, it was found to be uninhabited and no evidence of any former human occupation has so far been determined. Until we find evidence to suggest that the cocaine present in Egyptian mummies derives from a source other than the species indigenous to the Americas, where coca chewing was common practice, we must assume the New World to be the most obvious source of the drug.

that tobacco from Central America was also being shipped to the ancient world. The presence of tobacco and cocaine in the same Egyptian individuals would tend to support this supposition. Moreover, the strange relationship between the names used for tobacco smoking on both sides of the Atlantic implies a cross-fertilization of terminology, techniques, and quite possibly even plants and produce centuries before the age of Columbus. Only by establishing this ancient trade route can we go on to propose a means by which knowledge of the Caribbean islands, and the cataclysms they would seem to have suffered in some past age, can have reached the Mediterranean world prior to the age of Plato.

CONTINENT TO THE SOUTH

One tantalizing piece of evidence that suggests the true source of Africa's trade in drugs comes from the following, quite extraordinary account. The year after Columbus's triumphant return from the New World in 1493, King Ferdinand and Queen Isabella of Spain signed a treaty proposed by Don Juan, the king of Portugal, that effectively divided up the Atlantic Ocean, and the lands within it, between the two great powers. Spain would have everything found to the west of the demarcation, including all the territories Columbus had so far claimed in the names of the sovereigns of Castile and Aragon. Portugal, on the other hand, would receive all lands discovered east of the line, an agreement that effectively gave it only the Azores, the Madeiras, and the Cape Verdes. Yet in reality there is good reason to suppose that the king of Portugal was already privy to knowledge that spoke of the existence of a southern continent that lay within the territories allotted to him.

We are, of course, talking about South America, Brazil in particular, the existence of which would appear to have been common knowledge among the black African and Arab populations of West Africa. In time, this information was passed to Portuguese navigators and merchants, who in turn carried it back to their native country.[45] Having already missed out on the discovery of the West Indies, the king of Portugal was not about to make the same mistake again. It was for this reason that he devised the agreement between the two nations.[46]

Before signing the so-called Treaty of Tordesillas in 1494, Isabella and Ferdinand had employed spies to seek out new information regarding the rumored southern continent. Yet somehow the Spanish sovereigns greatly misjudged what these advisers had to say. Although Columbus did indeed discover the mainland on his third voyage to the New World in 1498, he never set foot on it, leaving the Portuguese navigator Pedro Alvares Cabral to lay claim to Brazil in the year 1500. As predicted, its coast lay east of the demarcation, meaning that, according to the treaty, it rightly belonged to Portugal.

This was undoubtedly a crushing blow for the Spanish sovereigns, who realized that they should never have signed the agreement. Moreover, one of the advisors who reported back on what was known about the continent to the south had earlier provided both them and Columbus with more than just confirmation of its existence. In a letter to Columbus dated August 8, 1495, Jaime Ferrer de Blanes, a distinguished Spanish geographer and trader in precious tones, stated that he had heard from "Hindooes and Arabs and Ethiopians [i.e., black Africans]" and from "many conversations I have had in the Levant, in Alcaire and Domas" that "within the equinoctial regions there are great and precious things, such as fine stones and gold and spices *and drugs.*"[47] (current author's emphasis) Furthermore, he added, "The inhabitants are black or tawny . . . when your Lordship finds such a people, an abundance of the said things will not be lacking."[48]

What kind of "drugs" had Ferrer in mind when he announced that they would be found in "abundance" within the "equinoctial regions"? Were they simply medicinal drugs, or were they something more exotic, such as tobacco and cocaine? We shall never know the truth of the matter, although this information really does open up the possibility that an age-old transatlantic trade route could well have existed between the West African coast and the Americas. More important, it would appear that one of the principal commodities that traveled between the two continents was drugs—drugs that could have found their way into Egypt by the beginning of the first millennium BCE.

Yet if the pharaonic Egyptians were indeed dealing in drugs such as tobacco and the coca leaf, who might have been responsible for these transatlantic shipments? Was it a seafaring culture of American origin, or were these precious commodities shipped into either the Mediterranean or Red Sea by a known seafaring culture of the ancient world? Since there seems to be no hard evidence whatsoever to substantiate the idea that any pre-Columbian culture of the Americas paid regular visits to the Old World, we must look for another solution to this mystery. In which case, we must ask ourselves this: were the Egyptians themselves in a position to establish trading links with the American continent, or were they merely receivers of class-A drugs that would appear to have originated in a tropical paradise that lay beyond the Western Ocean? It is with these thoughts that we must now take a closer look at the maritime capabilities of the ancient Egyptians.

9

Olmecs and Elephants

O n the southern side of the Great Pyramid there is a long, slim,
glass-fronted building known as the Boat Museum. Inside is one
of the two large funerary vessels discovered in stone-lined pits located
at the base of this wonder of the ancient world, built by the Pharaoh
Khufu around 4,500 years ago. Made of Lebanese cedar, this enormous
boat is more than 43.3 meters long and 5.9 meters wide, with an estimated weight displacement of forty-five tons.

Egyptologists tell us that the purpose of these vessels was to enable
the soul of the dead pharaoh—in this case Khufu—to make his final
voyage into the afterlife. Such funerary practices were common in
ancient Egypt. For example, up to twelve even-older burial boats, all
eighteen to twenty-one meters in length, have been uncovered within
the North Cemetery at Abydos in southern Egypt. They date to the
formative years of Egyptian history known as the Early Dynastic, or
Archaic Period, circa 3100–2700 BCE.[1] Other boat pits have been
found in Early Dynastic necropolises at places such as Saqqara and
Helwan.[2]

Gazing up at this proud ancient form is a breathtaking experience.
Its high prow, sturdy oars, and central cabin all exude an impression

of great confidence, coupled with a profound understanding of maritime knowledge spanning not hundreds but many thousands of years. It is easy to imagine it on the high seas, cutting through crashing waves toward some distant land.

This view, however, is extremely misleading since Khufu's boat was never intended for the high seas. The whole structure is stitched together using rope, with lines of mortise and tenon joints across the hull. It would have leaked badly and eventually disintegrated in the calmest of waters. Such realizations have led scholars to assume that Egypt simply borrowed its maritime expertise from foreign cultures. This might be so, but there is good evidence to show that the Egyptians really did possess large seagoing vessels that embarked on immensely long sea journeys.

There is, for example, the story of a Persian navigator named Sataspes, who circa 470 BCE was set the task of circumnavigating Africa by King Xerxes. Accepting the challenge, Sataspes proceeded to Egypt, where he acquired a ship and crew and sailed out beyond the Pillars of Hercules.[3] He passed the Libyan headland, "known as Cape Soloeis," without incident, and then continued southward. After "many months" of journeying, and "finding that more water than he had crossed still lay ever before him, he put about, and came back to Egypt."[4] On his return to the Persian court Sataspes claimed he had not been able to complete the journey "because the ship stopped, and would not go any further."[5] Xerxes, however, was not impressed, and so promptly had him impaled!

The plight of Sataspes was recorded by the Greek historian Herodotus, who said he had gained the story from the Carthaginians. If this was correct, we must see in it another attempt by this seafaring nation to promote rumors concerning shallow waters and treacherous seas in the hope of preventing any further foreign exploration of the outer ocean.[6] Regardless of this fact, the account does seem to confirm the obviously well-attested seaworthiness of Egyptian vessels at the time of the Persian empire. Furthermore, there is good evidence to indicate that this capability had existed in Egypt for at least 1,500 years prior to this age.

Plate 1. The philosopher Plato and his pupil Aristotle, c. 350 BCE. In their age rumors and stories abounded regarding an opposite continent, an impassable sea, and unknown islands that lay beyond the Pillars of Hercules. One of these islands was Atlantis.

Plate 2. The Athenian poet and chief legislator Solon (c. 638–558 BCE), whom Plato asserts learned of the story surrounding the destruction of Atlantis from a priest at the temple of Sais in the Nile Delta. Yet there is every reason to believe that Solon's role in Plato's Atlantis dialogues is not what it seems.

Plate 3. Map of Atlantis by seventeenth-century German Jesuit scholar and physicist Athanasius Kircher.

Plate 4. Atlas, the Greek god who supported the heavens on his shoulders and gave his name to a mountain range in North Africa. New evidence shows that his legend, integrally connected with the Atlantis story, derives from either Phoenician or Carthaginian sources.

Plate 5. An examination of the mummified body of Rameses the Great (pictured) in 1976 revealed that it contained significant traces of the tobacco plant. More recently, Egyptian mummies studied by German toxicologist Svetlana Balabanova have revealed the presence not only of nicotine but also of cocaine, a powerful drug derived from the coca plant native to the Americas.

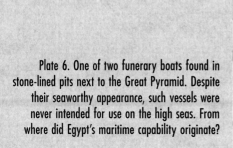

Plate 6. One of two funerary boats found in stone-lined pits next to the Great Pyramid. Despite their seaworthy appearance, such vessels were never intended for use on the high seas. From where did Egypt's maritime capability originate?

Plate 7. One of the several great stone heads found at key Olmec centers in Mexico, this one from La Venta in Tabasco province. Their resemblance to African individuals is irrefutable, but who were these noble ancestors and what role did they play in the introduction of the Atlantis legend?

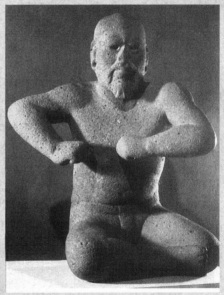

Plates 8, 9, and 10. African-style head (upper left) from Vera Cruz, Asian-like statue known as "the Wrestler" (upper right) from Uxpanapan, Vera Cruz, and a ceramic head of Mediterranean appearance (lower left) with beard and moustache from Tres Zapotes, Vera Cruz. Why did Mesoamerican cultures such as the Olmec and Maya depict individuals with such contrasting racial features?

Plate 11. Relief from Stela #21 at the Olmec site of La Venta showing the bearded figure nicknamed "Uncle Sam." American writer Constance Irwin argued that this carving showed a Phoenician seafarer from the eastern Mediterranean.

Plate 12. Ceramic head of Afro-Arabian appearance from the Mayan site of Comalcalco. Who does it represent? Certainly, it is not a member of the indigenous population as they were incapable of growing substantial facial hair.

Plate 13. Exterior wall of fired clay brick belonging to the Palace at the Mayan center of Comalcalco, near Villahermosa, in the state of Tabasco. Much of the city is constructed from fired brick, some of which bears marks that resemble an archaic script developed in the Indus Valley, where fired bricks were also used.

Plate 14. Cyclopean masonry photographed in the 1920s at Niebla, southwest Spain, by English archaeologist Elena Whishaw. In her opinion this wall formed part of an extensive seaport that thrived as early as 2500 BCE.

Plate 15. Bust of Christopher Columbus (1430?–1506), the discoverer of the New World, in the Capitoline, Rome. His crew from Palos in southwest Spain only consented to join the Genoese navigator on his celebrated voyage because they fully expected him to find the legendary island of Antilla.

Plate 16. Woodcut by the sixteenth-century French traveler André Thevet showing indigenous peoples of the West Indies smoking tobacco in the form of a cigar. Smoking was first encountered by members of Christopher Columbus's crew on the island of Cuba in October 1492.

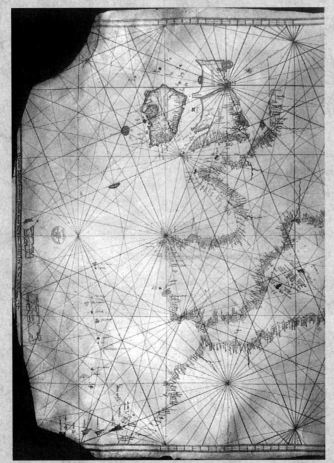

Plate 17. Benincasa map of 1476 showing Antilia (bottom left). Knowledge of its existence would seem to have been preserved by the Phoenicians, Carthaginians, and Moors long before this legendary Atlantic island began appearing on medieval sea charts.

Plate 18. The *Marine World Chart* of Nicolo de Canerio Januensis of 1502, identifying the main islands of the West Indies as the "Antilhas del Rey de Castella" (Antilles of the King of Castille). It confirms their association with the four islands of Antilia just ten years after Columbus's first voyage to the New World.

Plate 19. The Piri Reis map of 1513. Professor Charles Hapgood of Keene State College, New Hampshire, concluded that its truncated representation of Cuba was drawn using an ancient source map, supporting the theory of ancient sea journeys to the West Indies in pre-Columbian times.

Plate 20. Prince Henry the Navigator (right) of Portugal (1394–1460). More than anyone else he spearheaded the quest to discover the New World through his attempts to find Antilia and its legendary Seven Cities.

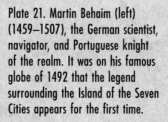

Plate 21. Martin Behaim (left) (1459–1507), the German scientist, navigator, and Portuguese knight of the realm. It was on his famous globe of 1492 that the legend surrounding the Island of the Seven Cities appears for the first time.

Plate 22. Hernando Cortés meets Montezuma, the great speaker of the Aztec nation, on his entry into Tenochtitlan in November 1519. What was the origin behind the ancient prophecies that led to Cortés being mistaken for the returning god Quetzalcoatl?

Plate 23. The ancient Mexican city of Teotihuacán, looking along the Avenue of the Dead toward the Pyramid of the Sun. Beneath this monumental structure archaeologists have uncovered a series of chambers corresponding to Chicomoztoc, the Seven Caves of the Mexica.

TALE OF THE SHIPWRECKED SAILOR

Among the Egyptological items found in the Imperial Museum of St. Petersburg is a papyrus of unknown provenance. Labeled as P. Leningrad 1115, it tells "The Tale of the Shipwrecked Sailor," an ancient account that has been linguistically dated to the Middle Kingdom of Egyptian history, circa 2135–1796 BCE.[7] If based on historical reality, it preserves the memory of long sea voyages undertaken by Egyptian mariners during, or even prior to, this distant epoch.

The account tells of a high official returning from a sea journey, during which he has failed to procure whatever the vessel was dispatched to find. He therefore dreads the reception that awaits him at the royal court. An attendant consoles the official, saying that he must celebrate the fact that he has returned to his homeland safe and well. The attendant then informs him of a time when he himself came near to death on a similar long voyage, and it is the finer details of this section of the story that are important here.

According to the attendant's story, he and the rest of the crew were dispatched to the king's mines, located in some foreign land, on a vessel 120 cubits (fifty-four to sixty-six meters) long and forty cubits (eighteen to twenty-two meters) wide.[8] These measurements, if accurate, speak of an enormous boat, larger than the ceremonial vessels found at Giza, and far greater than the merchant ships and caravels on which Christopher Columbus and his crews reached the New World.

The crew of 120 were said to have been "the pick of Egypt," and to confirm this statement the text states that "looked they at sky, looked they at land"[9] ("seen the heavens and seen the earth"[10] in another translation), implying that they had made similar long voyages before and were familiar with the art of celestial navigation. In addition to this, the crew could "foretell a storm before it came; a tempest before it struck,"[11] suggesting that they possessed a sound knowledge of maritime weather prediction.

The story relates how the attendant was shipwrecked after the vessel had encountered waves eight cubits (3.6 to 4.4 meters) high. All the crew except for him were killed, and after being cast onto the "island of the ka," he remained alone for three days before encountering a huge, bearded serpent thirty cubits (13.5 to 16.5 meters) in length. It addressed the sailor, telling him that it was the surviving member of a family of seventy-five serpents that had lived on the island before a "star fell, and they [the serpents] went up in flames through it."[12]

The monster said that a vessel would come to take the shipwrecked sailor back to his native land. Upon its arrival the Egyptian told his host that he would dispatch great riches to the island as a sign of his appreciation for the kind assistance he had received. The story continues: "Then he [the serpent] laughed at me for the things I had said, which seemed foolish to him. He said to me: 'You are not rich in myrrh and all kinds of incense. But I am the lord of Punt, and myrrh is my very own. That *hknw*-oil you spoke of sending, it abounds on this island. Moreover, when you have left this place, you will not see this island again; it will have become water.'"[13]

The above passage is often quoted by ancient mysteries writers to lend weight to the theory that the pharaonic Egyptians possessed their own concept of Atlantis: a paradisaical island abundant in fruits, game, and riches that was destroyed through fire and flood. Yet from our knowledge of Egyptian geography, we know that the mysterious land of Punt lay to the south of Egypt, beyond Ethiopia. In this knowledge, it has been suggested that the mythical "island of the ka" might have been located on the east coast of Africa, plausibly in the vicinity of what is today Somalia.[14]

The nature of the cataclysm responsible for the island's destruction will be dealt with in chapter 22. However, the importance of the story is that it would appear to confirm that the kings of Egypt regularly initiated daring maritime expeditions in an attempt to seek out and bring back mined commodities that presumably included rare metals and precious minerals. "The Tale of the Shipwrecked Sailor" also confirms that during the Middle Kingdom of Egyptian history, enormous seagoing vessels, like the ones described both in this text and by Herodotus in the story of Sataspes, were crewed not by foreigners but by skilled Egyptians.

We also know from wall inscriptions that in the reign of the Egyptian female king Hatshepsut (1490–1468 BCE), a flotilla of ships was dispatched to the fabled land of Punt. In the Deir el-Bahri mortuary temple of Hatshepsut in western Thebes, inscriptions speak of this celebrated expedition and record that, along with a large collection of exotic animals, live myrrh trees were brought back to Egypt for transplantation.[15] Lavish scenes depicting the wealth of this distant land are displayed on the walls of the temple, despite the fact that it still remains unclear where the fleet might have reached on its long sea voyage.

GRAFTON ELLIOT SMITH
AND THE EGYPTIANS

Having established the maritime capability of the Egyptians, we must go on to ask whether their vessels were in a position to have sailed the Western Ocean. If so, could they have reached the Americas? It is an extraordinary thought, and one that has captured the imaginations of scholars and mystics alike since the theory was first proposed during the seventeenth century by the German Jesuit scholar and physicist Athanasius Kircher (1602–1680) in his work *Oedipus Ægyptiacus.* This book postulated the Egyptian colonization not only of the American continent but also of India, China, and Japan.

Among the more adventurous scholars to have tackled the problem was Australian-born brain anatomist and Egyptologist Grafton Elliot Smith. In a book titled *Elephants and Ethnologists,* published in 1924, he argued for the diffusion of Egyptian culture into the Americas via India and China, citing as primary evidence of his theory a carved relief on a commemoration stela found in the Mayan city of Copan in Honduras. To him Stela B, as it is cataloged, showed the heads of two elephants, back to back, each with its own rider.[16] More conventional scholars have, however, demonstrated that they are not elephants but macaws, an apparent error of judgment that made Smith a laughing-stock. The truth is that nobody really knows whether they are macaws. As we shall see, evidence of ancient contact between Southeast Asia and Central America has come thick and fast in recent years.

THE OLMEC HEADS

The prospect of ancient Egyptians trading with, or at least reaching, the Americas was given a huge boost at the commencement of the 1970s by explorer Thor Heyerdahl, following the success of his Ra II expedi-tion from Morocco to the Caribbean island of Barbados. He opened the way for further speculation and discovery with respect to transatlantic contact in the distant past, a subject that was taken up by Indian writer Rafique Ali Jairazbhoy. Between 1974 and 1992 he penned three books that cite cultural, architectural, artistic, and religious parallels between the pharaonic Egyptians, China, and early Central American cultures, in particular the Olmec civilization that thrived in Mexico between circa 1200 and 400 BCE. It is this culture that produced the famous colossal stone heads regularly cited as proof positive of African contact with the Americas in prehistoric times. In all, some twelve of these colossal heads exist: four at the great Olmec center of La Venta in the state of Tabasco,[17] seven at San Lorenzo, on the Río Chiquito,[18] and another at Tres Zapotes, near Hueyapan, in the state of Vera Cruz.[19] They are fashioned from single pieces of basalt that weigh up to twenty tons apiece.

Of those present at the Parque-Museo La Venta in Villahermosa (the original La Venta site having been destroyed during commercial exploitation of the region), one stands 2.55 meters high and is 6.6 meters in circumference. Another, 2.7 meters high, has the top of its head flattened, showing that it was once used as an altar. A speaking tube runs from its ear through to its mouth, which enabled it to function as an oracle during ceremonies. The heads also bear strange headdresses, described variously as resembling a "helmeted dome,"[20] an upturned kettle, or a football helmet.[21] Some also have individual teeth, as well as earplugs that feature designs, such as carved crosses. On their discovery, the heads at La Venta were found to be facing east, toward the direction of the rising sun.[22]

Their broad faces, wide cheeks, rounded jaws, full lips, and flattened noses give them an uncanny resemblance to black Africans. More intriguing still is that their sheer size and weight, along with their prominent position at cult centers such as La Venta and San Lorenzo, tell us that they represented individuals with an extremely high status in Olmec society.

Foreign visitors first noted the Olmec heads' African features as early as 1862. A traveler by the name of José María Melgar y Serrano was passing through the province of San Andrés Tuxtla (the state of Vera Cruz) when he learned of the recent discovery at a site named Tres Zapotes, near Hueyapan, of a monolithic human form. He ordered it to be fully cleared of undergrowth and was amazed by what he saw. In the bulletin of the Mexican Geographical and Statistical Society, Serrano recorded that the colossal head was "a work of art . . . without exaggeration, a magnificent sculpture . . . but what most amazed me was that the type that it represents is Ethiopian [i.e., black African]. I concluded that there had doubtless been blacks in this region, and from the very earliest ages of the world."[23]

No other type of person is represented by the Olmec in a similar fashion, leading us to conclude that the individuals portrayed by the stone heads were either great leaders or revered ancestors. Furthermore, a number of smaller terracotta statues that also seem to represent black Africans have been found at various sites, belonging not just to the Olmec but also to other early Mexican cultures.[24] Like the giant heads themselves, the smaller statues bear distinctive features such as broad faces, thick lips, and flattened noses. In addition to these traits, many of them also have tight, curly hair and tribal scars. Further evidence of the presence among the Olmec of black Africans has come from the study of ninety-eight skeletons found in the preclassical cemetery of Tlatilco. A Polish craniologist named Andrzej Weircinski determined that 13.5 percent could be directly compared with the skeletons of African peoples.[25] A collection of twenty-five skeletons from a much later Olmec cemetery at Cerro de la Mesas produced a figure indicating that only 4.5 percent of those examined bore African traits, implying that in the intervening period intermarriage with the indigenous population had significantly reduced the number of foreign males present in the community.[26] The only conclusion to be drawn from this slender evidence is that black Africans appeared among the Olmec very early in the development of their culture, but that in later times their presence had dwindled considerably.

It was not until the 1950s that carbon-14 testing of organic materials was conducted in connection with the La Venta site. A joint expedition by the *National Geographic,* the Smithsonian Institution, and the University of California provided dates with an average reading of 814 BCE (+/−134 years).[27] It is now known that construction began at La Venta as early as circa 1100 BCE and ceased abruptly sometime around 400 BCE.[28]

If therefore the colossal heads and terracotta statues do represent black Africans, as so many writers have suggested, it would imply that some kind of transoceanic contact existed between Africa and the Gulf of Mexico as early as circa 1100 BCE and as late as 400 BCE. Understandably, scholars have tended to shy away from tackling this problem, although Jairazbhoy and others, such as the noted linguist, anthropologist, and author Ivan Van Sertima of Rutgers University, have concluded that black Africans arrived in Mexico from Egypt. In Jairazbhoy's case, he believes that they arrived here during the reign of Rameses III (1182–1151 BCE), who spoke of a maritime journey on the "inverted waters" bound for a mountain named Manu. This mountain was said to have been located "in the Far West at the edge of the Underworld."[29] Jairazbhoy saw this as signifying a sea voyage across the Atlantic Ocean to Mexico in "1187 BC," around the time of the foundation of the Olmec civilization.[30] Van Sertima, although agreeing with many of the points raised by Jairazbhoy in his books, considers that the stone heads represent Nubian kings who ruled Egypt circa 751–656 BCE and who established Olmec cult centers such as La Venta and Tres Zapotes.[31]

These are all bold and noble assertions that might eventually prove to be correct. Yet they all suffer from inherent problems that must be addressed if conclusions of this type are to be made. First, there is no reason to take Rameses III's legendary journey to the mountain in the "Far West" as a historical event. The story is far more likely to represent some kind of symbolic voyage to the *duat*-underworld, the subterranean domain through which the sun was said to pass from sunset to sunrise each night. In the religion of the ancient Egyptians the deceased pharaoh had to navigate this dark realm, traveling on a solar barque from west to east before he could fully enter the afterlife. Furthermore, although it was once thought that the genesis of the Olmec civilization was around 1200 BCE, the time frame of Rameses III's reign, it is now known that its first beginnings could have been as early as circa 1500 BCE. Quite clearly, this revised chronology brings into question Jairazbhoy's assertions, a problem he himself admitted in his 1974 book *Ancient Egyptians and Chinese in America*.[32]

Van Sertima's ideas fare little better. First, there is no reason to assume that the colossal heads at La Venta date from the time frame of the Nubian Egyptian dynasty of kings, circa 751–656 BCE. These dates fall somewhere within construction phases III and IV at the site, which took place between circa 800 and 400 BCE. It is far more likely that the heads date from building phase II, circa 1000–800 BCE, when the greatest amount of construction work took place at La Venta. It is even possible that the heads date from the earliest building phase, circa 1100–1000 BCE. It was during this period that the foundations of the great court were laid out and work began on La Venta's famous ten-sided pyramid, which is also cited by Van Sertima as evidence of Nubian contact with the Olmecs. In addition to this, the Nubian kings of Egypt are not known to have made long sea journeys to distant lands in the distant West. Furthermore, no obviously Egyptian item has ever turned up at an Olmec site, and no Olmec artifact has ever been found in Egypt.

Last, there is the enigma of the heads themselves. Even though Mesoamerican scholars accept that they are lifelike representations of either great leaders or highly revered ancestors, they are unable to accept that the heads show Negroid features. In their opinion, they depict the Olmec themselves, whose distinctive features are still to be observed among those who inhabit the same regions today. This might seem like denying the blatantly obvious, for whatever the colossal heads represent, it certainly isn't the indigenous population. Yet do the heads really depict black Africans?

BABY-FACED VISITORS

In addition to the clearly Negroid reliefs and statues in stone and terracotta, excavations at Olmec sites in Mexico have revealed a large number of figurines that clearly bear distinctive Mongoloid, or Southeast Asian, features. Many of these so-called baby-faced figurines, such as the so-called Wrestler of Uxpanapa, bear an uncanny resemblance to Chinese and Vietnamese individuals. Betty J. Meggers, a research associate of the Department of Anthropology at the Smithsonian Institution's National Museum of Natural History, has argued the case for contact between China's Shang dynasty and the Olmec culture. She has demonstrated that a large number of traits belonging to the Shang of circa 1750 BCE closely parallel those found in connection with Olmec sites currently dated to circa 1200 BCE. They include writing, the carving of jade, the use of batons as symbols of office, and similarities in styles of settlement and architecture, as well as several other comparisons relating to art and religion.[33]

Unexpected support for her theories came in 1996, when it was announced that two Chinese specialists on the Shang dynasty, Mike

Xu and Han Ping Chen, had found that they could "read" markings carved on celts, highly polished stone axes, unearthed at Olmec sites.[34] Amid the inevitable publicity that surrounded this announcement, Xu and Chen were severely criticized by scholars, yet they stood their ground and did not retract their initial statements on the matter. In the opinion of the Chinese scholars, "Recent discoveries of ancient relics from both Olmec land and Shang sites, plus intensive new studies on the Olmec and Shang writings and DNA testing, have proved Meggers's original ideas to be even more relevant, visionary, and correct."[35]

Strengthening the link between Southeast Asia and Mexico are the close parallels in the production of bark-cloth and papermaking techniques, a subject adequately investigated in the 1960s by Paul Tolstoy. He found that of 121 traits peculiar to this industry, ninety-two of them were shared by both Southeast Asia and Mexico. He further pointed out that no fewer than forty-four of these traits were employed only to increase the overall effect, so were therefore not essential to the main production of the material.[36]

In addition to this evidence, there is also the case of the eclipse calendar included in a Mayan astronomical work known as the Dresden Codex (the Maya of the Yucatán inherited aspects of their calendar system from the earlier Olmec culture). Not only does it work on precisely the same principles as an eclipse calendar used in China during the Han dynasty, circa 202 BCE–220 CE, but both incorporate exactly the same errors![37] A common origin seems to be the only explanation.

Then there is the discovery at an archaeological site in the Valdivia region of Ecuador, close to the Pacific coast, of very distinctive pottery "virtually identical" in design to that found in association with the Jomon culture of Japan, circa 3000 BCE.[38] Work on the Jomon-Valdivia relationship has also been championed by Meggers. She feels that there is enough evidence of a correlation between the two cultures on opposite sides of the Pacific to imply direct contact in prehistoric times.[39]

More significantly, studies in human lymphocyte antigens (HLAs)—proteins found in white blood cells—have revealed a direct correlation between certain peoples in Southeast Asia (as well as certain Afro-Arabian tribes) and native peoples of the Americas, such as the Ramah Navajo, the Mapuche, and the Nahua or Uto-Aztecans of the Mexican plain.[40] Since this link is purely genetic in nature, it can have stemmed only from cross-fertilization between these different cultures divided by the Pacific Ocean.

All this evidence suggests that if we are to look east for a solution to the colossal heads, we should also consider the possibility that a transpacific trade route existed between Southeast Asia and the Americas. Indeed, this is the one solution that the academic community is more open-minded toward. So in addition to displaying features of possible black African origin, the colossal heads bear undeniable Southeast Asian and even Polynesian facial traits.

Although most people scoffed at the theories proposed by Grafton Elliot Smith, history is now proving him correct. There is hard evidence to suggest transpacific contact between Mexico and places like China and Japan. Yet if he was correct in this respect, could he also have been right when he proposed that the Egyptian influence among the Mexican cultures had come not from across the Atlantic Ocean but via Southeast Asia? The answer seems to be yes. However, there are also good reasons to consider seriously the possibility of contact between the Olmec civilization and the peoples of the eastern Mediterranean.

A BEARDED MYSTERY

In addition to the colossal heads and multifaceted pyramid that were once located at La Venta, the cult center also possessed a number of curious stone reliefs that seem in stark contrast to the images of typically Olmec individuals. They show figures with pronounced Semitic, or at least eastern Mediterranean, features that include aquiline noses, high cheekbones, extended jaws, bushy moustaches, and full beards. Similar reliefs are to be seen at the Olmec site of Monte Alban.[41] Moreover, in addition to the statues and figurines that seem to resemble either black

Africans or Asians, many other examples in stone and terracotta appear to portray Semitic individuals with characteristic long faces and pointed beards, something highly irregular in Olmec art.[42] Indeed, the native peoples of Central America were incapable of growing substantial facial hair.

American archaeologist George C. Vaillant made a study of bearded faces in Mexican art and found several primary examples from various cultures of the pre-Columbian era.[43] Although he was not prepared to accept that this evidence demonstrated the presence in Central America of individuals from an ancient world culture, he did admit, "We are left in the perplexing position of having the same physical traits portrayed by artists of several different tribal groups, who evidently recognised a people different from themselves."[44]

One stone relief with apparent Semitic features found at La Venta has been nicknamed Uncle Sam by archaeologists. American writer Constance Irwin paid special attention to this relief, as well as another example found at the site, in her book *Fair Gods and Stone Faces,* published in 1963. In this landmark work she pointed out that, in addition to the obvious Semitic faces, trimmed beards, and Mediterranean-style dress, the individuals seen in the reliefs appear to be wearing "shoes with odd pointed upturned toes," something completely alien to conventional Olmec art.[45] Irwin noted that only three Mediterranean civilizations wore such shoes: the Etruscans, the Hittites, and the Phoenicians.[46] The Etruscans, she concluded, "would seem the least likely to have found their way to American shores,"[47] while the Hittites of Anatolia (modern Turkey) were a "land-bound" peoples.[48] This left only the Phoenicians, whom she proposed conducted sea journeys to the Gulf of Mexico and were responsible for introducing black Africans into Mexico.[49]

This conclusion on the part of Constance Irwin is incredible. Yet how else might we explain the presence at Olmec sites of statues, figurines, and reliefs that appear to show individuals with quite obvious eastern Mediterranean and black African features? As there seems to be no hard evidence to suggest that the Egyptians themselves ever reached the Americas, surely we must begin to look toward another culture altogether in order to discover those responsible for the hypothetical transcontinental drugs trade. As we saw in chapter 6, the most obvious navigational route across the Atlantic other than the Northwest Passage is to follow the North Equatorial Current from the Cape Verdes across to the Caribbean. Evidence suggests that both black Africans and Afro-Arabians were very much aware of the existence of the South American landmass long before the Portuguese navigator Pedro Alvares Cabral "discovered" Brazil in the year 1500. Furthermore, tobacco smoking seems to have been practiced on both sides of the Atlantic before Columbus, and one of the oldest known smoking pipes was found on Marajo Island, which lies at the mouth of the Amazon River in Brazil. It has been dated to circa 1500 BCE, the suggested foundation date of the Olmec civilization and just three hundred years before the artisans of northern Syria began fashioning stone smoking pipes.

Could all these facts be linked in some way? Could those renowned navigators, the Phoenicians, have been trading with the Olmec civilization, perhaps acting in concert with black African tribes that inhabited the Atlantic coast of West Africa? Could it really be the faces of Phoenicians that stare out from the carved stone reliefs found at cult centers such as La Venta, Monte Alban, and Tres Zapotes? If so, is it really possible that the true transatlantic dealers in exotic drugs, such as cocaine and tobacco, were not the Egyptians but the Phoenicians? Who exactly were the Phoenicians, and how far did their maritime capabilities extend?

10

THE MUREX
MERCHANTS

The land of the Phoenicians was made up of a series of city-states located on the Mediterranean Levant coast in what is today Syria and Lebanon. In the Old Testament, those who inhabited these territories were known collectively as the Canaanites, the peoples of Canaan, the "land of the purple," a title that translates into Greek as Phoenicia. It was an appellation derived from the deep crimson or purple dye extracted from the murex and purpura shellfish and used to color the expensive textiles so prized in the ancient world. Indeed, this dyed cloth was considered a luxury fit for royalty, surely the reason for the age-old connection between aristocracy and the color purple.[1]

The Phoenician nation evolved originally from a fusion of existing populations that inhabited the Middle East in the second millennium BCE. They included Semitic-speaking peoples from northern Syria and Iraq, as well as an indigenous Neolithic culture that had established a seaport at ancient Gebal, or Byblos, on the Lebanese coast sometime around 4500 BCE.[2] This same Byblos, or proto-Phoenician, culture was trading raw materials and other commodities with both Egypt and Crete as early as 3000 BCE.[3] How much farther afield its trade routes extended is a matter of speculation, although it is likely that its sailors were familiar visitors to coastal ports throughout the Mediterranean.

The earliest known Phoenician historian is the priest Sanchoniathon of Berytus (Beirut). He lived during the twelfth century BCE, and his important work, titled *The Theology of the Phoenicians,* is preserved in the writings of a first-century historian named Philo of Byblos. Despite its fragmentary form, Sanchoniathon's textual account provides us with some fascinating insights into the origins of the Phoenicians, who, he asserts, inherited their maritime capability from a dynasty of gods that founded Byblos during some bygone epoch.[4] These mythical individuals are said to have introduced civilized society and to have given birth to many sons and daughters who bore the names of later countries and city-states throughout the eastern Mediterranean. More curiously, it is said that one god named Taautus, a Phoenician form of the Egyptian moon-god Thoth, was granted the land of Egypt, where he created its first civilization.[5]

This tentative understanding of Levantine prehistory, from both archaeology and mythic tradition, enables us to understand why the later Phoenicians were able so easily to pull ahead of their neighbors in Egypt, Assyria, and Babylon to become the undisputed masters of the high seas. For unlike any other nation of the first millennium BCE, as experienced merchants and seafarers they established city-ports and settlements, many based around offshore islands located throughout the entire Mediterranean. They also had a port named Ezion-geber (modern Pharaoh Island, near Eilat) on the Red Sea, from where they set out on long journeys as far afield as Somalia on the East African coast, ports in the Arabian Gulf, and plausibly even India. All types of raw materials and commodities, from textiles to herbs, incense, spices, fish, timber, fruits, metals, jewelry, and trinkets, were traded from one port to another throughout the ancient world.

With the foundation circa 1100 BCE of the major city-ports at Gades and Tartessos in Iberia, the Phoenicians were able to spread their influence beyond the Pillars of Hercules. This position was strengthened greatly with the foundation circa 814 BCE of a sister colony at Carthage on the Mediterranean coast of Libya (modern Tunisia). As a nation it grew with such strength that, following the submission of the Phoenician city-states of Tyre and Sidon to the Babylonian King Nebuchadnezzar in the early sixth century BCE, Carthage seized the Phoenician trading ports in Iberia, which thereafter came under its control. Despite this takeover, most ancient writers continued to refer to Gades and Tartessos as ports belonging to the "Phoenicians."

In the centuries that followed, the Carthaginians and Iberic-Phoenicians explored the outer ocean and established island settlements, such as Cerne and Mogador on the Moroccan coast, in order to allow further exploration and trading exchanges with native peoples. Together they pushed out as far as the British Isles in search of tin and the Baltic coast of Germany in search of amber.[6] In chapter 5 we saw how the Carthaginian general Hanno explored the West Coast of Africa all the way down to the Gulf of Guinea, founding five cities along the way. We also know for certain that the Carthaginians traded with indigenous peoples of West Africa and how such trade exchanges were made.

Herodotus tells us that in Africa at least, when Carthaginian vessels arrived at the determined place of trading, the cargo would be transferred to the shore. Here the merchants would spread out their wares before lighting a fire and retiring to the ships. The smoke would mark out the spot, prompting local tribesmen to approach. They would place next to the goods an amount of gold deemed appropriate as payment, and then retreat. In due course the Carthaginians would return to see whether the offer in gold was sufficient. If it was, they would take the payment and go; if not, they would once more withdraw, allowing the tribesmen to add further gold to the existing offer. This bartering process would continue until the Carthaginians were satisfied that the correct price had been paid—the whole exchange taking place without any form of communication or misconduct between either party: hence the term "dumb commerce."[7]

AROUND THE CAPE

Only the Phoenicians and the Carthaginians would seem to have been in a position to trade directly with the Americas during the first millennium BCE. Moreover, the maritime influence of the Phoenicians on Egyptian history is well attested. Herodotus tells us that in an attempt to find a means of transferring vessels from the Red Sea to Egypt's Mediterranean ports, the Pharaoh Necho II (ca. 610–595 BCE) commissioned a group of "Phoenician men" to circumnavigate the African continent. This they accomplished by first departing from Ezion-geber, then journeying south along the East African coast until they reached the Cape of Good Hope. From here the vessels sailed in stages along the West African coast until, in the third year of their journey, they finally entered the Mediterranean. It is said that the fleet was able to sustain itself on the long voyage by setting up temporary settlements in the autumn and sowing and harvesting their own corn.[8]

As a footnote to the story, Herodotus tells us, "They declared—I for my part do not believe them, but perhaps others may—that in sailing round Libya [i.e., Africa] they had the sun upon their right hand."[9] This is in fact the one thing that proves the Phoenicians really did make the journey. We know this because the peoples of the ancient world would not, in theory, have known that in the Southern Hemisphere at latitudes below the Tropic of Capricorn the sun spends most of the day in the northern sky. So when the Phoenicians were navigating around the Cape of Good Hope at the southern tip of Africa, the sun would have been on their starboard side for much of the journey, exactly as Herodotus makes clear.

If the Phoenicians were able to achieve such extraordinary feats of seafaring ingenuity 2,100 years before Portuguese navigators would again make the same journey, just how far were they willing to go? If we might draw a comparison with Hanno's exploration of the African coast circa 425 BCE, the Phoenicians' circumnavigation of the same continent 175 years earlier was not for the purposes of seeing their names in the history books. Unquestionably, their own agenda was to establish settlements in order to enhance further their own trading capability, seemingly under the sponsorship of Egyptian kings such as Necho II. The Phoenicians were clearly seeking to exploit potential new sources of raw materials and saleable commodities that could be transported with relative ease to seaports both in the Mediterranean and on the Red Sea.

TRANSOCEANIC CONTACT

In chapter 5 we saw how evidence of the various island groups on the eastern Atlantic seaboard was known to the ancient world. We also saw how the Phoenician and Carthaginian mariners would appear to have established settlements in the Madeiras, and also on the island of Cerne, which lay either on the edge of the Western Sahara or near the mouth of the Senegal River. We also know that they reached the Azores and the British Isles. Yet did they go any farther? Did they reach the other side of the Atlantic Ocean? The answer would appear to be yes.

We have, for example, the writings of Pseudo-Aristotle and Diodorus Siculus, who both speak of Carthaginians settling on Atlantic islands with mild climates and navigable rivers. If these are not greatly exaggerated references to the Madeiras, they are allusions to Caribbean islands, very probably Cuba or Hispaniola. Not only do they have major navigable rivers, but, as we saw in chapter 6, they also would seem to have been synonymous with the mythical Hesperides, said by Statius Sebosus and others to have lain even beyond the Gorgades,[10] a mythical island group identified with the Cape Verdes.[11] If the Carthaginian settlement of Cerne really did lie at the mouth of the Senegal River, as historian Donald Harden has proposed,[12] it would have been in an ideal position to act as a staging post for transatlantic journeys. Here Iberic-Phoenician or Carthaginian vessels could have taken on board supplies, interpreters, pilots, and even a fresh crew before embarking on long journeys to the Caribbean.

Sir Edward Herbert Bunbury, a nineteenth-century Cambridge

geographer and fellow of the Royal Geographical Society, was of the opinion that the legend surrounding the Hesperides, as originally recorded by Hesiod in his *Theogony*, circa 700 BCE, was "almost certainly of Phoenician origin."[13] This lends weight to the view that it was their seafarers who first introduced knowledge of these islands to the ancient world.

In addition to the above accounts, we also have the testimony of Himilco, the Carthaginian general whose oceanic voyages and maritime lore are mentioned in the writings of the fourth-century Roman historian Rufus Festus Avienus. As detailed in chapter 2, there is every reason to believe that Himilco was very much aware of the Sargasso Sea and described it in extraordinary detail, saying that it could "barely be crossed in four months." If this was so, there seems little doubt that this distinguished Carthaginian navigator journeyed across the Atlantic Ocean and may thus have been familiar with the West Indies.

In all likelihood the Phoenicians and Carthaginians kept secret what they knew, not just about Atlantic trade routes but also the nature of the materials and commodities to be found in these tropical lands. Neither do we have to see the Phoenicians' circumnavigation of Africa under the Egyptian Pharaoh Necho II circa 600 BCE as the first time that they might have undertaken such a fantastic journey. Remember, this account has been preserved for posterity by Herodotus, who almost certainly learned of the story during his famous visit to Egypt. If this was the case, we have only the Egyptians' testimony that this event took place. From the Phoenicians and Carthaginians themselves there is merely a wall of silence when it comes to any knowledge of exactly where or how far their trading routes might have extended.

A perfect example of the great lengths to which the Iberic-Phoenicians would go to prevent any knowledge of the Atlantic trade routes becoming known to the outside world is demonstrated in a story told by the Greek geographer Strabo of a vessel outbound from the Iberian coast. Its destination was evidently the Cassiterides, which we will take to be either the Isles of Scilly or the southwest coast of

England. Here they were to exchange pottery, salt, and copper utensils for the tin and lead mined at no great depth by the inhabitants. Yet having taken to the open sea, the Phoenician ship's captain noticed that a Roman boat was tailing his vessel. Realizing that its intention was to learn the nature and destination of their voyage, he made the decision to alter course and head into "shoal water," probably the treacherous waters off the Isles of Scilly. Consequently, both vessels were wrecked, although the Phoenician ship's captain apparently survived by clinging to a piece of wreckage. On his return to port, he was handsomely compensated by the state for the value of his lost cargo. It is said, however, that by trying many times, the Romans did eventually learn the whereabouts of this trading market, as they probably did with many of the other routes used by the Phoenicians and Carthaginians.[14]

In the face of such extreme measures to protect their trading interests, it is very possible that shipmasters selected black African pilots, interpreters, and maybe even deck hands from among the Lixitae to accompany vessels on transatlantic journeys. In this way they could ensure that rumors or stories concerning the opposite continent did not spread among the Iberic or Semitic inhabitants of city-ports in Spain and Africa. However, any good secret is eventually going to be lost to the outside world, and this is very likely what happened during the early classical age.

THE PARAIBA CONTROVERSY

One of the most often cited examples of Phoenician contact with the Americas is the so-called Paraiba inscription. According to the story, on September 11, 1872, Viscount Sapucahy, the president of Río de Janeiro's Instituto Historico, received a package that, upon being opened, was found to contain a sheet of curious handwritten characters and a cover letter. This told of the discovery of a carved stone by black slaves working on a plantation owned by one "Joaquim Alves da Costa" of Pouso Alto, near Paraiba. Understanding its possible significance, da Costa had carefully copied the unusual inscription before duly dispatching it to the viscount.

A member of the institute named Ladislau Netto was given the task of translating and validating the written script, which was quickly identified as Phoenician. To this end he called on the expertise of the Brazilian emperor, Dom Pedro II, since he was the only person in the country with sufficient knowledge of the Semitic languages to even attempt a translation. Having made only partial progress in this respect, the two men decided that they should seek foreign assistance from a more formidable authority on such matters. It was the great French savant and historian Ernest Renan whom they contacted. He had conducted excavations in Lebanon and was an expert in Semitic languages. In an attempt supposedly to safeguard the full potential of the discovery, Netto decided to release only small sections of the text at any one time. Inevitably this aroused suspicion on Renan's part, and after having examined only part of the text the Frenchman decided that he was being duped, and so dismissed the whole episode as a hoax. As a result Dom Pedro withdrew his support, forcing Netto to admit to Renan that he had been mistaken in presuming the inscription genuine. The supposed perpetrator of the fraud, "Joaquim Alves da Costa," was never traced, adding weight to the conclusions drawn by Renan.

There the matter rested until 1967 when Cyrus H. Gordon, the director of Mediterranean Studies at Brandeis University in Massachusetts, decided to take up the case of the Paraiba inscription. One of his colleagues, a former graduate student in Hispanic studies, had chanced on a whole scrapbook containing material that related to the early history of the supposed stone, including a more accurate rendition of the inscription. Copies were sent to Gordon, and with some enthusiasm the two men engaged in a full investigation, which seemed to pay remarkable dividends. They were able to ascertain that it was written in a form of Semitic script apparently unknown in 1872.[15] After some difficulties a full translation was finally made. According to them it read as follows:

We are Sidonian Canaanites from the city of the Merchant King. We were cast up on this distant island, a land of mountains. We sacrificed a youth to the celestial gods and goddesses in the nineteenth year of our mighty King Hiram and embarked from Ezion-geber into the Red Sea. We voyaged with ten ships and were at sea together for two years round Africa. Then we were separated by the hand of Baal and were no longer with our companions. So we have come here, twelve men and three women, into "Island of Iron." Am I, the Admiral, a man who would flee? Nay! May the celestial gods and goddesses favour us well.[16]

The text speaks of a "Canaanite," or Phoenician, vessel that had apparently left the Red Sea port of Ezion-geber bound for the Cape of Good Hope, the same route taken by the Phoenician mariners who circumnavigated Africa on behalf of the Egyptian Pharoah Necho II circa 600 BCE. Yet instead of then turning north to sail along the West African coast, the vessel continued on a westerly course until finally it reached Brazil. As unlikely as this story might seem, the text matches what we know about the Phoenicians, including their unhealthy appetite for infant sacrifice.[17] Of more interest, however, was the reference in the inscription to the "hand of Baal," a saying similar to our own expression "hand of fate." According to Gordon, its use was unknown before the discovery on Cyprus in 1939 of a Phoenician inscription that contained this very same wording.[18]

After due consideration, Gordon decided that the "King Hiram" alluded to in the Paraiba inscription was Hiram III, who ruled the Phoenician empire circa 553–533 BCE.[19] In his book *Before Columbus,* published in 1971, he thus concluded, "The king can only be Hiram III," meaning that "the voyage from Ezion-geber began in 534, and ended in Brazil in 531."[20] These dates implied that the voyage must have taken place some two generations after the recorded circumnavigation of Africa by Phoenician mariners circa 600 BCE.

Since the 1970s Gordon has had a change of heart in respect to the authenticity of the Paraiba inscription.[21] Following considerable criticism from his contemporaries, he at last accepted that the king alluded to in the inscription was not Hiram III but Hiram of Tyre, the biblical king who assisted King David in building his "house."[22] The Old Testament also tells us that Hiram of Tyre entered a similar alliance with David's son Solomon, whom he helped to complete the temple in Jerusalem, circa 970 BCE.[23]

As a legendary biblical character, Hiram of Tyre is accepted to be the master mason of Solomon's Temple, the architecture and design of which is thought to embody the secrets of Freemasonry. In this role, the Phoenician king is revered by Freemasons as the spiritual founder of the Craft. It is therefore now believed that the Paraiba inscription was a fraud perpetrated by Brazilian Freemasons, connected with either the Instituto Historico at Río de Janeiro or Emperor Dom Pedro II.

With the Paraiba inscription's only academic ally having openly withdrawn his support, it can no longer be cited as reliable evidence of contact with the Americas. There are, however, quite separate indications that the Phoenicians and Carthaginians reached the Americas.[24]

ANCIENT ARTIFACTS

As early as 1787 workmen employed in the construction of the Cambridge-to-Malden road in Massachusetts are said to have unearthed a hoard of Carthaginian coins. Since none of the workmen present could identify them, the coins were given away to passersby who had gathered to marvel at the spectacle. Mercifully, the Rev. Thaddeus Mason Harris happened to chance by on his horse when the discovery was made and so was able to secure a selection of the coins for future study. Surviving specimens of the copper and silver pieces were finally identified as having been minted in the third century BCE. They bore short inscriptions in Kufic, a script used by the Carthaginians.[25]

Further coins, unquestionably minted in Carthage, were unearthed in more recent times by Frederick Gastonguat, a landowner from Waterbury, Connecticut.[26] Barry Fell, an epigrapher (a person who studies ancient inscriptions) and prehistorian, recognized them as belonging to "the earliest issue of Carthage." He translated their short inscription in Punic, the language of the Carthaginians, as reading OMMQNI, signifying the term "in camp," a reference to the fact that they were minted for military usage. They also bore the image of a horse's head, the motif of Carthage.[27] Although conventional American historians have been able to confirm the coins' North African origin, they are unable to accept them as evidence of a Carthaginian presence in the Americas. In their opinion, the coins must have been lost, discarded, or deliberately buried during colonial times, and so do not constitute archaeological evidence of any kind.

Such biased attitudes toward the discovery on the American mainland of historical artifacts originating in the ancient world are difficult to understand. Especially in light of a hoard of Carthaginian coins found in 1749 on the island of Corvo, which has been cited by historians as tentative evidence of this nation's contact with the Azores, even though no other evidence has ever come to light to confirm this supposition. Why, one might ask, have Carthaginian coins found under similar circumstances in the United States not been treated in a similar way? It just does not make sense, other than to assume that there is some kind of political motive for denying evidence of transatlantic contact with the Americas in ancient times. Furthermore, it is not just coins that have suggested a Phoenician presence in New England.

In 1948 an eastern Mediterranean oil lamp, dated to the third century BCE, was found at an American Indian site on Elm Street in Manchester, New Hampshire,[28] while in 1870 at Concord, New Hampshire, an ancient Iberian short iron sword blade was uncovered by Lyman Fellows as he helped dig the foundations for a railroad station. Its wooden hilt had decayed, although an etched inscription was just about visible. Barry Fell identified this as Iberian, and translated it as, "Hand wrought death dealing steel, able to cut through armor."[29] In

1993 the item appeared in an exhibition of pre-Columbian artifacts at Jamestown, Virginia.[30]

In addition to the discovery in North America of numerous ancient coins and out-of-place artifacts, there exists a whole range of inscribed stones that are seen as evidence of transoceanic contact with the ancient world. Too many of them exist to list individually, but some are incontestable and imply that foreign visitors from various cultures traveled to the Americas and left their mark in a number of different ways. What these items, all mostly found in New England, do not do, however, is provide us with any further confirmation of a Phoenician presence in Central America. To continue this line of enquiry we must go on to examine the evidence behind what is arguably one of the most politically sensitive and controversial cases of alleged pre-Columbian contact in the whole of the Americas—the discovery of actual wrecks from the ancient world.

11

SHIPWRECKS
AND SAILORS

In 1976 a young diver named José Robert Teixéira was spearfishing by some rocks at Ilha do Governador in the Bay of Guanabara, some twenty-four kilometers outside the busy port of Río de Janeiro. Searching the clear blue waters for prize fish to sell in the local market, his eyes caught sight of something unfamiliar protruding from the murky seabed. Upon closer examination he could see that it was a cluster of three huge jars, each more than a meter long, with double-handled necks. Curious to see what they were, he pulled one free from its resting place. As the fine sand fell away from its curved form, he saw that it was covered in crustaceans, so knew that it must have lain undisturbed for a very long time.

Teixéira retrieved all three of the giant vases that day in the Bay of Guanabara.[1] They fetched a better price than the fish would have done, so his labors had not been in vain. The antiques dealer who was lucky enough to have purchased these jars knew full well their real value, so he took them along to the Brazilian Institute of Archaeology for examination. For too long the scientists pondered over the huge terracotta containers before admitting, somewhat cautiously, that they were ancient "Greek" amphorae, used to transport commodities such as

163

olives or dates from one port to another in the ancient world.[2]

News of the find spread rapidly through Río de Janeiro, and soon it seemed that all the scuba divers in the city were heading out to Guanabara Bay to see if they, too, could find ancient jars. As might be expected, Brazilian scholars attempted to explain away the jars' presence by proposing that the amphorae were merely disgorged cargo from a colonial vessel inbound from the Mediterranean.[3]

It was not until five years later that the director of Río de Janeiro's Maritime Museum decided that they should take a closer look at the site where the amphorae were being discovered. They knew very well that ever since the 1960s a number of similar jars had been located by fishermen in the same general area, so it was quietly speculated that an ancient wreck might lie somewhere in the bay.[4] As a consequence, the director of the museum decided to bring in the expertise of world-renowned underwater archaeologist, shipwreck historian, and treasure salvor Robert F. Marx.

Having learned of the discovery of the amphorae, Marx remained skeptical. Yet after being introduced to one local diver who had no fewer than fourteen of the great jars in his garage, he began to think seriously about the matter. First, he determined that they were not Greek in origin. They were of a type manufactured around two thousand years ago at Kouass, near Tangiers, on the Atlantic coast of Morocco.[5] Marx borrowed one of the amphorae and showed it to oceanographers at two of Brazil's leading marine institutes. He was half expecting that they would confirm the thick encrustation to be of Mediterranean origin, showing that the jars had traveled to the New World in colonial times. Instead, the scientists explained that the encrustation was of a type unique to the waters around Guanabara Bay, meaning that it had built up in situ over thousands of years. So the answer was clear: the amphorae were unquestionably spilled cargo from a vessel that had traveled to Brazil when the Roman Empire was at the height of its power.

Sea growth removed from the broken amphorae found in the Bay of Jars, as the area had now become known, was sent by Marx to Ruth

Turner of Harvard University's Museum of Comparative Zoology and Walton Smith of the University of Miami's Marine Laboratory. Not only were they able to confirm the findings of the Brazilian scientists, but they also ascertained through carbon-14 testing that the encrustation was at least 1,500 years old.[6] Elizabeth Will of the Department of Classics at the University of Massachusetts and her colleague Michael Ponsich both concurred with these findings, yet suggested that the jars were of a type manufactured in the Moroccan port of Zilis (as opposed to Kouass), sometime during the third century CE.[7]

ITALIAN PIZZA VENDOR

Initially, Robert Marx was given the go-ahead by the Brazilian authorities to search for the exact location of the presumably Roman wreck. Although his expedition found no intact amphorae, it did manage to retrieve a large number of shards that included necks and handles, as well as a huge stone disc, perforated at its center. This, he concluded, could have been a weight anchor from the vessel.[8] Marx also called on the services of Harold E. Edgerton of the Massachusetts Institute of Technology, who conducted extensive sonar surveys in the vicinity of the hoped-for wreck. He quickly located two sunken targets on underwater reefs that were almost certainly the remains of one, and possibly even two wrecks lying on the sea bottom. However, following requests by Marx to explore the site more fully, the Spanish and Portuguese governments suddenly intervened and persuaded the Brazilian authorities to cease any further involvement in the affair.[9] They considered that confirmation of a Roman wreck in Brazilian waters would bring into question the validity not only of Pedro Alvares Cabral's claim to have "discovered" Brazil on behalf of the Portuguese sovereign in 1500, but also Spain's own claim to have "discovered" the New World in 1492.

With Brazil's upcoming quincentennial coinciding with the millennium celebrations, it seemed unwise to unlock a whole can of worms that might spoil Río de Janeiro's heavily publicized 2000 party. As a consequence of this extraordinary decision, Marx was refused permission to conduct any further investigations into the mystery of the amphorae found in Guanabara Bay.

The furor surrounding these events in Brazil eventually led to public slogans, such as "Cabral Sí, Marx No," as well as protests and marches against what was seen by the Brazilian people as Marx's wish to rob them of their national heritage. One Brazilian archaeologist who was asked by Marx to examine possible Phoenician jewelry rings found in Brazil not only confiscated these items but also added rather indignantly, "Cabral discovered Brazil, and let's leave it like that."[10] More incredibly, the then Brazilian minister of education apparently took Marx to one side at a Christmas party and said to him, "Every plaza in Brazil has a statue of Cabral, the real discoverer of Brazil, and we are not going to replace these with monuments to some anonymous Italian pizza vendor just because you have invented a Roman shipwreck where none exists."[11] In the wake of this fiasco, Marx accused the Brazilian government of deliberately suppressing vital information and materials that could confirm diffusion from the ancient world prior to the age of Cabral.[12]

As may be seen, the whole Bay of Jars affair degenerated into a sensitive issue of international and political concern that has now ruined any chances we have of confirming the presence of Roman wrecks on the seabed outside Río de Janeiro. This appalling situation makes me wonder just how many times national politics have stood in the way of the truth when it comes to presenting evidence of pre-Columbian contact with the supposed "New World."

Scholars rarely dispute evidence such as the Moroccan amphorae found in Guanabara Bay. How can they? Yet they explain the jars' presence in South American waters by admitting that every once in a while a seagoing vessel from the ancient world might just have been blown off course during storms and bad weather. Having reached the South American coast, it would probably have ended its days either floundering on uncharted shoals or rocks, or have been abandoned when the crew could go no farther. It is pointed out that Cabral himself discovered Brazil only after his vessel rounded Africa's Cape of Good Hope and was inadvertently carried across the ocean as he attempted to find the passage to India. Apparently, in the past century alone no fewer than six hundred African vessels have ended up being cast onto the South American coast, due either to bad weather or poor navigation.[13] This might well be true, but just how many vessels in past ages were able to make the return journey back to Africa? How many of their mariners were able to tell their people of this great continent that lay beyond the Western Ocean? How many of these stories prompted others, such as the Phoenicians and Carthaginians, to initiate their own voyages of discovery? This is the real enigma that must be addressed by historians.

THE COMALCALCO CONUNDRUM

Despite the cautious attitude toward ancient world contact with the Americas shown by academics, evidence does exist to suggest some form of contact between the Old World and certain Mayan sites located close to the Gulf Coast of Mexico. For example, on a plain in the state of Tabasco, around fifty-five kilometers northwest of Villahermosa, we find the great Mayan center of Comalcalco, which in the language of the Nahua peoples of central Mexico means "houses of the clay pans."[14] This curious appellation derives from the fact that instead of employing limestone as the main source of building material, those responsible for its enormous structures used fired clay bricks, the shape of which resembles the clay pans made by the Nahua.

Simply by looking at the towering walls that make up its North Plaza and Great Acropolis, there is a sense of recognition for those familiar with Roman architecture. These structures are made almost entirely of fired brlcks, resembling those used en masse during Roman times. In addition to this, some of the buildings possess buttresses, wing walls, and large, square windows, all of which "are relatively unknown in Maya architecture."[15] Yet similarity does not necessarily mean contact. We would need far more than comparison to suggest that an ancient world culture had introduced the Maya to fired bricks and new forms of architecture sometime around 200 CE.[16]

Amazingly, there are other connections between the buildings at Comalcalco and the ancient world. Two of the many temple mounds excavated by field archaeologist Neil Steede have revealed more than 4,500 fired bricks that bear marks incised on the wet clay before they were sun-dried. Many of these symbols are unquestionably of Mayan origin, yet a small percentage of them resemble signatures that appear on bricks and tiles from the Roman world. Furthermore, similar markings, which epigrapher Barry Fell identified as a form of alphabetic Libyan script, have been found on adobe bricks used to construct the Huaca Las Ventanas pyramids of northwest Peru.[17] These structures are accredited to the Mochica, or Moche, culture and are dated to somewhere between 300 BCE and 800 CE.

So could Romans have visited Mayan sites such as Comalcalco?

Steede conducted an extensive study into this subject and initially concluded that a Roman presence in Mexico might well explain the use of fired clay bricks at Comalcalco.[18] He also found a number of other parallels between the two cultures, including similarities in architectural design, artistic styles, and proposed astronomical alignments.[19] Furthermore, even though other local Mayan sites, such as Bellote and Jonuta, have brick structures, this particular building technique is unique to the area and is not found anywhere else in the pre-Columbian Americas.[20]

Surely these factors alone are strongly indicative that the presence of kiln-baked bricks at Mayan sites is evidence of intervention from the ancient world. Indeed they are, yet curiously the real answer is more complex, and might well lie outside the influence of the Roman Empire. Despite his earlier announcements to the contrary, which have appeared in professional journals, Steede has conceded that since no Latin inscription has ever been found at Comalcalco, there is no reason to assume that Romans ever reached Mexico.[21] In addition to this, English transoceanic specialist David Eccott, who has also made an extensive study of the evidence available at Comalcalco, considers that the knowledge regarding the use of fired clay bricks may have come from an altogether different location in the ancient world, the key being the maker's marks. Working alongside other colleagues in this field, he has determined that certain inscriptions found at Comalcalco indicate that the technology, and maybe even the expertise, behind the brick making could be part of a long tradition stretching back hundreds, if not thousands, of years. In his opinion, certain of the marks represent a form of ancient script familiar to Mesopotamia and the Indus Valley culture of northern India, circa 3000 BCE. This is thought to have spread gradually eastward to China, Sumatra, Easter Island, and then, finally, through transoceanic contact, to Peru, Panama, and Mexico.[22] Examples of this Indus Valley script have been identified both at Comalcalco and on the adobe bricks found at Huaca Las Ventanas in northwest Peru.[23] Yet regardless of the controversy surrounding the brickmaker's marks, there is still the lingering suggestion of a Roman presence in Mexico.

ROMAN CROSSINGS

Although a full twenty-four kilometers from the coast, Comalcalco is located on the Río Seco, a now silted tributary of the Río Grijalva, which flows into the Gulf of Mexico. Once a vessel could sail all the way to Comalcalco, and this is indeed what the Spanish conquistador Hernando Cortés attempted to do on his arrival on the Gulf Coast in 1519.[24] So there is no reason why Roman vessels inbound from Africa cannot have reached the region by first entering the Caribbean Sea and then following the Gulf Coast to the mouth of the Río Grijalva. Furthermore, other indications of a Roman presence in Mexico also exist. Take, for instance, the tiny sculpted Roman head professionally excavated in 1933 at a site named Calixtlahuaca, sixty-five kilometers northwest of Mexico City. This fascinating artifact is made of terracotta, and is just three centimeters in height. It is fashioned into the features of a Roman head that appears to be wearing a Phrygian cap, like the one worn by the god Mithras. A scientific process known as thermoluminescence, which dates ceramic objects with some accuracy, has determined that the head was manufactured around 200 CE. It was, however, found as a funerary offering, along with other grave goods, in a truncated pyramid structure dating to the twelfth century. This suggests that the head could have been in Mexico for up to a thousand years. Those experts who have studied this tiny artifact agree that it derives from the Hellenistic/Roman world.[25]

In addition to the Roman head of Calixtlahuaca, there is the case of the jar containing several hundred Roman coins found washed up on the northern coast of Venezuela. Their ages span an immensely long period from the reign of Caesar Augustus (63 BCE–14 CE) to around 350 CE. Since the hoard includes many duplicates, there seems very little likelihood that it could have been a discarded or buried collection of colonial origin, or that it might have been part of a national treasure trove on its way either to or from the New World. What seems more likely is that it is the wealth of a Roman trader lost overboard when his ship was wrecked sometime around 350 CE. Remember, a vessel that follows the North Equatorial Current westward from the Cape Verdes will be carried directly to the northern coast of Venezuela, almost precisely where the hoard was found. The coins are now in the possession of the Smithsonian Institution.[26]

Last, and somewhat more significantly, in 1972 scuba divers searching in waters off the coast of Honduras found an ancient hull with a cargo of "Punic" amphorae, suggesting that the vessel was of Carthaginian origin.[27] An accidental journey to the Americas might account for the apparent presence of a Roman vessel in Guanabara Bay, Brazil, or even one off the coast of Venezuela. Yet knowledge of a presumably far older wreck in the Gulf of Honduras, formerly a stronghold of the southern Maya, does not immediately suggest a chance, accidental journey across the North Atlantic Ocean. To have ended up at this location the vessel would have had to sail through the Lesser Antilles and Caribbean Sea, a voyage that must have been deliberate and not accidental. Exactly how old the wreck might be is unfortunately unclear, for it could date to either before or after the destruction of Carthage by the Romans circa 146 BCE. Since the Romans reoccupied ports such as Carthage and Mogador on the Atlantic coast of Morocco, they would have unquestionably reused old amphorae left behind by the Carthaginians. If the wreck dates to before the fall of Carthage, its discovery could constitute proof of Carthaginian journeys to the Americas in exactly the manner proposed in this book.

Yet as would seem to have happened in the case of the Roman discoveries in Brazil's Bay of Jars, the Honduran government stepped in and refused to grant anyone the right to investigate the site of the wreck. The underlying motive behind this decision was once again the fear that the discovery of an Old World vessel in American waters would undermine the achievements of Christopher Columbus. How many more wrecks might await discovery off the Atlantic coast of the Americas? How many more times will they be ignored in the name of political expedience and national embarrassment on the part of the Hispanic world?

Yet if the Romans really were making transatlantic journeys to the Mesoamerican world, why did they not formally record such maritime ventures? It can only be that, like the Phoenicians and Carthaginians before them, they wished to keep secret this lucrative trading market. Since the amphorae found in both Brazilian and Honduran waters are of North African manufacture, it is possible that the Romans gained their knowledge of transatlantic trading routes from the inhabitants of former Carthaginian ports and from the Lixitae—the nomadic Berber tribes of Morocco.

Was it through such voyages that the Romans came into contact with the Maya of Central America, in the same way that Phoenician and Carthaginian merchants would appear to have come into contact with the Olmecs, who inhabited the very same region several hundreds years beforehand?

In the next chapter we will return to the mysterious presence of psychoactive drugs in pharaonic Egypt. For we now have enough evidence to point a finger at those responsible not only for initiating the transatlantic trade in tobacco and coca but also for providing Plato with the source material behind the story of Atlantis.

12

ATLANTIC
VOYAGERS

From the evidence provided in the preceding chapters, it seems clear that at the beginning of the first millennium BCE the Olmec territories of Mexico were the destination of transoceanic voyagers. To the west lay the empires of China and Japan, while to the east were the Iberic-Phoenicians of Gades and Tartessos and the Carthaginians of North Africa, all of whom would appear to have left their mark on the pre-Columbian civilizations of Mesoamerica. Yet is it even realistic to suggest that the Olmec might have had a hand in supplying tobacco and coca to oceanic traders, who in turn would carry these valuable commodities halfway around the world for the pharaonic Egyptians to consume at their leisure? Let us look first at the problem of tobacco.

NO SMOKE WITHOUT FIRE

There is no known evidence to suggest that the Olmec practiced smoke inhalation, using either tobacco or any other kind of narcotic substance. This, however, proves nothing, since we know that tobacco smoking was widespread among the Olmecs' successors the Maya, who, according to conventional chronology, first established key centers in Mexico's

Yucatán Peninsula and in other parts of Mesoamerica circa 100 BCE. Indeed, our word *cigar* actually derives from the Mayan *sikar,* signifying either a cigar or tobacco.[1] Moreover, the Maya also depicted some of their gods wearing large hats and smoking fat cigars.[2] One such god, the black jaguar-headed God L, was the patron of merchants, in which role he was shown with a cigar in his mouth and a bundle of merchandise on his back (see fig. 12.1).[3] The origins of these gods are unknown. However, it is possible that they represent Olmec forebears, since we know that much of the Maya's cultural knowledge was inherited from the Olmec, who were probably seen as divine ancestors. If this was so, it seems inconceivable that the Olmec were not smokers, and if they were then they become the prime suspects in our case to identify those who supplied this valuable commodity to the ancient world.

Figure 12.1. God L of the Mayan pantheon smoking a cigar. Does this illustration imply that the earliest ancestors of the Maya introduced smoking to Central America?

If the Olmec were responsible for trading tobacco, might they also have introduced ancient world mariners to the delights of smoke inhalation? Remember, it must have been in this very manner that smoking was adopted by the first Spanish explorers and crewmen to reach the West Indies during the age of discovery. As mentioned in chapter 8, one of the oldest attested smoking pipes was found on Marajo Island, situated at the mouth of Brazil's Amazon River. It dates to circa 1500 BCE, just three hundred years before the northern Syrians began fashioning stone pipes made of hard stone. Since it seems likely that these pipes were used for smoke inhalation, there has to be a chance that the Phoenicians adopted the art of smoking from a Mesoamerican culture such as the Olmecs. If this was the case, it must have been the Phoenician merchants with their stone pipes who introduced the virtues of nicotine ingestion to the ancient Egyptians as early as circa 1200 BCE. Yet 1200 BCE is one hundred years before the official foundation date of Iberic-Phoenician seaports such as Gades and Tartessos in Spain and many hundreds of years before the establishment of Cerne on the West African coast. Can we really account for the presence in ancient Egypt of tobacco simply by supposing that it was supplied by Phoenician and Carthaginian traders?

It is a difficult question, and the most sensible solution is to suggest that the tobacco present in Egypt circa 1200 BCE was either indigenous to Africa or was transported via some other route, plausibly between the Americas and Southeast Asia. Yet a Pacific route of this sort would mean that, after its arrival in Asia, the tobacco would either have had to be carried overland, perhaps via the celebrated Silk Road that ran from China right across to Asia Minor (modern Turkey), or transported via a series of sea routes around the continent's southern coastline until it reached the Middle East. Both routes are possible, although the sea route probably makes better sense, as we know there was trade between Southeast Asia and India, and between India and the Persian Gulf, at a very early date. In many ways it brings us back to the ideas of transpacific contact suggested as early as the 1920s by Grafton Elliot Smith in his curious yet compelling book *Elephants and Ethnologists.* He proposed that the earliest civilizations of Mesoamerica were trading with the Chinese Empire, which was in turn trading with India and Egypt.

Since we know that the Phoenicians established ports on the Red Sea as early as 1000 BCE, and probably even earlier still, they might have traded at ports in the Persian Gulf with Asian merchants, who were themselves importing American tobacco via India and Southeast Asia. No other nation was in this same privileged position. Yet if this was so, why do we not see more evidence of the presence of tobacco among the cultures that inhabit these regions? This comes only from Africa, where a wild form of the plant is known to have grown. From West Africa through to Sudan and Egypt there is evidence of pre-Columbian tobacco medicine and smoke inhalation on a scale that appears nowhere else outside the Americas. Furthermore, the linguistic comparisons between the word *tobacco* in both Africa and Mesoamerica point toward some kind of pre-Columbian relationship involving transatlantic communication. It is therefore also possible that the tobacco entering Egypt as early as circa 1200 BCE came via transatlantic trade involving Phoenician merchants using ports in either Libya or Iberia.

PORTS OF SPAIN

Even though the Phoenicians are not considered to have begun Atlantic voyages until around the time of the foundation of Carthage circa 814 BCE, evidence for the presence of Bronze Age Iberic-Celts in North America as early as circa 1500 BCE hints strongly at transatlantic contact by this time.[4] Since we know that these same Iberian territories were in the hands of Phoenicians by circa 1100 BCE, there is every likelihood that the peninsula's earliest ports were established by a much earlier race of Mediterranean origin. Indeed, at Niebla, close to the former site of Tartessos, a complex of Neolithic galleried dolmens, temples, fortresses, hydraulic systems, and harbor works was recorded in the 1920s by Elena M. Whishaw, the director of the

Anglo-Spanish-American School of Archaeology.[5] Since they were contextually placed alongside Copper or Bronze Age artifacts considered to date to something in the region of 2500 BCE, Whishaw concluded that a seagoing maritime culture had occupied the Iberian peninsula during this early epoch. More intriguingly, since she concluded that no Mediterranean culture was making Atlantic journeys during this early age, those who founded the earliest port at Niebla must have been part of a trading colony belonging to the Atlantean empire described by Plato in the *Timaeus* and the *Critias*.[6] This extraordinary assumption led Whishaw to believe that the very earliest stone structures found here were in the region of between ten thousand and fifteen thousand years old.[7] Her views were expounded in a fascinating book titled *Atlantis in Andalucia,* first published in 1929.

Who might have built harbor works of stone in southwest Spain thousands of years before the arrival of the Phoenicians circa 1100 BCE remains unclear. What we do know, however, is that Strabo recorded that the Turdetans, the inhabitants of Tartessos, possessed records that went back six thousand years,[8] a fact that cannot have failed to influence the extraordinary theories of Whishaw.[9]

If we can assume therefore that transatlantic voyages took place as early as the second millennium BCE, there can be no problem in accepting that the tobacco found in the mummy of Rameses II was supplied by proto-Phoenician mariners who traded with Central and South American cultures, such as the Olmecs. Strengthening this view still further is our knowledge of coca production and distribution in the first millennium BCE (see fig. 12.2 on page 178).

As we saw in chapter 8, coca chewing was practiced in Peru as early as circa 2500 BCE, while the extended cheeks of the coca chewer appear on Colombian stone idols that date from circa 1500 BCE.[10] By this time the presence of coca was widespread throughout the Andes Mountains, from Colombia in the north right down to Chile in the south.[11] In Ecuador, for instance, traces of the lime used to unlock the cocaine

Figure 12.2. Scene from a pottery vessel belonging to
the Moche culture of Peru showing coca chewers (right)
summoning the spirit of the divine plant (left). Did the cocaine
found in Egyptian mummies come from Peru?

content of the coca leaf have been found in gourd-like vessels unearthed
at sites belonging to the Machalilla culture of Manabi province. These
items have been dated to between circa 1500 and 1000 BCE.[12]

Despite the extensive distribution of coca throughout the Andes
region, could it have found its way as far north as Mexico, where
the Olmec thrived between circa 1200 and circa 400 BCE? If so,
what possible culture might have been responsible for its transportation from the Andean highlands to Mexican cult centers such as La
Venta, Monte Alban, and Tres Zapotes? Is there any evidence that the
Olmecs might have been in contact with a South American culture
that traded in coca?

LAND OF THE CHAVÍN

The answer is likely to be yes, for it has long been speculated that the
Olmec were in contact with the Chavín, an important Peruvian culture
that thrived between circa 1200 BCE and circa 200 BCE. Various parallels exist between the two tropical forest cultures, most spectacularly

the preeminence they each gave to the cult of the jaguar, which included the use of extensive feline iconography.[13] In itself this might not seem like compelling evidence, especially as the jaguar motif is found among many Andean cultures during the same time period. However, it is the cult's presence among the Olmec that must be explained, for its form is strikingly similar to that of the Chavín. More significantly, it was during the formative years of the Chavín that maize was introduced to Peru from Central America, an undeniable fact that has prompted some scholars to suggest some form of cross-cultural contact with the Olmec civilization.[14]

As the American writer Constance Irwin observed in this respect, "It is indeed conceivable that . . . Mesoamericans, possibly Olmec, had ventured down to Peru bearing not only maize but also less tangible cultural gifts: architectural skill, some knowledge of astronomy, a feline deity, and possibly even an account of a bearded Fair God."[15]

So if the Olmec introduced maize to Peru, might we also conceive of some form of trade exchange in coca leaves via a relay route employing trains of llamas across the highlands of Ecuador and Colombia?

The Chavín produced a very distinctive art style using stone, pottery, and obsidian, and this has been identified at sites all over Peru.[16] Even though their main cult center at Chavín de Huántar is situated in the central highlands, Chavín artifacts have been found as far south as the plains of Nazca, showing that they were accomplished long-distance traders.[17]

Yet did the Chavín also trade in coca?

In many parts of the Andes coca was a highly valued crop produced in mid-valley zones, called *yunga,* that rise between a height of 500 and 2,500 meters and provide an ideal environment for cultivation.[18] Two main forms of *Erythroxylon,* the genus of the coca plant, were domesticated and grown in these specialized zones: *truxillense,* which thrives between a height of 200 and 1,800 meters, and another variant known simply as *coca,* cultivated between a height of 500 and 1,500 meters.[19] There is no doubt that coca was an important commodity in Peru's local and regional economy, especially among the Chavín. It was either exchanged for other bulk goods as part of an interzone trading network, or it was received at major ceremonial centers as tributes to local deities from worshippers belonging to outside communities.[20]

The main cultural and religious center of the Chavín in the central highlands of Peru was Chavín de Huántar, situated in the bottomlands between two mountain ranges—the Cordillera Blanca and the Cordillera Oriental, where the Huachecsa River converges with the larger Mosna River. This in turn flows north-northeastward into the much larger Marañon River, which is itself a branch of the Amazon. Although Chavín de Huántar was not the largest Chavín center, it was certainly the most impressive, with its extraordinary Old Temple complex and accompanying settlements, which thrived between circa 1200 BCE and circa 500 BCE.[21] As a key commercial center it became an important crossroads for the exchange of bulk goods.[22] Even though the Cordillera Blanca acts as a natural barrier to the parallel-running coast for a distance of around 180 kilometers, there are a number of passes that converge at Chavín de Huántar to form the meeting point of various pan-regional trade routes.

THE COCA CARTEL

The presence in settlements of refuse pits that have been found to contain forms of pottery from the south-central and northern highlands makes it clear that produce was received at Chavín de Huántar from all over Peru.[23] As a commercial center it must have acted as a clearing house, where commodities were received before being transported onward using natural corridors of trade.[24] As Richard L. Burger concludes in his impressive work *Chavín and the Origins of Andean Civilization*, "Thus, the early settlement of Chavín de Huántar was in an excellent position to gain access to exchange networks linking distant production zones, and to profit by regulating or controlling the use of these routes by other groups."[25]

It is known that one of the most important commodities that featured in Chavín de Huántar's trading network was coca, even though the site's elevated position would have made it impossible for the plant to have been grown locally.[26] So if coca really did form such a significant trading commodity, yet was not cultivated at Chavín de Huántar itself, where might it have come from?

One of the most well-known areas of coca production during the late Initial Period, circa 1200–1000 BCE, was Bagua, located in the northern highlands of Peru on a tributary of the Marañon River. At a height of around five hundred meters, the agricultural lands around Bagua proved to be ideal for cultivating coca. Furthermore, since its settlements were situated at a crossroads of communication routes west to the coast of Peru, north to the highlands of Ecuador and east into the Amazonian lowlands, it was itself a very important commercial center.[27] Exotic pottery found at Bagua demonstrates the extent of this trading network, which linked various economical zones inhabited by the Chavín.[28]

It is therefore conceivable that at least some of the coca received and subsequently exchanged at Chavín de Huántar, the cultural and ceremonial center of the Chavín, came from Bagua. Yet Bagua's own strategic position suggests that coca produced here could have been transported northward without it needing to pass first through Chavín de Huántar. In other words, coca could have been transported directly from Bagua via Ecuador and Colombia to the Central American territories of the Olmec.

All we can say for certain is that in the time frame suggested the most likely Andean peoples to have traded directly with the Olmec were the Chavín. Only they have been linked through clear cultural similarities with this ancient Mexican culture. In turn, the Olmec would appear to have established trading connections of their own with transatlantic traders such as the Phoenicians and Carthaginians.

It could, of course, be that the Phoenician merchants cut out the middleman and dealt directly with a South American culture such as the Chavín. On this subject Constance Irwin felt inclined to comment,

"If early mariners were, like later ones, seeking a westward passage, the Amazon would surely have beckoned, luring the traveller westward ever farther, until at last he reached its unnavigable headwaters, not far from Chavín de Huántar [or indeed Bagua]."[29] This remains a distinct possibility, as might some kind of direct or indirect contact between Southeast Asia and coca-producing cultures in Peru, Ecuador, and Colombia. It is possible also that a three-way trading cartel existed between the Chavín of Peru, the Olmec of Mexico, and the Phoenicians of the ancient world. This multicultural trading network probably included not only the supply of coca but also the knowledge of how to extract purple dye from tiny shellfish, a matter firmly developed in its entirety by the Phoenicians, and how to spin and weave cotton to make garments.

Another tantalizing avenue of research concerns the preColumbian distribution of the coca plant in other regions of the Americas. Not only was it cultivated in countries such as Chile, Bolivia, Peru, Ecuador, Colombia, and Brazil, but some species also were to be found in Guiana (modern Venezuela), Panama, and even in northern Mexico and Cuba (see fig. 12.3).[30]

Is it possible that the Olmec, or indeed the proposed transatlantic trading cartel, obtained their coca not from the Chavín of Peru but from a Central American country? Could one or more of the pre-Columbian cultures in countries such as Costa Rica, Panama, or Nicaragua have received coca from Peru before exchanging it on to more northerly tribes such as the Olmec? What about Mexico and Cuba, where species of *Erythroxylon* grew naturally; was coca chewing practiced in these countries as well?

Until further evidence of coca and cocaine ingestion comes to light, both in the Americas and in the ancient world, this is as far as we can go on the subject. In conclusion, it would appear that those responsible for supplying tobacco and coca to the Egyptian royal courts and temples from around 1200 BCE onward were in all probability the Phoenicians and Carthaginians. With their thirst for open commerce, their sense of exploration, and their accomplished maritime capability, they would

Figure 12.3. Map showing the extent of coca chewing and coca distribution in the Americas in pre-Columbian times. Did the trade in coca extend to the Olmec territories and also to West Indian islands such as Cuba, where species of the plant are known to have thrived before the discovery of the New World?

have held a unique position before other nations. So if it really was the Phoenicians and Carthaginians who were responsible for introducing Caribbean catastrophe myths to the Mediterranean world prior to the age of Plato, could these nations also have played some role in the creation of the Atlantis legend? Incredibly, the answer is yes.

THE LANGUAGE OF ATLANTIS

In Chapter 3, we saw how, in Plato's dialogue the *Critias,* Atlas—the first-born of the five twins of Poseidon—became the first king of Atlantis, while his twin brother was bestowed "the extremity of the island [of Atlantis] off the pillars of Hercules, fronting the region now known as Gadira."[31] We also learned that in Greek this twin's name was Eumelus, but "in the language of his own country [it was] Gadirus, and no doubt his name was the origin of that of the district."[32]

These words contain some very important facts. To begin with we can now assume that the immense size accredited to Atlantis, equal to that of Libya and Asia combined, does not relate to the extent of the landmass, but to the dominion over which the kings of the Atlantic island were seen to hold sway. Second, Gadira, or Gades, was, of course, the Phoenician city-port of this name founded in southwest Spain, circa 1100 BCE. Interestingly enough, Gadira is the only location, other than the Pillars of Hercules, singled out by Plato in connection with Plato's Atlantic island. It is a fact made doubly important when we read that "in the language of his [Eumelus's] own country [i.e., Atlantis] Gadirus" was his name. In other words, Plato believed that both "Gadira" and "Gadirus" derived from the Atlantean language. So how might we explain this apparent relationship between Gadira and Atlantis?

Gadira and Gadeira are Greek variations of the original Phoenician or Carthaginian name for the city-port. Pliny refers to it in the first century CE as "Gadir," which he says is Punic (i.e., Carthaginian) for "a fence,"[33] a name derived from the three-letter Semitic root *g-d-r,* meaning an "enclosure" or "an enclosure of stones." This can be interpreted to mean the "walled city" or the "city of walls," as in Geder, an unidentified Canaanite town mentioned in the Bible,[34] and Gedor, a town in the highlands of Judah.[35] Both derive their names from the same root as Gades.

Since the names Gadira and Gadirus are clearly Semitic in origin, this tells us that "the language of his [i.e., Eumelus's or Gadirus's] own country" was not Atlantean, as Plato thought, but Punic. In other words, the original language of the Atlantean tradition was Carthaginian, a variation of the Semitic-based Phoenician language. Of equal interest is the fact that those responsible for introducing the Atlantis legend to Plato used Gadira as a geographical reference point in order to explain better the extent of the Atlantean kings' oceanic dominion. Yet in naming Gadira, these storytellers have more or less given away their identity, for the most likely seafaring nations to have cited this Spanish city-port as a geographical reference point were, quite obviously, the Phoenicians and Carthaginians.

Even though Gadira, or Gades, is the only location singled out in connection with the extent of the Atlantean kings' influence, there are indications that other Carthaginian settlements also feature in the Atlantis narrative. For instance, Carthage itself has long been compared with the description given by Plato of his Atlantean city. Both were situated on low fortified hills, while Carthage's arrangement of docks and waterways has occasionally been likened to those that surrounded the Atlantic citadel.[36] We have also seen how there appears to be a close similarity between the concept of Plato's Atlantic island and the Carthaginian settlement of Cerne, situated off the West Coast of Africa. This small island, thought to have been located either in the proximity of the Western Sahara or close to the mouth of the Senegal River, was linked by Pseudo-Scylax with "parts" of the ocean "no longer navigable because of shoals, mud, and sea-weed," an allusion almost certainly to the Sargasso Sea.[37] Why associate Cerne with this region of the ocean if the ancient mariners who reported these hazards had not either commenced or ended their journeys in this island?

Nineteenth-century French geographer Felix Berlioux even came to the conclusion that Cerne actually was Plato's fabled Atlantic island. Using Diodorus Siculus's account of the Atlantioi (the Atlantes of Herodotus), among whom "mythology places the birth of the gods,"[38] Berlioux imagined an almighty Atlantean nation that arose out of Cerne and grew to become a huge Libyan empire.[39]

It seems more likely that Cerne's association with the Atlantis legend came about not because Plato's Atlantis was located off Africa but simply because this Carthaginian island settlement became confused with other stories concerning distant islands to be found many days' sail beyond the Pillars of Hercules. In all probability it was under these circumstances that the stranger aspects of Atlantic voyages became entangled with the core Atlantis legend, including perhaps the idea that elephants were present on the island. Remember, elephants were witnessed in a reed-filled lake by Hanno, the Carthaginian general who partially circumnavigated the African coast, around circa 425 BCE. Furthermore, it was on this same journey that he is alleged to have founded the island settlement of Cerne. Did such stories become so confused that eventually the African elephants to be found beyond the Pillars of Hercules were transferred out of the lakes of Mauritania and onto the celebrated island of Atlantis?

There can be no certainties in this business. Yet if we are to point a finger at those responsible for introducing the Atlantis legend to Plato's world, we need look no further than the Iberic-Phoenicians and their partners in crime, the Carthaginians. In them we have determined a much earlier source than Plato for the myth of the sunken island that lay beyond the Pillars of Hercules in the Atlantic Ocean.

Legends told to the first Spanish explorers to reach the West Indies of the submergence of the former Bahamian landmass and fragmentation of the Caribbean islands during some past cataclysm now cry out for further investigation. Yet before we can go on to do this, we must find out what the medieval world, immediately prior to the celebrated journeys of Christopher Columbus, knew about the true identity of lost Atlantis.

Part Three
CONQUEST

13

THE RETURN
TO PARADISE

Eighteen years before the Genoese navigator Christopher Columbus set out on his historic journey to the New World, he received a letter and sea chart from the Florentine astronomer and mathematician Paulo del Pozzo Toscanelli (1397–1482). Included in this correspondence was the transcript of a letter Toscanelli had sent to the canon of Lisbon Cathedral, Fernao Martins, who at the time was attempting to convince the king of Portugal to give his blessing to an exploratory voyage around the cape of Africa. Although the authenticity of this document has been challenged, there seems to be no point in ignoring its contents, for it alludes to what a navigator might expect to encounter on a sea voyage across the Atlantic Ocean.

From the city of Lisbon due west there are twenty-six spaces marked on the map, each of which contains two hundred and fifty miles [400 kilometers], as far as the very great and noble city of Quinsay [now Jangchow in China]. This city is about one hundred miles [160 kilometers] in circumference, which is equal to thirty-five leagues, and has ten marble bridges. Marvellous things are told about its great buildings, its arts, and its revenues. That city lies in the province of Mangi, near the province of Cathay [the northern part of the Chinese Empire], in which the king resides the greater part of the time. And from the island of Antillia, which you call the Island of the Seven Cities, to the very noble island of Cipango [i.e., Japan], there are ten spaces, which make 2,500 miles [4,000 kilometers], that is two hundred and twenty-five leagues. This land is most rich in gold, pearls, and precious stones, and the temples and royal palaces are covered with solid gold. But because the way is not known, all these things are hidden and covered, though one can travel thither with all security.[1]

It is perhaps pertinent to point out that when Columbus set out on his own epic voyage of discovery, very little was known about the western limits of the Atlantic Ocean. Although some cartographers and geographers of the medieval age accepted that ancient philosophers, such as Pythagoras, Plato, and Aristotle, had been correct in proposing that the world was in fact a sphere, what they believed lay beyond the uncharted waters of the Western Ocean was the Asian continent. Almost the only knowledge of the Orient circulating the Mediterranean world during medieval times was in the writings of the Venetian traveler Marco Polo (1254–1324), who had journeyed overland to Mangi and Cathay, and from whose book *The Description of the World* Toscanelli drew his own account of these exotic locations.

Despite this rather poor understanding of world geography, a number of navigational charts appeared during the fourteenth and fifteenth centuries that showed various mythical, or semimythical, islands that were thought to lie far out in the Western Ocean. They bore names such as Hy-Brazil, St. Brendan's Isle (after the legendary travels of an Irish monk of this name circa 520–577/8 CE), the Isle of Demons, the Hand of Satan, and, most significantly, Antilia. It was this island that Toscanelli identified in his letter with the so-called Island of the Seven Cities. So where exactly was "Antillia," and what were the Seven Cities?

THE EMERGENCE OF ANTILIA

The first allusion to Antilia can be found on a nautical chart compiled in 1367 by two Venetian brothers named Domenico and Francesco Pizzigani, or Pizzigano. In the proximity of where the Azores group should be placed is a legend that reads, "Here are statues which stand before the shores of Atulliae and which have been set up for the safety of the sailors, for they serve to show how far it is possible to navigate in these seas, and beyond these statues is the vile sea which sailors cannot navigate."[2]

Controversy has raged over exactly what, or where, "Atulliae" might have been. Originally geographers took it to be a corruption of the name Antilia. Yet this solution is now dismissed in favor of the all-important line reading *"ante ripas Getuliae,"* or *"ante ripas A(r)cules,"* with the last word being seen as a misspelling of Hercules.[3] This solution allows scholars to conclude that the legend relates merely to the "shores" of the Strait of Gibraltar, where anciently the Pillars of Hercules had once stood.[4] Yet simply by examining the all-important inscription on the original map one can see that the word in question is "Atulliae," and not "Getuliae," or "A(r)cules." Moreover, it is clear that the legend relates not to the Pillars of Hercules but to the farthest limits a navigator could journey in the outer ocean before he encountered a shoreline on which were statues of warning. Beyond this island were only uncharted waters and the impassable sea that had to be avoided at all cost.

I prefer to align myself with the study made of the 1367 Pizzigani map by the noted German cartographic specialist Konrad Kretschmer. After making a careful examination of the original map at the end of the nineteenth century, he concluded that the key name reads "Atulliae," a conclusion that has been accepted by some of the greatest geographers in the world.[5] Other suggested variations of the name are "Atilae" or "Atulae."[6]

Since the legend on the Pizzigani map of 1367 is in the exact spot where the Azores would later be discovered by Portuguese mariners, it has been suggested that Atulliae might have been an ancient name attached to one of the islands.[7] Support for this theory is found in the *Historia del Reyno de Portugal* of Manuel de Faria y Sousa (1590–1649), published in 1628. He recounts the supposed discovery on Corvo, the westernmost island in the Azorean archipelago, of a strange equestrian statue that just might be one of the statues of warning alluded to on the Pizzigani map. According to this Portuguese historian, "On the summit of a mountain which is called the mountain of the Crow [i.e., Corvo], they found the statue of a man mounted on a horse without saddle, his head uncovered, the left hand resting on the horse, the right extended towards the west. The whole was mounted on a pedestal that was of the same kind of stone as the statue. Underneath, some unknown characters were carved in the rock."[8]

It was not until the appearance in 1424 of a nautical chart compiled by a Venetian cartographer named Zuane Pizzigani, possibly a descendent of the Pizzigani brothers who compiled the Venetian map of 1367, that Antilia appears for the first time under its more familiar name. On this map, which bears an assortment of place names that belie its heavy Portuguese influence,[9] the island is shown as a rectangular landmass orientated approximately north–south—a form it takes on all subsequent charts of the fifteenth century. In size, it is approximately 450 kilometers by one hundred kilometers, and in distance it is around eight hundred kilometers from Portugal (although later maps place it at least 1,600 kilometers' distance from the shores of the ancient world).[10] Along its extended coasts is a series of seven bays, four on one side and three on the other, with a much larger eighth bay located at its southern end. Seven only of the bays are identified by name. These are: Asay, Ary, Vra, Jaysos, Marnlio, Ansuly, and Cyodue.[11] Many of the subsequent maps that appeared in the wake of the 1424 Venetian chart and that show Antilia contain variations of these seven place names.[12] Not one of these toponyms derives from real locations known in antiquity. Yet, as we shall see, the association of the number seven with the island of Antilia is of paramount importance to our investigations.

Even though the 1424 Venetian chart fixes the island name as "Antilia," in a legend that appears alongside the landmass it is written "Antlylia,"[13] demonstrating that at the time there was no fixed spelling. If the compiler of this chart was indeed a descendant of the earlier Pizzigani brothers, it seems likely that "Antlylia" was simply a modification of "Atulliae," the form it takes on the 1367 map.

From the 1424 chart onward until the end of the fifteenth century, Antilia appears on maps as part of an island group composed of Saya, Satanazes, Antilia, and Ymana, which eventually became known to geographers and historians as the islands of Antilia.[14] Their names also vary considerably on later maps, with Saya becoming Taumar, Satanazes becoming Saluagia, and Ymana becoming Roillo.[15] Always these four islands were located far out in the Western Ocean at a latitude that corresponds very well with the West Indies.

It is certain that Christopher Columbus would have been familiar with this somewhat sketchy knowledge of the Western Ocean prior to his initial voyage to the New World, particularly as his brother Bartholomew was a cartographer in Lisbon.[16] Since we also know that Christopher Columbus was aware of Antilia's supposed existence, there can be little doubt that he expected to encounter this island on his intended journey to Cipango and Cathay. Despite this knowledge, there is no real evidence to suggest that he might have been aware of the existence of the American continent before his arrival in the West Indies, or that he ever considered he had discovered the island of Antilia.

Curiously enough, the four islands of Antilia on the Battista Beccario map of 1435 are marked with the legend *Insulle a Novo Repte* ("Newly Reported Islands").[17] This statement unquestionably relates to the discovery of the first of the Azores group in 1427.[18] Yet a further map made by the Venetian cartographer Andrea Bianco in 1436 confirms that Antilia was located far to the west of the Azores. Here the island is positioned to the west of this more familiar archipelago, between which is a gap that bears the inscription *Questo xe mar. de baga* ("This is the Berry Sea"), a reference to the berry-like bladders of the *Sargassum bac-*

ciferum, the species of seaweed that dominates the Sargasso Sea.[19] Since the word *baga* is Portuguese, it implies that Portuguese navigators were familiar with the outer ocean as far as the Baga Mar, or Sargasso Sea, and perhaps even beyond it, and thus provided the core information for some of the earliest nautical charts of the fifteenth century. It tells us also that Antilia was expected to be found beyond the Sargasso Sea in the same geographical proximity as the Bahamian Islands.

It was shortly after the discovery of the West Indies (i.e., the Indies reached by the westward passage) that this archipelago became associated with the legendary Antillean islands for the first time. The *Marine World Chart* of Nicolo de Canerio Januensis, produced just ten years after Columbus's first voyage, identifies the three main islands of the West Indies as the Antilhas del Rey de Castella ("Antilles of the King of Castille").[20] Another, similar chart dating from around the same time also collectively identifies the islands of "Newe Spain" as "Antilie," (i.e., the Antilles),[21] while in 1511 Peter Martyr d'Anghiera, the Spanish chronicler, stated that they were known as "the islands of Antilia."[22] This, of course, is the name they retain to this day.

Yet how did early Spanish explorers come to identify the West Indies as "the islands of Antilia," especially as Columbus remained adamant that he had reached either Cathay or Cipango, even after his return to Spain? The answer would appear to lie in the fact that it was the Spanish crews that accompanied him on his voyage of discovery—and not Columbus—who came to believe they had encountered the fabled islands of Antilia. These men originated in the main from the Iberian port of Palos, from which Columbus's three vessels had set sail for the New World in the summer of 1492. Its local seamen possessed a long tradition of maritime experience that stretched back to the age of the Iberic-Phoenicians and Carthaginians. Indeed, Palos was just a few kilometers' distance from the sites of ancient ports such as Tartessos, Niebla, and Gades.

According to an obscure book titled *Historia de la Rabida,* written by Fray Angel Ortega, a Franciscan monk at the famous Monastery of La Rabida at Palos, local seamen preserved the memory of a great island called Antilia that lay across the Western Ocean.[23] Apparently, it was their belief in the existence of this world across the water, visited by their Iberic-Phoenician forefathers, that convinced them to join Columbus's expedition.[24] Among those who belonged to this seafaring community at Palos was Martin Alonso Pinzon, an experienced navigator who went on to captain one of the two caravels that accompanied Columbus's merchant vessel, the *Santa Maria*.[25] In this knowledge, it is easy to understand why the seamen of Palos should have become convinced that they had relocated Antilia on their arrival in the West Indies.

Ortega arrived at these extraordinary conclusions after consulting a considerable amount of contemporary documentation on the subject. In his opinion, "These Andalucian adventurers had already frequently set forth to seek Antilia because they knew and applied in their navigation all the science and progress of their time. It is the height of injustice to describe these men, as so many historians have done, as poor ignorant fishermen, and still more to suggest that their skill at sea was due to their pursuing the profession of pirates."[26]

SEARCH FOR THE SEVEN CITIES

In 1492, the year in which Columbus set sail for the New World, a German geographer and navigator named Martin Behaim (1459–1507) produced the first geographical globe. Yet unlike modern examples, Behaim's able attempt to draw the entire Earth lacked the presence of three major landmasses—Antarctica, Australia, and America. Instead, a huge segment, taking up around a third of the globe, was filled with an enormous ocean containing literally dozens of small islands of different sizes, shapes, and colors. More important, at a latitude just north of the equator, close to the center of the vast Atlantic Ocean, he placed the familiar, rectangular-shaped island of Antilia, which, when compared with the infinitely larger island of Cipango to its west, was small indeed. Next to Antilia on Behaim's globe is a legend that insists that in "1414 a ship from Spain got nighest it without being endangered."[27] If this was true, it perhaps bears out the claims made by the seamen of Palos who seemed convinced that their forebears had discovered Antilia many years before Columbus's own landfall in the West Indies.

There is nothing out of the ordinary about Antilia's appearance on the Behaim globe. By this time it had become standard practice to include it on navigational charts. What is significant, however, is that next to the island is an extraordinary legend that makes compelling reading: "In the year 734 of Christ, when the whole of Spain had been won by the heathen (Moors) of Africa, the above island Antilia, called Septe [sic] citade (Seven Cities), was inhabited by an archbishop from Porto in Portugal, with six other bishops, and other Christians, men and women, who had fled thither from Spain, by ship, together with their cattle, belongings and goods."[28]

What exactly were these Seven Cities that had earlier been alluded to in the Toscanelli letter of 1474, and how did they relate to the island of Antilia? It is the so-called Weimar map of 1461/9 that first shows the "septe civit" ("Seven Cities") in direct association with Antilia.[29] Yet it is Martin Behaim's globe that contains the oldest reference to the legend of the Seven Cities, which had apparently been the impetus for various Portuguese expeditions to find Antilia in the years leading up to the discovery of the New World.

A curious account of a vessel reaching the Seven Cities is given by the Portuguese historian António Galvão in his book *The Discoveries of the World*. He records that in 1447 a Portuguese ship was driven westward by storms and eventually found its way to the Island of the Seven Cities. Its inhabitants, speaking in Portuguese, asked "if the Moores did yet trouble Spaine,"[30] a reference to the conquest of Spain and Portugal by the Moors of North Africa at the time of the flight of the seven bishops. He also states, "The boateswaine of the ship brought home a little of the sand, and sold it unto a goldsmith of Lisbon, out of the which he had a good quantitie of gold."[31] Galvão's inscription concludes with the words: "There be some that thinke, that those Islands whereunto the Portugals were thus driven, were the Antiles, or Newe Spaine, alleaging good reasons for their opinion, which here I omit, because they serve not my purpose. But all their reasons seem to agree, that they should be that countrey, which is called Noua Spagna."[32]

It is clear that the English also had their sights set on the discovery of Antilia. In a letter received by the sovereigns of Castille and Aragon from the Spanish ambassador to England dated July 1498, he states that the "merchants of Bristol have for the last seven years annually sent out ships in search of the island of Brazil and the Seven Cities."[33] Where exactly these vessels might have reached is not recorded, although the crowning glory of these uncertain ventures on behalf of the English Crown was the rediscovery in 1497 of the Northwest Passage by the Venetian navigator Giovanni Caboto, better remembered under the anglicized name John Cabot. According to a document discovered in 1896, Cabot's principal sponsor was one Richard Amerycke, the high sheriff of Bristol,[34] which at the time was England's leading port.

One writer who took it upon himself to record instances of supposed attempts to find Antilia and the Island of the Seven Cities was Ferdinand Columbus, the son and biographer of Christopher Columbus. He not only included the Toscanelli letter in the introduction to the annotated diaries of his father, but he also recorded the following information in respect to the same archaic tradition:

> Pseudo-Aristotle in his book *On Marvellous Things Heard* reports a story that some Carthaginian merchants sailed over the Atlantic to a very fertile island (as I shall presently relate in more detail); this island some Portuguese showed on their charts under the name of Antillia, but in a different situation from Aristotle, though none placed it more than two hundred leagues [960 kilometers] due west of the Canaries and the Azores. And they hold it for certain that this is the Island of the Seven Cities, settled by the Portuguese at the time the Moors conquered Spain from King Rodrigo, that is, in

the year AD 714. They say that at that time seven bishops embarked from Spain and came with their ships and people to this island, where each founded a city: and in order that their people might give up all thought of returning to Spain they burned their ships, riggings, and all else needed for navigation. Some Portuguese who speculated about this island conjectured that many of their nation had gone thither but were never able to return.[35]

The Atlantic island referred to by Pseudo-Aristotle circa 300 BCE (and again by Diodorus Siculus circa 8 BCE), we will recall, is the one said to have been settled exclusively by Carthaginians. It had "wood of all kinds," "navigable rivers," "all other kinds of fruits," and an indigenous population.[36] We must presume that this same knowledge had been available also to Ferdinand's father Christopher before he embarked on his own journeys of discovery. Yet the fact that Ferdinand goes on to dismiss the theory that this island with "navigable rivers" could ever have been one of the West Indies is wholly understandable. The thought that this island group could have been discovered thousands of years beforehand by Carthaginians undermined the great achievements of his father.

It is further stated by Ferdinand, "In the time of the Infante Dom Henrique of Portugal [most probably in 1447, making this a variation of the account told by Galvão] there arrived at this island of Antillia a Portuguese ship, driven there by a storm."[37] Upon going ashore the crew joined the islanders for a church service, but being afraid that they might be detained once knowledge of their presence became more widely known, the Portuguese seamen returned to their own country. It is said that when Prince Henry the Navigator learned of this voyage to the Island of Seven Cities, he ordered the crew to embark once again for the island, at which they all promptly disappeared! Like Galvão, Columbus informs us that sand taken for use in the ship's "firebox" was found to contain a third part gold.[38]

That the island of Antilia with its Seven Cities was during the

Middle Ages believed to exist does not seem in doubt. Whether it be in legends surrounding its initial discovery by the Portuguese following the Moorish conquest of Lusitania (ancient Portugal) or in stories concerning its supposed rediscovery by Spanish and Portuguese mariners during the fifteenth century, there is enough evidence to show that it was a popular subject among cartographers, geographers, and navigators of the day.

Antilia was very much a Portuguese enigma. This can be determined if we examine the derivation of its name. In Latin *ante* means "counter," "before," or "in front of," while *illa,* or *ilha,* is Portuguese for "island." When placed together, Antilia thus implies an island located before, or in front of, something else, perhaps even a great continent. In March 1487 the Portuguese king Joao II had granted two sea captains, Fernao Dulmo and Joao Affonso, permission to seek "a great island or islands or coast of a continent which presumably is the island of the Seven Cities."[39] Since Spanish and Portuguese historians of the sixteenth century were happy to identify the islands of Antilia with the West Indies, there is no reason why we should not conclude that this "great island or islands" was believed to lie in the proximity of the then unknown American continent.

Yet was Antilia really to be found in the West Indies, or did it lie elsewhere in the Western Ocean?

SEVEN CITIES IN THE AZORES?

Some medieval cartographers and navigators unquestionably identified Antilia, and thus the Seven Cities, with the Azores. This idea was drawn from the island's positioning on certain charts and the knowledge that Antilia was said to have possessed statues of warning like the one described in connection with the island of Corvo. Furthermore, as we saw in chapter 2, a legend found on the island of São Miguel speaks of the Seven Cities as lying at the bottom of two volcanic lakes connected to each other by a small gap in a narrow causeway.[40] There are even seven villages situated near the shores of these expanses of water, known collectively as the Lake of the Seven Cities (Portuguese: *Lagoa das Sete Cidades*).[41] Yet not one of these points in favor of Antilia being found among the Azores holds any weight. We know, for instance, that the island of Antilia moved around on navigational charts, which, we must not forget, were drawn by cartographers who had little, if any, maritime experience of the outer ocean (Martin Behaim being the one notable exception).

We can also be quite sure that the association between the Azores and both the legendary statue of warning on Corvo and the supposed existence of the Seven Cities on São Miguel evolved only after the first Portuguese and Flemish settlers began colonizing the archipelago during the 1460s. We know this because when the earliest Portuguese navigators reached the Azores in 1427 the islands were found to be devoid of both fauna and human life. This is despite the fact that the archipelago appears on an old chart purchased in Venice by the Portuguese in 1428, as well as on an even earlier Genoese map from 1351.[42] It therefore seems certain that these stories sprang up only after the Portuguese began exploring the islands. The volcanic lakes mentioned in connection with the legend of the Seven Cities were probably singled out for this distinction because of the air of mystery they exude. Their waters reflect the image of the nearby rim of a volcano, and so give the impression that a hidden landscape awaits discovery within the lakes' unfathomable depths—a perfect setting for any lost city.

That the islands of Antilia were not the Azores group but representations of islands much closer to the American mainland is a conclusion that some more open-minded geographers have been willing to accept over the past century. For example, in 1954 Portugal's celebrated University of Coimbra published a scholarly work on the then newly rediscovered Venetian chart of 1424. Titled *The Nautical Chart of 1424 and the Early Discovery and Cartographical Representation of America*, it was authored by Armando Cortésao, a former counselor for the History of Science Division at UNESCO and vice president of the International

Academy for the History of Science. Accompanying the text was a foreword by Professor Maximino Correia, the university's rector.

As an expert on medieval nautical maps, Cortésao was specifically requested to make an examination of the 1424 chart, which had originally formed part of the Phillipps Collection, assembled by the Englishman Sir Thomas Phillipps (1792–1872). After a five-year study of the map Cortésao felt he was ready to announce some staggering conclusions in respect to the identification of the islands of Antilia, for as he notes in the introduction to the book, "I began my study with an entirely open mind, without any preconceived idea or prejudice; I have tried never to depart from scholarly honesty, to be guided only by scrupulous scientific method, and to base my reasoning on facts whenever possible. I have come to the conclusion that Antilia and the other westernmost isles figured on the 1424 Chart are intended to represent the easternmost part of the American hemisphere, but I fear that general agreement will never be reached on this controversial question; I know it only too well, alas."[43]

In the book's summary, Cortésao adds that in his opinion, "There are many and good reasons for concluding that the Antilia group of four islands shown for the first time in the 1424 Chart should be regarded as the earliest cartographical representation of any American lands."[44] I am sure that Armando Cortésao expected his remarkable discoveries to shock the academic world. Unfortunately, it was simply not ready for such announcements, and neither is it today.

ISLAND IN THE SEA

Finding the true geographical location of Antilia, and thus the Island of the Seven Cities, was also the challenge taken up by American geographer William H. Babcock, the author of *Legendary Islands of the Atlantic: A Study in Medieval Geography,* first published in 1922. To this end, he concentrated on the Battista Beccario map of 1435, which clearly defines the four islands of Antilia. These Babcock identified finally as Jamaica, the Florida peninsula, the Bahamian islands, and, in the case of Antilia, Cuba.[45] So having dismissed Hispaniola and Puerto Rico as possible candidates for Antilia, Babcock chose instead Cuba, the largest of the three main islands of the Greater Antilles. L. Sprague de Camp, in his critical work *Lost Continents: The Atlantis Theme in History, Science, and Literature,* acknowledged Babcock's assertions in respect to Antilia, saying that the legendary island "corresponded so closely in size, shape, and direction with the real Cuba that when the latter and its neighbors were finally found they were promptly named the Antilles. . . . Babcock the geographer thought that the pre-Columbian Antilia was evidence of a pre-Columbian voyage that actually touched Cuba—not, perhaps, entirely impossible."[46]

Further support for Babcock's theory comes from the famous Piri Reis map of 1513, produced in Turkey some twenty-one years after Christopher Columbus first reached the West Indies. Here Cuba appears as a rectangular-shaped island that is strikingly similar to how Antilia is shown on navigational charts of the fifteenth century (see fig. 13.1). A number of coastal and inland features on the Piri Reis map match exactly the known topography of Cuba, yet other quite obvious

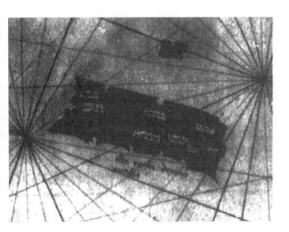

Figure 13.1. The island of Antilia from the Venetian chart of 1424 alongside the truncated form of Cuba as found on the Piri Reis map of 1513. Do the pre-Columbian and post-Columbian maps both show the same island?

features of the island are clearly missing. Professor Charles Hapgood of Keene State College, New Hampshire, realized that the Piri Reis map showed only the eastern part of Cuba; the western half simply did not appear at all. This fact led him to conclude that the mapmaker in question must have been working from an ancient source map that showed only half of the island.[47] Believing perhaps that this alone was the complete representation of its coastline, the Turkish cartographer had gone ahead and drawn a truncated form of Cuba in its approximate geographical position.

For Hapgood this was a very exciting discovery. He knew full well that by the date attributed to the Piri Reis map (i.e., 1513), nearly all nautical charts showed the entire Cuban coastline based on early maps made by the first scholars and navigators to visit the West Indies. None of these charts displayed any kind of major fault in their detail of Cuba. Since the Piri Reis mapmaker had quite obviously been unaware of the very latest cartographic knowledge reaching the Mediterranean world, it suggested that his sources were pre-Columbian in origin. As a consequence, Hapgood concluded that Cuba must have been "well known in Europe before the first voyage of Columbus."[48]

Does the island of Antilia's distinctive rectangular shape denote that it, too, represents a truncated form of Cuba, perhaps derived originally from the same age-old source maps? More important, if Cuba really was the role model for Antilia, how did it relate to the legends surrounding the Island of the Seven Cities?

THE LUST FOR GOLD

After exploring several small Bahamian islands during his initial voyage to the New World in October 1492, Christopher Columbus was directed by the local Lucayan American Indians to search for a much larger island known as Colba, or Cuba.[49] This, he concluded, must be Cipango (that is, Japan), where he would find the "city of gold" belonging to the great khan.[50]

It was on Sunday, October 28, that his vessel came within sight of Cuba for the first time. After surveying one of its navigable rivers, Columbus sent a party of envoys into the island's interior with a letter of introduction from the Spanish sovereigns. Yet when the search party returned several days later it reported that neither the great khan nor the "city of gold" could be found. Instead, American Indians directed his envoys to a local cacique, or tribal chief, to whom samples of cinnamon, pepper, and other spices were shown in the hope that they could be brought to them in abundance. In response, the cacique explained that none of these commodities were to be found there. He suggested that they search farther south, perhaps even on another island altogether.[51]

Having failed to find gold in the quantities desired, Columbus lost interest in Cuba. Instead, he set his sights on another large island that the indigenous peoples knew as Bohio. It turned out to be Hispaniola, or La Espanola as Columbus christened it.[52] It was here that he would later found La Navidad, the first city of the New World.

Columbus returned to Spain and basked in the glory he felt he justly deserved before setting sail again for the West Indies, this time with mass colonization in mind. In total he made four voyages to the New World, in 1492, 1493, 1498, and 1502. His brother Diego was eventually made governor of La Espanola, while Cuba, which was christened Juana, after a Spanish prince of this name, was at first left relatively untouched.

Yet in 1511 Cuba's peace was shattered forever as the conquest of paradise began in earnest. For it was in this year that Diego Columbus appointed as its first governor a maniacal Spaniard named Diego Velasquez, who had sailed with Columbus on his second voyage to the West Indies in 1493. His task was to initiate colonization at any cost,[53] and it was a challenge he took up with an unimaginable zeal.

With a contingent of three hundred fully armed conquistadors, Velasquez departed La Navidad with four caravels in November 1511. As the Spaniards pushed farther and farther into Cuba's mountainous interior they were surprised to encounter fierce resistance from the indigenous peoples. Led by a cacique named Hatuey, the native peoples managed to hamper Velasquez's progress for many months. Yet despite their fighting spirit, the American Indian warriors, with their wooden spears and near-naked bodies, were simply no match against the armor, halberds, muskets, and swords of the conquistadors, and amid some of the most gruesome barbarity ever inflicted on humankind one by one the tribal provinces fell. Hatuey was caught and burned alive. Before his death, a Catholic friar who accompanied the expedition offered to redeem Hatuey's soul by allowing him to renounce his faith and convert to the Church of Rome. In response to this bizarre request, Hatuey purportedly called out that he would rather go to hell than "to a place where he would ever meet again such cruel and wicked people as Christians."[54]

Blood-soaked and unrepentant, Velasquez marched on, ever pursuing his lust for gold. He, too, never quite found what he was looking for, yet the genocide he initiated resulted, within a matter of ten short years, in the annihilation of almost the entire native population of Cuba. Many who did not submit to the saber blade, musket, or cannonball committed suicide.[55] It is estimated that around two hundred thousand individuals were either put to death or died through malnutrition, exhaustion, hunger, suicide, and European diseases, or through standing in rivers up to twelve hours a day, panning the sand for gold.[56] By 1521 there were so few inhabitants left on Cuba that it was necessary to import thousands of black African slaves, who upon their arrival were dispatched to work either on the sugar plantations or in the gold mines opened by the Spaniards.[57]

Leaving aside the hideous crimes against humanity he was unquestionably responsible for in the name of colonization, it is quite clear that Velasquez believed he would encounter far more than fierce opposition from the indigenous population in the heart of Cuba. Everything suggests that he was searching for the Seven Cities and their gold-bearing sand. There is no proof of this supposition. However, during the thirteen years that he spent as governor of Cuba prior to his death in 1521, Velasquez laid the foundations of exactly "seven cities,"[58] each with its own province, which still exist today. This alone makes it clear that he considered Cuba to be the original Island of the Seven Cities, recalled so vividly in the legend of the seven bishops who managed to escape the persecution of the invading Moors some eight hundred years beforehand.

EL DORADO—LAND OF THE GOLDEN MAN

Inevitably there were those who could not come to terms with the fact that the West Indies, as the islands of Antilia, had produced no evidence whatsoever for the existence of the gold-bearing Seven Cities. As a consequence, navigational charts of the sixteenth century began placing them in new locations. The Seven Cities were shown, for instance, in the heart of Brazil, which was by then in the hands of the Portuguese. Other maps placed them farther west, in Colombia, Peru, and even in Ecuador.[59] Still others located them in North America, generally in the region of either Florida or California.[60] Between 1538 and 1542 various Spanish expeditions departed Mexico in search of the legendary "Seven Cities of Cibola," which were thought to be located somewhere in the vicinity of the Colorado River. None of them succeeded in achieving anything other than bloodshed and misery.

The Seven Cities were never found, yet the mystery surrounding their whereabouts not only lingered but also transformed into a quite different quest altogether. For it is fair to say that during the 1530s the search for the Seven Cities, or the "golden cities" as they had become known by this time, was responsible for the rapid emergence of rumors regarding the existence of a fabled empire of immense wealth attached to the legend of El Dorado, "the Golden Man."[61]

In the wake of the discovery in 1519 of the Aztec Empire by Hernando Cortés (1485–1547/54) and the conquest in 1532 of the Inca Empire by Francisco Pizarro (1475–1548), it was believed that an even greater empire awaited discovery somewhere in the heart of South America. Legends spoke of a revered lagoon on which great heaps of gold and emeralds were offered to the water's presiding deity. Apparently, during the inauguration of a *zipa,* or supreme monarch, the chosen heir would be escorted to this sacred lake and there his garments would be removed. His body would be coated with a gluey earth, following which a pipe would be used to blow gold onto his skin, giving him the appearance of a sun-god. Remaining perfectly still, the heir would then be floated out onto the lagoon on a raft of rushes. With him would go a company of four subject chiefs wearing gold finery. When the raft finally reached the center of the lagoon, the priests would make offerings of gold to the water deity, throwing out each item in turn until the raft was empty.[62]

In one version of the story the Golden Man would dive into the water, allowing the gold dust to fall from his body until he was totally cleansed. The zipa's return to the surface marked his transition from chosen heir to supreme monarch, the point at which large quantities of gold would be cast into the water.[63] Quite obviously, the sediment at the bottom of the lagoon was considered to contain a thick layer of gold, as well as unimaginable treasures made as offerings to the god of the lake over hundreds, if not thousands, of years.

Among those who searched in vain for the golden city was the Elizabethan navigator Sir Walter Raleigh. Having become convinced that it awaited discovery deep within the interior of Guiana following the capture of certain Spanish reports that spoke of "Nuevo Dorado" and the lost kingdom of "Manoa," he set out in search of El Dorado in 1595.[64] After journeying up the Orinoco River for a distance of around four hundred kilometers and finding nothing, he turned back content that he had accumulated enough evidence to convince the English sovereign, Elizabeth I, to give her blessing to a more substantial expedition. Yet the queen was not amused when he arrived back in England empty-handed, forcing him to abandon any plans he might have had of returning to Guiana. Instead, he spent his time writing a book based on his adventures, which was published in 1596 under the title *The Discoverie of Guiana.* It became an instant bestseller, with three impressions in the first year alone and immediate translations into German, Latin, and Dutch.

Seven years later Raleigh was accused of taking part in a plot to overthrow the new monarch, James I. As a result he was promptly made a prisoner in the Tower of London and sentenced to death. Yet he ever dreamed of making a fresh attempt to find the lost empire of Manoa, and in 1617 he was finally able to convince the king to allow him to mount a second expedition. Once again he failed to find El Dorado, and this time all that awaited Sir Walter on his return to London was the chopping block!

In the meantime, Spain claimed sovereignty of the as yet undiscovered "province of El Dorado," while the search for the lagoon began to focus on a lake high up in the Colombian Andes, not far from Bogota. Known as Guatavita, it was thought to match the description of the lagoon into which the Golden Man had offered the gold to the presiding deity. Moreover, local tradition asserted that the lake contained the wealth of a powerful kingdom ruled by a people known as the Chibcha.[65] Yet despite high expectations, all attempts to retrieve the supposed gold that lay at the bottom of the lake failed.

The whereabouts of El Dorado still eludes the world. Yet what seems certain is that the search to discover this unknown empire was originally inspired by much earlier traditions surrounding the legendary Seven Cities. For instance, an Italian world chart of 1510 actually shows "Antiglia," undoubtedly an allusion to Antilia and the Seven Cities, in northwest Venezuela, close to the location of the Guatavita lake.[66] Moreover, Antilia's gold-bearing sand might easily be compared with the gold dust that was said to have been scooped up from the ground and used to cover the body of the Golden Man as part of his inauguration ceremony.

In conclusion, it would seem that the transference of the Seven Cities out of the ocean and onto the mainland became the impetus for the creation of fresh legends concerning the existence of mysterious golden cities deep in the interior of the American continent. Rumors and stories told by coastal American Indian tribes of sacred and forbidden ruins must have spurred on European explorers to mount fresh expeditions of discovery, yet all the time in vain. Their vision of finding a lost city of gold was fictitious, a creation of their own sense of adventure. Yet whether the object of their quest was Antilia, El Dorado, Cibola, or Manoa, there must have been a common thread to these stories that obviously convinced them of the existence of this lost golden empire. Perhaps the indigenous peoples of these regions preserved the memory of a former high culture that saw the number 7 as playing a significant role in their society, perhaps through its importance in local creation myths. Yet every time this sacred number cropped up in the tales and stories told by native people to Europeans, it was eagerly seized on as evidence that the American Indians had some knowledge of the whereabouts of the Seven Cities. If this is correct, it might well explain why their location moved around so frequently on nautical charts of the Middle Ages.

ENCIRCLED ISLANDS

So if the Seven Cities have never been found, are we to assume that they never existed in the first place? Was their existence merely the product of medieval fantasies born out of the naiveté of the earliest European cartographers and explorers in respect to what lay on the other side of the Western Ocean?

It is a fact that some medieval world charts would occasionally show, far out in the Western Ocean, a ring of land surrounding a body of water. Inside it would appear a collection of tiny islets, like boats enclosed within a circular dock. On a Catalan map of 1375, nine are shown, while on other variations of the same basic map, seven can be counted.[67] On this subject, Babcock commented, "These miniature islands have sometimes been thought to represent the seven cities of the old legend; but islets are not cities, and there seems no reason why each city should require an islet. However, the coincidence of number, exact or approximate, is suggestive."[68] Islands, or islets, are certainly not cities, although the link is a real one, with the clear connection being the number 7. Remember, too, that Antilia is quite separately shown with seven lobed bays along its elongated eastern and western coastlines, and seven place names positioned on the island itself, facts that cartographical scholar Armando Cortésao believed were linked to the tradition of the Seven Cities.[69]

If Babcock's observations were accurate, this suggests that knowledge of Antilia and the legendary Seven Cities might originally have been detached from the story of the seven Portuguese bishops fleeing the Moors in the eighth century CE. Then toward the end of the fourteenth century these separate traditions, which probably derived from the same root source, were combined to become one single island with a preponderance of the number 7.

All the evidence points toward the fact that the legends surrounding Antilia and the Seven Cities predate the exploration of the Western Ocean during the age of discovery by many hundreds, if not thousands, of years. Where exactly the earliest European cartographers and explorers might have obtained this valuable information of unknown Atlantic islands is more difficult to ascertain. It is, however, a subject that we must now address in our attempt to find the true origins behind the story of Antilia and its legendary Seven Cities. Only by doing this can we go on to comprehend the island's relationship to Plato's Atlantis.

14

THE EXALTED ONE

The date is January 2, 1492. The scene is the famous Alhambra Palace, built chiefly in the fourteenth and fifteenth centuries and unquestionably the finest remaining example of Arab architecture in the whole of Spain. Blood-soaked bodies litter the ground, most of them Moorish soldiers and civilians, some Christian Crusaders. This ancient citadel, the last stronghold of Islamic occupation, has fallen.

Crowds begin to gather. A group of Christians climb the roof and tears down the building's crescent-tipped pinnacle, which shimmers in the sunlight above the gilded dome. It is wrenched out of its socket and crashes to the ground, the faith of the infidels banished from Spanish soil, forever.

It is an imagined scenario based on very real events. Yet somehow there is a strange irony in the fact that the fall of Granada took place the same year as the discovery of the New World. For it now seems certain that without the great wisdom and enlightenment of the Moors there is every likelihood that the Americas might have lain undisturbed for many years to come. The departure of the Moors from Western European soil was indeed a tragic affair. Not only did they help initiate the age of discovery, and thus catalyze the Renaissance, but their presence in Spain and Lusitania, the ancient name for Portugal, would also appear to have been instrumental in the emergence of legends surrounding Antilia and the Island of the Seven Cities.

THE END OF ANDALUCIA

The Moorish occupation of al-Andalus (Andalucia), the name they gave to Spain, had begun almost eight hundred years earlier. In the seventh and eighth centuries the Arab armies pushed forward from Persia across to the Atlantic coast of Africa, and with them had come new ideas in culture and religion. Among the races that embraced the ways of Islam was the Lixitae, from the Berber tribes of Mauritania.

Known to Europeans as the Moors, this Afro-Arabian culture advanced across the Strait of Gibraltar in 711 CE and began the conquest of Spain, which at the time was ruled by a Germanic tribe known as the Visigoths. They had seized control of the country following the collapse of the Roman Empire. The Moors pushed forward as far as France, but in 732 were forced to withdraw to Spain following a decisive defeat against an army led by France's great cultural hero, Charles Martel. Four years later, in 736, they established the Umayyad emirate (later a caliphate), which took as its capital the ancient city of Córdoba. Other great Arab centers included Toledo, Seville, Merida, and, of course, Granada.

For four whole centuries the Moors ruled supreme in Andalucia. Yet power struggles among the contenders for the caliphate weakened their grip on the country. Steadily the Christian armies began to take back Spain. First they gained control of its northern territories, and by the summer of 1139 they held Lusitania, a decisive victory that led to the inauguration of Alfonso I (1096–1185) as the first king of Portugal. Then in 1236 the Crusaders took Córdoba, the Moorish capital. Some thirteen years later the Christians regained the Algarve with the assistance of the military fighting machine known as the Knights Templar. For another 243 years the Crusade continued until one day in 1492 the Moors lost Granada, their final stronghold.

PORTUGAL'S GOLDEN AGE

As an independent kingdom Portugal thrived. In the reign of King Joao I (1385–1433), it began to expand its influence overseas, following an extensive series of maritime expeditions under the charge of an enlightened figure named Prince Henry the Navigator (1394–1460). In 1418 and 1420 Portuguese navigators Joao Goncalves Zarco and Tristao Vaz Teixeira rediscovered the islands of Porto Santo and Madeira. In 1427 Diogo de Silves, the pilot of the Portuguese king, reached the Azores, although it would be another four years before the Portuguese explorer Goncalves Velho Cabral would make landfall on the islands.

In Africa, the Portuguese journeyed along its western coast until they reached the Gulf of Guinea, where they established innumerable settlements. From here they advanced westward, and in 1460 the Venetian navigator Alvise Cadamosto, sailing on behalf of Prince Henry, discovered the Cape Verde Islands, some 640 kilometers out from Cape Verde in Senegal. Furthermore, in 1488 navigator Bartolomeu Diaz succeeded in rounding the Cape of Good Hope, while exactly ten years later another Portuguese vessel under the command of Vasco da Gama (1450–1524) not only circumnavigated Africa but also climbed the east coast and established a passage to India. Curiously enough, it is a fact that in 1420 an Indian junk had been successful in crossing the Indian Ocean and then rounding the Cape of Good Hope in search of islands that legends said were inhabited separately by men and women. These facts are inscribed on a map produced between 1457 and 1459 by a Venetian priest named Fray Mauro at the request of Portuguese king Alfonso V.[1]

It is clear that long before Columbus's monumental journey to the New World, expeditions commissioned by Prince Henry the Navigator regularly explored the Western Ocean beyond the Azores. Here they encountered, like every vessel before them, the "Mar de Baga" (the Berry Sea), the name the Portuguese gave to the Sargasso Sea.[2]

It even seems possible that Diogo de Teive, one of Prince Henry's most able sea captains, very nearly discovered the island of Newfoundland in 1452, fifty-five years before it was claimed in the name of the English sovereign Henry VII by John Cabot. Having set out on a northwesterly course from the Azores, de Teive managed to sail across the Gulf Stream before entering a region where harsh, cold winds blew in from the north. Realizing that the vessel was heading into dangerous waters, he set a southeasterly course back to the Azores. It was only afterward that geographers realized that, against all odds, he had reached a latitude of 50° and had therefore come within just a few hundred kilometers of the east coast of Newfoundland.[3] This account, given by de Teive himself, is in stark contrast to the alternative version of what is presumably the same journey recounted by Ferdinand Columbus. He records that the main objective of de Teive's expedition was to discover the Island of the Seven Cities.[4]

Prince Henry had every reason to commission expeditions to relocate the lost Seven Cities. Their discovery would have enabled Portugal to claim sovereignty over the island, not only through conquest, but also through the right of inheritance. This would have been of paramount importance when it came to convincing other countries, such as Spain and England, that Portugal could rightfully lay claim to such territories. For example, the Spanish chronicler Gonzalo Fernándaz de Oviedo y Valdez claimed that if the West Indies really were the Hesperides, they rightly belonged to the Spanish sovereign. This was because the Roman writer Statius Sebosus had said that the Hesperides were the daughters of Hesperus, a legendary "Spanish" king, whom Oviedo saw as a distant ancestor of the Spanish monarch.[5]

Britain, on the other hand, attempted to lay claim to the Americas by asserting that they had been discovered by Madoc, the seafaring son of a Welsh king named Owen Gwynedd, in the year 1170. John Dee, the mathematician, mapmaker, and court astrologer to Queen Elizabeth, promoted this idea during the 1570s in an attempt to establish a firm foundation for what he termed the "Brytish Empire." In summary, he believed that Madoc's journey enabled the British to lay claim to "all the

Coasts and Islands beginning at or abowt Terra Florida . . . unto Atlantis going Northerly," and beyond that to all the islands as far as Russia.[6] The mention of the all-important *A* word is not without significance, for Dee became convinced that North America was Atlantis, and even marked it thus on navigational charts he produced during this period.

PRINCE HENRY THE NAVIGATOR

There is no doubt that by the end of the fifteenth century Portuguese navigators were among the most capable in Europe. Yet so many of their naval achievements can be accredited to the extraordinary leadership and foresight of Prince Henry the Navigator. In 1419 he had founded an academy, or school, of navigation within the confines of his polygonal stone fortress at Sagres in the Algarve. Located on a desolate promontory overlooking the Atlantic, it stood on the very edge of the known world. Here Prince Henry advocated an education in cartography, geography, and physics, and set up as the school's first director a Majorcan named "Master Jacob."[7] Under the influence of the Catalans, Majorca had thrived during the thirteenth and fourteenth centuries as a maritime center with an extensive trading network. Prince Henry had therefore wanted to capitalize on its ancient traditions, which included the production of high-quality nautical charts and instruments.[8]

In an attempt to create the greatest, and most cosmopolitan, seagoing nation of all time, Prince Henry invited to Portugal expert sailors, cartographers, cosmographers, navigators, and astronomers from all over the Mediterranean world. He can be said to have succeeded in this aim, for there is little doubt that his efforts paved the way for the greatest discovery of all—the relocation of the New World. According to tradition, Vasco da Gama, Ferdinand Magellan, Bartolomeu Diaz, Pedro Alvares Cabral, and even Christopher Columbus all passed through Sagres's school of navigation.

Prince Henry was not afraid to push new boundaries when it came to oceanic exploration. He unquestionably knew about the undiscovered southern continent spoken of by Moorish pirates and black African seafarers. He would have known, too, that Antilia and the Island of the Seven Cities lay beyond the Mar de Baga. He must also have been aware that a nautical chart produced in 1448 by Andrea Bianco, who had spent time in Portugal, showed southwest of Cape Verde a mysterious land next to which was a curious inscription that read "authentic island [that] is distant, 1500 miles [2,400 kilometers] to the west."[9]

According to the chronicle of Diogo Gomes, one of Prince Henry's captains and close associates, "The Prince wishing to know about the far away regions of the western ocean, whether there were any islands or continent (*terra firme*) besides those described by Ptolemy [a well-known Alexandrian astronomer and mathematician of the second century CE], sent caravels to discover."[10] It is even clear from a letter dated July 14, 1493, to King Joao II of Portugal from a doctor in Nuremberg named Hieronymus Monetarius that Prince Henry had attempted during his lifetime "to demonstrate the sphericity of the earth."[11]

What motivated Portugal's wish to explore the outer limits of the ocean during the fifteenth century? Was it simply to expand their trading network and sovereignty, or could Prince Henry have been privy to knowledge unavailable to the rest of the maritime world? If so, did it concern the whereabouts of Antilia and the Island of the Seven Cities?

EMERGENCE OF A LEGEND

According to the tradition surrounding the foundation of the Seven Cities, it was in 714 CE that the advancing Moorish army laid siege to the city of Merida, the old capital of the Roman province of Lusitania (which is today a town over the Portuguese border in Spain). As a result, seven bishops and their flocks decided to escape persecution by securing a fleet of ships and setting sail into the unknown. They traversed the Western Ocean until one day the fleet came on an island known as Antilia, where they established Sete Cidades, the Seven Cities.

This is the basic story as told by cartographers, historians, and navigators of various nationalities during the late fifteenth and early sixteenth centuries. Yet as we have seen, there are basic problems in accepting these accounts as straightforward historical fact. No evidence of a pre-Conquest Portuguese colony has ever come to light on any Atlantic island. There is not one scrap of evidence to suggest the former existence of the Seven Cities, either in the West Indies or anywhere else for that matter. So why were the Portuguese so eager to mount long-distance maritime voyages in an effort to find them?

The only answer is that they considered these stories to be actual history. Yet if this was so, why exactly did they believe in them so fervently? Were they transmitted to the Portuguese by those who could rightly claim that their most distant ancestors had some knowledge of these events that had supposedly taken place in their country several hundred years beforehand? If so, who might this have been? Since the kingdom of Portugal did not exist in the eighth century and the Visigoths who occupied these territories at the time of conquest had long since been vanquished, the only people in a position to have recounted these legends were the Moors.

Such a solution might seem at first like an odd one, especially as the Moors were quite obviously being evicted from a land they felt could very easily be called their own. However, it is a fact that throughout the Moorish occupation of Spain and Lusitania a considerable amount of contact existed between Arabs and Christians. Many Europeans clearly recognized the wisdom to be gained from the secret teachings of Islamic mysticism and philosophy that thrived in the Moorish centers of learning, such as Córdoba and Toledo. New knowledge that included algebra, astronomy, cartography, geography, geometry, mathematics, navigation, and classical philosophy was accessible to those willing to put aside racial and religious intolerance. There is no question that the Moors introduced many of these key sciences to the medieval world.

Islamic cities also became the focus of alchemists, occultists, mystics, and freethinkers who descended on Spain in the hope of gaining ultimate enlightenment, not only from the established schools of learning but also from back-street opportunists who at the right price would reveal their own brand of the forbidden sciences.

THE KNIGHTS TEMPLAR

Among those who recognized the importance of the Moorish centers of learning were members of clandestine military orders such as the Knights Templar. According to the stories, they had frequently trafficked with the Saracens during the Crusades in the Holy Land. The Order of the Knights of Christ and the Temple of Solomon, as they were more correctly titled, was founded in 1128 to protect pilgrim routes in and out of the Holy Land. Yet in a matter of a few short years they grew to become the most powerful fighting force in the whole of Christendom. With preceptories, tithes, and estates in virtually every country of Europe, they gained the favor of kings, protecting their wealth and instituting the first international banking system. Yet they also became a law unto themselves, owing allegiance to no one but the pope, and worse still they dabbled in forms of Christian mysticism that turned out to be their undoing.

By the beginning of the fourteenth century, the French King Philip the Fair owed them vast sums of money. So with the aid of the pope, Clement V, he had every Templar in France arrested at dawn on Friday, October 13, 1307. At the same time other monarchs were ordered to arrest their Templars and bring them to justice. The Templars were accused of blasphemy, heresy, and denying the divinity of Christ. Many were tortured into giving false confessions, and when the knights were finally brought to trial in France they were found guilty of the charges made against them. Many were put to death, including the grand master, Jacques de Molay, who was burned at the stake in March 1314.

The pope officially dissolved the Order in 1312, and all Templar lands reverted to the sovereign of the countries in question. Yet the results of the trials outside France varied considerably. In Scotland, for instance, the evidence against the Templars was deemed inconclusive, so the case against them was dropped, while in Spain, Portugal, Germany, and Switzerland they were fully acquitted of all charges.

The trials themselves lasted for several years and produced literally thousands of official documents that contain some fascinating insights into the apparent relationship that existed between the Templars and their Arab adversaries. One account speaks of the "Master of The Temple and the other chiefs of the Order" paying homage to Saladin (1137–1193), the sultan of Egypt and Syria when Jerusalem fell to the Saracens in 1187.[12] Another witness's testimony states that at times of truce, when no battles were being fought, Templars paid serviture to the "Soldan," that is, the sultan, and also "kept them friendly."[13] In another case a witness confessed that "he had heard that the Christians had suffered much from the great familiarity that existed between Bello Joco, then Master of the Order and the Soldan and Saracens, but he believed the contrary."[14] Last, it came to light during the trials that item no. 119 of the order's regulations prescribed that the master of the Order should take a "Saracen scribe" as an interpreter.[15]

Although much of what the Templars were accused can be dismissed as fabricated charges, the trial documents show how strong the rumors were regarding the Order's connection with the Arab world. There seems little question that this relationship extended to the Moors, particularly at their great centers of learning in Spain and Portugal. So what did the Templars learn from the Moors, and how much of this knowledge might have passed into the hands of the military orders that succeeded them?

KNIGHTS OF CHRIST

The Knights Templar led the crusading armies to victory in the Portuguese Algarve and were rewarded in this respect by being given estates and tithes right across the country. After the departure of the Moors, it is likely that the Templars became the custodians of at least some of the libraries that existed in the Arab centers of learning. Exactly how this curious relationship might have influenced their development or interests remains uncertain, although it is what happened to the Templars of Spain and Portugal after the dissolution of the Order that is of key importance here.

As previously stated, the ruling councils in both countries acquitted the Templars of all charges. Despite this, the Order was disbanded, so, to fill the gap, new organizations were established to take its place. The Spanish sovereign created the Knights of Santiago, a key chivalric order greatly influenced by Templar tradition. In Portugal, King Dionysius I announced the creation in 1317 of an order to be called the Christi Militia, or the Knights of Christ, which was given a bull of approbation by Pope John XXII in 1319. Curiously enough, it was also in 1317 that the Portuguese king appointed the Genoese navigator Emmanuel Pezagno as hereditary admiral of the country's fleet, an act that marked the commencement of a new era in Portuguese naval power. All former estates, tithes, and properties belonging to the Order of the Temple were henceforth handed over to the Knights of Christ, and quite naturally the Portuguese Templars flocked to join its ranks. It is said that only a candidate with four generations of hereditary nobility was eligible for investiture, ensuring that the Order consisted only of handpicked brethren who could be trusted implicitly by the aristocracy.[16]

Like the Templars before them, the Knights of Christ outwardly opposed the Moors. Having decided that the Order would take to the high seas they launched, under the command of Prince Henry, a series of naval expeditions against Moorish pirates. The Order's decisive victory at the battle of Ceuta on Africa's Mediterranean coast in 1415 signaled the beginning of Portugal's overseas exploration. Two years later, Prince Henry was appointed grand master of the Order, a post he was to hold until his death in 1460. Chivalric rites of initiation and enlightenment unquestionably took place in his remote castle fortress at Sagres. We can only guess at the relationship there might have been between investiture into the different grades of the Order and the advancement of maritime scholarship.

Under Prince Henry's influence, Pope Leo X granted the Knights of Christ the right of presentation to all bishoprics overseas, meaning that the Order was to be given full status in whatever country its cavaliers might enter. Can we see in this right Prince Henry's desire to present his Order to the seven bishoprics that were assumed to exist on the Island of the Seven Cities?

There seems little doubt that by the middle of the fifteenth century the Knights of Christ, under the patronage of Prince Henry, had grown to become one of the most powerful military organizations in Europe. Yet in many ways the Order was merely a reconstituted form of the Knights Templar, with its center now in Portugal instead of France. The familiar red cross ensign of the Templars was borne on the sails and flags of the Order's hundreds of vessels, while everywhere they went the Knights of Christ established military commanderies—454 in all, with thirty-seven in Africa alone.[17]

Some of the most famous Portuguese navigators were members of the Knights of Christ. Even Christopher Columbus's name has been linked to the Order. His vessel the *Santa Maria* is said to have sailed under the Order's red cross ensign, an enigma that has perplexed historians to this day. It has even been suggested, without any kind of substantiation, that Columbus was himself a member of the Knights of Christ and that the Order supplied him with navigational charts and maps on Atlantic trade routes.[18] There are no official records to this effect, even though it is a fact that following the death of his Portuguese father-in-law, Bartolomeu Perestrello, the first governor of Madeira and a knight of the realm, Columbus received as part of his inheritance "writings and sea charts." These told of the different voyages of discovery in which Portugal was currently engaged.[19] Indeed, it is quite clear that Columbus's frequent journeys to Portuguese settlements on the Guinea coast helped him to become a proficient navigator in his own right.

BEHAIM'S INVESTITURE

There seems to be an integral relationship between the Knights of Christ and Portugal's interest in the rediscovery of the Island of the Seven Cities. This can be determined if we examine the life of Martin Behaim, the German navigator and merchant who in 1492 produced the world's first globe. His expertise as a scientist and navigator brought him to Lisbon in 1484, where he continued to live periodically until his death in 1507. Almost immediately after his arrival in Lisbon Behaim joined two separate maritime expeditions to West Africa. The Behaim family archives state that in between these long voyages he was invested as a knight of the realm on February 18, 1485, by King Joao II.[20] This important ceremony, which took place in the Church of St. Saviour in the town of Alcacovas, was sponsored not only by the king but also by three key members of the aristocracy. Moreover, the event was said to have been conducted "in the presence of all the Princes and Knights [of the Order], and of the Queen."[21]

It is not specified which military order Behaim embraced as a cavalier, although the fact that so many knights, dignitaries, and members of the royal family attended the ceremony strongly suggests that it was the Knights of Christ. This same conclusion has been drawn by various historians, although it has, however, been questioned by Behaim's biographer, E. G. Ravenstein, in his book *Martin Behaim: His Life and His Globe,* published in 1908.[22]* Despite such shortcomings, what we do know is that just a few months after the date given for his investiture, Behaim would appear to have been asked to join an expedition to go in search of the Island of the Seven Cities. Under the joint command of two Portuguese sea captains named Fernao Dulmo and Joao

---

*Ravenstein points out that Behaim could not have belonged to the Order since he is never shown in portraits bearing its red-cross insignia. He further asserts that shortly after Behaim's supposed investiture, he married his second wife. Since knights were only permitted to marry after a constitution was passed to this effect in 1495, it proves that Behaim could not have been a member at that time.

Affonso, the expedition was scheduled to depart Terceira in the Azores during March 1487. Moreover, a deed of partnership, sanctioned by the king and dated July 12, 1486, states that the two sea captains were to be joined by a "*cavalleiro alemao*" (German knight).[23] Since the only German knight to whom this description could at the time have applied was Martin Behaim, it was almost certainly he who was being considered for this prestigious role on behalf of the Portuguese crown.[24]

The eventual fate of this bold venture is not recorded, and Behaim's role in the expedition remains unclear. All we can say is that just five years later his famous globe bore an inscription that outlined for the very first time the story behind the foundation of the legendary Seven Cities on the island of Antilia.

This catalog of events is strangely suggestive of some kind of connection between Behaim's investiture as a Portuguese knight of the realm, his apparent invitation to join a vessel bound for Antilia, and his subsequent knowledge of the legend surrounding the Island of the Seven Cities. Might it have formed part of some kind of secret discourse to which a cavalier in, say, the Knights of Christ became privy on his investiture? Once again, there is no proof of this supposition, although the tantalizing evidence surrounding the apparent relationship between the Knights Templar and the Arab world makes this possibility extremely attractive indeed. Yet if this was the case, where might the Moors have obtained knowledge of this island in the west?

THE LISBON WANDERERS

Shortly after their conquest of Spain and Lusitania, the Moors began their own exploration of the Western Ocean, the fruits of which were recorded by an Arab geographer, Muhammad al-Idrisi (ca. 1099–1164). In his celebrated work titled *Geography,* circa 1154, he detailed the discovery of several Atlantic islands.[25] In fact al-Idrisi believed there to be an incredible twenty-seven thousand islands located in the Western Ocean, some of which he attempted to highlight on a world map, wrought in silver and made for Robert, the king of Sicily. Sadly, this extraordinary item has not survived.

Al-Idrisi also spoke of the Al-Khalidat, or the Fortunate Isles, on which he said were bronze statues on tall columnar pedestals that faced out toward the west. Curiously enough, al-Idrisi spoke of there being six of these statues, with one of them being located at Cadiz, ancient Gades.[26]

This information alone confirms the role that the Moors must have played in introducing a knowledge of Atlantic islands to the medieval world, for it is not until some two hundred years later that any reference to these alleged statues of warning reappears. As we have seen in chapter 13, similar statues are mentioned in the legend on the Pizzigani map of 1367 in connection with an Atlantic location named as "Atulliae," very probably an early form of Antilia. Since this is also the oldest known reference to the island's existence, might it be seen as further evidence that the Moors were instrumental in bringing Antilia to the attention of the medieval world?

Al-Idrisi also tells us of the amazing exploits of the eight Maghrurins ("deceived men"), also known as the "Lisbon Wanderers," who undertook a maritime journey of discovery to find out "what is it that encloses the Ocean, and what its limits are."[27] They are said to have departed from the port of Lisbon, then obviously under Moorish rule. After a number of days' sail, the ship is said to have entered the "Sea of Darkness and Mystery," almost certainly the Sargasso Sea.[28] Afterward, the expedition discovered various Atlantic islands, including one known as Al-Ghanam, the "Isle of Sheep," which, rightly or wrongly, has been identified as Madeira.[29] Later, the Moorish vessel is said to have changed its course and come across another island group, very possibly the Canaries. Having disembarked on one of its islands, the Moorish sailors were imprisoned by the local inhabitants, arguably the Guanches, the indigenous population of the Canary Isles. Yet after securing their release, the Maghrurins were able to navigate their way to the African coast before eventually setting a course back to Lisbon.[30]

The Moors certainly possessed the capability to explore the outer regions of the North Atlantic Ocean. They discovered key island groups, such as the Azores, the Canaries, and possibly even the Cape Verdes, which they knew as the "islands of the two wizards."[31]

Is it possible that the Moors, as the descendants of the Lixitae, gained at least some of their maritime knowledge and capability from the Carthaginians, as well as the Spanish descendants of the Iberic-Phoenicians who occupied the coastal regions of Andalucia? Could the original inspiration for the legends surrounding Antilia and the Island of the Seven Cities have come from the Phoenicians and Carthaginians? If this was so, then the Moors might therefore have been the care-takers of oceanic knowledge and lore that stretched back for at least 1,700 years before the Arab conquest of Spain and Portugal. To take the matter further we must examine the origins of the name Antilia.

TO ENDURE, OR NOT TO ENDURE

Scholars suggest that the name Antilia derives from the Latin *ante,* "in front of," and the Portuguese *ilha,* meaning "island." Yet this transla-tion is based on its final form only. On the Pizzigani map of 1367 it appears as "Atulliae," which seems to have been its more formative spell-ing. Other, later variations of this same basic spelling include "Atilhas," found on a map dated 1518,[32] "Ateallo," from a Catalan map dated circa 1448,[33] and "Attiaela," which appears on another Catalan map of the fifteenth century.[34] If this is the more correct spelling, the name does not derive from *ante-ilha,* but comes from a much older variation of uncertain origin. Since it has been proposed that details on Catalan maps like the ones mentioned here may well have been taken from Moorish sailing charts,[35] could it be possible that the original form of Antilia was Afro-Arabian in origin?

In the 1830s Alexander von Humboldt (1769–1859), the celebrated German naturalist, traveler, and statesman, proposed that "Antillia" and its variations were derived from "Al-tin," Arabic for "the dragon."[36] If correct, it would imply that the island was home to a fabulous beast of this description (bringing to mind the dragon that guarded the golden apples on the islands of the Hesperides). Support for this theory comes in the knowledge that at least one mythical island in Arab folklore was actually known as the Island of the Dragon.[37] So was this the answer? Almost certainly not, for the transition from Al-tin to Antilia is far too severe for it to make linguistic sense.

If not obviously Latin, Portuguese, or Arabic, from where might the name Antilia have originated? Could it be either Phoenician or Punic, the language of the Carthaginians? With this prospect in mind, I made a search of known place names in common usage during biblical times and came across something very interesting indeed. My eyes were drawn to an entry in a biblical dictionary for "Attalia," or "Attaleia," a port at Pamphylia in Asia Minor, modern Turkey, built by Attalus II, the king of Pergamon (159–138 BCE). The first syllable was sufficiently close to the formative spellings of Antilia for a comparison to be made. The origin of the word "Attalia" is unknown, although it could be Greek. However, what intrigued me most about this place name is that it later was altered to Antalya, the form by which this Turkish port is known today.[38]

The purpose of this exercise has been to demonstrate how easily the name Antilia could have evolved from the earlier spelling of "Atulliae," or "Atilae." Moreover, when stripped of its inferred vowels and the superfluous second letter *l,* the linguistic root of the formative spellings of Antilia is composed of just three consonants: *a-t-l.* As we saw in chapter 3, the root *atl,* as in Atlas, Atlantis, or Atlantic, is commonly thought to derive from the Greek *tlâo,* "to endure" or "to bear."

The controversy surrounding the origin of the linguistic root *atl,* so crucial to our understanding of the Atlantis mystery, is one that has raged for a century and a half. Seven years before the American congressman turned historical detective Ignatius Donnelly launched his monumental work *Atlantis: The Antediluvian World* onto an unsuspecting public, a scholarly article appeared in the *Cincinnati Quarterly*

Journal of Science. Titled "Atlantis: A Statement of the 'Atlantic' Theory Respecting Aboriginal Civilization," the paper, penned by American historian L. M. Hosea, addresses the linguistic origin behind the proper name Atlas, which he acknowledges is thought by language scholars to derive from the Greek word *tlâo*.[39] In his words:

> This derivation, however, appears hardly reasonable, since the name would seem to have existed before the duty [of supporting the heavens] was imposed upon the god, and was no doubt imported into the Greek through maritime intercourse with the African nations. It is more probable that the original signification of Atlas . . . was gradually lost as commerce declined and the tradition of the existence of the islands [under his domain] became indistinct, and was ultimately merged in the secondary idea of "keeper of the pillars which hold heaven and earth asunder"—which stood upon the western horizon where the eye would naturally turn in looking toward the fabled islands, and thus became crystallised in the mythology of the day. It is, therefore, more reasonable to suppose that the few Greek words, and there are but few, which contain the radical *atl* or *tl,* all of them involving the idea of supporting a burden, are themselves derived from this secondary signification of Atlas.[40]

What Hosea is trying to say here is that the Greek root *atl* is unlikely to have derived from a word created to express Atlas's punishment of having to bear the heavens on his shoulders. Almost certainly it existed prior to this time and was only later modified into the meaning it possesses today. So if this is the case can we find a more suitable solution to this problem, one that might be acceptable to the scholarly world?

RAISED ON HIGH

Greek belongs to a family of languages known as Indo-European, which is derived from some of the earliest written and spoken languages of western, central, and southern Asia. So in theory the origin behind the name Atlas should be found in one of the core Indo-European languages, such as Sanskrit. Although native to India, it is considered to be one of the oldest forms of this language group. I therefore put the matter to Clifford Wright, professor of South Asian Studies at the School of Oriental and African Studies in London. In his opinion, the only word in Sanskrit that resembles the linguistic root *atl* is *tul,* or *tol,* which means "to weigh."[41] Since this implies an act whereby an item is lifted to determine its weight, Wright could understand how a Greek-language scholar might conclude that the word *tlâo,* "to bear" or "to endure," might stem from this Indo-European root. Furthermore, he pointed out that this same Sanskrit word was the root behind the Latin *tollo,* "to lift," "to raise," and "to weigh." Yet to Wright, the act of weighing implied by this word did not fully explain the idea of bearing or enduring a heavy weight suggested by Atlas's penance of having to support the heavens on his shoulders.[42] Furthermore, the name begins with the letter *a,* which when used as a prefix in Greek words reverses the original meaning. So *tlâo* prefixed with an *a,* as in *atlâo,* becomes "to not endure" or "to not bear," making complete nonsense of how Atlas is supposed to have gained his name. What is more, the Latin *tollo* obviously dates to a slightly later period and might have been influenced by the Greek word *tlâo.* So was there an alternative linguistic root for Atlas?

It is accepted that certain proper names found in the Greek language are not Indo-European in origin, but West Semitic. This is a language branch that includes Arabic, Hebrew, Phoenician, and Punic (that is, Carthaginian). Indeed, it is Herodotus who informs us that it was the Phoenicians who first introduced "writing" to the Greeks. They "shaped their letters" using an existing sixteen-character alphabet. Furthermore, "Afterwards, in the course of time, they [the Greeks] changed by degrees their language, and together with it the form likewise of their characters."[43] Could the *atl* root behind both Atlas and Antilia therefore be of Semitic origin?

Extraordinarily enough, an examination of this language group does provide some useful answers. The word root *atl* appears in the vowel-less language of the Hebrews, where it means "exalted," as in "elated" or "raised" on high. For example, it is present in the Hebrew name Atalyah, meaning "Yah is exalted." This is composed of the root *atl,* "exalted," and *yah,* meaning "God."[44] The same word root *atl* is present also in the Arabic language, where it too means "exalted" or "raised." More significantly it is found in Akkadian, an East Semitic language that thrived in ancient Iraq as far back as the third millennium BCE.[45]

Most important of all, the *atl* word root appears as a proper name in Punic. Jo Ann Hackett, professor of Biblical Hebrew at Harvard University, informed me that it appears on a dedication stone from Carthage written as "ATLA."[46] However, it is not recorded whether this personal name actually means "exalted" or "raised," yet there is every reason to assume that it does. Even though the exact age of this dedication stone is unknown, it was probably manufactured sometime between the fourth and second centuries BCE.[47]

This is where it starts getting interesting, for in addition to meaning "exalted," the Hebrew word *atl,* and indeed its variations, can also mean "elevated," which a standard English dictionary tells us means "raised; at or on a higher level; lofty in style."[48] This adjective is, of course, derived from the noun *elevation,* which denotes "the act of elevating; the state of being elevated; an elevated position or ground; height above sea level; the height of a building," and, lastly, "the angular altitude of a heavenly body above the horizon."[49]

If we turn now to Lemprière's standard *Classical Dictionary* and look at the entry for "Atlas," we find it reads, "The fable that Atlas supported the heavens on his back arises from his fondness for astronomy, and his often frequenting *elevated* places and mountains, whence he might observe heavenly bodies.[50] (current author's emphasis)

Since we know that Mount Atlas was deemed to be the petrified Titan supporting the heavens on his shoulders, Atlas's name is therefore intrinsically linked with his action of having elevated or raised up these misty heights. Clearly, then, this connection strongly suggests that the name Atlas does not derive from the Indo-European language of the Greeks but from West Semitic, most obviously the Punic language of the Carthaginians. Furthermore, it seems clear that the word root *atl* does not mean "to bear," as is suggested by its Greek word root, but "to elevate" or "to raise." If correct, it means that the mountain must therefore take its name from the fact that its "heavens" are "elevated" above ground level, an act seen as having been performed by the mighty stone giant. In this respect, Atlas thus becomes the personification of this act, in a sense the one who raises or elevates the heavens into the air. If this was the case, it tells us that, as a noun, Atlas, and indeed ATLA, might well translate as "the elevator," "the exalter," or indeed "the exalted one."

HOMER AND HESIOD

So if Atlas derives his name from the Carthaginians, it now seems certain that both Atlantis and Antilia stem from the same linguistic root. Yet as the *atl* root is found also in ancient texts written in the East Semitic language of the Akkadians, this tells us that its usage long antedates the first references to the hero-god Atlas in classical literature. Such works include Homer's *Odyssey,* composed circa 800–600 BCE,[51] which speaks of Atlas upholding the heavens, and Hesiod's *Theogony,* written circa 700 BCE,[52] which tells of Atlas's association with the Hesperides.

Unfortunately, there is still no way of telling which came first, Atlas the Titan or Atlas the mountain. All we can say is that both were associated with ancient Mauritania, the land of the Moors and Carthaginians, and that Atlas was additionally connected with astronomy, navigation, and the watery depths that lay in the direction of the setting sun. It is almost certainly due to this connection that the Greek islands located in the Western Ocean were considered to be "daughters" of Atlas, or Atlantides, their existence being preserved either in mythical form or as speculative maritime lore. Even as late as the sixteenth century, Atlantic islands were still referred to as "Atlantides." António Galvão in his *The Discoveries of the World* states that in the *Timaeus* Plato records that there existed "in ancient times in the Ocean sea Atlanticke certaine great Islands and countries named Atlantides."[53]

There can now be little doubt that it was the Carthaginians, and not the Greeks, who introduced the *atl*-derived names, such as Atlas, Atlantis, and Antilia, to the ancient world. Support for this theory comes from Sir Edward Herbert Bunbury, the nineteenth-century Cambridge geographer and fellow of the Royal Geographical Society, whose book *A History of Ancient Geography* remains a standard benchmark in all major universities. Having made an exhaustive study of the Greek myths exposed to the world for the first time by the likes of Homer and Hesiod, he became convinced that those that feature Atlas and the Hesperides were "almost certainly of Phoenician origin."[54] He further added, "We find in the earliest Greek records many vague and dimly-traced ideas as to the wonders of 'the far west,' which are in all probability derived from Phoenician sources."[55]

Adding still further weight to this argument is the knowledge that the concept of the Elysian Fields or Elysium, the mysterious isle of the dead located in the Western Ocean, is Phoenician in origin.[56] The same might also be said of Oceanus, the Ocean River, first found mentioned in Homer's *Iliad*.[57] In the words of noted nineteenth-century Swedish geographer A. E. Nordenskiöld, "The name οχεανοζ [okeanos] is probably of Phoenician origin."[58]

It is my opinion that some semblance of this legendary maritime knowledge remained in the possession of the ancient Lixitae, who as the Moors carried this understanding of Atlantic islands into Spain and Portugal sometime between the eighth and fourteenth centuries. Among their traditions was a fragmentary knowledge of a mysterious Atlantic island called Atulliae. Somehow this tradition came to the attention of the medieval cartographers and navigators of Portugal, who updated the name of this island to Antilia, *ante-ilha,* the island "before" or "in front of" something else, most probably the unknown American continent.

This is not to say that the concept of the Seven Cities was the creation either of the Moors or the Portuguese, only that the true origins of this tradition had somehow been lost along the way. Seven is the number that predominates in the legend of Antilia and for the islands of the Western Ocean in general. Seven cities, seven named bays, seven bishops, seven islets, seven Atlantides, seven Pleiades, seven islands sacred to Proserpine (after Marcellus), and seven divisions, or "circles," of the Atlantean city as envisaged by the Neoplatonist named Amelius.

Were the Seven Cities simply an elaboration of some much more archaic tradition connected directly with the core legends behind both the Atlantis myth and the medieval traditions of Antilia? It is a tantalizing possibility, and one that we begin to explore in the next chapter.

Yet for the moment we return briefly to the pioneering work of American historian L. M. Hosea. Having queried the linguistic root of the name Atlas, he went on to propose, "If . . . we can find a country, in the spoken language of which the word Atlantis has an indigenous root, there it is said we are justified in seeking traces of the long lost race."[59]

Having made this statement Hosea goes on to suggest that the "country" in question was the "lovely vale of Anahuac," the pre-Conquest name for Mexico. Quoting the Abbé Brasseur de Bourbourg, an accomplished nineteenth-century French philologist and language scholar who made an in-depth study of Mesoamerican religion and mythology, he informs us, "Here, too, [in Anahuac] we find the radical *tl* or *atl*," meaning "water," and from which was "derived Atlan, *on the border or in the midst of water*."[60]

Is there any way that a language spoken by the indigenous peoples of central Mexico could have any connection with the naming of the West Indies by Phoenician and Carthaginian traders? As we shall see, exploring this fascinating although linguistically difficult line of enquiry will reveal some remarkable insights into the possible origins of Antilia, the Island of Seven Cities.

15

FAIR GODS
FROM AFAR

The date is November 18, 1519. After months of daring exploits rivaling anything the pages of history had ever seen, the Spanish conquistador Hernando Cortés entered Tenochtitlan, the gleaming island metropolis of the Aztec Empire. Tens of thousands of Aztec citizens, brightly attired in colorful robes, lined either side of the long causeway into the city. Advancing between them was a column of several hundred fully armed Aztec warriors in animal skins and plumed headdresses. They were the royal guards of the Aztecs' Great Speaker Motecuhzoma II—better known to the world as Montezuma—who was being carried on a golden litter by four attendant noblemen moving at a slow, deliberate pace.

Cortés, dressed in full armor, was mounted on a well-groomed horse. He was accompanied by a trusted band of cavaliers, and in file behind them was a company of no more than three hundred disciplined foot soldiers marching to the sound of pipes and drums. Some carried colorful banners, including Cortés's own by now tattered standard, which had united his motley army on so many occasions since they had landed in New Spain.

Trailing behind the Spaniards were four thousand fierce, feather-clad warriors from the eastern province of Tlaxcala. Having been defeated no fewer than four times by the Spaniards, they had become Cortés's greatest allies in his plan to seize outright control of the Aztec nation.

There is no question that this was the latest, and greatest, act of sheer lunacy orchestrated by Cortés and his noble company. At any moment Montezuma could have given the signal for the entire population of Tenochtitlan to attack Cortés's army. Those not killed outright would have been captured and offered up as human sacrifices in the temples already stained with the blood of thousands upon thousands of victims. Yet Cortés was no ordinary Spanish general.

Hernando Cortés was born in 1485 at Medellin, a town in the province of Estremadura in western Spain. From an early age he displayed a fighting spirit, able wit, and good intelligence, which his father had wanted to channel into the study of law. Yet the young cavalier had other ideas. Having already shown a fondness for military action, he seized the opportunity in 1504 to depart for the New World. Seven years later he accompanied Diego Velasquez and his vicious conquistadors on their brutal colonization of Cuba. Later he was to become Velasquez's secretary. Yet Cortés disagreed fundamentally with the governor's ill-conceived and bloody policies, which in 1518 he attempted to bring to the attention of the ruling council on Hispaniola. He and his coconspirators were arrested, although he managed to escape and claim sanctuary in a church. Eventually, the two men settled their dispute, and Cortés was granted an estate with arable lands in the neighborhood of St. Jago, and for a short while he adopted an agricultural lifestyle.

DISCOVERY OF NEW SPAIN

Fueled by reports reaching Cuba of a great empire in New Spain, the name given to the American mainland, Cortés set his sights on conquest. His motives are said to have been gold, glory, and the conversion of the people in the name of the Church of Rome. Expectations had been raised by the return from the Yucatán of an expedition led by Hernandez de Cordova in 1517. His vessel had been blown off course from Cuba en route to the Bahamas, and by chance it had made landfall on the coast of the Yucatán. Here the Spanish crewmen encountered hostile inhabitants, unquestionably Mayan warriors, who were much better equipped and organized than the peoples so far encountered in the West Indies. Moreover, they constructed buildings and temples made of stone, something that had not been seen on any of the islands of the West Indies. Most curious of all, Cordova was of the opinion that "thereabouts were the Seven Cities,"[1] a point that cannot have gone unnoticed by the Cuban governor Diego Velasquez and his young secretary Hernando Cortés.

A second expedition under the command of Juan de Grijalva left Cuba bound for the Yucatán on May 1, 1518. It, too, experienced an unfriendly welcome from the local Maya, although Grijalva pushed on and reached as far as the modern state of Tabasco on the Gulf of Campeche, close to the site of the Mayan city of Comalcalco. He then journeyed north along the Gulf Coast and came across two offshore islands. One of them he named the Isla de los Sacrificios, following the discovery there of skeletal remains and a bloodstained temple that could only have been used for human sacrifice—the first time this practice had been encountered in the New World.[2]

Fired by such reports, Cortés planned an entire mission to New Spain, complete with a fleet of eleven vessels, one hundred shipmasters, pilots, and sailors, an army of around five hundred men, sixteen horses, and sufficient quantities of arms and armor, all without the knowledge of Velasquez. Despite the governor's late attempts to prevent the expedition from leaving Cuba, the fleet departed Cape St. Antonio bound for the Yucatán on February 18, 1519. After successfully defeating the Maya in various skirmishes, Cortés sailed southwestward and finally reached the Gulf Coast on April 21, 1519. With the help of the local population, he built an extensive settlement as a base camp as well as a place of refuge should it be needed in the months to come. On the site of this encampment grew the modern city of Veracruz.

The events that were to follow Cortés's first landing in New Spain are quite remarkable. Having decided to burn his ships so that there might be no going back, he decided to make his advance toward the Aztec capital, even though Montezuma had forbidden it. Cortés had also ordered the Totonac of nearby Cempoala to arrest Aztec tribute collectors, and then had them secretly released in order to gain the respect and admiration of the great speaker. Cortés had also torn down pagan idols inside sacred temples in front of frantic crowds and replaced them with wooden crosses and images of Mary and the Infant Savior. Moreover, he had led his troops against armies of one hundred thousand or more Tlaxcalan warriors as if it were a simple skirmish, and yet he had always won the day. Now Cortés seemed intent on tearing the heart out of the Aztec Empire in the name of the Spanish sovereign Charles I. All that stood in his way was the god-like Montezuma and every Mexican subject still loyal to him.

THE GREAT SPEAKER

The great speaker's personal army came to a halt as the golden litter, its canopy of green feathers bedecked with gold, silver, pearls, and green stone, was slowly lowered to the ground.[3] Montezuma, aided by his brother and nephew, went to greet the white strangers, as noblemen strew cotton mats before him so that his feet would not make contact with the bare earth. As he passed, all eyes lowered, for it was forbidden to look directly into those of the monarch. Others, overawed by the great speaker's presence, prostrated themselves.

Montezuma was about forty years of age. He was tall and thin, with a long dark face, straight black hair that covered his ears, and groomed stubble. On his head he wore an elaborate plumed headdress that consisted of a green fan of feathers taken from the sacred quetzal bird. It trailed down his back and was worn as a symbol of kingship and to denote that he had been a great military commander in his earlier days.

For more than 150 years the Aztecs had been fighting to carve out an empire that embraced all the tribes and peoples of Anahuac. After the fall circa 1200 CE of the Toltec Empire, the entire country had been plunged into conflict and chaos. Yet since the founding of Tenochtitlan in 1345, the Aztecs gradually won the day, and the country had finally begun to stabilize. The great speakers saw themselves as descendants of the Toltec ruling dynasty. Their empire had risen to power around 900 CE, and for a period of some three hundred years they had reigned supreme from the ancient city of Tula, which lay to the northeast of Tenochtitlan (where Mexico City would eventually be founded). Even earlier, Anahuac had been ruled by an unknown race who built the sacred city of Teotihuacán, located north of modern Mexico City, and left as a legacy the awesome Pyramid of the Sun and Pyramid of the Moon. Officially, this extraordinary cult center thrived somewhere between 300 and 900 CE, although its foundations were infinitely older and more mysterious. Now the land of Anahuac was under the rule of the Aztecs, the last of the great Mesoamerican civilizations.

For the intended meeting with Cortés, Montezuma wore a cotton girdle and square-cut blue cloak clasped at one shoulder. On his feet were sandals of solid gold, decorated with sparkling emeralds. His approach toward Cortés, in the company of several noblemen who walked in front of him, was with a sense of dignity and trust. This was despite the fact that he had made repeated attempts to outwit and slay these white men from the East ever since their arrival on the shores of his world. In many ways he considered Cortés his nemesis and felt that the fate, not only of himself and his family, but also the entire Aztec nation, now lay in the hands of this man in shining metal who sat on an animal that resembled a great deer.

Upon seeing Montezuma's approach, Cortés dismounted and handed the reins of his horse to a page before slowly advancing in the company of his most trustworthy companions. Finally, he said in some haste, "Is this not thou? Art thou not he? Art thou Montezuma?"[4] To which Montezuma replied in his native language, "Indeed, yes: I am he."

Following cordial greetings, Cortés took hold of a gold cord containing a series of margarita stones in many colors and slowly placed it around Montezuma's neck. Instinctively, the general moved to gently hug his adversary but was immediately rebuked and restrained from doing so by the shocked attendants, since it was protocol not to make physical contact with the great speaker.[5] Montezuma accepted the gift from Cortés as garlands of flowers and gifts of gold were showered on Cortés and his entourage.

There then followed an address from Montezuma to the Spanish general, of which the following is considered to be a faithful report:

O our lord, thou hast suffered fatigue, thou hast endured weariness. Thou hast come to arrive on earth. Thou hast come to govern thy city of Mexico; thou hast come to descend upon thy mat, upon thy seat, which for a moment I have watched for thee. For thy governors are departed . . . who yet a very short time ago had come to stand guard for thee, who had come to govern the city of Mexico . . . I have been afflicted for some time. I have gazed at the unknown place whence thou hast come—from among the clouds, from among the mists. And so this. The rulers departed maintaining that thou wouldst come to visit thy city, that thou wouldst come to descend upon thy mat, upon thy seat. And now it hath been fulfilled; thou hast come; thou hast endured fatigue, thou hast endured weariness. Peace be with thee. Rest thyself. Visit thy palace. Rest thy body. May peace be with our lords.[6]

Following a return speech from Cortés, the Spanish general seized Montezuma's hand as if to reassure him, after which the Spaniards were led away to the quarters that had been prepared for them during their uneasy stay in the capital city.

MONTEZUMA'S SPEECH

Why had Montezuma made such a curious speech? Why was he in such reverence of Cortés, the man he had attempted to capture or kill for so many months? Why did the great speaker insist that they had always known he would one day return "to govern thy city of Mexico" and descend "upon thy seat," kept warm for him by Montezuma's ancestors, almost as if the great speakers had merely prepared the way for his coming?

The answer came the following day when Cortés and his knights paid Montezuma a visit in his great Hall of Audience. Having removed their boots as a sign of respect, the Spaniards were ushered forward by noblemen. Montezuma graciously received them, and after formal pleasantries and a further exchange of gifts, Cortés got down to the main purpose of the meeting—the conversion of the Aztec nation to the faith of Rome. It was his intention to convince Montezuma that his subjects should desist from conducting their barbarous rites to mere pagan idols, which bore the likeness of devils. Everywhere they had seen evidence of the mass slaughter of human individuals, whose hearts were wrenched from still-writhing bodies and offered up to demons of hell.

Through his interpreter, Doña Marina, Cortés explained the mysteries of the Catholic Church. Montezuma—who was himself a priest of the god Tezcatlipoca, in his form of the fire-god Huitzilopochtli—listened attentively to the account of the white god said to have died on a cross and risen from the dead after three days. He even accepted that this Jesus must indeed be a powerful god to have protected the Spaniards against the wrath of the gods whose idols the Spaniards had destroyed both in his country and in the land of the Maya. Only after Cortés had finished his own address did Montezuma deliver his return speech. Thankfully, it is preserved among the famous *Letters from Mexico* written by Hernando Cortés to the Spanish sovereign in 1519. What he said is of great importance.

For a long time we have known from the writings of our ancestors that neither I, nor any of those who dwell in this land, are natives of it, but foreigners who came from very distant parts; and likewise we know that a chieftain, of whom they were all vassals, brought our people to this region. And he returned to his native land.

And we always held that those who descended from him would come and conquer this land and take us as their vassals. So, because of the place from which you claim to come, namely, from where the sun rises . . . we believe and are certain that he is our natural lord.[7]

Another version of the speech is more revealing and alludes specifically to the identity of the great leader who it was believed would one day return.

In a word, we believe that the great Prince to whom you pay obedience, is a descendant of Quetzalcoatl, Lord of the Seven Caves of the Navarlaques, and lawful sovereign of the 7 nations that gave rise to the Mexican Empire. For from the tradition he left these countries to conquer new regions in the east, with a promise that in the process of time his descendants should return to new-model our laws and reform government. We have therefore already determined that everything shall be done for the honour of a Prince who is the offspring of such an illustrious progenitor.[8]

Cortés was fully aware that Montezuma, the Aztec nation, and all the other tribes of New Spain held him in awe because he supposedly resembled a god named Quetzalcoatl who had arrived with his followers on a boat that had come from the direction of the rising sun. He had brought civilization to Anahuac. His homeland was known as Tlapallan, the "red land,"[9] and it was to here that he had departed after his ministry. The name Quetzalcoatl derives from two words in the Nahuatl language: *quetzal,* "feathered" or "plumed," and *coatl,* "snake," more specifically the rattlesnake. According to Aztec tradition he was the seventh son of his father Itzac-Mixcohuatl, whose name means White Grass Snake Nebula.[10] The term *nebula* alludes to the river of stars known as the Milky Way. Quetzalcoatl's celestial form is determined by the second syllable of his name, *coatl*, which also can mean "twin," a reference to his role as Venus personified as the morning star. His dark twin, Xolotl, was seen as Venus in its form as the evening star.

Quetzalcoatl was originally a great culture hero of the Toltec peoples and was still revered in many parts of Mexico at the time of the Conquest. According to the earliest Spanish chroniclers, who made a point of learning about this Quetzalcoatl, in his earthly form he was said to have been tall in stature, with long dark hair and a flowing beard.[11] Many also assumed that he possessed white skin, although this assertion is dismissed by scholars as a creation of the Spaniards, who wanted to see themselves as fulfilling the prophecy of Quetzalcoatl's return.[12]

THE CROSS AND TUNIC

More difficult to understand was Quetzalcoatl's connection with the cross, which supposedly adorned his black tunic (see fig. 15.1).[13] For five

Figure 15.1. The Toltec god Quetzalcoatl atop a teocalli pyramid temple.

hundred years Christian writers and historians have seized on this religious symbolism to suggest that Quetzalcoatl was an early Christian seafarer, such as the apostle Thomas, whom the Spanish clerics of the sixteenth century were convinced reached the Americas.[14] The truth of the matter is that the cross had been a symbol important to both Mesoamerican and South American cultures long before the advent of Christianity, and most likely it served as a sign of either the Milky Way or a star constellation of some kind.

LORD OF TLAPALLAN

Quetzalcoatl was said to have appeared on the Gulf Coast, close to where Cortés made his own celebrated landfall in 1519. Like Cortés, Quetzalcoatl protested against the barbaric ways of the native peoples and preached against human sacrifice. He was said to have taught of a divinity called Opu, the Invisible, or Yohalli Ehecatl, "night wind," who was to be offered oblations in the hours of darkness in a sacred enclosure removed from all noise even on the coldest of nights. Furthermore, every twenty days, large conch shells would be used to announce the commencement of a ceremony in which devotees would present on an altar an aloe spine stained red with their own blood.[15]

For twenty years Quetzalcoatl stayed in the ancient city of Cholula instructing the Toltec in the arts of metalworking, agriculture, and government administration, all things that were apparently unknown before this time.[16] He also founded the Toltec city of Tula, or Tollan (another name for Tlapallan), in honor of his homeland.

Yet there had been those who looked on Quetzalcoatl's presence in the land of Anahuac with great disdain. Among them was a vengeful magician named Tezcatlipoca, who in place of one foot had a circular mirror fashioned from the black volcanic glass known as obsidian—hence his name, "Smoking Mirror." This black-faced god, the patron of Tenochtitlan and the Aztec nation, craftily persuaded Quetzalcoatl to consume a draft of an alcoholic beverage known as *pulque*. It so intoxicated him that he forgot his oath of chastity and slept with his sister Quetzalpetlatl. As self-punishment for this misdeed, the Feathered Serpent decided to abandon Tollan—a decision that was to have grave consequences. Upon his departure, Quetzalcoatl is said to have razed the houses and buildings built by him. He also buried his treasure of gold and banished all birds of rich plumage.

At a location named as Coaapan, Quetzalcoatl was met by some of the gods of Anahuac, who asked him, "Where do you go?"

"I go to Tlapallan whence I came."[17]

"For what reason?"

"My father the Sun has called me thence."

"Go, then, happily," they bade him, "but leave us the secret of your art, the secret of founding in silver, of working in precious stones and woods, of painting, and of feather-working, and other matters."[18]

Quetzalcoatl refused to hear their words and continued his journey eastward, until he reached Tabasco on the Gulf Coast.[19] From here he departed for Tlapallan on a raft made of snakes.[20]

After this time, the dark lord Tezcatlipoca reigned supreme and was worshipped by Toltec and Aztec alike. So that Smoking Mirror might continue to permit the sun to rise each morning, and thus allow the empire to prosper, this grim god gorged on the steaming hearts of countless human sacrifices, offered up daily on the altars of Tenochtitlan's Great Temple.

Yet because Quetzalcoatl was not killed, but simply went away, those who followed him firmly believed that one day he would return to the land of Anahuac. He would punish those who had turned their back on him—a threat that hung like a sword of Damocles over the Aztec Empire. Its priests and ruling dynasty knew full well that their bloody allegiance to Tezcatlipoca would thus ensure their downfall and at the same time plunge the world into chaos and disorder.

Montezuma considered it possible that Cortés was an incarnation of Quetzalcoatl. So much so that after the Spaniards had established their settlement at Veracruz, Montezuma dispatched, in addition to a welcoming party, a proficient artist, whose task it was to paint an accurate picture of the general. When Montezuma beheld Cortés's image for the first time and saw for himself the pale face, black beard, and metal helmet, like the conical hat worn by Quetzalcoatl, he must have been tempted to admit that this was indeed the returning god. Even stranger was the fact that Cortés bore on his chest a white shell set in gold, which greatly resembled the so-called wind jewel worn by Quetzalcoatl.[21] This took the form of the cross-sectioned whorl of a conch shell, which regularly features in Aztec art and sculpture as the insignia of the god.

PROPHECIES OF DOOM

If all this was not enough to unnerve the great speaker, a series of rather unusual portents and signs had already suggested that the return of Quetzalcoatl was imminent.[22] For instance, in 1510 Lake Tezcuco, on which Tenochtitlan was built, became violently agitated without any form of tempest or earthquake. As a consequence its banks had overflowed, flooding the streets of the city. The following year the turrets of the metropolis's Great Temple, sacred to Tezcatlipoca in the form of the fire-god Huitzilopochtli, spontaneously caught fire and continued to burn despite frantic attempts to subdue the blaze. In the years that followed no fewer than three comets were seen in the skies, while shortly before the arrival of the Spaniards a mysterious "sheet" or "flood" of fire had appeared in the sky. According to one account the luminous mass had eventually become "thickly powdered with stars."[23] Most bizarre of all was the rumor that spread quickly through the Aztec capital to the effect that Montezuma's sister had returned to life four days after her death to warn the great speaker of the dark cloud that now hung over the future of his empire![24]

In addition to these supposed supernatural events, it was considered by Aztec priests and astronomers, including Montezuma, that Quetzalcoatl would return to wreak destruction when the year Ce Acatl (One, Arrow Reed), his name as the morning star, coincided with the day Chiconaui Ehecatl (Nine Wind), the birth date of the first Quetzalcoatl.[25] This moment occurred only once in every fifty-second year, and by strange fate, if indeed this is what it might be called, these two calendar events combined during the spring of 1519, shortly before Cortés made his landfall at Veracruz.

Yet the age-old prophecies and strange portents did not preclude the idea that Quetzalcoatl might arrive on the shores of Mexico with a group of companions who also bore a similar resemblance. Nahuan peoples encountered by Cortés and his men during his toilsome journey to Tenochtitlan in 1519 spoke of the return of "white" men in plural. For example, the Tlaxcalans, whom Cortés beat decisively, came to accept that "the Spaniards might be the white and bearded men foretold by the oracles."[26]

Who were these "white and bearded men foretold by the oracles"? What part did they play in the rise of Mesoamerican civilization and the development of its mythic traditions?

Whether Montezuma truly believed that Cortés was an incarnation of Quetzalcoatl, and his fellow Spaniards fair gods from afar, is impossible now to say. Neither can we be sure about the authenticity of Montezuma's famous speech (of which there is more than one version and differences of opinion regarding when and where it was given).[27] It has been suggested that what he had to say about the returning god was falsified by Spanish historians in order to justify the conquest of Mexico, something I find difficult to comprehend. All that can be said with any degree of certainty is that Montezuma believed Cortés to be of the same lineage as himself,[28] while it was debated whether the Spaniards were of the "family of Quetzalcoatl."[29] These facts are recorded by the earliest Spanish chroniclers, who either accompanied Cortés during the conquest of Mexico or wrote of these matters shortly after this time.

The greatest enigma is why Montezuma did nothing to save his empire once Cortés and his army were firmly within his grasp. From the moment that the Spaniards first set foot in Tenochtitlan, Montezuma could have just snapped his fingers and they would have been seized and killed by the royal guard. Indeed, following Montezuma's subsequent arrest at the hands of Cortés, the emperor was transported through the streets on his royal litter escorted by attendants and Spanish soldiers. Crowds began to gather, roused by the thought that the white men were carrying off their great speaker by force. There is little question that the Spaniards would have been lynched had not Montezuma "called out to the people to disperse, as he was visiting his friends of his own accord; thus sealing his ignominy by a declaration that deprived his subjects of the only excuse for resistance."[30]

Had Montezuma been too proud to act, or had he in some way come to accept that the hand of fate was on him and that nothing he could do would save his empire? If this was the case we must return to the sheer potency of the prophecy of Quetzalcoatl's return and attempt to understand why one of the greatest rulers of history succumbed so easily to superstitious fear and belief.

Why did Cortés's arrival become confused with the prophecy of Quetzalcoatl's return? Who exactly was Quetzalcoatl, and, indeed, what did he really represent? More important, where was Tlapallan, his ancestral homeland, to which he departed at the end of his ministry? Answering these questions will permit us to understand the Mesoamerican vision of an original homeland, which, as we will see, has strange parallels with Old World traditions concerning Atlantis, Antilia, and the Island of the Seven Cities.

16

PEOPLE OF THE
SERPENT

According to the creation myth of the Mexica peoples, before the first dawn there had been four previous suns. Tezcatlipoca had been the chief god of the first sun, and those who lived on Earth were giants devoured in the last days by jaguars. Ehecatl, the wind god (and a form of Quetzalcoatl), had watched over the second sun, although this world was destroyed by wind and its inhabitants became monkeys. The rain god Tlaloc presided over the third sun, but this one was obliterated by fiery rain and its inhabitants became butterflies, dogs, and turkeys. The water goddess Chalchiuhtlicue controlled the fourth sun, Nahui Atl (Four Water), although this world was engulfed by a flood and its inhabitants became fish (i.e., they drowned).

Afterward there came a fifth sun, or age, jointly initiated by Tezcatlipoca and Quetzalcoatl, who elevated the heavens by transforming themselves into great trees. The two gods then slayed the caiman (or crocodile), from whose body they fashioned the present world.

Quetzalcoatl, in the company of his twin Xolotl, then descended into the underworld in search of the bones of those who had drowned in the previous world age. Having fooled Mictlantecuhtli, the god of death, into giving up these remains, the twins proceeded to Tamoanchan,

246

which means the "Place Where the Serpent People Landed." Here the bones were ground like corn into a fine meal before being mixed with blood to produce the first human beings, whose descendants ruled Anahuac as the Aztec nation.

There exist important variations of this story that might help us to locate Tlapallan, the ancient homeland of the Feathered Serpent. They speak of the ancestors of the Mexica emerging from a place called Chicomoztoc, the Seven Caves, generally thought to be situated beneath Colhuacán, the "Crooked Mountain." One version speaks of a lightning staff being struck on the Seven Caves, while another describes the ancestors' escape from inside the Earth only after the sun had fired an arrow of sunlight into the House of Mirrors, another name for this sevenfold cave.[1]

During the sixteenth century a Mexican chronicler named Don Fernando de Alva Ixtlilxóchitl wrote a mythical history of the Nahuan peoples titled *Obras o Relaciones Históricas (Works or Historical Relations)*. He recorded that human beings emerged into the world only during the third age. Chief among them were two tribes—the Olmec ("rubber people") and Xicalanca—who were said to have made landfall in the land of Papuhá.[2] Where they came from is not stated, although Ixtlilxóchitl records that afterward the two tribes founded the city of Cholula and settled in the state of Tabasco. The land of Xicalanco extended from Campeche in the Yucatán south to the mouth of the Tabasco River, although the ancient town of this name stood on the point of an island, situated between the sea and the immense Lagoon de Terminos.[3] Tradition asserts that it was also in this same region that Quetzalcoatl departed for Tlapallan after quitting the land of Anahuac. It is interesting therefore that Ixtlilxóchitl places the coming of Quetzalcoatl during the same epoch as the arrival of the Olmec and Xicalanca.[4]

The concept of the Feathered Serpent was unquestionably known to the Olmec, for its likeness has been detected among the formative architecture at La Venta in the state of Tabasco. Monument 19 contains a sculpted image of a rattlesnake bearing an avian beak and a plumed crest, which scholars consider to be an early representation of Quetzalcoatl.[5]

After the first Quetzalcoatl came many more, for it became a title applied to at least one Toltec lord, who is remembered as Ce Acatl Topiltzin Quetzalcoatl. Moreover, the successors of the Toltecs, the priest-kings or great speakers of the Aztec Empire, also adopted the title Quetzalcoatl.[6] In this way they saw themselves as lineal descendants of the Feathered Serpent, the reason perhaps why Montezuma was willing to consider that Cortés and the Spaniards were also of the "family of Quetzalcoatl."

FACES OF THE SERPENT

The Feathered Serpent also appears in the mythology of the Quiché of Guatemala. They are one of a whole group of mountain tribes known collectively as the southern Maya because they adopted the language, lifestyle, architecture, administration, and sophistication of the Yucatec Maya. The creation myths and early history of the Quiché are preserved in a remarkable work known as the *Popol Vuh,* or "Council Book."[7] Here Quetzalcoatl becomes the "Sovereign Gucumatz," or "quetzal serpent," one of the seven creator-gods who were thought to have fashioned the first human beings from a ground mixture of white and yellow maize.[8] Dennis Tedlock, the translator and editor of what is arguably the most definitive version of the Popol Vuh, said that these gods were located either "on or in the sea in the primordial world."[9]

Later in the Popol Vuh, Gucumatz reappears as "a true lord of genius" who ruled the Cauec, the first-ranking Quiché lineage, during the fourth generation of their historical period. He possessed three companions who were also seen as "lords of genius," and together they are described in the following quite revealing manner: "They knew whether war would occur; everything they saw was clear to them. Whether there would be death, or whether there would be famine, or whether quarrels would occur, they knew it for certain. . . . But it wasn't only in this way that they were lords. They were great in their own being and observed great fasts. As a way of cherishing their buildings and cherishing their lordship, they fasted for long periods, they did penance before *their* gods."[10] (current author's emphasis)

The expression "their gods" implies that these lords of the Quiché were not native to the tribe but came from elsewhere with foreign customs and beliefs. Could the Quiché's Feathered Serpent have belonged to the tribe spoken of in the Popol Vuh as the Gumatz, or "serpents," who along with twelve other tribes, including the Quiché, arrived out of the east before the first dawn?[11] What we can say is that in the language of the Quiché the name Gucumatz is identical to that of Quetzalcoatl, suggesting that originally these two culture heroes were one and the same. Yet the concept of founding civilizers in the guise of walking serpents was not exclusive to the Nahua and Quiché, for it reappears also among the Mayan tribes of the Yucatán.

SERPENT OF THE EAST

According to the Chilam Balam of Chumayel, one of the sixteen books of Chilam Balam ("Jaguar Translator"), written in the Roman alphabet by priestly scribes wishing to preserve the sacred history of the Maya following the conquest of the Yucatán, the peninsula's original inhabitants were known as Ah-Canule, the "People of the Serpent." Their priestly elite were known as Chanes, "Serpents," Canob, "Serpents' Wise Men," or Ah-Tzai, "People of the Rattlesnake."[12] This race was said to have come out of the east on boats in the company of a great leader named Zamna, or Itzamna, who bore the title Lakin-Chan, "Serpent of the East."[13] One account speaks of him arriving in the company "of a considerable number of priests, warriors, and artists of all professions, apparently chosen from among those most capable of helping their leader in his noble enterprise of initiating the barbarians."[14] He also introduced the people to the arts and sciences, as well as legislative laws

and the characters of writing.[15] Like Quetzalcoatl, he and his companions "did not make human sacrifice," "had knowledge of only one God,
Hunal (or Hunab)-Ku, who created heaven and earth and all things,"
and made offerings only of flowers and fruit.[16] The first town that he
built was Mayapan, situated on the slopes of the Mani Mountains.[17]
Itzamna went on to found many other cities, each with its own province, before at the end of his days he went to live by the sea. At the place
where Itzamna died, the great center of Izamal grew up.[18] Maya from all
over the peninsula would come here to offer up prayers and gifts at his
shrine, where miracles and cures were frequently reported. His hand,
known as Kab-ul, the "guiding hand," became the symbol of his faith,
and this alone could be used as a protection against the evil eye.[19]

One of the sixteen books of Chilam Balam known as the Chilam
Balam of Chumayel records that the People of the Serpent, whom it
names as "the First People," were said to have made landfall on Cozumel
Island, which lies beyond the east coast of the Yucatán. From here they
spread to other parts of Mexico, where they founded various cities,
including Chichén Itzá, which means "the Mouth of the Wells of the
Itzaes."[20]

Here, of course, we find the pyramid temple known as the Castillo,
noted for its amazing lighting effects. On the two equinoxes each year
the triangular shadows cast on the northern stairway, which termi-
nates at ground level in serpents' heads, appear to undulate with the
movement of the sun, giving the impression of a snake ascending at the
spring equinox and descending at the autumn equinox.

Yet this city was equally celebrated as the cult center of Kukulcan,
the Mayan form of the Feathered Serpent, who, according to the
sixteenth-century Spanish historian Bartolomé de las Casas, arrived in
the Yucatán "from the east" in the company of "20 illustrious leaders"[21]
who were "dressed in long, flowing clothes and had big beards."[22]

Itzamna was not the same person as Kukulcan, who would appear to
have been the Mayan equivalent of Quetzalcoatl or Gucumatz. Indeed,
Kukulcan's descendants, the priest-kings known as the Cocomes (*cocom*

is the plural of "snake" in Nahuatl), were direct rivals of the Itzaes, the descendants of Itzamna, from whom they seized control of the Mayan territories shortly before the time of the Conquest.

The Itzaes' priesthood, the Chanes, venerated the rattlesnake and saw as particularly sacred a species known as *Crotalus durissus durissus,* which has a distinctive crisscross design along the entire length of its back.[23] This pattern is replicated on the exterior facades of a number of key Yucatec temples, including Chichén Itzá. The rattlesnake is also connected with calendrical cycles, since it is commonly thought to shed its fangs every twenty days, a time period amounting to one *uinal* in the Mayan calendar system.[24] Moreover, in Mayan astrology, the rattlesnake was represented as a starry constellation in which the seven stars of the Pleiades formed its sevenfold rattle.[25] Indeed, *tsab,* the rattles of the snake, is listed in Mayan dictionaries as the name of the Pleiades.[26]

WHERE THE SERPENT PEOPLE LANDED

Edward H. Thompson, the celebrated U.S. consul and explorer, wrote a book titled *People of the Serpent: Life and Adventure among the Maya.* Published in 1932, it contains some remarkable insights into the religious beliefs of the native Mexican peoples. He asserted that the People of the Serpent landed on the Gulf Coast at Tamoanchan, the Place Where the Serpent People Landed. This mythical location was thought to lie at the mouth of the Panuco River, on the Gulf Coast, south of Tampico in the province of Tamaulipas.[27] Remember, it was also to Tamoanchan that Quetzalcoatl and his twin Xolotl brought the bones of those who had died in the floods that destroyed the fourth sun or age.

Thompson presents a rather flamboyant account of the Chanes' arrival on "strange craft" that "shone like the scales of serpents' skins, and to the simple natives who saw them approaching they appeared to be great serpents coming swiftly toward them."[28] He goes on to describe the appearance of the individuals: "In these craft were light-skinned beings, and some of the traditions have it that they were tall of stature and blue-eyed. They were clad in strange garments and wore about their foreheads emblems like entwined serpents. The wondering natives who met them at the shore saw the manner of their coming with the symbol of the Sacred Serpent, which they worshipped, on their brows, and knew the strangers to be their gods come down from their home in the sun to teach and guide them."[29]

Thompson wrote that the local inhabitants of Mexico and the Yucatán accepted the Chanes as their guides and teachers, through whom civilization arose in these regions.[30] He also believed that they probably separated into two distinct groups "in the furtherance of a concerted plan," one moving northward to lead the peoples of the land of Anahuac and the other moving southward to Chiapas and Guatemala in order to unite the mountain tribes there. He was also convinced that the People of the Serpent were the founders and ruling dynasty of the Olmec and Toltec civilizations, which gave rise to great Mayan centers such as Chichén Itzá.[31] His conclusion was that the People of the Serpent conquered "not by force and strange weapons, but by binding the primitive peoples to them by force of their power and wisdom."[32]

What we see here is the arrival among the indigenous peoples of Mexico of what appears to have been an elite group, remembered as being serpentine in nature or appearance. They used their knowledge, organizational skills, and great wisdom to unite tribal communities with a common cause—the foundation of civilization. In return, these priest-kings, lords, or rulers were seen as divine and remembered by later generations as gods or great wisdom-bringers.

It therefore becomes crucial to establish the whereabouts of their original homeland, and the most immediate clue appears to be Quetzalcoatl's link to Tamoanchan. Since it was thought to have been located on the Gulf Coast, it suggests that Chicomoztoc, the Seven Caves, where Quetzalcoatl and Xolotl obtained the bones of the former human race, lay beyond here in the direction of the rising sun.

Indeed, we find that it was at Panuco, where Tamoanchan was traditionally situated, that the Nahuan tribes are said to have arrived following a journey across water on seven boats that the early Spanish chronicler Fray Bernardino de Sahagún said were collectively known by the name Chicomoztoc.[33] On this journey they were accompanied by wise men, known as Amoxoaques (from Nahuatl *amox,* meaning "books"), a name suggesting they had extensive knowledge of sacred texts.[34] According to Bartolomé de las Casas, their leader was Quetzalcoatl himself, implying that the region around the Panuco River was where the Nahua first established themselves on the mainland after leaving Chicomoztoc.

IN SEARCH OF CHICOMOZTOC

One of the only representations of Chicomoztoc is found in a codex known as the *Historia Tolteca-Chichimeca,* which dates from the sixteenth century. Here it is shown as a seven-lobed cave with an entrance corridor. Sitting on top of it is the curled form of Colhuacán, the Crooked Mountain. Inside each bay, and in the earth that surrounds them, are the bones of those who died in the floods of the fourth age, along with various tribal symbols such as birds' heads, hands, reeds, and feathers. These show that Chicomoztoc is the place of the ancestors of the seven tribes (and sometimes eight or even thirteen clans/tribes) that emerged from here at the beginning of the present world age.

Unfortunately, Nahuan tradition does not give a precise location for Chicomoztoc. Moreover, there appears to be confusion as to where it was thought to have been situated in the mythical world. One version of the story reads, "This is the beginning of the record of the coming of the Mexicans from the place called Aztlan. It is by means of the water that they came this way, being four tribes, and in coming they rowed in boats. They built their huts on piles at the place called the grotto of Quineveyan. It is there from which the eight tribes issued. . . . It is there where they were founded in Colhuacán [the "Crooked" or "Curved Mountain"]. They were the colonists of it since they landed there, coming from Aztlan."[35]

The "grotto of Quineveyan" is a form of the Seven Caves, and it is to here that the Mexica embarked on a journey across water from Aztlan, which translates as "Place of Whiteness," "Place of Herons,"[36] or "Place of Reeds."[37] It is from this place name that the Aztecs derived their own appellation. They were the "People of Azt," just as the Toltecs were the "People of Tol," after Tollan, or Tula, the name given to both their capital city and Tlapallan, Quetzalcoatl's homeland.

In drawings, Aztlan is shown as an island surrounded by water, over which a single person rows a canoe away from the shore. Located on the island is a teocalli, or stepped pyramid temple, around which are six other temples, making seven in total—an allusion to the symbolism of the Seven Caves (see fig. 16.1).

Despite the reference to the "grotto of Quineveyan" being located on the mainland, the sixteenth-century Spanish historian Diego Durán

Figure 16.1. Illustration recording the flight of the Mexica from Aztlan, their legendary island homeland, from an Aztec codex in the Boturini collection. What is the true relationship between Aztlan and Plato's Atlantis?

recorded that it was anciently believed by the Aztecs that their fore-fathers had come from "that delightful place" Aztlan. Here could be found "a great hill in the midst of the waters" called Colhuacán, as well as the "caves or grottoes" called Chicomoztoc. More significantly, he recorded that the Mexica abandoned this homeland *and came to the mainland.*[38] (current author's emphasis)

This shows that some traditions placed the Seven Caves in Aztlan, which was itself located overseas. However, Mesoamerican scholars have proposed other ideas about the Mexica's original homeland. For instance, anthropologist Paul Kirchhoff identified Colhuacán, the Crooked Mountain, beneath which Chicomoztoc was located, as San Isidro Cuilacán, which lies 270 kilometers northwest of Mexico City.[39] He therefore concluded that Aztlan was nearby and that the Seven Caves must lie slightly to the east.[40]

Professor Wigberto Jiménez Moreno accepted that the Seven Caves lay to the northwest of the Valley of Mexico, but proposed that Aztlan was once located in a lagoon at Mexcaltitán, on the northwest coast of Mexico.[41] In its waters is a small island that Moreno felt corresponded with the pictorial representations of Aztlan. He also pointed out that on the banks of Mexcaltitán is a site known locally as Aztatlan, which might once have been surrounded by water.[42] This he felt was the true origin behind the mysterious island homeland of the Mexica.

Other scholars have had different ideas. For instance, Rudolph Van Zantwijk proposed that if Aztlan signified the "White Island," then it had to be Cuitlahuac (modern Tlahuac) in northern Mexico, which even to this day is known locally as the White Island.[43]

Such views have allowed scholars to perpetuate the view that the earliest nomadic peoples to reach central Mexico came originally from North America. Here they are considered to have lived hunter-gatherer lifestyles since crossing the Bering Strait land bridge, which connected Siberia with Alaska until it was swallowed up as the sea level rose at the end of the last Ice Age, sometime circa 8500 BCE. I do not contest that some of the earliest inhabitants of Mexico arrived from North America.

Yet the religious beliefs and creation myths of the Mesoamerican peoples suggest that the real picture is more complex. The development of these various tribal cultures resulted most probably from the emergence of an elite group that arrived not overland from North America but by boat from across the water. Moreover, we can say with some certainty that their totemic symbols, or distinguishing features, upon arrival in the country were the quetzal bird and the rattlesnake.

IN THE MIDST OF THE SEA

Returning to the question of the Mexica's mythical homeland, Mesoamerican scholar Nigel Davies was prepared to admit that the various theories concerning its suggested whereabouts raised "the question of whether there were, perhaps, two Aztlans."[44]

Or indeed three, four, or even five? All the indications are that those sites proposed on the mainland were merely symbolic representations of an ancestral homeland that existed somewhere out to sea. Although the Aztec codices speak only once of Aztlan's placement beyond "the mainland," there does exist an ancient folktale that throws considerable light on the matter. It records that the Aztecs' former homeland might be likened to a great disc surrounded by "the water of heaven," in that it "touched the sky at the horizon."[45] The story in question additionally says, "From across those waters came the people in canoes or on the backs of huge turtles. The dead too had to be carried over them by dogs as they had no boats."[46]

In my personal opinion, "the water of heaven" is a reference to the infinite reaches of the sea, since an island that lies beyond sight of land will be in waters that, in every direction, touch "the sky at the horizon." Moreover, the ancient idea that some of the "people" arrived "on the backs of huge turtles" is suggestive of sandbanks, cays, or islands that might have acted as stepping-stones to reach the mainland.

In the knowledge that Aztlan might have been located overseas, is it not possible that this is simply another allusion to Tlapallan, or

Tollan, the mythical homeland of the Toltecs, the ruling elite whom the Aztec great speakers saw as their ancestors? Linguistically, Tollan can be written variously as *tulan, tlan, atla,* or even *atlan.*[47] Aztlan, on the other hand, is a word made up of just two glyphs—the heron feathers, which denote the sound *azt,* and another glyph that evokes an *a* sound.[48] The linguistic root of this word was a matter discussed by American historian William H. Prescott in his monumental work *History of the Conquest of Mexico,* first published in 1843. He pointed out that Tollan was derived from *tolin,* meaning "reed," thus signifying, like Aztlan, the "place of reeds."[49]

As we have already established, the *atl* word root features prominently in the Nahuatl language, where it signifies "water," "war," and, more curiously, the "top of the head."[50] From these derivations the French philologist and language scholar the Abbé Brasseur de Bourbourg determined that the Nahuatl *atlan* meant "on the border or in the midst of water." In this respect, he pointed out that a "city named Atlan existed when the continent was discovered by Columbus, at the entrance of the Gulf of Uraba, in Darien [on the northern coast of Colombia], with a good harbour; it is now reduced to an unimportant pueblo named Acla."[51] We might also cite Professor Wigberto Jiménez Moreno's Aztatlan, the place name attached to an area of land next to a lagoon at Mexcaltitán, on the northwest coast of Mexico. From the above exercise in Nahuatl linguistics, it would imply that the name Aztatlan can be translated as "herons/whiteness/reeds on the border, or in the midst, of water."

What all this suggests is that memories were preserved among the tribes of Mesoamerica regarding a single island landmass, called variously Aztlan, Tollan or Tlapallan, from which came a seafaring people who formed the ruling dynasties of the earliest populations to inhabit the region. This view is easily confirmed if we now take a closer look at the creation account of the Quiché-Maya tribe of Guatemala, for they also preserved the memory of an exodus from a former homeland containing a sevenfold cave of emergence.

THE POPOL VUH

The Quiché text known as the Popol Vuh speaks of seven creator gods, one of whom, as we saw in chapter 16, was known as the Sovereign Gucumatz. They agreed to make four men from a ground paste of yellow and white maize, and once this had been done their creations were allowed to fall asleep. Four women were then placed beside the men.[52] Afterward the ancestors of the Quiché were led in the darkness before the first dawn to find a place called Tulan-Zuyua, in which was Wucub-pek, the Seven Caves. Here each of the men was allotted the patronage of an individual god, who was carried out of the cave in the form of an idol. This idea of a movable god is found also in Aztec myth, which speaks of "an idol called Huitzilopochtli" being "borne by four guardians [teomamas—"bearers of the god"],"[53] who came out of Aztlan in the company of the seven clans of the Mexica.

The Popol Vuh tells us that it was in the Seven Caves that the four men and the four women suddenly found that they were unable to comprehend each other's words, since they now spoke different tongues.[54] Amid this confusion, they departed Tulan-Zuyua and went in search of a more favorable region in which they could worship the sun god Tohil. He was the patron deity of Balam-Qitzé, the first leader of the Quiché. Constantly it poured with rain, putting out the sacred fires lit in Tohil's honor. Somehow they were able to cross a great sea, a matter that the authors of the Popol Vuh attempt to explain in the following manner: "They crossed over as if there were no sea. They just crossed over on some stones, stones piled up in the sand. And they gave it a name: Stone Courses, Sand Banks was their name for the place where they crossed through the midst of the sea. Where the waters were divided, they crossed over."[55]

Still in perpetual darkness, the ancestors of the Quiché came upon a mountain named Hacauitz.[56] Here the god Tohil informed them that they would soon see the sun, which at last appeared. Very gradually, the face of the Earth, which had been both "soggy" and "muddy," was dried by the unbearable heat, and it was here, on this sacred mountain, that they built the first citadel.[57]

These are the basic elements of the Quiché creation myth. As to the direction of the Seven Caves, this is made quite clear. In book four of the Popol Vuh we read, "Their hearts [i.e., those of the first four men] did not yet harbor ill will towards the gods who had been taken up and carried away when they all came from Tulan Zuyua, there in the east, and who were now in the forest."[58]

Further on in the text the descendants of the first ancestors of the Quiché decide to go in search of Tulan-Zuyua, with the words, "We are going to the east, where our fathers came from."[59] Later, those who embark on this long journey tell us, "'We're not dying. We're coming back,' they said when they went, yet it was these same three who passed over the sea."[60]

So in the knowledge that the Mexica also located the Seven Caves overseas, there can be little doubt that we are dealing with one place of emergence for the two quite separate nations. Obviously, this is not the conclusion of Quiché scholars who associate Tulan-Zuyua with the ruined city of Utatlán, west of the modern town of Santa Cruz del Quiché.[61]

THE ANNALS OF THE CAKCHIQUELS

Despite the conservative attitudes of these scholars, a belief that the Seven Caves were located on a landmass beyond the sea is also present in the creation myths of the Cakchiquel, a Guatemalan mountain tribe related to the Quiché-Maya. The Popol Vuh states that the Cakchiquel are one of the tribes that came forth from the original ancestors who departed in darkness from Tulan-Zuyua following the confusion of tongues in the Seven Caves.[62] *The Annals of the Cakchiquels* speak of their departure from the same ancient homeland, which was known to the tribe as either "Pa-Tulán, Pa-Civán"[63] or Civán-Tulán: "We came to the shore of the sea. There were gathered warriors of *the Seven Cities*, and many perished before our eyes. 'How shall we cross the sea?' they said. 'Who will help us?' There was a forest there of red-trunked trees [pines]. We made some poles and, pushing off with them, went out to the open sea, into the boundless waters."[64] (current author's emphasis)

Here it is stated that the "warriors" must "cross the sea" and enter "the boundless waters." Elsewhere in the same text it states that the Cakchiquel came originally "from the other side of the sea to the place called Tulán,"[65] not to be confused with the otherworldly location of the same name. Furthermore, we learn from another sixteenth-century Cakchiquel text known as *Title of the Lords of Totonicapán* that, along with the rest of the seven tribes and thirteen clans, the tribe's first ancestors departed "from the other part of the sea, from the East."[66] So there is no mistake as to where this homeland lay, the text also states, "When they arrived at the edge of the sea, Balam-Qitzé [the first elected leader in both Cakchiquel and Quiché tradition] touched it with his staff and at once a path opened, which then [after they had reached the other side] closed up again."[67] Since it also says that Balam-Qitzé achieved this Moses-like feat because the Cakchiquel were "sons of Abraham and Jacob," I feel it is safe to assume that the text's construction has been corrupted by Christian influences. Despite this, the Cakchiquel quite obviously believed, similar to all other Mesoamerican tribes, that their ancestral homeland lay across "the boundless waters" to the east.

More significantly, the Cakchiquel believed that Civán-Tulán was the ancient homeland of the tribe's own Feathered Serpent, whose name was Nacxit.* Before their departure, this great "Lord" is said to have given Balam Qitzé a "gift" known as the Giron-Gagal,[68] a name denoting a powerful stone kept wrapped in a bundle. This sacred item, prob-

---

*Nacxit is an abbreviation of the name Topiltzin Acxit Quetzalcoatl, which is mentioned in both Quiché and Cakchiquel documents. He is also mentioned in the *Chilam Balam of Chumayel* texts under the name Nacxit-Xuchit (Recinos and Goetz, *Annals of the Cakchiquels,* 64, 64 fn, and 84 fn).

ably fashioned from either obsidian or rock crystal,* is said to have been used during incantations in order to instill fear in rival tribes.[69]

In addition to learning that the Cakchiquel's ancient homeland lay "on the other side of the sea,"[70] we also find that there appears to have been some kind of urgency to their departure, almost as if they were being forced to leave in haste. What is more, like the account preserved in the Quiché's Popol Vuh, the Cakchiquel's departure was in total darkness.[71] Did this suggest that some kind of disaster had taken place—one that necessitated a rapid departure from this foreign land?

CROSSING THE CAUSEWAY

So where might we start looking for this island homeland spoken of in so many creation myths of the Mesoamerican peoples (see fig. 16.2 on page 262)? The Popol Vuh tells us that the thirteen tribes crossed "over on some stones, stones piled up in the sand," which were subsequently named "Stone Courses, Sand Banks." We are further told, "Where the waters were divided, they crossed over."[72] As Dennis Tedlock has pointed out, the original Quiché words used in this passage give the impression of a causeway across a body of water.[73] The Cakchiquel likewise spoke of having crossed through the sea, almost as if it had parted before them. Moreover, *The Annals of the Cakchiquels* speaks of the tribes passing "over the rows of sand, when it widened below the sea and on the surface of the sea."[74] Is it possible that these accounts record a migration route that took in a series of small islands, sandbanks, and cays that acted like stepping-stones from the proposed island landmass across to the mainland?

---

*The Giron-Gagal is probably the same artifact as the Chay, or Obsidian Stone, "created by the wondrous Xibalbay" and given to the Cakchiquels (Recinos and Goetz, *Annals of the Cakchiquels,* 9 fn, 45, 45 fn). Rock crystal was used extensively by Carib shamans for cures and by the Maya to fashion votive objects such as goblets and crystal skulls (see Zerries, "Primitive South America," 248, for an account of the Makiritare Carib use of rock crystal).

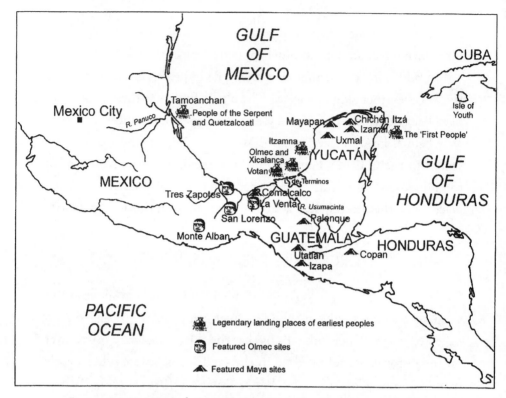

Figure 16.2. Map of Central America showing principal Olmec and Mayan sites as well as the legendary places of landfall attributed to early civilizers such as the Feathered Serpents. These sites generally took the form of offshore islands close to key river estuaries on the Gulf Coast.

As anthropologists Jose M. Cruxent and Irving Rouse commented in respect to the islands, banks, reefs, and cays that today stretch between the Greater Antilles and the Honduran coast, "When the sea level was lower a few thousand years ago, the chain formed a nearly continuous series of stepping-stones leading [from the mainland] to the Greater Antilles."[75] We know also that, up until a matter of four thousand to five thousand years ago, the Mosquito Coast of Honduras and Nicaragua extended out in the direction of Jamaica for a farther 250 kilometers, although this, too, was submerged by the rising sea level. Was the ancestral homeland of the Mesoamerican peoples in the Caribbean?

SEASHELLS AND SERPENTS

There is a major clue to be found on the exterior walls of the Temple of Quetzalcoatl at Teotihuacán. Its facades are adorned with stone heads of the plumed serpent attached to serpentine bodies that undulate in and out of various types of seashell. The problem here is that Teotihuacán is 320 kilometers away from the Gulf Coast, and, as Mesoamerican scholar George C. Vaillant realized, the seashells shown on the temple walls are unique to the Caribbean.[76]

Vaillant could make no sense of this curious mystery, although his observations were noted by American writer Constance Irwin. In her opinion, "It is almost as if the builders who bestowed such infinite care on this temple were trying to convey the message that Quetzalcoatl had come to these parts out of the Caribbean."[77]

The identity of those who constructed the great city and religious center of Teotihuacán in the final centuries before the Christian era remains a mystery. Yet this distinction was claimed by the Totonac peoples of eastern Mexico in their own sacred history.[78] More significantly, these annals speak of their race arriving in the land of Anahuac from Chicomoztoc, the Seven Caves. I was therefore intrigued to discover that in 1971 archaeologists uncovered "several" hewn chambers directly beneath the Pyramid of the Sun at Teotihuacán. They are described as forming a virtual cloverleaf arrangement, which, when seen in concert with a long entrance chamber, gives them the sevenfold symbolism of the cave of emergence so familiar to Mesoamerican tradition.[79]

If the chambers uncovered beneath Teotihuacán's Pyramid of the Sun do represent Chicomoztoc, we can be pretty sure that they are copies of an earlier structure that signified the true place of emergence of those who built this magnificent city. This is confirmed by the fact that the familiar teocallis, or pyramid temples of Mexico, are accepted to be physical representations of world mountains, such as Colhuacán, the Crooked Mountain, beneath which the Seven Caves were thought to have been located.[80]

Since the Seven Caves symbolism appears to be present at Teotihuacán, the clear connection between the Temple of Quetzalcoatl and the Caribbean cannot be ignored. Did the founders of this race come, as the Totonac annals imply, from an island landmass in the Caribbean Sea? Was this where we would now have to continue our search for the ancestral homeland of the Feathered Serpents? This surmise was cannily predicted by American historian Robert B. Stacy-Judd, the author of *Atlantis—Mother of Empires,* published in 1939. Having reviewed all available material on the origins of Quetzalcoatl, Itzamna, Kukulcan, and Gucumatz, he concluded, "As the traditions of the Aztecs frequently refer to their original homeland as 'on a great water' perhaps we may assume, as fact, that Tollan-Tlapallan, the land from which Quetzalcoatl came, was situated in ancient Antillia, of which the present Greater and Lesser Antilles are now all that remains."[81] By "ancient Antillia" he was alluding to the theory proposed by early-twentieth-century Scottish mythologist Lewis Spence that the final portion of a much greater Atlantean continent existed in the region of the West Indies. To this smaller landmass Spence had allotted the name Antillia, after the legendary island of the same name. Yet how might we better pinpoint this original homeland?

BEYOND COZUMEL

The Chilam Balam of Chumayel tells us that the First People, or the People of the Serpent, came out of the east in boats and made landfall on the small island of Cozumel, located off the east coast of the Yucatán. This would have been the most obvious spot for any vessel to have landed following a journey from the east. Indeed, in 1518 the expedition led by Juan de Grijalva left the Cuban port of St. Jago de Cuba and, having been blown slightly off course, finally came upon Cozumel Island. He followed its western coastline before moving on to the Gulf of Campeche, where the Olmec and Xicalanca were considered to have first made landfall. The same thing happened a year later when Cortés set out on his own monumental expedition to conquer Mexico. He, too, visited Cozumel Island before continuing his journey to the Gulf Coast and making landfall at what is today Veracruz.

Where might vessels belonging to the People of the Serpent have come from before they likewise reached Cozumel Island?

Due east of the Yucatán at a distance of no more than 250 kilometers is Cuba, where both Grijalva and Cortés had set out on their own respective voyages to New Spain. Was it possible that the legendary founders of the Mesoamerican tribal dynasties came originally from Cuba?

In the book *Devocionario de Nuestra Señora de Izamal y conquista espiritual de Yucatánci,* published in 1633, Franciscan friar Bernardo de Lizana provides a valuable early history of the Yucatán along with an account of the beliefs and practices of its inhabitants. Based on the testimonies of the local Mayan population, Lizana records that the earliest inhabitants of the peninsula had arrived from Cuba, where they had settled after leaving Haiti.[82] Other Spanish authors concluded from stories related to them by the Nahua that Chicomoztoc could be found either in Florida or on the island of Cuba.[83]

Clearly, there appeared to be differences of opinion among the early Spanish commentators on the subject. Had the People of the Serpent come from Cuba, Haiti, Florida, or some other location altogether?

One possible way of rectifying the situation was to find the Seven Caves. There had to be an outside possibility that, if such a place once existed, it might have continued to be revered even after the ancestors of the Mesoamerican ruling dynasties had departed their homeland. Was there any sacred place or archaeological site that matched the description of the Seven Caves anywhere in Florida, the Bahamas, or the Caribbean?

Just one site fits the description perfectly, and this is Cueva #1 (Cave no. 1), found among a group of "seven caves"[84] at Punta del Este on the Isle of Youth, which lies some one hundred kilometers south of the Cuban mainland.

The caves in question were discovered by accident in 1910 after a French vessel was wrecked in the vicinity of the island.[85] A surviving sailor named Freeman P. Lane found himself on the shores of Punta del Este and, upon entering the nearby swampland, quite literally stumbled across the complex. Inside he found that the walls and ceiling of the main cave were covered in petroglyphs, described today as "paintings of a celestial and tribal nature."[86]

Could this obscure grotto be the place of emergence spoken of with such reverence in the creation myths of the Mesoamerican peoples? If so, what might it tell us about the origins of the elite group described as "feathered serpents," who brought civilization to the various indigenous tribes, and how might this knowledge relate to the story of Atlantis?

17

THE OLD, OLD RED LAND

The American Indians who came out to greet Christopher Columbus and his crew when the *Santa Maria* approached the northeast coast of Cuba on October 28, 1492, belonged to a culture known today as the Taino. In contrast to the peoples of Mesoamerica they were fairly primitive, with a basic lifestyle comparable to the Neolithic farming communities of Eurasia.

The Taino were, however, accomplished fishermen and regularly journeyed between islands in their dugout canoes. They made decorated pottery, cultivated plants such as maize, cotton, yucca, and tobacco, and lived on a diet of fish, crab, conch, birds, reptiles, and small mammals. Their native religion included the worship of celestial deities and communication with ancestral spirits, which they represented in the form of personal idols, or *zemis,* carved from stone, shell, and clay. The Taino lived for the most part in communal settlements, which would often consist of up to three thousand individuals. Like the great cult centers of Mesoamerica, each village would have its own ball court in which members of the community played a rubber-ball game.[1]

The Taino's earliest ancestors had arrived on Cuba from South America, via a long and arduous migrational course that had taken

in the Lesser Antilles and Puerto Rico. Each step had involved settling on one or more islands before embarking on the next stage of
their ceaseless journey to find the ultimate homeland. Estimates suggest they first left the region surrounding the mouth of the Orinoco
River, in Venezuela, sometime around the time of Christ and arrived on
Hispaniola around 250 CE.[2] They are thought to have made the final
crossing to Cuba circa 450–600 CE. Traces of Taino culture are found
also in the Bahamas, which they reached circa 600–700 CE,[3] although
here the indigenous peoples were known as the Lucayans.

There is very little to connect the Taino with the development of
Mesoamerican civilization. As we saw in chapter 15, when the Spaniards
arrived in the West Indies they found no evidence that the native people built stone structures, even though they unquestionably traveled
as far as the Yucatán. When Bernal Díaz, an early Spanish chronicler,
landed on the Yucatec coast with a group of conquistadors in the sixteenth century, he was met by a young American Indian woman who
spoke to them in a language native to Cuba (it was probably Arawak,
the language of the Taino). Upon being asked where she came from,
the woman related how, two years previously, she and ten others had
been fishing in a canoe off Jamaica when it had been carried out to sea
by strong currents. Finally, they had reached the land of the Maya.[4] If
nothing else, this story demonstrates just how easy it is for a small vessel, such as a canoe, to use prevailing currents to travel from the Greater
Antilles to the coast of Central America.

Despite the easy means of contact between Cuba and the Yucatán it
would seem that the lifestyle, sophistication, and culture of the highly
advanced Maya had no lasting impact on the Taino, who were content
to be little more than fishermen and farmers. Yet the Taino were not
the first inhabitants of Cuba. In the early years of colonial rule, explorers penetrated deep into the country's interior and reported seeing all
manner of strange monuments, as well as grotesque carvings and stone
idols that were utterly alien to Taino culture.

This same sentiment was voiced by the Abbé Brasseur de Bourbourg in 1857 when he wrote, "Modern travellers assure that they have seen sculpted rocks and ruined buildings around Havana indicating the presence of ancient civilized populations on this Island."[5]

Little by little it emerged that Cuba had been occupied by a much earlier, and far more advanced, culture that had left its mark in entirely different ways.

THE BLACK IDOL

A little more than a century ago, Daniel G. Brinton, professor of American archaeology at the University of Pennsylvania, wrote an important paper for the journal *American Anthropologist* titled "The Archaeology of Cuba."[6] He drew on information contained in much earlier articles that describe curious finds made in several parts of the island. Among the strangest of these was the discovery by nineteenth-century Cuban archaeologist Don Miguel Rodriguez-Ferrer of a black marble idol found among the mountains in the eastern province of Santiago. It stood a meter high and was carved into "the upper portion of a human figure, the face bearing a mild expression."[7] Rodriguez-Ferrer subsequently presented the statue to the University of Havana, "where it yet should be."[8]

It goes without saying that this black idol had nothing whatsoever to do with the Taino, who did not use stone in this manner and almost exclusively occupied coastal regions of the island. Furthermore, since marble was not indigenous to Cuba, it meant that the stone used to fashion the idol must have come from elsewhere, plausibly neighboring Hispaniola, where marble is found in the southern part of the island.[9] It is even possible that it came from farther afield, perhaps from the Central American mainland. To this day the origin of the black idol remains a mystery.

Brinton also referred to two localities in the eastern part of Santiago province, one known as Pueblo Viejo, the other being La Gran Tierra de Maya, where Rodriguez-Ferrer had discovered "circles, squares, mounds, and enclosures." These were said to resemble the general character of earthworks in the Mississippi Valley of the United States.[10] The use of the word *Maya* does not necessarily relate to the civilization of this name, for, as RodriguezFerrer made clear to Brinton, it was also a word that featured in the native Arawak language.

More interesting was Rodriguez-Ferrer's suggestion that the earthen monuments in Cuba's Santiago province resembled those found along the Mississippi Valley. The great river of this name rises in streams that empty into Minnesota Lake before flowing south to the Gulf of Mexico. Some of the earthen monuments that litter the valley in various states of preservation are of an extraordinary nature and date to as early as circa 4000–3000 BCE.[11]

Aside from these curious archaeological enigmas, Brinton spoke also of the discovery of huge anthropomorphic forms carved on rock faces in the river valleys of central Cuba, as well as "monolithic statues" that seemed to have had no obvious connection with the Taino.[12]

THE JADE CELT

Then there is the remarkable jade axe, or celt, found within a cave located in the extreme eastern limits of the island.[13] At nineteen centimeters in length, it is perfectly symmetrical, highly polished, and beautifully finished. Brinton said that at the time of its discovery it was acknowledged to be "the finest object of its kind from America the members [of the Berlin Anthropological Society] had seen."[14] The cave in question was one of a number that overlooked the sea and were found to be "particularly rich in bones, pottery, and stone implements."[15]

Jade is not indigenous to the Caribbean. It was, however, used extensively by Mesoamerican cultures from the time of the Olmec civilization through to the time of the Conquest. The exact age of the celt found in Cuba remains unknown, although similar examples made of blue-green jade have been found in Costa Rica.[16] The fashioning of jade artifacts was also a specialty among the artisans of Vera Cruz and

Tabasco States on the Gulf Coast of Mexico, linked not only with the Olmec and Xicalanca but also with traditions concerning the departure of Quetzalcoatl to Tlapallan.

HISTORY OF THE CIBONEY

Clearly there had been a much earlier culture present on Cuba—one that sculpted in stone, built earthen monuments, possessed a more sophisticated religion, and penetrated deep into the country's interior. So who were these people?

The first clue appears to be the enormous number of natural caves found in many parts of Cuba, most of which contain clear evidence of both domestic and ritual usage from the prehistoric age onward. Cut out of limestone, or "reef rock," by the action of water tens of thousands of years ago, these caverns seem to have held an enormous importance for a pre-Taino culture known as the Ciboney.

The history of the Ciboney is not easy to understand, although they are considered to fall into two quite separate cultures defined by the time frames in which they thrived on the island.

One is the Cayo Redondo, who inhabited Cuba from around 200 CE until the time of the Conquest. Archaeologists classify them as Mesoamerican Indians, in that their culture is considered to have reached a stage of development comparable with the Mesolithic peoples of Eurasia who thrived between circa 9600 and 4500 BCE. The Cayo Redondo are seen as a transitional phase between the Neolithic-style farming communities of the Taino and the more primitive Paleo-American Indians who occupied Cuba between circa 5000 BCE and 200 CE.[17]

The other Cuban culture is known as the Guayabo Blanco. These Paleo-American Indians are thought to have occupied caves and temporary settlement sites. They are considered to have reached a stage of development comparable to that of the Upper Paleolithic hunter-gatherers who inhabited Eurasia circa 40,000–9600 BCE (although some anthropologists categorize them as Mesoamerican Indians). The Guayabo Blanco also fashioned tools and artifacts of flint, bone, and shell. Yet, as we shall see, some of the Guayabo Blanco, or at least those who would seem to have lived alongside them, developed a high culture with a level of sophistication beyond that attributed to the Cuban Paleo-American Indians.

Interestingly enough, the Guayabo Blanco were not the earliest inhabitants of Cuba. Recently, tantalizing evidence has come to light of an even earlier Paleo-American Indian culture thought to have been present on the island as early as 6000 BCE.[18] Archaeologists have labeled them the Levisa after a rock shelter close to the mouth of the Río Levisa in Cuba's Holguín province.[19] What relationship they might have to later cultures is at present unknown. It is likely, however, that the Levisa were absorbed into the Guayabo Blanco culture sometime after the latter's arrival circa 5000 BCE.

MEGALITHIC MONUMENTS

Even though anthropologists and archaeologists have assigned neat appellations and timescales to the earliest peoples of Cuba, something is clearly amiss. As previously noted, in the nineteenth century Rodriguez-Ferrer came across a series of "circles, squares, mounds, and enclosures" in Cuba's Santiago province, located due south of Holguín province. While at a four-thousand-year-old occupational site linked with a cave named Cueva Funche at Guanahacabibes in Cuba's western province of Pinar del Río, archaeologists in 1966 uncovered a large earthen structure of surprising sophistication.[20] If these monuments are not the work of Cuba's Taino population, or the Mesoamerican Indians or Paleo-American Indians that preceded them, then they must be the product of a more sophisticated mound-building culture that once existed on the island.

This was a staggering realization, and one that has made archaeologists reconsider earlier documented accounts of earthworks found in other parts of the island. Were these monuments constructed by this same faceless culture that must have lived alongside the Paleo-American Indians of Cuba some four thousand years ago? Might these peoples also have been responsible for the carving of the black marble idol, the jade celt, and the monolithic statues discovered on the island by early explorers and archaeologists? So who exactly were the Cuban mound builders?

PREVIOUSLY ESTABLISHED CULTURE

During their research to find the original homeland of the prehistoric peoples of Hispaniola, archaeologists José M. Cruxent and Irving Rouse realized something of immense importance concerning the origins of Cuba's earliest inhabitants. In their opinion a direct comparison could be made between artifacts found at Guayabo Blanco occupation sites on the island and a mound-building American Indian culture that thrived near the headwaters of the St. Johns River in Florida, circa 2000 BCE.[21] At a number of sites in the St. Johns River area, one of the principal scraping tools found in abundance was the shell gouge, made by breaking off a triangular section from the outer part of a conch whorl and then grinding one edge of it.[22] They pointed out that very similar shell tools are found in abundance at sites attributed to Cuba's Guayabo Blanco culture. This led Cruxent and Rouse to conclude, "Cuba's early Paleo-Amerindian complex was derived from Florida, although we know too little about the pre-pottery cultures of Florida to state this as a certainty."[23] So were the Guayabo Blanco Cuba's mound builders?

Cruxent and Rouse were not the only ones to realize the apparent relationship between the Guayabo Blanco and the archaic American Indians of the mainland. Cuban archaeologists Ramón Dacal Moure and Manuel Rivero de la Calle, in their 1986 book *Arqueologia aborigen de Cuba* (Aboriginal Archaeology of Cuba), drew comparisons between the burial customs of the Mississippi mound builders and the funerary mounds of Cuba. This followed a detailed study of earthworks located in Camaguey and Ciénaga da Zapata.[24] More intriguingly, they pointed out that the configuration and design of the earthen structures found on the island suggested that they were the handiwork of "a previously established culture."[25] Even more controversial was Moure and de la Calle's conclusion that burial customs associated with Cuba's mounds demonstrated the presence on the island of a sophisticated Neolithic culture that far exceeded the state of development of its Mesoamerican Indian and Paleo-American Indian inhabitants.[26]

THE CAVES OF CUBA

Further evidence of the presence on Cuba of a prehistoric culture of immense sophistication is the remarkable cave art and, indeed, the caves themselves. These have been found to contain a rich variety of unique petroglyphs (i.e., abstract forms) and pictographs (animal and human forms) that adorn their walls and ceilings in either ochre-red or charcoal-black.

Dating the cave art is dependent on the recognition of a certain style. For instance, all the stickmen, animals, and fish found drawn on the walls in some caves are considered to be fairly recent and were probably executed by Taino artists prior to the time of the Conquest. There are even depictions of what appear to be black-skinned individuals, which are thought to have been painted by African slaves who took refuge in the caves after escaping from either the sugar plantations or mines founded by Spanish colonists.

More intriguing are the abstract geometric designs that adorn the walls and ceilings of some of the caves. These include concentric rings, spirals, triangles, boxes, and diamonds. This style is recognized as being much older and is usually accredited to the Guayabo Blanco people. Where they are filled with geometric forms, it is clear that these caves were the domain, almost exclusively, of the earliest inhabitants of the island. Moreover, where geometric designs are found, circular skylights are often cut into the cave ceiling, allowing shafts of sunlight to penetrate the dusty interiors. Cuban archaeologists have recognized the magico-religious significance of these deliberately fashioned light holes and relate them directly to the presence of the petroglyphs, which become illuminated on certain dates in the solar calendar.[27]

In many ways the Cuban cave skylights resemble the holes cut into underground rooms by the Olmec civilization. These so-called zenith tubes permitted rays of sunlight to penetrate the darkened interior at midday on the vernal and autumnal equinoxes. One example can be found among the mountaintop ruins of Monte Alban, an Olmec site in the Valley of Oaxaca.[28] The idea of the emergence of human life from caves was an important religious concept to the Olmec.[29] If, as Edward H. Thompson has suggested, the Olmec priest-kings were descended from the People of the Serpent, it is possible that their magico-religious understanding of sunbeams penetrating the darkness of caves was inherited from their island ancestors on Cuba.

ART OF THE ANCIENTS

More of a mystery is the exact age of the earliest prehistoric cave art on Cuba. Since much of it is accredited to the Guayabo Blanco culture, it could be several thousand years old. There seems to be no evidence that it might date any earlier than this period. That said, several caves on Mona, a small island that lies in the Mona Passage between Puerto Rico and Hispaniola, were found to contain a whole series of petroglyphs and pictographs similar to those on Cuba. These painted caverns extend for hundreds of meters underground and include a variety of different artistic themes, including "finger paintings" that represent "human figures, and heads, serpents, geometrical figures, and undulating lines," all of which are "depicted with great subtlety and elegance."[30]

Most scholars accept that these paintings belong to an unknown culture that preceded the arrival of the Taino circa 250 CE and were remembered by them as the Arcaicos, the "ancients."[31] They are thought to have come originally from Cuba and thus are most probably linked to the Guayabo Blanco. If this is true, the cave art on Mona probably dates back to somewhere between circa 5000 BCE and 250 CE. Infinitely more puzzling are the conclusions made in respect to the cave art on Mona by Professor Pedro Santana Vargas of the Humacao Regional College at the University of Puerto Rico. Rather surprisingly, he is of the opinion that the designs, "the first found outside Europe," could be as much as thirty thousand years old![32] Assuming that the printed date should not read three thousand instead of thirty thousand, I can only assume that Vargas's assessment of the petroglyphs is based on their apparent similarity to the well-known Upper Paleolithic cave art found in France and Spain, some of which may well be thirty thousand years old.

Since no cultural artifacts have been discovered in the Caribbean that might confirm the presence of early man in the Greater Antilles before circa 6000 BCE, it is perhaps safer to conclude that its earliest cave art dates to between circa 5000 BCE and 250 CE.

IN SEARCH OF THE RED LAND

All the evidence presented by the mythological traditions of the early cultures of Mesoamerica points toward the islands of the Greater Antilles being the original homeland of their earliest ancestors and wisdom-bringers, described repeatedly as "serpents" or "feathered serpents." What I needed, however, was confirmation of this hypothesis from Cuba itself. This could come only from an examination of the apparent relationship between Cuba's geology, geography, and prehistory and mythical locations such as Aztlan, Tulan, and Tlapallan. In their mythical form, all are said to have been landmasses that were thought to have been located in the sea. More curiously, Tlapallan, as we know, means the "red land," a name that may have been connected with the island's overall appearance.

Some scholars might argue that, in Mesoamerican tradition, the color red had a symbolic value alone. We know, for instance, that in the religion of the Maya, red was connected with the east.[33] In addition to this directional color coding, the Maya believed that a spirit named Ah Musen Cab, "the Secret Red of the Earth," governed the "eastern section of the subterranean world."[34] For "subterranean world" substitute either the otherworld or simply the primordial world, strengthening the view that a sacred land beyond the sea was associated with the color red.

Can we look toward Cuba for an explanation to this mystery?

If we make an examination of the three principal islands of the Greater Antilles, the first point we realize is that Cuba's geology is unique. Whereas Hispaniola and Puerto Rico are almost entirely rugged and mountainous, Cuba is noted for its vast plains, which are often at a height just above sea level. Moreover, climatic weathering, coupled with the underlying geology of the island, has produced a lateritic or oxidized soil that is quite literally blood-red in color. It is found in many parts of the island but is most visible on the rich and fertile plains that stretch westward between Havana and the western tip of the island, on which grows the tobacco for Havana's famous cigars. Cuba also once produced more sugarcane than any other country.[35] With the help of Cuba's rich soil, its cane yields a higher content of sugar than anywhere else other than Mexico.[36]

It must be pointed out that iron-enriched soil of the type found on Cuba is not exclusive to the island. It can also be found in other parts of the Antilles, although the nature of their geology means that it appears only sporadically and in very isolated patches. Of all the islands only Cuba is well known for its distinctive red earth.[37] It is therefore conceivable that a memory of Cuba's fertile plain could have reached Mesoamerica, making it an obvious candidate for the title *huehue tlapallan,* the "old, old red land."

If Cuba *was* Tlapallan, I find it strangely ironic that Cortés, seen by Montezuma as a virtual incarnation of Quetzalcoatl, should have departed on his quest to conquer Mexico from the Feathered Serpent's ancient homeland. It might even be suggested that Cortés unconsciously acted out an archetypal role set in motion by a highly superstitious nation—one that became convinced its world was about to be destroyed by an avenging angel named Quetzalcoatl. Such is the potency of self-fulfilling prophecies.

THE ISLE OF CRANES

Moving from Tlapallan to Aztlan, we find certain descriptive features that seem to make sense of Cuba's identification as the Mexica's ancestral homeland. As we saw in chapter 16, scholars of Mesoamerican history have interpreted the name Aztlan as meaning "Place of Reeds" or "Place of Herons." However, the heron feathers glyph used to denote the main component of the word Aztlan can relate also to the crane, thus implying an additional translation of the "Place of Cranes." In this knowledge, I find it strangely coincidental that, although various species of sandhill cranes inhabit North America, only one subspecies is found in the Greater Antilles, and this is the critically endangered Cuban sandhill crane (*Grus canadensis nesiotes*).[38] There are now thought to be just a few hundred birds left on the island, with most of these being found in the pine-palmetto savannas and swamps on the Isle of Youth.[39]

Strangely enough, the sighting of Cuban sandhill cranes on the Isle of Youth by Columbus's crewmen in May 1494 may have led to the belief that Christian holy men inhabited the island. The story goes that, having anchored off the isle's coast, Columbus sent in a group of crossbowmen to hunt game in the pine forests.[40] Upon their return they declared that their party had encountered "light-complexioned natives wearing white tunics which reached to their knees."[41] For some bizarre reason, Columbus concluded that they were Christians of "Ethiopia."[42]

A search party was sent to investigate, although all they found were cranes "twice the size of those of Europe."[43] The discovery led the crewmen to presume that the crossbowmen had mistaken these huge birds for pious holy men![44] Whether correct or not, the incident would seem to have had a profound effect on Columbus, for he went on to christen the island La Evangelista (The Evangelist).*

In the light of this information, is it possible that the presence on the Isle of Youth of sandhill cranes remained strong in the racial memory of the ancestors of the Mexica, or Aztecs, following their proposed migration to the mainland? The fact that these cranes were once common on the island singles it out for special attention and begins to make sense of why Chicomoztoc, the Seven Caves, might indeed have been located there.

The Spanish historian Diego Durán related the story of how Montezuma I attempted to establish the whereabouts of Chicomoztoc. To this end he consulted an aging historian named Cuauhcoatl who spoke of the great speaker's ancestors as having come from Aztlan. Here was to be found "a great hill in the midst of the waters, and it is called Colhuacán because its summit is twisted. . . . In this hill were caves or grottoes [i.e., Chicomoztoc] where our fathers and grandfathers lived for many years. . . . However, after they abandoned that delightful place and came to the mainland, everything turned against them."[45]

It is difficult to conceive of Colhuacán as "a great hill in the midst of the waters" unless we identify it as an offshore island close to Aztlan. Can this account be describing the Isle of Youth, which does indeed contain great hills, beyond which, as we shall see, is the most likely candidate for the site of Chicomoztoc, the Seven Caves?

ISLE OF PINES

Turning to the creation account of the Cakchiquel, we read that on the departure from the original homeland, the warriors of the "Seven Cities"

---

*It must be pointed out that due to a confusing entry in Columbus's diary for this period it is unclear whether his vessel had laid anchor off the Isle of Youth or in the Bay of Batabanó, off mainland Cuba, when this incident occurred. However, the pine forests, cranes, and local traditions that were mentioned all suggest that this incident did indeed occur on the Isle of Youth (Fallon, *Guide to Cuba,* 223).

debated on how they might cross the "boundless waters" of "the open sea."[46] To this end they entered "a forest there of red-trunked trees" and from these were made "some poles" which they used to push out their vessels, presumably rafts, into deeper waters.[47] The "red-trunked trees" would seem to have been pines.

Today two species of pines are known on the Isle of Youth, *Pinus caribaea* and *Pinus tropicales*. More important, there are only two areas of Cuba where pines proliferate—Pinar del Río in the west of the country and on the Isle of Youth, which used to be known as the Isle of Pines. Pines do exist on some of the Bahamian islands, such as Andros, the largest of the group, as well as on Hispaniola. However, their preponderance on the Isle of Youth is strangely significant and adds further support to the idea that this island and its caves played a special role in the creation myths of the Mesoamerican peoples.

These might all seem like slender pieces of evidence in favor of Cuba's role as the mythical homeland of both the Feathered Serpents and the ruling dynasties of Mesoamerica. Yet when seen in the context of proposed migrations from the Greater Antilles in prehistoric times, they take on a greater role as we recall that the various tribes that emerged from the Seven Caves are supposed to have built the Seven Cities. Although this cannot have referred to cities of mortar and stone, the fact that the Cakchiquel promoted this view of their creation account implies that they themselves believed in the existence of actual cities built by their earliest ancestors.

That Portuguese maritime tradition preserved the memory of an Atlantic island, called Antilia, on which stood the Seven Cities is too much of a coincidence. In chapter 14 we traced back this age-old tradition through the Moors to the Carthaginians and the Iberic-Phoenicians. We have also seen how the etymological root of Antilia appears to be identical with that of Atlantis, and that both names derive from the Semitic word root *atl,* and, quite possibly, the Punic proper name ATLA.

Cuba emerges as the most likely identity not only of Antilia, but also of one of the surviving remnants, along with Hispaniola and Puerto Rico, of Plato's Atlantean empire. Since it also seems likely that Cuba was the island homeland of the Mesoamerican races on which the Seven Caves or Seven Cities are said to have been located, I feel there has to be a direct relationship between these seemingly quite separate traditions.

Mesoamerican creation myths involving the Seven Caves may have existed as early as the second or first millennium BCE and, if these dates are correct, they could well have been made known to early Atlantic voyagers visiting Caribbean islands such as Cuba. They in turn could have carried these abstract mythological ideas back to Spain and North Africa, where they gestated for many hundreds of years before emerging as the legend of the Sete Cidades. As the Seven Cities were assumed to be located on the island of Antilia, and Atlantis possessed a city divided into seven divisions, there had to be a reason why these legendary place names were so similar to *atlan,* the root behind names such as Tollan and Tulan. This word, as the Abbé Brasseur de Bourbourg was at pains to point out, translates as "on the border or in the midst of water," a perfect appellation for an island landmass located in the open sea.[48]

The sheer fact that these similar-sounding names all seem to relate to the same island (i.e., Cuba) does suggest some kind of shared phonetic usage, most obviously through the Semitic root *atl.* If this surmise should prove correct, it could imply that only when these names entered separate languages did they take on individual spellings and meanings.

In advance of traveling to Cuba with the express purpose of visiting the Isle of Youth to examine the Punte del Este cave site, I wanted to explore one other possibility—that certain elements of Plato's Atlantis account referred specifically to the country. However, I knew that, in this respect, I had serious competition, for shortly before my intended visit to the island I became aware that a world-renowned scientist was making similar claims in respect to the neighboring island of Hispaniola. I knew very well that Hispaniola was important to the

Atlantis story and had every right to stake its claim as the shining jewel of Plato's island empire. So, as I readied myself to jet off to the Caribbean, it became clear that I was about to enter an important academic battle, the consequences of which would be recognition of either Cuba or Hispaniola as the true site of lost Atlantis.

18

HISPANIOLA
VERSUS CUBA

In an important paper delivered to members of the Royal Historical Society in June 1885, American historian Hyde Clarke proposed that the Atlantean empire's "head seat," or island, was Hispaniola.[1] At the moment he made this curious statement, he could not have been aware of its true import. We can now be pretty sure that the three islands of "immense extent" spoken of by the Roman geographical writer named Marcellus as surviving portions of Plato's Atlantis are in fact the three principal members of the Greater Antilles—Cuba, Puerto Rico, and Hispaniola. Moreover, we can also be pretty sure that the inhabitants of the central island, sacred to Poseidon and identified by Geoffrey Ashe as Hispaniola, preserved a memory of the disaster and flood that had led to the submergence of the Atlantean landmass.

From these points alone I could understand why the smart money was already on Hispaniola being the true site of lost Atlantis. This placed Cuba somewhat at a disadvantage, even before my pro-Hispaniola contestant has been introduced. Yet I still felt confident that I could make a convincing case in favor of Cuba being Atlantis. The American geographer William H. Babcock had proposed that Cuba was Antilia. Since Antilia appeared to be a medieval form of Atlantis and both derived their names from the same Semitic word root, I felt Cuba, and not Hispaniola, was being singled out as the island of special importance.

I knew, too, that Antilia was the Island of the Seven Cities and that this tradition echoed Mesoamerican legends regarding a mythical homeland called Chicomoztoc, within which were the mythical Seven Caves. Out of these had come the original seven tribes that had gone on to found the "seven cities" mentioned in Cakchiquel tradition. Chicomoztoc with its fabled Seven Caves I had also located on Cuba's Isle of Youth. Furthermore, the Atlantean island was divided into seven circles according to the third-century Platonist Amelius. This also echoed the sevenfold symbolism expressed in Mesoamerican creation myths.

Having already studied the geology, geography, climate, history, and topography of the Greater Antilles, I felt in a strong position to counter any points put to me in favor of Hispaniola. Despite this confidence, there were also natural feelings of hesitation. In some ways it seemed like a dangerous exercise attempting to make direct comparisons between Plato's description of his Atlantic island, as outlined in the *Critias,* and actual Caribbean islands. Many others had already tried and failed to win the crown of Atlantis because they wrongly considered as fact much of Plato's very visual description of his Atlantean city. There was always a chance that either I or, indeed, my opposite number would deliver statements that had no geographical or historical validity, and so would only help to throw the whole debate into confusion.

BACKGROUND FORM

My opponent was a formidable one. Indeed, he is a leading authority in his chosen field of study. His name is Emilio Spedicato. As the professor of operations research, a mathematical discipline, at the University of Bergamo in Italy, he lectures on theoretical physics in some of the greatest universities of the world. Spedicato is most celebrated for his pioneering work into the mechanics, historical framework, and effects of impacts with so-called Apollo, or Earth-crossing, objects, most usually asteroids.

For his insights into this compelling subject, Spedicato has gained the admiration and respect of other pioneers in this field. They include Victor Clube and Bill Napier, as well as great thinkers such as transatlantic seafarer and author Thor Heyerdahl. Above and beyond his work on Apollo objects, Spedicato has proposed astounding new theories regarding the origins of stellar and planetary systems, which are also now challenging mainstream science.

That so renowned an authority should come forward to advance the theory that Hispaniola, one of the islands of the Greater Antilles, was Plato's Atlantis is in itself quite extraordinary. As we know, the usual academic line on Atlantis is that it is a memory of the Aegean island of Thera, or indeed Crete, devastated by a volcanic eruption some 3,450 years ago. If the Italian professor is being proved correct with respect to his scientific theories on Apollo impacts, his proposal that Hispaniola was Atlantis cannot have been made lightly.

I first became acquainted with Spedicato when he contacted me after having read my earlier work *From the Ashes of Angels*. He applauded me on my own controversial theories and discoveries in respect to the genesis of civilization, for which I felt most gratified. It was shortly after this time that a copy of his all-important paper on Apollo objects and the Atlantis theory arrived by post from Italy. This was despite the fact that he had no idea I considered Cuba to be the principal island of the Atlantean empire. Titled "Apollo Objects, Atlantis, and Other Tales: A Catastrophical Scenario for Discontinuities in Human History," Spedicato's lengthy essay was first published in 1985, although it has since been revised and expanded on more than one occasion.[2]

THE CASE FOR HISPANIOLA

This essay, then, would be Spedicato's main line of attack as he attempted to justify Hispaniola's role as the crown jewel of Atlantis. Like me, the Italian professor had fully realized that Plato's Atlantis dialogues related not to a single landmass the size of Libya and Asia combined, but to the extent of the proposed island empire. He had also concluded that the geographical account of the Atlantic island given in the *Critias* appeared to describe an actual location that could not have been submerged simply through earthquakes and floods. In other words, it still existed today. More important, he realized that Plato had left a trail of clues suggesting that his Atlantic island stood in front of another continent that lay across the ocean and that it had been accessible in the past to voyagers from his own world. With all this in mind Spedicato had focused his attentions on the islands of the Greater Antilles and had concluded, finally, that Hispaniola matched Plato's description of Atlantis. His reasoning can be summarized as follows:

1. The coasts of Atlantis are said to have been particularly precipitous, a description that applies very well to Hispaniola's entire coastline. Moreover, because there have been no major changes to the shoreline since the termination of the last Ice Age, geologists can safely say that this is how the island would have looked in the time frame proposed by Plato for the destruction of Atlantis.[3]

2. Plato states that the Atlantean city was built in a central position on a large rectangular plain. On Hispaniola a roughly rectangular-shaped plain exists in the southeastern corner of the island. Like the irrigated plain described in the *Critias,* it is shielded to the north by a range of hills.[4]

3. One possible candidate for the location of the Atlantean city would be the lowland region of Hispaniola known as the Plaine de Cul-des-Saca. It is bordered north and south by mountains. Moreover, it possesses several lakes, including Lake Enriquillo, the surface of which is currently below sea level. There is every reason to suggest that the lake contains coralline structures, today covered by sediment, which might well help to explain the red, white, and black stone said by Plato to have been used to construct the city.[5]

4. Plato asserts that the size of the Atlantean plain is six hundred by four hundred kilometers. This comes close to matching the overall size of Hispaniola, which is oriented east–west and measures approximately 650 by three hundred kilometers.[6]

5. The Taino of Hispaniola referred to the island as Quisqueya, the "Mother of Lands." Did this denote its importance as a mythical homeland to the peoples of the Caribbean archipelago during prehistoric times?[7]

6. If Hispaniola is Atlantis, then the other islands said by Plato to have formed the Atlantean empire would constitute the principal islands of the Greater Antilles, namely Cuba and Puerto Rico.[8]

These then were Emilio Spedicato's points in favor of Hispaniola being the principal island of Plato's Atlantean empire. Even though he seemed unaware of the earlier findings of Hyde Clarke or Geoffrey Ashe, he had produced some serious ideas that now challenged Cuba's claim to the same title. Yet having read and absorbed the various statements made by Spedicato, I felt in a commanding position to counter his proposals.

The date for the two-way debate was set for May 21, 1998, with the venue being the Department of Theoretical Physics at Cambridge University. Spedicato was to lecture there during the early afternoon and afterward we had agreed to meet. The day came, and after some pleasant moments passed in cordial greetings we settled down for our scholarly discussion in a small, quiet canteen on the ground floor. In preparation, I placed down a pocket cassette recorder on the low table before us in order to record the proceedings.

Before we had even started the debate, I became aware that the whole episode would have an unexpected witness. As I turned my head, I saw Professor Stephen Hawking, arguably one of the most outstanding cosmologists of our time, being guided in his wheelchair by a helper to a table just a few paces away from where we sat in the otherwise empty canteen. Here he would remain for the larger part of our lively exchange.

Now that I was ready to respond suitably to each of Spedicato's points, we got on with the matter at hand.

MOUNTAINS AND PLAINS

First, I fully appreciated that Hispaniola's coastline is particularly precipitous in a manner described by Plato in the *Critias*. However, Plato alludes to this rugged coastline only beyond the mountain range that embraced the Atlantean plain on its northern, western, and eastern sides. To the south, where Spedicato also accepted that the Atlantean plain and city were situated, the coastline must have been either at or very close to sea level. We are told, for example, that a roofed canal was built from the sea through to Atlantis's central islet. This waterway was in length fifty furlongs (ten kilometers), in breadth three hundred feet (91.5 meters) and in depth one hundred feet (thirty meters). As explained in chapter 4, from the description given by Plato the canal would seem to have entered the island from the south, showing that there could not have been any mountains or precipitous cliffs between the southern shoreline and the city. So if we assume that the thirty-meter-deep canal was half filled with water, it would mean that the great plain could not have been any more than fifteen meters above sea level. This does not fit the description of Hispaniola's southern coastline. Moreover, since we know that the sea level has risen at least sixty meters since the end of the glacial age, circa 9600 BCE, it means that the Atlantean plain must now be deep underwater.*

---

*This projection is based on the view that between circa 14,000 BCE and circa 2000 BCE the sea level rose by as much as 105 meters. Unfortunately, very few marine geologists agree on the rate or amount the sea level rose following the termination of the last Ice Age (Hine and Steinmetz, "Cay Sal Bank, Bahamas," 157, regarding rises in the Bahamas and Caribbean). More important, there is good reason to suggest that the rate of rise was infinitely greater somewhere between circa 10,200 and 9000 BCE (Emiliani, "Paleoclimatological Analysis," 1083–88).

Cuba, on the other hand, is much better suited to Plato's description of the island's fertile plain as outlined in the *Critias*. If we examine its coastline we find that, except for the southwest, it, too, can be described as "precipitous." Furthermore, if we focus on western Cuba we can see that its northern limits are dominated by the Cord de Guaniguanico mountain range. This completely shields the rich and fertile plain that stretches from Havana westward to Pinar del Río, a distance of around 540 kilometers. More significantly, until some eight thousand to ten thousand years ago, the plain extended south to the Isle of Youth, giving it an estimated breadth of 160 kilometers. What is more, if Plato's Atlantis account contains a memory of a real fertile plain on one of the islands of the Greater Antilles, we must assume that he was alluding to an island renowned for its plains. If so, then the only island that makes complete sense is Cuba. Hispaniola cannot be described in a similar manner.

Spedicato's proposal that the Atlantean city might have been located on Hispaniola's Lake Enriquillo is an interesting theory. Yet Plato does not say the city was built on a lake, only that constructed waterways encircled its central islet where once had been "a mountain which was nowhere of any great altitude."[9] Although I accept that the idea of the Atlantean city being located on an island within a lake is appealing, it is not to be found in Plato's narrative.

As to the suggestion that coralline structures currently buried beneath Lake Enriquillo's sediment might account for the supposed presence of red, white, and black building blocks, said by Plato to have been used to construct the Atlantean city, this must remain an unsubstantiated theory. What is more, the hope of finding coralline structures in three different colors seems improbable.

MOTHER OF LANDS

I was initially intrigued to learn that the Taino had referred to the island of Bohio, their name for Hispaniola, as Quisqueya, meaning the "mother of lands" or the "mother of islands." This did indeed suggest that the island held some special significance in the minds of its inhabitants. We must not forget, however, that the Taino arrived on Hispaniola only circa 250 CE, so their understanding of its sacredness probably relates not to its connection with Atlantis but to the fact that it was the first major island they reached after departing Venezuela.

In 1497 Christopher Columbus dispatched the Jeronymite Friar Ramón Pané to make a record of the religious beliefs of the Taino who inhabited the Macorís territory of north-central Hispaniola.[10] He discovered that the villagers spoke of a sacred mountain called Cauta that lay in a region of the island known to them as Caonao.[11] Here were two caves, one named Cacibajagua, "Cave of the Jaguar," and the other Amayaúna, "Without Importance."[12] From the former emerged "most of the people who inhabit the island,"[13] while from the latter came all other races.[14]

Creation myths of this order are not unusual in any part of the world. The idea of humanity's emergence from caves in sacred mountains is a universal one, reflecting the rebirth of life from the swollen womb of the Earth. Yet mythological concepts such as this always become localized to the landscape into which a tribe or culture emerges. This means that the Taino could only have adopted a local mountain as the place of emergence of its people after their arrival in Hispaniola. Yet once achieved, this association would have satisfied the spiritual needs of the various communities. Upon being asked, "Where do we come from?" the storyteller could justifiably allude to a distant mountain and say that their first ancestors emerged from there. As much as this might be true, it does not preclude the possibility that the Taino carried the basic theme behind this myth from their own original homeland, which would appear to have been the region at the mouth of the Orinoco River.

Unfortunately, no similar survey of the religious beliefs of the native Cuban cultures was carried out before Diego Velasquez was given free rein to decimate the local population in 1511. So even though Cuba is the largest island of the Greater Antilles, we know very little about the myths and legends of those indigenous peoples present when Columbus arrived off its northern coast in October 1492. What we do know is that the French Jesuit priest, traveler, and historian Pierre François Xavier de Charlevoix (1681–1762) spoke of the indigenous inhabitants of Cuba as believing that the world had been created jointly by three celestial personages and that afterward it had been devastated by a universal deluge in which everything was drowned except for one old man.[15]

The only likelihood that the name Mother of Lands, used to describe Hispaniola, might have had anything to do with the Atlantean tradition is that the incoming Taino preserved the memory of an island homeland once occupied by their most distant ancestors. For this to be right, we would have to accept that the original inhabitants of the Greater Antilles were forced to migrate to the mainland, before much later making a return journey to the islands. Even if this was the case, and I do agree it is an attractive proposition, we have no way of knowing whether they returned to the correct island landmass.

ATLANTEAN PLAIN

I could see no convincing reason to sway my interest away from the conclusion that Cuba was the best candidate by far for Plato's Atlantis, despite the findings of Hyde Clarke and Geoffrey Ashe. Indeed, as I now made clear, Cuba's counterclaim seemed to highlight the immense significance of its own western plain, bordered on its northern side by the Cord de Guaniguanico mountain range. We know also that the plain once extended southward, across what is today the Bay of Batabanó, to the Isle of Youth, the proposed site of the Seven Caves. Here then was evidence of a vast plain, originally 540 by 160 kilometers in extent, which may well have been drowned, in part at least, during the time frame allotted by Plato. Admittedly, he stated that the plain of Atlantis was the equivalent of six hundred by four hundred kilometers in size, which is slightly larger than Cuba's own great plain. However, drawing comparisons between the Atlantean plain and that of Cuba seemed justified.

Using his own interpretation of Plato's Atlantis narrative, Spedicato was proposing that Hispaniola's precipitous coastline has remained unchanged for the past 11,500 years. However, I do not feel that we can simply ignore Plato's assertion that Atlantis, or at least some part of its island landmass, sank beneath the sea. Since the low-lying Atlantean plain would have been the first part of the island to submerge, the fact that we have a location of this description on Cuba cannot be ignored.

Cuba's Cord de Guaniguanico can also be compared with the mountain range that Plato tells us shielded Atlantis's great plain from northerly winds. As we know, Cuba, and the Greater Antilles as a whole, is subject to the cool, moist breezes that accompany the north-easterly trade winds blowing in from the Atlantic Ocean. They affect vegetation, rainfall, and public health. Without them, life on the islands would be more or less intolerable. In Cuba's case, they provide the necessary moisture to generate cultivation on its vast fertile plains.

Yet between November and February each year, Cuba is itself subject to north winds, known as "los nortes," or "northers," which before they arrive in the Caribbean bring intense blizzards to the eastern United States.[16] Although these cold fronts reach exposed regions of the Cuban landmass, the Cord de Guaniguanico completely shields the western plain from these harsh winds, which would otherwise damage winter crops. This situation fits exactly Plato's statement to the effect that "all through the island this level district [i.e., the plain] faced the south and was thus screened from the cold northerly winds."[17]

FINDING DEAD CENTER

In the knowledge that Cuba's great plain might be compared with Plato's Atlantean plain, what then could I say about Plato's description of his marvelous citadel? Prior to the inundation of the Bay of Batabanó, the Isle of Youth would have been an elevated, hilly landscape located in the middle of the southern extreme of Cuba's extended plain. Curiously enough, the Punta del Este caves, which are positioned on a headland at the southeast end of the island, would have been placed approximately halfway along the plain's southern shore (see fig. 18.1). Indeed, they would have occupied a position very similar to where they are today, just a few hundred meters from the beach. Plato, we shall recall, placed the city close to the center of the island's southern shoreline.

If this might be considered a reasonable comparison, then the Isle of Youth would match the position of the Atlantean citadel, while the Punta del Este caves would serve as the grotto wherein Leucippe gave

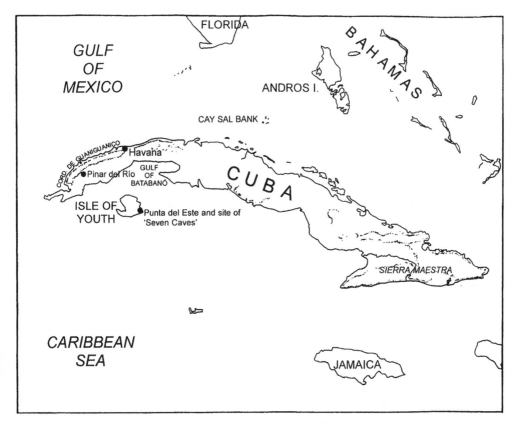

Figure 18.1. Map of Cuba showing the position of the Punta del Este cave site on the Isle of Youth. Ancient traditions found on both sides of the Atlantic Ocean strongly hint at Cuba's role in the development of the Atlantis legend.

birth to Clito, the progenitor of the Atlantean royal dynasty. As basic as these comparisons might seem, they could well reflect some element of the core Atlantis legend, which, I propose, was originally transmitted to the Mediterranean world by Phoenician and Carthaginian traders.

Sadly, no evidence of a true Atlantean city has yet been found in Cuba's Bay of Batabanó. More important, we have no Atlantean kings, no circular hydraulic systems, no canals, and no evidence of maritime activity before the arrival of the earliest Paleo-American Indians sometime around circa 6000 BCE. Yet absurdly enough we do have unfathomable evidence for the presence of bulls on the island.

BOVINE ART

Among the books I was able to study on the archaeology and prehistoric art of Cuba was Moure and de la Calle's *Arqueologia aborigen de Cuba*. Spread throughout its pages are line drawings of the primitive art to be seen on the walls and ceilings of different caves in Cuba. Yet among them are two pictographs that contradict everything we know about pre-Columbian Cuba, for they show, quite clearly, stickmen hunting large bovine creatures. In the first example, we see two men—one carrying a knife, pole, or short spear and the other with a similar weapon held point downward. Facing toward him is a horned creature that is unquestionably a long-coated bull. Unfortunately, the picture is not captioned, so there is no note on where this remarkable scene might be viewed.[18]

The other example in Moure and de la Calle's book shows the thick body of an enormous horned bull facing toward an unarmed stickman, who appears to be on the other side of a barrier made of sharp poles, angled toward the approaching beast.[19] The picture is enlarged on the preceding page and bears a caption informing the reader that it is a pictograph from the Cueva del Aguacate at Guara in the province of Havana (see fig. 18.2).[20]

Both images seem to show bovine creatures being hunted or provoked by humans in a manner that might be compared with, on the one

Figure 18.2. Pictographs from two Cuban caves showing bull baiting. Top, from an unknown cave site on the island, and bottom, from the Cueva del Aguacate at Guara in the province of Havana.

hand, Spanish bullfights and, on the other, prehistoric art connected with the cult of the bull. For instance, some of the Upper Paleolithic cave art in Spain and France shows very similar bovine creatures being hunted, while on a wall in the Neolithic city of Çatal Hüyük in southern-central Anatolia we see a striking fresco that shows a bull hunt circa 5800 BCE.[21] With these thoughts in mind, we are, of course, reminded of Plato's statement concerning the presence of bulls in the Atlantean citadel's sanctuary of Poseidon. These, we learn, were periodically captured using "wooden clubs and cords only but no implement of iron," before being slaughtered as sacrificial victims.[22]

I am simply at a loss to explain the presence of bovine imagery in the caves of Cuba. The only logical explanation is to assume that the pictographs are the work of Taino artists and that they depict bulls introduced to the island in the wake of the Spanish Conquest. Certainly there was a bullring at Regla, a suburb of Havana, although surely this was built after Cuba's native population had been annihilated by the forces of Diego Velasquez. Indeed, Havana itself was not founded until circa 1519, eight years after he began colonizing the island.[23] Yet if the pictographs are representations of bullfights, perhaps done by black African slaves, why do we rarely find similar representations of other colonial features and activities such as men riding horses, galleons sailing into port, and the outlines of stone buildings? Why might the bullfight have been singled out for special attention? Admittedly, there is a Christian priest stickman depicted next to a Calvary cross in the Cueva de Ambrosio, located close to what is now the holiday resort of Varadero. However, the style in which it is drawn suggests it was executed by a Christian pilgrim and not by a Taino or African artist.

If, however, these pictographs do not represent Spanish bullfights, we have a major problem on our hands. It would imply that, at some point in the past, large bovine creatures were either present on the island or they were witnessed by the cave artists on the American mainland. Since no remains of bulls or bison have ever surfaced during excavations at occupational sites belonging to the Taino, we can take the matter no further. If, however, Cuba's bovine cave art does turn out to be pre-Columbian it would be very significant indeed.

The three largest islands of the Greater Antilles would appear to have been known to the ancient world as the Hesperides, and can conceivably be considered surviving remnants of lost Atlantis. However, only Cuba and Hispaniola, the two largest members of the group, would appear to have played a more significant role in the memory of Plato's principal island landmass, and of these it is Cuba that I feel most resembles Atlantis's overall description.

Cuba's memory as the mythical homeland of the Mesoamerican peoples must also not be forgotten, for its significance in this respect may also have influenced the part it played in the development of the core Atlantis legend, plausibly at the hands of Phoenician and Carthaginian traders.

Even though I consider Cuba, and not Hispaniola, to be the Atlantean flagship, the sheer fact that an academic of Emilio Spedicato's caliber is willing to accept that Plato's Atlantic island was one of the Greater Antilles is itself remarkable.

During our meeting, I felt that I had adequately presented Cuba's case for being the true site of lost Atlantis, while Emilio Spedicato had done the same for Hispaniola. The final judgment must now be the responsibility of the individual reader. Yet nothing either Spedicato or I had brought to the table that fateful day at Cambridge University in May 1998 can explain key elements of Plato's Atlantis account. For instance, there is no evidence yet of a sunken kingdom (although see the new preface and epilogue), and, more pressingly, there are unanswered questions concerning the supposed fate of the Atlantean island empire. Both matters would have to be dealt with sufficiently before anyone could accept that Cuba, or indeed Hispaniola, deserves to take the crown of Atlantis.

That a major cataclysm occurred in the Caribbean during prehistoric times had been alluded to by Geoffrey Ashe, following his assessment of the statements made by Marcellus with respect to the three islands of "immense extent." Plus we have the account mentioned earlier of Pierre François Xavier de Charlevoix, which speaks of the indigenous inhabitants of Cuba believing that three celestial personages created the world jointly and that afterward it was decimated by a universal deluge in which everything was drowned except for one old man. Yet myths of cataclysm and flood are universal. They are preserved in the folk memories of indigenous peoples all around the globe. Literally thousands of legends exist that speak of a time before the current world age when the waters rose up and drowned every earthly inhabitant, save for a chosen few who either climbed mountains, ascended trees, or built arklike vessels to escape the all-encompassing deluge.

Whether flood myths have any basis in historical reality is still a matter of conjecture among scholars. Yet in this case we are dealing with one single story that speaks of the supposed submergence of an island landmass that once occupied the Caribbean. For the folk memories of the Taino of Hispaniola and Cuba and the Carib of the Lesser Antilles to have any real meaning, we would need to determine whether a catastrophe really did befall the region in prehistoric times. A gut feeling told me that a key to this mystery awaited discovery in the Punta del Este caves on Cuba's Isle of Youth.

Plate 24. The Temple of Kukulcan at Chichén Itzá in the Yucatán. This great cult center of the Yucatec Maya was said to have been founded by Kukulcan, the Feathered Serpent, who arrived "from the east" in the company of "20 illustrious leaders," each one bearded and dressed in "long, flowing clothes."

Plate 25. Photograph of a stone frieze from an unknown site in the Yucatán, taken by Mayan scholar Teobert Maler (1842–1917) and formerly in the possession of American author Robert B. Stacy-Judd. Does it show a Noah-like flood hero departing Tulan, the mythical homeland of the Maya, amid the cataclysms recalled in the Chilam Balam of Chumayel?

Plate 26. The heads of plumed serpents on the Temple of Quetzalcoatl at Teotihuacán. Note the carvings of seashells identified by Mesoamerican scholar George C. Vaillant as specifically Caribbean in origin. Do they indicate the direction of the Feathered Serpent's original homeland?

Plate 27. Chicomoztoc, the Seven Caves of the Mexica, from the *Historia Tolteca-Chichimeca* codex. From here emerged the first human beings at the beginning of the current world age, but where was it located and could it be found today?

Plate 28. A four-thousand-year-old occupational site at Guanahacabibes, located in Cuba's western province of Pinar del Río. Who constructed this monument of a type so similiar to those found at mound complexes in the United States?

Plate 29. Cueva #1, the most important of the "seven caves" at Punta del Este on the Isle of Youth, south of the Cuban mainland. Its walls are adorned with dozens of petroglyphs many thousands of years old. Do they tell of catastrophic events that devastated the western Atlantic seaboard around 12,800 years ago?

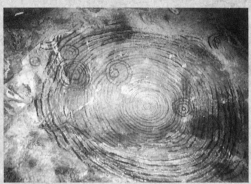

Plates 30 and 31. Two examples of the prehistoric cave art found inside Punta del Este's Cueva #1 on the Isle of Youth. The first picture (left) shows the main "target" design pierced by an arrow or daggerlike symbol, which is traced by the sun at the time of the equinoxes. The second example (right) shows a serpent or cometlike feature, highlighting the clear celestial nature of the many designs found in the cave.

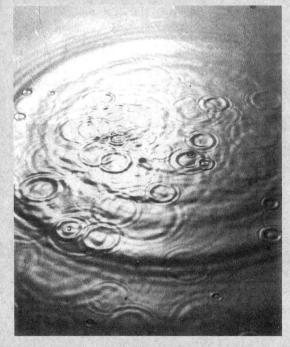

Plate 32. Rain falling on water. Its similarity to the cave art of Punta del Este's Cueva #1 is undeniable, but what does it mean? Is it a key to unraveling the mystery behind these extraordinary designs?

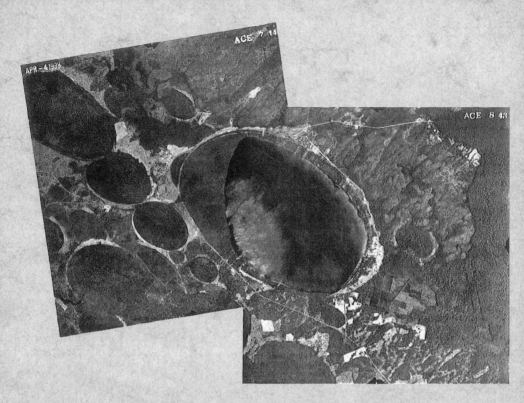

Plates 33 and 34. Two examples of Carolina Bays: White Lake Bay in Bladen County, North Carolina (above), and more bays at Myrtle Beach, South Carolina (below). Countless thousands of these elliptical scars cover large parts of Georgia, Virginia, the Carolinas, and other areas of the East Coast. What kind of impact might have been responsible for their formation around 12,800 years ago?

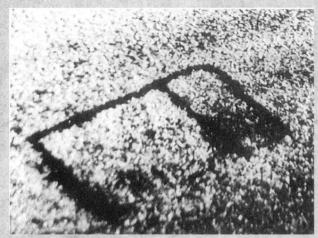

Plate 35. The "temple" site first located north of Andros Island in the Bahamas by pilots Robert Brush and Trigg Adams during the summer of 1968. Do these stone foundations constitute evidence of a prehistoric Bahamian culture, or are they simply the low walls of a modern sponge pen built in the 1930s?

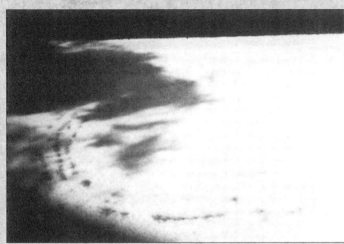

Plate 36. A huge one-hundred-meter triple-circle of loose stones first noticed off the southwest coast of Andros Island by pilot Robert Brush in the late 1960s. Is this strange structure natural or artificial?

Plates 37 and 38. Two examples of masonry discovered either on or close to the Bimini Road. Left, a black granite slab removed from the sea-bottom by dive shop owner Bill Keefe in 1995 and, right, David Zink examines a tongue-and-groove stone found during his Poseidia expedition in 1975. Are all such stones simply discarded ships' ballast, or do they constitute hard evidence of an antediluvian Bahamian culture?

Plates 39a and b. Photomosaic of part of the Bimini Road site, west of Paradise Point, North Bimini, made in 1969 by underwater surveyor Dimitri Rebikoff (above and opposite top). Geologists dismiss this curious feature as an outcrop of offshore beach rock, but Atlantean researchers continue to cite evidence for its artificial construction, so what is the true answer?

Plate 40. Explorer and marine archaeologist J. Manson Valentine. Before his death in 1994 he identified no fewer than sixty sites of possible archaeological interest located on the submerged Great Bahama Bank.

Plate 41. Just one of the curious underwater features investigated by J. Manson Valentine and his team. Here we see a series of hexagonal cells located in shallow waters close to Moselle Shoal, north of Bimini. Are such sites of artificial construction?

Plate 42. One of the many cut, dressed, and drilled stones lying in shallow waters close to Moselle Shoal, north of Bimini. Their presence has frequently led to unsubstantiated claims that Atlantean temples await discovery in the shallow waters of the Bahamas.

Plate 43. Decorated underwater cave found off the east coast of Andros Island by diver Herb Sawinski in 1963. The rise in sea level that followed the cessation of the last ice age would suggest that this prehistoric art could be many thousands of years old.

Plate 44. Reconstruction of the Andros Platform found off the coast of Nicholls Town, Andros Island, in the Bahamas. It consists of what appears to be three tiers of a breakwater enclosing a harbor formed of massive blocks. Who used this structure before it was submerged beneath the waves several thousand years ago?

Plate 45. Large blocks forming part of the Andros Platform underwater feature off the coast of Nicholls Town, Andros Island. Did it function as a breakwater or harbor for ocean-going boats and vessels thousands of years before the arrival in the Bahamas of Christopher Columbus in 1492?

Plate 46. Section of the Brown's Ruins underwater feature located near the islands of North Cat Cay and South Cat Cay, close to the western edge of the Great Bahama Bank. Was this structure originally located on land and destroyed by a super-tsunami triggered by a comet impact around 12,800 years ago?

Part Four
DESTRUCTION

19

THE OLE MOON BROKE

Never before had I ventured so far in pursuit of the truth. In the fume-filled time warp that is Havana, I found myself wasting time, money, and effort trying to purchase air tickets to the Isle of Youth. Once this was achieved, my traveling companion and I got out of the capital and headed by car toward Pinar del Río, the great cigar-manufacturing center where the cost of living would be cheaper. The journey was pleasing in that we had a chance to survey Cuba's great western plain from one end to the other. I was particularly interested in the Cord de Guaniguanico mountain range, which includes a number of peaks that are strangely truncated or curved in the style of Colhuacán, the Crooked Mountain, of Aztec myth. Regularly, I stopped to take photographs of these sugarloaf mountains, which border the northern limits of the plain.

Just as curious was the plain's distinctive red earth, which penetrates to a depth of at least two to three meters. I occasionally pulled the vehicle over onto the hard shoulder in order to gather samples, much to the amusement of the local population. At one point on the motorway, while examining a layer of red earth, I was stunned to see a man emerging from the nearby field of sugarcane carrying a live crocodile! It was a meter in length and had presumably been caught in the swamplands that border the Bay of Batabanó to the south.

Almost every available acre of cultivated land between Havana and Pinar del Río is covered with sugarcane, although the nearer we got to our destination the more the fields contained tobacco. By the time we had reached Pinar itself, there were tobacco plantations virtually everywhere.

I needed to know what I could expect to find inside Punta del Este's Cueva #1 on the Isle of Youth. From the few pictures available in archaeological books, I had become convinced that it held major clues regarding the origins of Mesoamerican civilization. The quality and character of its petroglyphs were simply outstanding. More important was the fact that two Cuban archaeologists, Ernesto E. Tabío and Estrella Rey, had stated that, in their opinion, the complexity of the cave art in Cueva #1 did not conform with the known styles of the Guayabo Blanco culture.[1]

Yet if the cave art in Punta del Este Cueva #1 was not the handiwork of the Guayabo Blanco, then who had been responsible for creating this veritable Sistine Chapel of the prehistoric world? Could it have been the Levisa, the relatively unknown culture who were present on Cuba circa 6000 BCE? Or was it the more enigmatic mound builders who would appear to have lived alongside the Guayabo Blanco and had links with the Mississippi Valley and St. Johns River cultures of the United States?

A SUDDEN SEPARATION

If the site of the original Seven Caves was to be found on the Isle of Youth, could there be a connection between the knowledge of a flood preserved in Aztec tradition and the cataclysm recalled in the folk memories of the Taino of Hispaniola and Cuba and the Caribs of the Lesser Antilles?

French historian Paul Gaffarel in his *Histoire de la découverte de l'Amerique*, published in 1892, stated that native Caribs of the south Caribbean islands told the Spanish chroniclers that "the Antilles had at one time formed a single continent, but they [the islands] were *suddenly* separated by the actions of the waters."[2] (current author's emphasis) Gaffarel also recorded that the indigenous population of Haiti spoke of how the islands of the Antilles were formed during a *sudden* flood.[3] (current author's emphasis)

In addition to the work of Gaffarel, Sir James Frazer's *Folk-lore in the Old Testament* stated that, "The Caribs of the [Lesser] Antilles had a tradition that the Master of Spirits, being angry with their forefathers for not presenting to him the offerings which were his due, caused such a heavy rain to fall for several days that all the people were drowned: only a few contrived to save their lives by escaping in canoes to a solitary mountain. It was this deluge, they say, which separated their islands from the mainland and formed the hills and pointed rocks or sugar-loaf mountains of their country."[4]

Clearly, these legends do not appear to convey the idea of the gradual submergence of low-lying islands and landmasses in the manner prescribed by marine geologists. Furthermore, in the creation account of the Cakchiquel, the tribe's departure from Civán-Tulán exudes a note of desperation and a sense of urgency, almost as if they were being forced to leave their original homeland in haste.

Is it really possible that there is a major piece of information missing from our knowledge regarding the final submergence of the low-lying regions of the Bahamas and Caribbean so many thousands of years ago? Did an almighty cataclysm really wreak havoc in the Western Hemisphere in the manner described by the indigenous peoples of the Greater and Lesser Antilles? Were the survivors those who reached higher ground, entered caves, or abandoned their original homeland before the catastrophe took place? More pertinently, was the memory of this cataclysm echoed in Plato's account of the destruction of Atlantis by earthquakes and floods in a single night and day? This is what I intended to find out while here in Cuba.

Prior to embarking on my quest to find the Seven Caves, I had attempted to pin down other catastrophe myths related by the American Indians of the Bahamas and Caribbean. My search had not gone unrewarded, for I turned up some important new piece of evidence. For instance, the Spanish chronicler Peter Martyr d'Anghiera in his book *De Orbe Novo,* published in 1511, recorded the following: "The natives themselves declare that there is such a tradition transmitted to them by their ancestors. [They say that] little by little, violent tempests submerged the lands, and separated them one from another by arms of the sea.[5]

These words seem clearly to contain the memory of climatic and oceanic events that caused destruction in the West Indies at some point in the distant past. Is it really possible that such poignant information might have been passed down from generation to generation, and from one culture to another, across many thousands of years?

TALES FROM TOBAGO

Another curious tradition of a quite similar nature is preserved among the Afro-Caribbean community of Tobago, an island situated at the southern end of the Lesser Antilles. They would appear to have inherited stories regarding a localized catastrophe from the native Carib population, which survived on some of the islands of the Lesser Antilles until the end of the sixteenth century. In his book *Secret Cities of Old South America: Atlantis Unveiled,* Harold T. Wilkins includes a letter in which a friend in Tobago retells a folktale she heard from "Negro workers on my husband's estate in the hills." According to the folklore, she writes, "very, very big men" lived on the islands in the past. *"But there wasn't no sea then.* Then everything got smashed up . . . the ole moon broke . . . the sea rushed in. After a time Tobago came dry again, but very small, small. How long ago was it? It was long before anybody's grandfather could remember. No, not British white men, these BIG MEN who lived in these days so long, long ago. But *not* black men, either!"[6]

This old tale emphasizes the lingering presence in the Caribbean of archaic memories concerning the sudden drowning of lands—an event that can only be linked to the final submergence of the low-lying islands, reefs, and banks in the Antillian chain. This accepted, we must also ask ourselves who the "very, very big men" might have been and what the islanders could have meant when they said that "the ole moon broke."

First, the "very, very big men." Obviously, we can only but speculate on such statements. However, I am reminded of the stories surrounding the People of the Serpent, who in Mayan tradition arrived out of the east in boats. According to Edward H. Thompson, these individuals were said to have been "light-skinned beings . . . [who were] tall of stature."[7] Such a statement suggests that those who were believed to have inhabited the Lesser Antilles at the time of this alleged cataclysm were unlike any known Mesoamerican population type and might well have been of increased height when compared against those who inhabited the archipelago in more recent times.

With such thoughts in mind, we move on to the use of the curious phase "the ole moon broke." What could this mean? It is a quite specific statement, and one that we must assume has an importance relative to the story being told. In other words, there is a connection here between the "ole moon" breaking and the catastrophe that splits asunder, or at least drowns, parts of the Antilles.

One last statement in the folk account from Tobago drew my attention. This was the suggestion that "the sea rushed in" and then receded again, leaving behind only part of the island landmass that had formerly occupied the same position. Does this not suggest that the catastrophe was caused by a massive tsunami (of the sort that, since the writing of this book, have been responsible for terrifying natural disasters, such as the catastrophic devastation and loss of life seen in Southeast Asia in 2004 and in Japan in 2011)? Although this seems a likely explanation for the surviving account of the cataclysm that supposedly befell the Lesser Antilles during some distant epoch, tsunamis are merely secondary effects of violent geological processes such as earthquakes, volcanic eruptions, and landslides. What is more, after a tsunami engulfs everything in its path, the waters will recede, leaving behind thick sediment that can completely consume low-lying areas.

Something was therefore amiss in the folk story preserved by the islanders of Tobago, suggesting that it might relate to more than one event—one a catastrophe involving a super-tsunami and another that somehow caused the permanent drowning of the low-lying regions of the Caribbean.

THE EAGLE-SERPENT PEOPLE

Moving to the American mainland for a moment, we find that among the American Indian tribes who preserve a memory of the destruction of a previous world age by floods and devastation are the Yuchi tribe of Oklahoma. In the nineteenth century, the U.S. government relocated the Yuchi from the Gulf Coast of Alabama to their present home. Yet it is the knowledge that their original homeland lay across the sea that could well hold vital clues regarding a cataclysm that overtook the Bahamas and Caribbean in prehistoric times.

Joseph B. Mahan, who until his death in 1995 was the executive director of the Institute for the Study of American Cultures, spent many years studying the cultural history of the Yuchi. He concluded that they were the legendary Shawano, the "Eagle-Serpent People," who provided a secular and religious leadership to many of the American Indian tribes of the Southern states. Mahan also produced compelling evidence to show that the Yuchi were descendants of the enigmatic mound-building culture that inhabited Florida and later occupied the Mississippi Valley.[8] As we have seen in chapter 17, there appears to be a direct relationship between the mound builders of Cuba and both the St. Johns River people of Florida and the Mississippi Valley culture.

In June 1957 Mahan was granted an audience with the Yuchi's hereditary chief, Samuel W. Brown Jr., so that he might be allowed to prepare a written account of the tribe's sacred history. According to

Mahan in his fascinating book *The Secret—America in World History before Columbus,* the chief spoke of the tribe's origins in the following manner: "The Yuchis have a persistent legend that their original homeland was an island somewhere to the east. Their chief recorded a more concise statement of this legend for me asserting that the Bahama Islands are remnants of the legendary island which was destroyed ages ago in an enormous natural catastrophe."[9]

Brown alluded further to this catastrophe, stating that the land was "destroyed by fires and clouds of different colors which came from the west and the north."[10] According to Mahan the great island then sank beneath the sea and "only a few survivors" managed to reach "the cape," identified by Brown as Florida. He seemed in no doubt that this former landmass was in the vicinity of the Bahamian archipelago, and even singled out the island of Andros in particular.[11]

Andros is the largest island in the Bahamas, and we shall review its mysteries in chapter 23 (and see also the epilogue, which reveals discoveries made more recently off its coast). However, what Brown related to Mahan is quite remarkable, for it appears that the Yuchi tribe's earliest ancestors were displaced forcibly from an island landmass that was drowned during an almighty cataclysm involving fire and other unusual aerial phenomena.

The most obvious identity of the "great island" spoken of by Brown is the Great Bahama Bank, of which Andros is the largest surviving remnant. Is it possible that this enormous low-lying landmass, which has the likeness of an inverted horseshoe and is the size of England, Scotland, and Wales combined, was truly drowned in the manner described?

Once again there are inconsistencies in the story. As already stated, tsunamis of the sort described in the Yuchi account do not permanently drown landmasses. Moreover, marine geologists consider that the Great Bahama Bank submerged very gradually between circa 8000 and 3000 BCE.[12] Clearly, the Yuchi were not referring to this event, but to one that engulfed large areas of the Bahamas in an instant of time. Can this be right, or are they fusing together more than one event?

Attempting to understand what Brown might have meant when he said that the catastrophe that engulfed his people's former homeland took the form of "fires and clouds of different colors which came from the west and the north" is even more difficult to determine. One explanation is to suppose that these effects were caused by atmospheric debris being thrown high into the sky by a severe disturbance at ground level. It is known, for instance, that volcanic eruptions can expel so much debris that they can cause atmospheric disturbances and strange colorations of the sky for many days, if not weeks, after the initial event.

So is this what occurred—the Great Bahama Bank was overcome by the effects of a volcanic eruption that completely devastated this former landmass? Unfortunately not, for there are no volcanoes whatsoever in the Bahamas. The closest examples are to be found in the Greater and Lesser Antilles, and these are unlikely to have caused the type of destruction suggested in Brown's account.

Despite its contradictions, there is a vividness to the Yuchi story that reaches far beyond the idea that their tribal flood myth is simply an idealized view of how their earliest ancestors emerged from the mythical world. If the Yuchi really have preserved a racial memory of an event that devastated the Bahamas thousands of years ago, we would have to explore the possibility that, prior to its final submergence, the former Bahamian landmass, known to marine geologists as the Great Bahama Bank, had been occupied. We will also have to consider the possibility that the Yuchi, as the Eagle-Serpent People and the former inhabitants of this sunken landmass, might just turn out to be linked with Plato's Atlantean race.

Such thoughts go completely against everything that archaeologists tell us about the prehistory of the Bahamas. In their view, the first peoples to occupy this archipelago were the Lucayans, a branch of the Caribbean Taino, who migrated to the region via the Greater Antilles sometime around 600–700 CE.[13] We shall see, however, that the archaeologists are entirely wrong in this respect.

ENTERING THE SEVEN CAVES

After spending time at Pinar del Río, my traveling companion and I returned to Havana and caught the flight out to the Isle of Youth. The date was Thursday, September 2, 1998. As described in the prologue, we landed at Nueva Gerona airport and finally hired a four-wheel-drive vehicle for the day. Yet having realized only once we were on the island that the Punta del Este caves were located in a military zone and that a special permit was required to pass an army checkpoint, we secured the services of local archaeologist Johnny Rodriguez and a driver from the hire firm. Neither of them spoke much English, although their assistance proved invaluable in helping us to obtain permission to pass unhindered through the checkpoint and reach the hazardous swampland at the southeastern corner of the island.

A flight of steps beyond a more or less derelict telecommunications station took us down to the level of the sandy swampland, home to sand crabs, crocodiles, vultures, mosquitoes, and the occasional Cuban sandhill crane. Being careful to avoid some poisonous shrubs for which we had no antidote, the four of us made our way toward Cueva #1, which is located on slightly raised ground within a low cliff face engulfed by trees. Modern debris was scattered about outside the cave mouth, although a metal plaque on the right-hand side confirmed we had reached our final destination. After months of careful planning, and with some trepidation, I set foot in what might well have been the site of the original Chicomoztoc, the Seven Caves of Mesoamerican tradition.

20

RATTLING
OF THE
PLEIADES

The long wait was worth it. What lay before us in the depths of Punta del Este's Cueva #1 was something quite special. The entrance is perhaps seven meters in width and three meters in height, and inside is a central chamber around twelve to fifteen meters deep. Positioned around its walls are a series of separate bays of different shapes and sizes, and a long corridor off to one side. It possessed roughly seven bays or compartments, perhaps reflecting the septuple symbolism of Chicomoztoc, the Seven Caves.

The corridor, or chamber, on the right-hand side was around ten meters in length and of undoubted human manufacture. Johnny Rodriguez, the Cuban archaeologist, pointed out that here the skeletons of Guayabo Blanco women had been found. Each one, more than two thousand years old, was laid out in a fetal position and covered in red ochre.

From this knowledge alone, it seemed clear that the Guayabo Blanco venerated this cave site as a womblike structure. If this was true, it made sense of why Chicomoztoc was seen as the place of emergence of the present human race.

THE TRANSIT OF VENUS

Strewn across the cavern's dusty floor were fragments of conch shell left behind by the last Taino to occupy, or use, the grotto. Overhead were two circular skylights, like the "zenith tubes" found at Olmec sites to mark the arrival of the sun at the time of the equinoxes. Beneath the one closest to the entrance was a circular concrete dais, where, according to Rodriguez, a stone platform would have been set in the ground. The rear skylight was difficult to approach, since it was now directly above a mound of earth displaced during excavations. Yet its apparent function was interesting indeed. According to those scholars who had studied these skylights, it marked the 584-day cycle of the planet Venus. How this might have been achieved was not made clear.

Should the skylight really mark the transit of the planet Venus, then this was extremely important. Quetzalcoatl was seen as the Morning Star, while his twin, Xolotl, was viewed as the Evening Star, names given to the dual aspects of Venus.

Had we really found the original site of the Seven Caves? Did this riddle, preserved by the Aztecs, relate in some way to the manner in which Cueva #1 was able to catch the planetary influence of Venus, which, together with the seven stars of the Pleiades, determined the fifty-two-year calendar cycle marking the birthday of Quetzalcoatl? If this was correct, might there also be a connection between the seven-fold symbolism of the Seven Caves and the seven stars of the Pleiades? Remember, aside from being known as Ah-Canule, People of the Serpent, those who established high culture in Mexico and the Yucatán were known also as Ah-Tzai, "People of the Rattlesnake."[1]

As a constellation, the rattlesnake was composed of a series of stars that emanated from the Pleiades, which formed its sevenfold rattle. Quetzalcoatl's own serpentine body was that of the rattlesnake. Moreover, the entire cult of the Chanes, or "serpents," appears to have revolved around a species of rattlesnake known as the *Crotalus durissus*

durissus.[2] So in this knowledge, did the rattlesnake play a hitherto unknown role in this gradually unfolding story?

ORBIT OF THE SUN

I have saved until now the description of the dozens of mesmerizing petroglyphs that adorn the walls and ceiling not only of Cueva #1's central chamber but also of the side corridor where the female burials were unearthed by archaeologists. They are composed of many series of concentric rings, geometric forms, and other strange devices, either in charcoal black, ochre red, or two-tone black and red. Many series overlap with others, while some are grouped together inside further concentric shapes like dumbbells.

One point that struck me almost immediately was that Cueva #1 contained neither stickmen nor animals of the type that indicated the handiwork of Taino artists. Even though the Taino had unquestionably occupied the cave, it would seem as if they considered it too sacred to be defaced, as was done in the decorated caves on the Cuban mainland.

In the side corridor was a cross formed out of a series of angled concentric rings, making me recall the labyrinth designs found among the Hopi art of the Four Corners region in the United States. On a straight edge nearby were a series of linear strokes of various sizes painted in lines. In my opinion they bore a resemblance to the Celtic script known as ogham, which has been detected at a number of American Indian cave sites in the southern United States.

Of all the petroglyphs in Cueva #1, the most stunning is a huge targetlike design composed of somewhere in the region of between fifty and fifty-five concentric rings, alternating in black and red. I cannot be more specific with the ring count as one side appears to have more circles than the other. Superimposed on this incredible design are another nine series of concentric rings, as well as a double arrow that begins in the center of the image and reaches out beyond the largest ring, which is approximately a meter in diameter. Other series of concentric rings surround the overall design, and it is difficult not to view the whole thing as a representation of the orbit of planets, with the main two-tone target representing the sun.

Confirmation of this surmise was offered by Rodriguez. On the equinoxes, he said, a beam of sunlight penetrates the cave through the forward skylight and slowly crosses from the center of the target to its edge via the arrowlike image. His description of this remarkable solar event reminded me of the "sun daggers" that illuminate geometric designs at rock sites in the southwest United States. For instance, in a cave at Holly Canyon, near Hovenweep Castle in the southeast corner of Utah, a shaft of light enters on the summer solstice and proceeds to pierce a carving of three concentric rings, which are said by the local Pueblo American Indians to represent the sun.[3] At another site on an outcrop of rock close to the entrance of Chaco Canyon, New Mexico, named Fajada Butte, a "dagger of light" enters between a gap in three stacked slabs of stone and penetrates a large spiral pattern on various dates of the year. On the summer solstice it pierces the center of the tar-getlike design. On the midwinter solstice two "daggers of light" are cast on the spiral, one either side of its outer rim, while on the equinoxes a dagger passes through the right-hand edge of the image.[4] According to the Navaho, these features were created long ago by the people known as the Anasazi, the "old ones."[5]

What relationship this celestial art might have to the geometric designs in Punta del Este's Cueva #1 is unclear. All that can be said with any certainty is that the Anasazi reached the peak of their power during the twelfth and thirteenth centuries CE and that their ruling elite are thought to have come originally from Mexico. They may thus have been related to the Toltec, who were also at the height of their power during this same period of time.

All of these solar events seem uncannily representative of how the present human race emerged from the Seven Caves only after the sun had shot an arrow of sunlight into its darkened interior. Did the entry of the "sun dagger" into Cueva #1 signify some kind of penetration of an earthly womb and the subsequent rebirth of life? Could those who created this clear religious symbolism in Cueva #1 have carried it to Central America?

SIGNS OF SERPENTS

That there was a relationship between the petroglyphs of Cueva #1 and celestial bodies, such as the sun, moon, and planets, did not seem in doubt. Indeed, these celestial images appeared to determine certain fundamental religious concepts obviously held by those who most anciently revered this cave site. These would seem to have included the symbolic regeneration and reemergence of the human race from the womb of the Earth following its penetration by a dagger, or arrow, of sunlight. The sexual union of Sky Father and Earth Mother is a universal concept.

All this was deduced from just a few minutes of listening to Rodriguez and examining the petroglyphs of Cueva #1. To me, however, the great targetlike design suggested something else—the idea of ripples caused as raindrops fall on water.

I ventured into the side corridor where the female burials were found and had another look at the various designs that adorned its ceiling. One now drew my attention. It was composed of a series of concentric rings adjoined to a strange S-shaped tail enclosed by even more concentric rings. For some reason it bore a resemblance to a comet, leading me to rethink the imagery in the main chamber. What if the water ripples suggested by the concentric rings were not being made by raindrops? What if they were really something else hitting water, like stones falling from the sky? What if this cave imagery was recalling some kind of catastrophic impact, or series of impacts, caused either by an asteroid or a comet?

These were bizarre thoughts, but I felt I should ask our archaeologist friend whether anyone had ever considered that the geometric designs in Cueva #1 represented comets. He quickly affirmed that this was indeed the case.

I thought further on the matter and recalled that comets have also been discerned in rock art found at various Neolithic and Bronze Age sites in Britain. Catastrophe scientists Victor Clube and Bill Napier, in their book *The Cosmic Serpent,* published in 1982, examined examples of cometlike "cup and ring" markings at megalithic sites across the British Isles. Among them were carvings on a large flat slab at Ardmarnoch in western Scotland that show "serpent-like lines with haloes." In their opinion, "It is possible therefore that the Ardmarnoch array shows a family of comets moving through a star field."[6]

A further example of a cometlike object composed of concentric rings and a series of lines that emerge from a central design is depicted on a rock taken from a site named Traprain Law at Haddington in East Lothian, Scotland. It is currently housed in the National Museum of Antiquities of Scotland in Edinburgh. To Clube and Napier it bore "the appearance of a long curved comet tail and a huge halo surrounding a comet head that was probably as bright as the full moon."[7] I was simply stunned by the similarity between the Traprain Law carving and Cueva #1's main target design, right down to the fact that both examples have arrowlike devices emerging from their centers.

That comets were anciently seen as fiery serpents in the sky might also be of interest here, for I already knew that in the mythology of the Maya the rattlesnake had a celestial counterpart that was said to have sprung from the seven stars of the Pleiades. Since the rattlesnake is not indigenous to the Greater Antilles, the importance implied by Cueva #1's sevenfold symbolism and snakelike imagery lay not in the creature itself but in the apparent association between comets and the constellation of the Pleiades.

The Mayan text known as the Chilam Balam of Chumayel spoke of an almighty cataclysm during which the "Great Serpent" was "ravished from the heavens, together with the rattles of its tail," so that its "skin and pieces" of its "bones fell here upon the Earth"[8] Since the seven stars of the Pleiades were viewed in Mayan astronomy as the rattlesnake's sevenfold rattle, did this suggest that a comet responsible perhaps for a cataclysm on Earth was seen as a cosmic serpent that came from the direction of the Pleiades?[9] So that no one would ever forget the direction from which the fiery serpent had emerged, did the stars marking this spot come to represent the celestial snake's rattle, which, remember, warns a potential victim it is about to strike?

Other cultures of the Western Hemisphere would seem to have preserved a memory of how a fiery serpent that brought to a close a previous world age was connected with the Pleiades constellation. For example, the Carib population of Surinam (formerly Dutch Guiana), located on the northeast coast of South America, believe in a supreme being called Amana. She is described as a virgin mother and water goddess who has "no navel" and is "a beautiful woman whose body ends in a serpent. She is the essence of time, has borne all things . . . and exercises her power from the Pleiades. She is also called a serpent spirit and a sun serpent. . . . She renews herself continually, by sloughing her skin like a snake."[10]

Amana gave birth to twin brothers, Tamusi and Yolokan Tamulu, the first born at dawn, the other at dusk. Of the two brothers—who, like Quetzalcoatl and Xolotl in Aztec myth, were personifications of the planet Venus as the morning and evening star—Tamusi became the principal god of the Caribs, and like his mother he ruled from the Pleiades. His adversaries, the fiends, were signified by a celestial serpent "which has already several times devoured the Pleiades and thus brought the world to an end. Each time Tamusi created the world anew, and he will do so once again."[11] According to one Guianan Carib tribe this destruction took the form of "a great fire and a deluge" sent by the god Puráa,[12] and we have already seen how the Antillean Caribs saw a similar cataclysm as having split apart a former island landmass existing in the vicinity of the Lesser Antilles.

This then was the knowledge preserved in the sevenfold symbolism of Chicomoztoc, the Seven Caves, from which humanity emerged following a time of darkness and destruction that ended a previous world age. Yet those who inhabited Mexico, the land of Anahuac, during the rule of the Aztec great speakers, forever feared the arrival of another fiery snake that would, once again, emerge from the Pleiades and destroy the world. So much did they believe this that at the beginning of November each year, when the Pleiades rose in the evening for the first time, the Aztec priests would gather to appease the great snake with human sacrifice, something they would do at midnight when its stars reached a point overhead.[13] This gruesome ceremony was enacted so that the Aztec nation would never forget that on this day in the past "the world had been previously destroyed," since "they dreaded lest a similar catastrophe would, at the end of a cycle, annihilate the human race."[14]

Curiously, an age-old Hebrew legend asserts that the Great Flood was caused after "the upper waters rushed through the space left when God removed two stars out of the constellation Pleiades."[15] More extraordinary still is the fact that the Jews believe this event occurred on a date corresponding in the Gregorian calendar to November 17, very close to the annual date acknowledged by the Aztecs for this very same reason.[16] Nineteenth-century mythologist R. G. Haliburton made a special study of the Pleiades in myths and legends worldwide. He thought it beyond coincidence that separate races on two different continents honored the catastrophe that brought about the Great Flood in the very same calendar month. He therefore proposed a common origin for this belief in a global catastrophe connected quite specifically with the constellation of the Pleiades.[17]

Plato himself, in the preamble leading up to his account of the destruction of Atlantis in the *Timaeus* states, "There have been, and will be hereafter, many and diverse destructions of mankind, the greatest by fire and water."[18] He goes on to say that the primary cause of such conflagrations and floods "is a deviation of the bodies that revolve in heaven round the earth,"[19] an allusion to the passage of comets, such as Phaeton, the "child of the sun," that "once harnessed his father's chariot but could not guide it on his father's course and so burnt up everything on the face of the earth."[20] Was Plato in fact alluding to the destructive might of a comet that once brought absolute devastation to the world, including the disappearance of Atlantis in "one terrible day and night" of "earthquakes and floods"?

EVIDENCE OF IMPACTS

For the moment I could offer little more on the subject. Yet in the wake of my all too brief visit to Punta del Este's Cueva #1, the feeling that at some time in prehistory the Bahamas and Caribbean had been devastated by a comet impact would not leave me. It made complete sense of the various legends told by the indigenous peoples of the Caribbean, as well as the story related by Brown of the Yuchi tribe, who believed that his earliest ancestors had migrated to Florida from the former Bahamian landmass. Moreover, I became convinced that Cueva #1 was like some kind of ancient shrine preserving, through the use of symbolic mnemonic devices, both the memory of this catastrophic event and the eventual reemergence of humanity once order had been restored in the outside world.

After returning to the United Kingdom I checked again for any evidence of an impact that might have devastated the western Atlantic seaboard in prehistoric times. What we certainly know is that the asteroid, or meteor, now thought to have been responsible for the extinction of the dinosaurs at the end of the Cretaceous period, some sixty-five million years ago, probably created the huge impact crater discovered in 1991 on the edge of the Yucatán Peninsula. It has a diameter of 160 kilometers and, due to the rising sea level, part of its rim now lies beneath the Gulf of Mexico. Clearly the so-called Cretaceous Tertiary, or KT, boundary event has nothing whatsoever to do with any lingering folk memories of comet impacts in the Caribbean. However, the fact that one of the world's most famous asteroid impacts occurred in precisely the region under scrutiny is curious, to say the least.

In addition to the proposed KT boundary event crater, there is other evidence of impacts in the Caribbean. A number of so-called bediasites have been found on some of the islands.[21] These are solidified particles of molten rock debris, usually silica in nature, ejected into the atmosphere at the point of an impact, which then harden suddenly before falling back to Earth. What kind of event might have been involved remains uncertain, although scientists have proposed that these glass-like objects (also known as tektites) are the residue of an impact-strewn field that stretches from the Indian Ocean across the Pacific to the Caribbean.[22]

The volume of debris material thrust into the upper atmosphere during an impact event would remain at high altitudes for weeks, if not months or even years, causing the sun to become obscured and other strange atmospheric effects to take place—something scientists refer to as a "nuclear winter." This might go some way to explain the "fires and clouds of different colors" that Brown said destroyed the Bahamian landmass.[23] We must also not forget that the Quiché-Maya and Cakchiquel tribes of Guatemala spoke of their departure from the ancient homeland during the perpetual darkness that prevailed before the first dawn. The Quiché additionally recorded that rain fell perpetually, and when the sun finally appeared its fierce heat dried the land, which had become "soggy" and "muddy."[24] A form of lethal acid rain will accompany a nuclear winter caused by an oceanic impact event, which would obviously vaporize large quantities of seawater.

An oceanic impact would also help explain why the indigenous peoples of the Caribbean, from Hispaniola to the Lesser Antilles, appear to have preserved the memory of a sudden inundation of the islands. A comet or asteroid impacting with the ocean would create successive tidal waves many hundreds, if not thousands, of meters high. These would completely devastate island landmasses and low-lying coastal regions. Yet could I find any additional evidence that such an event had taken place? Had anybody ever proposed such a theory? I searched long and hard and finally came across a scientific paper written in 1954 that seemed to echo exactly these sentiments.

EXTRATERRESTRIAL CHUNKS

The article in question, published in the *International Anthropological and Linguistic Review,* was written by Alan H. Kelso de Montigny, a brilliant anthropologist of Dutch extraction, who lived for many years in Cuba before migrating to the American mainland. Titled "Did a Gigantic Meteorite, i.e., an Asteroid, Fall into the Caribbean, and Thus Create the Lesser Antilles about 6,000 Years Ago?"[25] it begins by reviewing earlier material that the author had presented in the same journal regarding the origin and nature of lunar craters.[26] The article goes on to propose that "as the earth is much larger and heavier than its satellite, the gravitational pull of the earth is also several times as great as that of the moon, i.e., the earth must have attracted at least ten times as many gigantic meteorites and asteroids as its satellite."[27]

Kelso de Montigny points out that, aside from the constant bombardment of smaller "extraterrestrial chunks of matter," the Earth must have suffered from greater impacts caused by much larger "projectiles," or "gigantic chunks."[28] Consequently, every several thousand years or so, an asteroid would thus cause an "immense cataclysm," along with "floods, a glacial epoch, and a wholesale extermination of humans and animals."[29]

Kelso de Montigny felt he had detected evidence that just such an event had occurred in the Caribbean "in 4000 or 3000 BC."[30] Moreover, he tantalizingly alluded to the fact that he had found:

> some confirmation of this thesis in numerous Indian traditions that said that many centuries ago "a moon" fell out of the sky onto the earth, looking—during its passage through the sky—like A FIERY SNAKE (the fiery tail of the burning asteroid), that there were terrible earthquakes (the impact of the asteroid), that the day turned into a permanent night (the dust, smoke, and water vapor produced by the impact), that there was a gigantic flood and a formidable rain that lasted many, many days (the seawater, displaced, as well as

evaporated by the impact of the asteroid), and that the only people that were saved were those that succeeded in reaching mountain peaks and finding shelter there in caves.[31]

Everything I had conceived of having occurred in the Caribbean many thousands of years ago was here presented in one paragraph, written by an astute anthropologist who had himself lived in Cuba! Here also was the reason behind the expression "the ole moon broke," used in the folk account preserved among the islanders of Tobago in the Lesser Antilles. By the "ole moon" they meant an extraterrestrial object, a comet fragment perhaps, that fell into the ocean, causing mass devastation on a scale of the type expressed in the various myths and legends preserved by the indigenous peoples of the Caribbean.

Unfortunately, Kelso de Montigny failed to provide details of the primary sources consulted during the preparation of his article. For instance, there was no indication whether the reference to the "moon" falling might relate to the folk account preserved on Tobago, or to something else. Regardless of this, he goes on to write, "When the present writer travelled, many years ago, in Venezuela, he made the acquaintance of an Indian medicine man from the western part of that country, who spoke some Spanish. He stated that his father had taught him that ages and ages ago, a gigantic snake of fire had passed through the sky, and that then the world had almost come to an end, because there came an interminable night with a terrible flood and fearful rains. That nearly all the people had been drowned, except a few that could escape into the mountains."[32]

The "medicine man" would appear to have preserved a memory of what can only be described as an impact event that caused mass destruction on an unimaginable scale. The description of the incoming object as a "gigantic snake of fire" could not be more pertinent to the sevenfold symbolism and cave art of Punta del Este's Cueva #1.

Faced with so much circumstantial evidence from oral traditions coming from different areas of the Caribbean, Central America, and

South America, it seemed highly likely that an impact of immense proportions had indeed occurred in the vicinity of the Caribbean during some past age of humanity. However, such stories were simply not enough. What I needed was hard scientific evidence to substantiate such bold claims.

METEORIC REMAINS

In an attempt to back up his bold hypothesis, Kelso de Montigny proposed that although marine geologists consider the breakup of the islands of the Lesser Antilles to have taken place between ten thousand and twenty thousand years ago, this event must have occurred in more recent times. He cited as evidence the fact that on several of the islands there exists a species of poisonous snake called the fer-de-lance (*Bothrops atrox* or *Lachesis lanceolatus*), which is also found in Central America.[33] Since this species is unlikely to have been introduced to the islands by human hands, he believed that this supported his contention that "a solid stretch of land," a kind of land bridge stretching between the South American mainland and the uppermost islands of the Lesser Antilles, had existed until circa 4000–3000 BCE. He pointed out that if it had been broken up any earlier, then the fer-de-lance snakes would have evolved so differently that their common ancestry would have been lost.[34]

The only other support presented by Kelso de Montigny for an impact in the Caribbean was the simple fact that the curve formed by the Lesser Antilles chain is highly suggestive of an impact crater. He also pointed out that the waters at the center of this circle (or ellipse) are the deepest in the southern Caribbean.[35] He recommended that this region of the sea "should be investigated for meteoric remains under the mud of the sea bottom."[36] The American anthropologist concluded his article by predicting, "If such remains of the impact of a gigantic chunk of extraterraneous matter were still found, and that giant catastrophe thus proven to the hilt, we would immediately have an explanation for the last Ice Age of America and Europe."[37]

Alan H. Kelso de Montigny is no longer with us. He died in 1972. So having tracked down his son, Alan H. Kelso de Montigny, an artist who lives in Miami, I asked him to tell me more about his father's work. He informed me that the article published in the *International Anthropological and Linguistic Review* was the only one his father wrote on the subject. However, I was intrigued to discover that right until his death, Kelso de Montigny believed that the asteroid he proposed had devastated the Caribbean was responsible also for the destruction of Plato's Atlantis.[38]

As tempting as it might be to accept the idea of an impact in the Caribbean somewhere around 4000–3000 BCE, there is actually very little evidence to support such a theory. Having read various scientific papers on marine geology, sediment levels, climate changes, and sea level rises in the Bahamas and Caribbean over the past fifteen thousand years, I could find no significant evidence that any dramatic changes had taken place in the Western Hemisphere at this time.

This was quite obviously a major blow, since I knew that this was the earliest possible time period for any migrations from the Greater Antilles to the Central American mainland. To make matters worse, there is no other evidence whatsoever to confirm the theory put forward by Kelso de Montigny that until circa 4000–3000 BCE the Lesser Antilles had been a land bridge linking the South American mainland with the northern end of the present island group. Thus the species of fer-de-lance snake found on various islands of the archipelago either retained their unique characteristics for much longer than Kelso de Montigny surmised or the earliest inhabitants really did introduce them, which seems unlikely.

In addition to these facts, there is currently no supporting evidence to suggest that the rim of the Lesser Antilles was formed by an asteroid impact in the location proposed by Kelso de Montigny. No impact debris has ever been found, and, to my knowledge, no independent scientist has ever come up with a similar scenario regarding the deepest chasms of the Caribbean Sea. This is not to say that he was wrong, only that at the present time his claims cannot be substantiated.

THE SECRET OF ATLANTIS

Not a little disappointed by these findings, I looked again for hard evidence of an impact in the vicinity of the Bahamas and Caribbean. In the meantime, I read for the first time a work on Atlantis that, I must confess, had lain undisturbed on a bookshelf throughout the entire preparation of this book. Titled *The Secret of Atlantis,* its author was Otto Heinrich Muck, one of the most enigmatic figures ever to enter the field of Atlantology. Born in Germany, he was the inventor of the U-boat snorkel and before his death in 1965 held no fewer than two hundred patents under his name. Yet more significantly, in World War II he had been a member of the infamous Rocket Research Team at Peenemünde, Germany, where the V-1 and V-2 rockets were developed, tried, and tested.

In a manner similar to many others before him, Muck had reviewed the evidence for Plato's Atlantic island before going on to propose that it had been a landmass of enormous size that had sat astride the Mid-Atlantic Ridge, the theory first postulated by Ignatius Donnelly in the nineteenth century. What caught my attention, however, was not his placement of Atlantis, but the means by which he conceived of its disappearance. Muck's conclusions are best summed up by historical writer Peter Tompkins in his introduction to *The Secret of Atlantis:* "At 8 p.m. on June 5, 8498 BCE, the accused, named Asteroid A, did wildly go off its course, break into pieces, plunge into the Atlantic's Bermuda Triangle, and engender a holocaust worse than 30,000 hydrogen bombs, dragging with it, like some Lucifer, an entire island civilization and the better part of mankind on the planet."[39]

Such a grand explanation might at first reading seem ludicrous, and an exact date and time for the event scholarly suicide. Yet intrigued by Tompkins's words, I read Muck's book and was utterly astonished by what I read, for it would appear that this German ex-rocket scientist may well have stumbled on the mechanism behind the destruction of Atlantis.

21

COSMIC PINBALL

What the allies found when they overran the Peenemünde research establishment at the end of World War II was a world away from the science laboratories of Britain and the United States. Indeed, its highly talented Rocket Research Team was considered so important that some 120 of its top scientists, including Wernher von Braun, agreed to leave Germany and join the United States' own rocket program.

Yet what we also know is that the highly advanced work of the research team at Peenemünde was influenced by bizarre scientific views promoted in Nazi Germany during the 1920s and 1930s. They included the opinions of Austrian mechanical engineer and inventor Hans Hoerbiger, who in 1913 published a book titled *Glazialkosmogonie*, which expounded his so-called cosmic ice, or world ice, theory.[1] This proposed that the current moon was originally a planet orbiting the sun, which was captured by the Earth's gravitational field some 12,500 years ago. Prior to this age, another moon, described as the "Tertiary satellite," had occupied the same position. Yet over tens of thousands of years its orbit had brought it closer and closer to the Earth until finally it had broken up, causing catastrophic devastation right across the planet. Before the Tertiary epoch of Earth's geological history (which began after the KT boundary event of sixty-five million years ago and ended around five hundred thousand years ago), even earlier moons had, according to Hoerbiger, been captured and then destroyed in a similar manner, a pointer therefore toward the ultimate fate of our present moon.

Since Hoerbiger had concluded that moons are covered in ice, the destruction of the Tertiary satellite must have sent enormous chunks of ice on a collision course with the Earth. Their disintegration on impact would have caused catastrophic earthquakes, volcanic eruptions, fiery rains, and periods of darkness.

Quite naturally, Hoerbiger, and his English prodigy, the writer H. S. Bellamy, saw the cosmic ice theory as explaining the universal myths regarding the destruction of previous world ages. In his 1936 book *Moons, Myths and Man: A Reinterpretation,* Bellamy cited folk myths preserved by the Botocudos and Tupi tribes of western Brazil, which, like those found on the Caribbean island of Tobago, spoke of the old moon falling to Earth.[2] He felt that these stories helped support Hoerbiger's views concerning the destruction of the Tertiary satellite. Bellamy also cited many examples of legends concerning fiery serpents as explaining the comet-like appearance of the present moon on its capture by the Earth's gravitational field. More important, Bellamy believed that this same monumental event had created the universal flood responsible for the destruction of Atlantis.[3]

Hoerbiger's cosmic ice theory has now been disproved. We know that the moon's surface is not covered with ice. Furthermore, the rock samples brought back from the moon by the Apollo landing missions make it clear that our lunar satellite could not possibly have been "caught" by the Earth's gravitational pull just 12,500 years ago. Yet since Germany's Nazi Party readily embraced the cosmic ice theory and its implications for the world, scientific research into catastrophe theories, cosmic impacts, and the destruction of former civilizations was eagerly encouraged.

It was out of this distorted vision of prehistory that, after the end of World War II, Otto Muck emerged to make his own literary contribution to the problem of Atlantis. Picking up on the work of Alan H. Kelso de Montigny, he began to explore hydrographic charts of the ocean floor and noticed two large holes, elliptical in shape and oriented northwest to southeast, that lay in deep water, east of Florida and north of the Bahamas.[4] As Muck pointed out, "It must have been an indescribably powerful force that drove these deep holes in the sima of the Atlantic basin. . . . In the age of the atom bomb one is tempted to think of it in terms of a colossal submarine nuclear explosion."[5]

To him these deep holes in the sima, a layer of silica-magnesium found beneath the earth's surface, represented not "enormous sink-holes," as marine geologists might have supposed, but "the unhealed scars left by two deep wounds inflicted on the Earth's crust by the impact of a celestial body of considerable size."[6] Moreover, their northwest to southeast orientation implied that the fragments of the object had been on this trajectory when they had struck the ocean.[7]

THE CAROLINA BAYS

The approach of such a celestial body would, in Muck's opinion, have "grazed the remaining land in the northwest," that is, the southeast United States.[8] He added, "In searching for evidence on the strip of land that has remained, we would expect to find a field of craters, preserved through the thousands of years that have passed since the catastrophe."[9] He therefore switched his attentions to the American coastal plain and chanced upon something of immense importance to his argument.

In 1930 Myrtle Beach Estates, a timber company in Harry County, South Carolina, commissioned an aerial survey of the company's pine resources in order to facilitate the sale of its timber. For this purpose, it engaged the services of Fairchild Aerial Survey, which photographed some eight hundred square kilometers of land in the Myrtle Beach area. Upon development of the films, Edwin H. Corlett, one of Fairchild's engineers, noticed something highly unusual about the landscape under scrutiny. It was quite literally pockmarked with hundreds of elliptical depressions, some so large that they dwarfed surrounding agricultural fields. There were elongated dry "bays," a local term used to denote depressions, as well as huge egg-shaped lakes and ponds, some superimposed on others.

Corlett was perplexed by the mystery, and so brought the photographs to the attention of Frank A. Melton, a geology professor at the University of Oklahoma. Spreading out the photomosaic, Corlett let him ponder over the possible cause of these bays before sharing his thoughts on the matter. In his view, they were meteoritic scars caused by the impact of literally thousands of what he took to be "comets." Melton was suitably impressed, and with William Schriever, a professor of physics at Oklahoma, he conducted a further aerial survey of the strange features before initiating on-site investigations of the elliptical bays around Myrtle Beach. The two men singled out some forty-three examples for study and prepared a detailed report, presented at the 1932 annual conference of the Geological Society of America. It was published the following year in the *Journal of Geology* under the title "The Carolina 'Bays'—Are They Meteorite Scars?"[10]

Melton and Schriever concluded that there were at least three thousand of these shallow, perfectly formed depressions, almost all of them oriented northwest to southeast. In their estimates the depressions covered an area of around 160,000 square kilometers and could be found in three separate states: Georgia, North Carolina, and South Carolina.[11] At the southeastern end of many of the bays examined was a pronounced sandy rim, often up to two meters in height.[12] This was indicative of the low trajectory of the incoming meteorites, which must have appeared in quick succession, accounting for the overlapping of some bays.[13] In the two men's final opinion, the bays represented an immense crater field produced by a whole "swarm" of objects that had approached from the northwest and struck the American southeast from "50,000 to a million years ago."[14]

These were bold statements for their time. However, even Melton and Schriever underestimated the full potential of the so-called

Carolina Bays, as they quickly became known. For it is now known that there are an estimated half a million such depressions in at least seven states.[15] Aside from Georgia and North and South Carolina, they are also to be found in other eastern states, including New Jersey, Maryland, Virginia, and Florida.[16] Their frequency is astonishing. One area of Bladen County, North Carolina, that is eight kilometers by 6.4 kilometers in size, has a 67 percent covering of bays.[17] Other areas of the Carolinas have as much as 50 percent bay coverage.[18] No fewer than forty thousand of these are of moderate to large size, with lengths of more than 152.4 meters.[19] One of the biggest depressions is Big Swamp Bay in central South Carolina, which is six kilometers from one end to the other.[20] Other examples found nearby are small by comparison, measuring between ninety-one and 122 meters in size.[21] By contrast, there is even evidence of bays more than eleven kilometers long.[22]

Many of the depressions are elongated in shape, while others, usually much smaller in size, are almost circular.[23] Yet there is a definite pattern to their appearance, orientation, and arrangement, which varies in accordance with their placement.[24]

IMPACT CRATERS?

In the wake of Melton and Schriever's announcements regarding the origins of the Carolina Bays, alternative theories as to their cause came thick and fast. They included vulcanism, glaciation, artesian springs, fish spawning grounds, buffalo wallows, wind erosion, and dust devils.[25] Despite these bold attempts to explain away the depressions in terrestrial terms, other academics immediately stepped forward to support Melton and Schriever's meteorite "swarm" hypothesis.[26] The greatest objection to this idea came from Douglas W. Johnson, a geologist with Columbia University, who from 1934 onward argued that the bays were formed through the actions of wind on artesian wells.[27]

Yet it was always going to be the most glamorous theory that stole the show. In 1933 Edna Muldrow, a writer for the popular magazine

Harper's, used Melton and Schriever's published paper as the basis for a seven-page feature on the likelihood of a "comet" striking the Earth— one of the first occasions that this topic was highlighted in such a public manner.[28] She attempted to conjure the image of a "bad half hour when the whole heavens burst into one blinding flame," causing mass destruction across the United States.[29]

AERIAL DETONATION

Quite obviously, the orthodox scientific community in the 1930s did not greet the promotion of "crackpot" ideas of this type too kindly. Charles Darwin's theories of evolution, based on the notion of the survival of the fittest, saw fauna, including the human species, as having developed over many millions of years. In the minds of the neo-Darwinists of the time, catastrophe theories were nothing more than a popular myth.

The 1950s, however, saw a shift away from the scientific belief in a gradual transition of world ages, most probably because humanity had now seen the effects of atomic bombs and so realized just how easy it is to raze cities and destroy countless human lives. With this change in outlook came even more ambitious theories concerning the origins and nature of the Carolina Bays. In February 1952, William F. Prouty, a geologist at the University of North Carolina, proposed that the bays were created by powerful airshock waves produced by the impact of incoming meteors toward the end of the Pleistocene epoch of geological history, circa 9600 BCE.[30] In an attempt to prove his case, he conducted a series of experiments whereby he shot bullets into a layer of powder at a low angle from a distance of nine meters. The air-shock waves created elliptical craters more or less identical to those of the Carolina Bays.[31] He also pointed out that on-site surveys of a large percentage of the bays demonstrated that they possessed magnetic anomalies that hinted strongly at the meteoric origin of the depressions.[32]

To some degree, Prouty's revised meteorite theory for bay

330 Destruction

construction drew inspiration from the scientific community's new knowledge of an incident that had shaken an inaccessible part of central Siberia, in the upper basin of the Podkamennaja Tunguska River (latitude 60° north, longitude 101° east), on June 30, 1908.[33] According to one witness account:

> About eight o'clock in the morning, I had been sitting on the porch with my face to the north, and at this moment in the northwest direction appeared a kind of fire which produced such a heat that I could not stand it. . . . And this overheated miracle I guess had a size of at least a mile [1.6 kilometers]. But the fire did not last long, I had only time to lift up my eyes and it disappeared. Then it became dark, and then followed an explosion which threw me down from the porch about six feet [1.8 meters] or more . . . but I heard a sound as if all houses would tremble and move away. Many windows were broken, a large strip of ground was torn away, and at the warehouse the iron bolt was broken.[34]

When finally a team led by a Russian scientist, Professor Leonid A. Kulik, reached the site in 1927, a massive area of forest twenty-four to thirty-two kilometers in diameter was found to have been scorched bare and laid flat in an enormous radical fanlike effect. At the blast's epicenter, where they expected to find an impact crater, Kulik and his team found only an area of denuded trees that still stood upright, suggesting that the celestial body had detonated aerially, directly above the location. Despite returning to the site three years running, Kulik was unable to find any conclusive evidence to show that the devastation was caused by a meteorite.[35]

Mercifully, the area around the point of impact had been completely devoid of human habitation, so there were no human casualties as a result of the aerial blast. Yet had this celestial visitor rendezvoused with the Earth just four hours later, it would have decimated St. Petersburg, leveling the city and wiping out its entire population.

If the Carolina Bays were caused by the disintegration of a single celestial body, as their parallel alignment seems to indicate, then the event in question must have been of unimaginable proportions. From the sheer number of depressions, it perhaps equaled something like one hundred thousand Tunguska-style aerial detonations, all occurring either synchronously or in direct succession. Some evidence of the effects of just one of these detonations came to light on a farm at Camden, South Carolina, close to some of the bays. During the construction of a drainage ditch, excavators exposed, at a depth of 4.3 meters, a mass of prostrate trees. They all bore the same alignment and looked as if they had been subject to a "massive blowdown," indicating that the trunks had been uprooted during an almighty cataclysm that bore distinct similarities to the aftermath of the 1908 Tunguska event.[36]

FURTHER DEPRESSIONS

More intriguingly, huge elliptical depressions, or lakes, of a type very similar to those labeled as Carolina Bays exist close to Point Barrow, in Alaska. They are found in the permafrost, the frozen subsoil of the polar regions, and range in size from fourteen kilometers by five kilometers to 1.6 kilometers by eight hundred meters.[37] They cover an area of around seventy-two thousand square kilometers and number in their thousands, with an average trend in orientation of twelve degrees west of north.[38] In common with the Carolina Bays, the troughs of Point Barrow are always shallow. Moreover, some overlap each other, showing that they were not created simultaneously, but in succession.

In addition to the elongated depressions near Point Barrow, other similar examples exist at Harrison Bay, Alaska, as well as on the Old Crow Plain in the Yukon area of Canada.[39] They are also found in the Beni department of northeast Bolivia, distributed over a region spanning seventy-two thousand square kilometers.[40] The depressions in all these cases are elongated, shallow, and regularly have axial orientations west of north.[41]

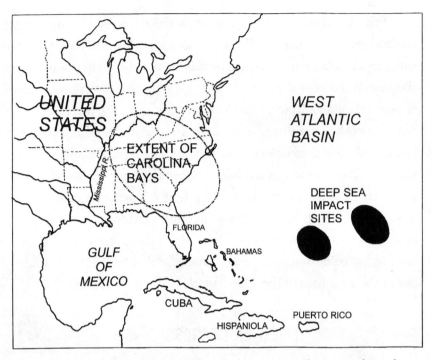

Figure 21.1. The United States and western Atlantic seaboard
showing the extent of the Carolina Bays (after William F. Prouty)
and the suggested impact site of much larger fragments of a
celestial object (after Otto Muck).

As no suitable terrestrial solution exists to explain these elliptical
depressions in the Western Hemisphere, there is every likelihood that
they were produced by shock waves from aerial detonations caused by
a disintegrating extraterrestrial object. But what sort of object, and
exactly how were they formed, and when (see fig. 21.1)?

ASTEROID A

Otto Muck dismissed the notion that meteorites could have been
responsible for creating the Carolina Bays. They would have made circular depressions, like the famous Meteor Crater of Arizona (also called
Devil's Crater). He likewise dismissed the notion that the depressions

could have been produced by a comet head, since it "is much too small and too deficient in mass. Its explosion might have caused an impressive display of celestial fireworks in the marginal zone of the nitrogen envelope, but these illuminations high up in the atmosphere would have had no consequences on Earth."[42]

In an attempt to understand fully the nature of the celestial body involved with the Carolina Bays event, Muck used the statistics from an estimated ten thousand depressions to make various theoretical calculations. Assuming that an average trough had a diameter of five hundred meters, he worked out that the ten thousand fragments involved would have possessed a mass volume of five hundred cubic kilometers.[43] Using these figures and assuming that the specific gravity of their mass was around two tons per cubic kilometer, "the weight of the solid core of the exploded celestial body" would have been "in excess of 10^{12} tonnes."[44] If the presupposed nickel-iron core of the object had equaled this weight, he estimated that the total mass of the object had originally been in the region of six hundred to seven hundred cubic kilometers, "which corresponds to a sphere about 10 kilometres in diameter."[45] In view of these calculations, Muck concluded that the "Carolina Meteorite," as he referred to it initially, must have had "an energy density" at the point of impact five million times greater than the Tunguska object of 1908.[46] If this was the case, then he felt it could better be described as an asteroid, or a minor planetoid, and so named it "Asteroid A."[47]

Asteroids are huge rocky bodies that generally orbit the sun between Mars and Jupiter, and are probably the remains of a planet or at least the constituents of a planet that never came to be. Yet not all asteroids are to be found in the belt between these two planets. Occasionally, collisions send large fragments careering off into other parts of the solar system. Some end up on courses that cross the Earth's orbit, making them potential "global killers." It may well have been one of these stray asteroids that hit Arizona, creating Meteor Crater, or, indeed, caused the KT boundary event that wiped out the dinosaurs sixty-five million years ago.

CLUES FROM TUNGUSKA

Since the 1950s, when Muck's book was mostly researched, opinion has swayed away from the Carolina Bays being created by either a meteorite swarm or a disintegrating asteroid. No meteoric fragments have been found in connection with the depressions, and no suspected large meteorite, or asteroid, impact site in any other part of the world is known to have left up to half a million elliptical depressions over an enormously large area.[48] Furthermore, other telltale evidence that is usually present at impact sites has been noticeably absent from the Carolina Bays. For instance, they were not found to contain what scientists term "shatter cones," or high-pressure changes in quartz grains.[49] Moreover, no noticeable differences could be found between the mineralogy of sediment cores taken from the bays and samples extracted from beyond the rim.[50]

Obviously, these findings have led scientists to conclude that the cause of the craters was somehow terrestrial in origin. Yet at the same time new evidence has emerged concerning the cause of the 1908 Tunguska event. When Russian scientist Leonid Kulik and his team reached the site of the aerial blast in 1927, they found no evidence of meteoric fragments. What they did find, however, was that the whole area had been pockmarked by a series of "shallow, funnel-shaped depressions of variable width but not more than four or five metres in depth." According to Kulik, there were "innumerable 'shell-holes' or craters which vary in diameter from one to perhaps 50 yards in diameter, scattered all over the central area. Their edges are mostly steep, the bottoms flat and swampy, and sometimes with traces of a central elevation."[51]

What could have caused these depressions if it was not either a meteorite or an asteroid? All sorts of rumors abounded. A fragment from a supernova, a mass of antimatter, and even an exploding UFO have all been proposed to explain the Tunguska explosion. None, however, makes any scientific sense. So what was the real answer?

In 1961 another scientific team managed to reach the remote site of the Tunguska event, and this time it did retrieve what seemed to be physical evidence of the assumed impact event. Tiny spheroids were found mixed among soil samples taken from the epicenter, and after careful analysis, they were found to be grains of non-icy "dirt" from a comet fragment.[52]

If this was indeed the case, it meant that the aerial detonation that caused the Tunguska explosion, and left in its wake a series of shallow impressions, was in fact a small, but highly volatile comet nucleus.[53] Since the countless shallow depressions found in various regions of the American continent compared favorably with the shape and depth of the much smaller Tunguska depressions, some geologists began to suspect that the Carolina Bays were the result of aerial detonations caused by a disintegrating comet fragment.[54]

DIRTY SNOWBALLS

Astronomers generally believe that comet nuclei consist of an icy core mixed with dust, the so-called dirty snowball theory first proposed by Fred L. Whipple of Harvard University during the 1950s. In size they can be as much as several kilometers in diameter or as small as a house. Indeed, it was very probably a comet of this smaller size that caused the Tunguska event of 1908.[55]

Many comets belong to our solar system. They have long elliptical orbits that take them far out beyond Pluto, a distant dwarf planet, before they arc around to begin their return journey toward the inner solar system. Some of these comets have orbits of just a few years. Comet Encke, for example, comes around every 3.3 years. Others have orbits that take them so far out into deep space that they can be tens of thousands of years in duration.

Still others come out of nowhere and cross through our solar system. Many do so without being disturbed, while a few are affected either by the gravitational pull of the sun or by one or more of the planets, usually the largest, Jupiter, which was spectacularly hit in July 1994 by twenty-one fragments of Comet Shoemaker-Levy 9. When this slingshot action takes place, a comet can be catapulted onto a new course, which could send it careering toward any one of the planets of the inner solar system, including the Earth. This game of cosmic pinball is most likely to occur after a comet has swung around the sun during its perihelion (i.e., the closest point it comes to the solar orb) and is in retrograde, in other words, when it is on its way back out of the inner solar system. Should it cross the Earth's orbit at such a time, it would enter the atmosphere both at a very acute angle and at an extremely high velocity.

If these same data are applied to the Carolina Bays mystery, the bays' characteristic appearance, arrangement, orientation, and relationship start to make sense. Could it be possible that we have evidence here of a high-velocity, low-altitude comet nucleus that entered the Earth's atmosphere on a retrograde course somewhere over the Asian continent before heading southeastward toward the American continent? If this is correct, did its core break into countless pieces as the Earth's gravitational field drew it gradually downward? Did its gradual disintegration low in the atmosphere, above Canada and the United States, produce massive aerial detonations that in turn caused immense fireballs and air-shock waves that left behind countless elliptical craters and areas of devastation along its path of destruction?

Quite clearly, the axial orientations of the Carolina Bays reflect the proposed trajectory or flight path of the incoming comet fragments. So long as these individual aerial detonations continued to take place, a shallow impact depression would form. Such an effect helps to explain not only the estimated five hundred thousand bays located along the United States's eastern seaboard, from New Jersey all the way down to Florida, but also why the elliptical depressions have pronounced rims at the southeastern ends and why some are superimposed on their neighbors.[56]

As the proposed comet nucleus continued to disintegrate, large fragments would have broken away and veered off at a tangent, separating even farther as they careered closer and closer toward the Earth. The resulting air blasts would have produced further elliptical craters, aligned not with the trajectory of the nucleus but with the course of the smaller fragments that had departed from the main core. This therefore accounts for the slightly different orientation of bays, lakes, and depressions across the United States. All this would appear to have been caused by the fragmentation of a single comet nucleus that quickly dissolved into, quite literally, millions of pieces that would have lit up the sky in a manner more terrifying than anyone on Earth today could ever imagine. This, in my opinion, is currently the most likely hypothesis behind the formation of the Carolina Bays.[57]

An example of the modern understanding of the mechanism behind the formation of the Carolina Bays is provided by Henry Savage Jr. in his definitive work *The Mysterious Carolina Bays,* published by the University of South Carolina Press in 1982. After summarizing the available evidence associated with the bays, he proposed:

> These half million shallow craters represent the visible scars of but a small fraction of the meteors that fell to earth long ago when a comet smashed into the atmosphere and exploded over the American Southeast. Countless thousands of its meteorites must have plunged into the sea beyond, leaving no trace; while other thousands fell into the flood plains of rivers and streams that soon erased their scars. Millions must have smashed into the less friable, more resistant surface soils and rocks of the hills and mountains of the western Carolinas, Georgia, and Virginia, eastern Tennessee, and Kentucky, to be generally volatized in the terrific heat of impact, leaving only surface scars, soon eroded from the hills and mountains that generally characterize those regions.[58]

Despite Savage's suggestion that thousands of comet fragments (he calls them "meteorites") "must have plunged into the sea beyond," to my knowledge no geologist or astronomer has ever embraced Muck's claims regarding the origins of the two deep elliptical holes in the West Atlantic Basin. This surprises me, for their shape and northwest–southeast orientation hint clearly at an association with the Carolina Bays event.

It could be argued that if comets are simply masses of icy dirt, then once the nucleus has vaporized there would be no fragments left to plunge into the Atlantic Ocean. However, NASA scientists are no longer willing to accept that comets are simply "dirty snowballs." There is good reason to suggest that some of them do contain solid cores that, once the icy nucleus has burned away, resemble what can only be described as typical asteroids.[59] Indeed, there is now growing evidence to suggest that some asteroids are really "comets in disguise."[60] Should this be the case, there is no reason why the comet nucleus that seems to have created the Carolina Bays did not contain a solid core. If it did, then we must ask ourselves whether two of its fragments created the deep holes identified by Muck in the West Atlantic Basin.

Even if the Carolina Bays comet was not responsible for these elliptical trenches, from Savage's own words it is clear that thousands of fragments would have plummeted into the Atlantic Ocean, causing untold devastation. If this truly was the case, then how might this new information affect our knowledge of the destruction of Plato's Atlantis?

RAVISHING OF THE GREAT SERPENT

Although much of the data contained in this chapter was unavailable to Muck when he wrote *The Secret of Atlantis,* the German rocket scientist believed he had discovered the mechanism behind the disappearance of Atlantis. Indeed, he was quite amazed that there had been "no mention of Atlantis" in connection with the extraterrestrial event surrounding the formation of the Carolina Bays.[61]

Yet Muck also knew that earlier authors had already used worldwide catastrophe myths to help confirm the reality of Plato's Atlantis account. Perhaps the first person to do this was Ignatius Donnelly, the American author of *Atlantis: The Antediluvian World,* originally published in 1882. Just one year later a sequel appeared under the title

Ragnarok: The Age of Fire and Gravel. Although it did not match the success of the first book, its extraordinary contents, inspired by the extensive archive research Donnelly had already conducted in connection with Atlantis, were explosive in their implications. The book demonstrated that a fiery comet had shattered the relative calm of the Pleistocene epoch, bringing about an almighty conflagration, period of darkness, mini–Ice Age, universal deluge, and decimation of the human race of the sort recorded in catastrophe legends worldwide.[62]

Following this same line of enquiry Colonel Alexander Braghine, in his thought-provoking book *The Shadow of Atlantis,* first published in 1940, cited various myths and legends from across the Americas in an attempt to prove that an extraterrestrial object, remembered in terms of a fiery serpent, had been responsible for the destruction of Atlantis.[63]

In this fascinating work, Braghine devoted a whole chapter to the Mayan text known as the Chilam Balam of Chumayel, which we encountered in chapter 16 in connection with the coming of the First People, or Ah-Canule, the People of the Serpent. Yet this ancient book—written in the Latin alphabet and accredited to J. J. Hoil, a Mayan scribe who lived in the second half of the eighteenth century—also speaks of the events that supposedly preceded the departure of the People of the Serpent from their original homeland.[64] For instance, in book V it states:

When the Earth began to waken. Nobody knew what was to come. . . .

And the Thirteen Gods were seized by the Nine Gods. And a fiery rain fell, and ashes fell, and rocks and trees fell down. And He butted trees and rocks against each other.

And the Thirteen Gods were seized and their heads were cut off, and their faces were slapped, and they were spat out, and weights were placed upon their shoulders.

And their Great Serpent was ravished from the heavens, together with the rattles of its tail and also with their quetzal feathers. . . .

And then their skin and pieces of their bones fell here upon the Earth. And then their heart hid itself, because the Thirteen Gods did not wish to leave their heart and their seed. And the arrows struck orphans, aged ones, widowers, and widows, who lived, not having strength for life.

And they were buried on the sandy shores, in sea-waves. And then, in one watery blow, came the waters. And, when the Great Serpent was ravished, the sky fell down and the dry land sank. Then Four Gods, the Four Bacab, destroyed everything. . . .

And the Great Mother Seiba arose amidst recollections of the destruction of the Earth. She rose straight up and elevated her head, begging for herself the eternal foliage. And by her branches and by her roots she called her Lord.[65]

Everything about these words appeared to speak of a terrible cataclysm that had accompanied an unimaginable aerial spectacle surrounding the "Thirteen Gods" of the Maya and Ahau Can, the Great, Lordly Serpent. References to "their skin and pieces of their bones" falling "upon the Earth," mentioned in the same breath as a fall of ashes, the crashing down of "rocks and trees," as well as the collapse of the sky and a sudden inundation, hint clearly at an event like that now thought to have caused the Carolina Bays.

This was also the conclusion drawn by Muck with respect to the Chumayel account, for he stated, "It is very detailed and originates in a country not far from the coast that was struck by the Carolina Meteorite. . . . It is difficult to think of any other image that could so vividly and accurately describe this event, the nature of which was almost beyond the power of words to portray."[66]

What Muck seemed unaware of is that the Chilam Balam of Chumayel describes events that occurred before the People of the Serpent left their original homeland. As I have shown in these pages, the creation myths of the Mesoamerican tribes point clearly toward

Cuba being the main source of these ancient memories. There also exist various stories that speak of the forerunners of the Yucatec Maya arriving on the peninsula following a great deluge.[67]

One post-Conquest account of the arrival of the People of the Serpent was recorded by the fanatical Catholic Diego de Landa, bishop of the Yucatán. Between 1549 and 1563 he worked in the province attempting to stamp out the native beliefs of the Maya, a crusade that apparently included the public burning of whole piles of sacred texts in the ancient town of Mani. However, after he was seriously criticized for his treatment of the Maya, Landa had a change of heart and in 1566 penned a valuable work on Mayan history and religion titled "Relacion de las casas de Yucatán." In this he states, "Some of the old people of Yucatán say they heard from their ancestors that this land was occupied by a race of people who came from the east and whom God had delivered by opening twelve paths through the sea."[68]

Also, the Mayan books of Chilam Balam and the *History of Zodzil* by Juan Darreygosa, which is based on another text titled *The Unedited Documents Relating to the Conquest of New Spain,* affirm that the earliest inhabitants of the Yucatán arrived after the sea level rose, for it states, "The most ancient people who came to populate this land [i.e., the Yucatán] were those who populated Chichén-Itzá . . . and [they] were the first after the flood."[69]

Furthermore, we know that the cataclysms recounted so vividly by the indigenous people and Afro-Caribbean communities of the Antilles speak of the breakup of a former landmass through disaster and flood, followed by the sudden emergence of individual islands. The Chilam Balam of Chumayel's reference to "sea-waves" covering the "sandy shores" in "one watery blow" seems remarkably like the description of the super-tsunamis that would unquestionably have accompanied such a catastrophic event.

As we will also recall, the Yuchi tribe of Oklahoma spoke of the destruction of their Bahamian homeland "by fires and clouds of different colors which came from the west and the north," causing it to sink beneath the sea.[70] The directions in which these "fires and clouds of different colors" are said to have traveled are so close to the southeasterly trajectory of the Carolina Bays comet that a connection between the two events seems highly probable indeed.

Had the Yuchi, the Maya, the Quiché, the Cakchiquel, the islanders of the Antilles, the Venezuelan "medicine man" encountered by Kelso de Montigny, and the native peoples of Brazil all been describing the very same sequence of events that had brought absolute devastation to the Western Hemisphere thousands of years before recorded history? How many more ancient myths and legends from tribal cultures all over the Americas are abstract memories of these same terrifying events?

THE DESTRUCTION OF ATLANTIS

It is worth recalling at this juncture the words of Plato regarding the destruction of Atlantis, for they now become much more pertinent to the matters under discussion: "There was a time of inordinate earthquakes and floods; there came one terrible day and night, in which all your men of war were swallowed bodily by the earth, and the island of Atlantis also sank beneath the sea and vanished."[71]

If the two deep sea holes in the West Atlantic Basin really are impact craters connected with the proposed Carolina Bays event, then whatever caused them would have drowned, temporarily at least, any low-lying island landmasses located in the North Atlantic Ocean (see fig. 21.2). The Bahamas lie just one thousand kilometers away from Muck's proposed impact site, while Cuba and Hispaniola are situated at a similar distance to the southwest. Puerto Rico, on the other hand, would have been just seven hundred kilometers south of the epicenter, and so is therefore likely to have suffered the full effects of the devastation.

At the same time almighty earthquakes, caused when the core fragments penetrated the ocean floor, would have shaken the entire

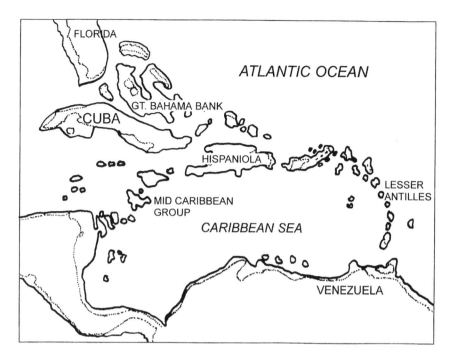

Figure 21.2. Map showing the extent of the Bahamas and Caribbean Sea prior to the Carolina Bays impact event. The Great Bahama Bank represented a huge low-lying landmass that equaled the size of England, Scotland, and Wales.

eastern Atlantic seaboard, creating even further tsunamis and pushing Bahamian and Caribbean flora and fauna to the point of extinction.

If the Greater Antilles did once form part of the Atlantean island empire, then Plato's words become much more poignant. Somehow, he would appear to have preserved a recollection of the aftermath surrounding the proposed comet impact in the West Atlantic Basin.

Muck made the same connection, although he placed Atlantis elsewhere in the Atlantic Ocean. In his opinion, the oceanic impact of the two huge core fragments of Asteroid A would have triggered submarine volcanic explosions all along the weak fracture lines of the tectonic plates marked by the north–south orientated Mid-Atlantic Ridge. Within just twenty-four hours, "one terrible day and night," the plates would have split apart, allowing the Earth's magma to come into contact with the waters of the ocean. The resulting explosion would have blown the island landmass skyhigh. Any part of it that remained would have sunk down into the cracks and hollows that opened up in the ocean floor.

As Muck triumphantly concluded, "The previous day, that bed had been a large island with high mountains and splendid buildings. Today Atlantis lies some 2 miles (3 km) lower, in the center of the depression . . . a submarine landmass, a mysterious broadening of the Atlantic Ridge, which is no longer so mysterious now that its origin has become clear. All that remains visible of Atlantis is nine small islands rising above the sea, displaying their bare slopes to those who pass in ships. The Azores."[72]

As explained in chapter 2, there is no convincing evidence to suppose that an Atlantean landmass ever existed on the Mid-Atlantic Ridge, meaning that the Azores are not the surviving tips of the lost continent's highest mountains. Muck chose to believe in a utopian Atlantis of modern conception, and thus its destruction had to be one of such enormity that it would explain why no trace of its former presence can be traced today. The view that the Bahamian and Caribbean archipelagos were the real components of Plato's Atlantean island empire, with Cuba as its crown jewel, allows us to conceive of a more realistic vision of what Plato seems to describe in his Atlantis narrative. Although low-lying landmasses or regions would have been drowned temporarily in the aftermath of the Carolina Bays event, islands as a whole would have stayed very much the same as they were before the tsunamis had struck.

END OF AN ERA

The Carolina Bays event does more than simply provide us with a possible mechanism behind the destruction of Atlantis. Among those who have realized its greater significance is Emilio Spedicato. In his all-important paper on Apollo objects he proposes that both the end of Atlantis and the termination of the Ice Age were the product of a single oceanic impact:

> We conjecture that the location [of the impact] was in the North Atlantic, somewhere east of the Carolinas. . . . The evidence from the Atlantis story . . . points to a great tsunami and a flood originating from the Atlantic area. We also remark . . . that elliptical flat depressions (the Carolina bays), filled with water, with major axis pointing southeastward to the Atlantic, characterize in number of thousands the Carolina coast (extending also from New Jersey to Florida). The time of their formation is not certain, but can well be the end of the last glaciation.[73]

Is this possible? Is it conceivable that there is a relationship between these two quite separate events in the history of our planet? Was the last Ice Age brought to a close by the same comet impact that destroyed Atlantis?

What we do know is that at the termination of the Ice Age immense ice sheets, which had engulfed a large part of the North American and Eurasian continents for many thousands of years, vanished suddenly, leading to a two-thousand-year warming of the climate, circa 13,000-11,000 BCE. There are powerful indications that dramatic events were occurring around this time across the American continent. For instance, in the glacial "muck" pits of Alaska, Frank C. Hibben, professor of archaeology at the University of New Mexico, discovered overwhelming evidence to show that tens of thousands of animals had suddenly met with the most hideous of deaths. In his book *The Lost Americans,* published in 1946, he states, "In the dark gray frozen stuff is preserved, quite commonly, fragments of ligaments, skin, hair, and even flesh. . . . The evidences of violence there are as obvious as in the horror camps of Germany. Such piles of bodies of animals or men simply do not occur by any ordinary natural means."[74]

Hibben also writes:

Mammoth and bison alike were torn and twisted as though by a
cosmic hand in Godly rage. In one place, we can find the foreleg
and shoulder of a mammoth with portions of the flesh and the toe-
nails and the hair still clinging to the blackened bones. Close by is
the neck and skull of a bison with the vertebrae clinging together
with tendons and ligaments and the chitinous covering of the horns
intact. . . . The animals were simply torn apart and scattered over
the landscape like things of straw and string, even though some of
them weighed several tons. Mixed with the piles of bones are trees,
also twisted and torn and piled in tangled groups; and the whole is
covered with fine sifting muck, then frozen solid.[75]

Such horrific scenes can only have been caused by violent upheav-
als of an unprecedented nature, a theory supported by layers of black
ash found in both Alaska and Siberia and corresponding to the end of
the Pleistocene age.[76] In Hibben's estimates more than forty million
animals perished on the American continent alone. Whole species,
including the giant beaver, mammoth, mastodon, sabertoothed tiger,
giant sloth, Alaskan lion, American camel and horse, and many others became extinct almost overnight.[77] At the same time, Pleistocene
megafauna disappear almost entirely from the Greater and Lesser
Antilles. This included a species of giant ground sloth (*Megaelocsus*)
that had formerly thrived in Cuba.[78] Since these island groups were
supposed to have been devoid of human life until circa 6000 BCE,
it indicates strongly that these animals could not simply have been
hunted to extinction as many paleontologists suppose. Were they too
destroyed in the cataclysm?

We must listen when Hibben tells us, "The Pleistocene period
ended in death. This is no ordinary extinction of a vague geological
period which fizzled to an uncertain end. This death was catastrophic
and all-inclusive. . . . The large animals that had given the name to the

period became extinct. Their death marked the end of an era. But how did they die? What caused the extinction of forty million animals?"[79]

Could the Carolina Bays comet really have been responsible for the termination of the Ice Age? Did it cause the mass devastation of animal life described so graphically by Hibben in the 1940s? More pertinently, had it really been instrumental in creating the dramatic ending to Plato's Atlantis?

22

END OF THE ICE AGE

O nce upon a time the sun, whose name was Ta-vi, roamed the Earth at will. He would spend long periods inside a cave, during which time the world would become dark and cold. On one such occasion his brother, the hare god Ta-wats, waited so long that he fell asleep by his campfire. When the wayward sun finally reemerged, he brushed so close by Ta-wats that his shoulder was scorched. Realizing the anger this would arouse in his brother, the sun fled back inside the cave.

For many years the hare god sought out Ta-vi, and after several adventures he finally came to the edge of the world. As he stood waiting, the sun emerged from his cave. Seizing the opportunity to avenge himself, Ta-wats raised his bow and shot an arrow at his brother's brilliant face. Yet the fierce heat scorched and then consumed the arrow. The hare god fired another arrow, and then another, but always the heat burned them up. Only one arrow now remained, and this was a magical arrow that never missed its mark. So Ta-wats brought the barb to his eye and, after baptizing it with a tear, let the arrow find its target. It struck his brother "full in the face, and the sun was shivered into a thousand fragments, which fell to the earth and caused a general conflagration."[1]

Ta-wats decided that he must get away from the destruction he had caused, and so fled quickly as the flames consumed first his feet, then his legs, then his body and hands, and finally his arms. Only his head now remained, and this tumbled over and over, crossing burning mountains and rolling through fire-engulfed valleys until eventually, swollen with heat, his eyes burst and tears gushed forth that then covered the Earth and quenched the flames.

Ta-vi, the sun god, had been conquered, and for the part he played in causing the world to be consumed by fire, the council of gods sentenced him to encircle the sky forever, thus creating day and night, until the end of time.[2]

This is the tale that was once told by the Ute tribe of the North American Southwest to explain why the sun, Ta-vi, and the moon, Ta-wats, cross the sky each day. Yet this curious account also appears to contain elements that go far beyond merely explaining the sun and moon's daily course. It seems to preserve vital information about an intense conflagration and deluge that the Ute believed had befallen the primordial world.

Can we see in the wandering sun a bright incoming comet that disintegrated into a "thousand fragments, which fell to the earth," causing fierce infernos? Was the sun's disappearance inside a cave the recollection of a dark nuclear winter brought about by such a catastrophe? Were the tears that issued forth from Ta-wat's eyes an abstract memory of all-encompassing floods that engulfed the North American continent in the wake of the devastating impact event?

I would not be the first writer to draw attention to the significance of this powerful American Indian folktale. Ignatius Donnelly included it in his compelling work *Ragnarok: The Age of Fire and Gravel,* first published in 1883. "Here we have the succession of arrows, or comets," he asserted. "And here, again, we have the conflagration, the fragments of something falling on the earth, the long absence of the sun, the great rains and the cold."[3]

Indeed, we have. Donnelly knew he was on to something of immense importance when he was writing this book. The folktales he collected from all over the North American continent and beyond spoke clearly

of a cometary impact of incredible magnitude, linked in some inextrica-
ble way with the catastrophic events that accompanied the cessation of
the Ice Age. Yet in 1883 he had no scientific proof to back up what he
believed had occurred during this dramatic period in the Earth's long
history. The Tunguska event was still another twenty-five years away,
and it would be three-quarters of a century before the full implications
of the Carolina Bays would be realized, and more than a century before
the fragments of Comet Shoemaker-Levy 9 would crash, one after the
other, into the surface of Jupiter, making it blatantly clear that impacts
of this sort not only occur, but can happen at any time.

A FIERY CHARIOT

One might doubt the ability of indigenous peoples to preserve the
memory of catastrophic events that occurred so long ago. It is, however,
worth pointing out that the American Indians of Arizona recall how
once their ancestors watched as a fiery chariot fell on Coon Mountain.
At the exact spot they say it crashed is the famous Meteor Crater, or
Devil's Crater, formed perhaps twenty-thousand years ago.[4] It is one
kilometer across, some two hundred meters deep, and is thought to have
been made by a meteorite around one hundred meters in diameter.[5]

If the Ute really have provided us with an abstract account of
the cosmic visitor that wrought havoc across the American continent
around the end of the Ice Age, is it possible that the indigenous peoples
of the Bahamas and Caribbean also preserved a memory of this same
terrifying event? Might this explain Plato's statements concerning the
supposed destruction of Atlantis by earthquakes and floods?

As we saw in the last chapter, academics such as Emilio Spedicato
are willing to consider that, in his Atlantis account, Plato had been
alluding to events surrounding the termination of the Ice Age. This is
very promising indeed. Yet to access the picture fully, we must determine what exactly happened in the Caribbean and Bahamas at the
end of the last Ice Age, and before we can do this it will be necessary

to establish the exact age of the Carolina Bays to know where to start looking for this evidence.

SEARCHING FOR SEDIMENT

In the 1950s a scientific survey team, funded by Duke University, collected a large number of sediment cores from Carolina Bays as much as 160 kilometers apart. These showed that at the base of some of the depressions there was a layer of blue-grey clay, which had been blown into the bays after a sudden deforestation and desiccation of the region.[6] This proved to be the key to dating the bays, for the bottom sediment directly beneath this clay layer revealed pollen spectra relating specifically to the tundra forests that had dominated North America until the end of the Ice Age, circa 13,000 BCE. Yet in contrast, the sediment layer immediately above the blue clay produced carbon-14 dates many hundreds of years after the ice sheets had finally receded.[7]

Over the years, the age of the Carolina Bays has been hotly debated. Melton and Schriever were of the opinion that they were formed between "50,000 and a million years ago."[8] Yet there are strong indications that the bay formation process occurred at a more recent date, for as William F. Prouty pointed out in 1952, those examined seemed to be placed on what he called "late Pleistocene terraces,"[9] confirming their creation around the end of the last Ice Age.

Carbon-14 dating of the bays has varied considerably, not helped by the now obligatory recalibration of all carbon-14 dates, due to inconsistencies in the manner that carbon-14 is released from organic matter. One survey conducted by the University of South Carolina in the 1970s provided dates between circa seventy thousand years and six thousand years BP (before present),[10] while another set of tests showed dates that ranged between 18,460 and 8,355 years BP.[11] Henry Savage noted that five individual test samples examined by the university produced an average date in the region of "10,500 years ago" (approximately 10,640 BCE with modern recalibration of Carbon-14 dates), which, as he pointed out, "is well within the range of origins of tribal legends."[12] This date accords very well with the sequence dating of the bays deduced by Duke University in the 1950s, as well as with the observations of geologists such as William F. Prouty, who concluded that the bays "cannot be older than late Pleistocene if formed by meteorites."[13]

From this information it becomes clear that the bays' formation took place sometime around the close of the Pleistocene age, circa 11,000–10,500 BCE, when the temperatures in the Northern Hemisphere were slowly rising again and the ice sheets were finally beginning to recede. What this means is that whatever caused them must have struck the North American landmass at this time. Even if this was correct, could I find any evidence linking the Carolina Bays comet impact with the proposed inundation of the low-lying regions of the Bahamas and Caribbean, which presumably occurred around the same time? The answer, unbelievably, is yes.

THE EMILIANI CONTROVERSY

In 1957 Cesare Emiliani of the Department of Geology at the University of Miami noted that deep-sea core samples from the Gulf of Mexico displayed clear evidence of sharp temperature rises circa 9000 BCE,[14] a date that can today be raised to circa 11,000 BCE using up-to-date carbon-14 recalibration. This can only have come from a rapid melting of the ice sheets on the North American continent that, by this time, were already in retreat due to the increase in temperature at the end of the last Ice Age. Then in 1975 a team of geochemists and marine scientists led by Emiliani[15] set out to show that analysis of core samples from the De Soto Canyon area of the Gulf of Mexico could now "identify an episode of rapid ice melting and sea-level rise at about 9600 years BCE,"[16] circa 11,500–11,000 BCE using modern carbon-14 dating techniques. This finding was determined by a dramatic increase in sedimentation resulting from the outpouring of ice meltwater leaving the Mississippi River at this time. Clearly, something major was making the ice sheets melt much quicker than had previously been the case, although what exactly this could have been was beyond the remit of Emiliani's work at this time. Despite this, he and his colleagues used these findings to propose that the rapid melting of the ice, with its consequential outpouring into the Gulf of Mexico, "in spite of its great antiquity in cultural terms, could be an explanation for the deluge stories common to many Eurasian, Australasian, and American traditions. Plato . . . [in his story of Atlantis] set the date of the flood at 9,000 years before Solon, equal to 9600 years BCE or 11,600 years BP: this date coincides, within all limits of error, with the age of both the highest concentration of ice meltwater in the Gulf of Mexico and the Valders readvance."[17]

The Valders readvance is the name given to the sudden resurgence of the ice sheets that occurred quite unexpectedly following the retreat of the very same ice sheets at the end of the last Ice Age. It came on very suddenly, in a matter of a generation or so, and prevailed for a period of approximately 1,200 years, resulting in a mini–Ice Age that ended as quickly as it had begun. In Europe this same event is known as the Younger Dryas event (a term used universally today). At the time when this book was written, the Valders readvance was thought to have begun around 9600–9000 BCE and come to an end around 8300–8000 BCE. However, with the necessary recalibration of carbon-14 dates employed today, it is now thought to have started circa 10,800 BCE and to have ceased circa 9600 BCE.

Emiliani's findings suggest that at the onset of the Valders readvance something else was happening as well—a massive surge of ice meltwater flowing down the Mississippi River and emptying out into the Gulf of Mexico. So what caused this sudden melting of the ice sheets, which at the time still covered large areas of North America? Was it fragments of a comet crashing into them? Did this cause the vast volumes of water they held to be instantly released into the local river systems, which in turn outpoured into the Mississippi? Did the evaporation of the water locked up in the ice sheets rise into the upper atmosphere and fall back down as torrential rain that continued unabated for weeks, if not months on end, resulting in additional flooding across the Northern Hemisphere? And, finally, did this meltwater cause the sea level to rise rapidly, leaving low-lying regions of the globe to be drowned beneath the waves forever?

This was strong stuff from the scholarly world, especially one headed by a scientist of Emiliani's caliber. Moreover, his findings cannot be underestimated. Along with his colleagues at the University of Miami he had managed to propose a solution explaining the destruction of Atlantis in a manner that no other academic had dared before. During the mid-1970s, when Emiliani and his colleagues' paper appeared in the prestigious magazine *Science,* historians saw Atlantis as a memory of the volcanic eruption that had destroyed the Mediterranean island of Thera and devastated the Minoan civilization of Crete, circa 1450 BCE. Emiliani's findings overturned these old ideas and showed that Plato had been correct about the destruction of Atlantis. He did not mention any kind of impact event, but he did find a suitable mechanism to explain the drowning of Atlantis in approximately the same time frame offered by Plato. To the international media these findings were like manna from heaven. They seized on Emiliani and his associates' conclusions and rather prematurely announced that scientists had at last confirmed the reality of Atlantis.

Not unnaturally, the academic community reeled and so readied itself for a concerted attack on this American scientist who dared to suggest that Atlantis had existed exactly as Plato had imagined in his famous dialogues. To spearhead the assault, the critics called on no less an authority than Herbert E. Wright Jr. He himself had ably demonstrated how sediment cores extracted from lake sites in the North American Midwest showed that the transition from glacial spruce forests to postglacial hardwoods had been "abrupt," implying "a marked shift in ecological conditions" at the end of the Valders readvance,[18] which today we know occurred around 9600 BCE.

WRIGHT'S ATTACK

It was in an important article written for the authoritative work *Atlantis: Fact or Fiction?* edited by Edwin S. Ramage and published by the Indiana University Press in 1978, that Wright chose to deliver his attack on Emiliani and his colleagues.[19] After reviewing the manner in which Atlantologists distort scientific evidence to fit their own theories, Wright questioned Emiliani and his colleague's belief that the ice meltwater surging into the Gulf of Mexico from the Mississippi River occurred during the Valders readvance, and not afterward, when the temperature rose and the ice sheets started to melt. Wright pointed out that surges of meltwater are caused not by snow "accumulation and wastage, but rather an abrupt change in the physical factors controlling ice flow."[20] This, of course, is correct. However, all Emiliani and his colleagues had suggested was that these events occurred during the readvance of the ice sheets, which was very strange indeed. In his words, "This age coincides with that of the Valders readvance; because this readvance was accompanied by a rapid rise in sea level, it was apparently a surge, which brought ice to lower latitudes and caused rapid melting."[21]

Wright went on to query the effects an increase in the sea level of the sort implied by Emiliani and colleagues might have had on low-lying regions. In Wright's opinion, if it had occurred in a matter of a few brief years, coastal areas would have been affected only slightly. Such an outpouring of ice meltwater would hardly, as Emiliani was implying, have drowned whole islands such as fabled Atlantis![22] Yet what Emiliani and his associates actually said was that, according to their calculations, there would have been an "accelerated rise in sea level, of the order of decimeters per year."[23] As anyone can work out, over a two-hundred-year period an increase of this order would have caused, as they say, "widespread flooding of low-lying areas, many of which were inhabited by man."[24]

Also queried was Emiliani's date of 9600 BCE for the high point of the surge of ice meltwater reaching the Gulf of Mexico. In Wright's opinion the Valders readvance took place as early as 11,000 BCE, completely invalidating the case.[25]

Wright's argument here is petty and pedantic. Back in the 1970s the lack of understanding regarding the recalibration of carbon-14 dates meant that the different dating techniques available could produce a wide range of often-contradictory dates for a single event. As mentioned above, it is now considered that the Younger Dryas mini–Ice Age began as early as circa 10,800 BCE, and not around 9600 BCE. This means that Wright was in fact correct. However, this realization detracted nothing from Emiliani's argument.

Not helping their case was Emiliani and colleague's presumption that the greatest surge of ice meltwater occurred exactly halfway "between 12,200 and 11,000 years ago, that is, about 11,600 years ago," i.e., 9600 BCE, the popularly accepted date given by Plato in the *Critias* for the destruction of Atlantis.[26]

As a consequence of these findings, Wright concluded that by citing a date of 9600 BCE Emiliani and his colleagues had encouraged a spurious link between the events surrounding the Valders readvance and Plato's Atlantis account.[27]

"In view of the numerous difficulties in relating glacial events to short-term global sea-level changes," Wright concluded, "Atlantists will have to look elsewhere for their catastrophes," that is, in the Mediterranean.[28] For in his words, "The scientific documentation of the magnitude and chronology of the explosion and collapse of Santorini [i.e., Thera] . . . establishes this locale as a leading contender for Atlantis,"[29] bringing us full circle back to the hardline academic view on the Atlantis myth.

By removing the significance of Emiliani's chosen date for the sudden surge of meltwater pouring into the Gulf of Mexico from the Mississippi River, that is, 9600 BCE (ca. 10,800 BCE using modern recalibration techniques), and dismissing the evidence presented for this event at the beginning of the Valders readvance, Wright felt he had successfully demolished any scientific grounds for confirming the existence of Atlantis during this distant epoch. This was regrettable, for it really does seem as if Emiliani and his associates at the University of Miami recognized the true mechanism behind the rapid drowning of low-lying regions of the Bahamas and Caribbean, the very heartland of the Atlantean island empire.

Yet all the indications are that the events described by Emiliani and his colleagues in their *Science* article, along with the evidence of the Carolina Bays comet impact, provide compelling proof that something catastrophic did indeed occur at this time. Clearly, it was an event of terrifying proportions that was kept alive in the myths and legends of the indigenous peoples of the North American continent, as well as those of the Caribbean islands, until finally it came to the attention of Phoenician and Carthaginian voyagers during the first millennium BCE. They, in the current author's opinion, carried this knowledge back to the Mediterranean world, where, finally, it was picked up on by Plato and used as material for his account of the destruction of Atlantis.

ZERO DAY ONE

Yet how can we justify proposing that Atlantis might have been destroyed by earthquakes and floods perhaps as much as 1,200 years earlier than Plato's assumed date of 9600 BCE? Well, in actuality, Plato never states this is the date of Atlantis's destruction. As outlined in chapter 3, in the *Critias* he records that the Atlantic island was submerged nine thousand years before the dialogue in which the subject of Atlantis is debated by Socrates, Timaeus, Critias, and Hermocrates.[30] As this fictitious meeting is set in the year 421 BCE, it provides a hypothetical date for the island's destruction of 9421 BCE.

Earlier, in the *Timaeus,* the war between the Atlanteans and Athenians, along with the destruction of Atlantis, is said by Plato to have taken place only after the foundation of Egyptian civilization. Since the old priest of Sais tells us that the sacred records of the temple were already *eight thousand years old* by the time of Solon's visit to Egypt circa 570 BCE, this means that Atlantis cannot have been submerged before circa 8570 BCE. So each dialogue contradicts the other. In other words, we should not rely on Plato to provide us with an accurate date for the destruction of Atlantis.

Otto Muck chose a much later date for the destruction of Atlantis in *The Secret of Atlantis*. By using a rather unorthodox interpretation of the Mayan long-count calendar—suggested by the work of Professor H. Ludendorff of the Astrophysical Observatory at Potsdam, Germany—Muck concluded that the asteroid he saw as having destroyed Atlantis struck the Atlantic Ocean on "Zero Day One." This date, he said, corresponded with June 5, 8498 BCE, in the Gregorian calendar.[31]

No other scholar of the Mayan calendar has been able to verify these calculations, and most authorities are of the opinion that the long-count calendar has a start date of August 13, 3114 BCE.[32]

It would be ridiculous to ascribe any single date to the catastrophic events that appear to have twice drowned large parts of the Bahamas and Caribbean, once through the destruction caused by a super-tsunami, triggered most likely by a comet impact event, and, a second time, by a sudden outpouring of ice meltwater into the Gulf of Mexico and the rapid rise in sea level following the impact event. Yet it is clear from the various dates provided by those who have recognized signs of a massive natural catastrophe that occurred at the termination of the Ice Age that these flood events must have taken place circa 10,800 BCE, that is, around the commencement of the Younger Dryas mini–Ice Age.

KING-LISTS AND CHRONOLOGIES

As we saw in chapter 1, Plato most likely derived his own Atlantean timeline from dates preserved in pharaonic king-lists such as the Royal Canon of Turin. If correct, it is perhaps significant that ancient Egyptian texts speak of the age of the gods being brought to a close by dramatic events that bear a striking similarity to the already cited American catastrophe myths featuring fire, flood, and periods of darkness.

For example, the foundation texts carved on the walls of the Ptolemaic temple of Edfu in southern Egypt state that during *zep tepi,* the first period of building construction in Egypt, an "enemy serpent" known as the Great Leaping One appears out of nowhere.[33] Its actions plunge the world into a state of darkness at which point a flood engulfs the so-called Island of the Egg, a primeval homeland of the gods called also Wetjeset-Neter. Mass devastation follows, bringing desolation and decay, and once the waters have finally receded, the divine inhabitants of the island are now no more than "ghosts," implying that they have been killed during the period of floods and darkness.[34] We are told that life returns to Wetjeset-Neter, and soon a second phase of building construction commences. This is conducted by divine beings known as the Shebtiw and Netjeru,[35] the latter of which go on to lay the foundations of Egyptian civilization.[36]

There is every reason to link the symbol of the Great Leaping One, which brings darkness, destruction, flood, and decay, with the aftermath of a catastrophic comet impact. We must also not forget the Middle Kingdom text known as "The Tale of the Shipwrecked Sailor," reviewed in chapter 9. It contains the story of an Egyptian sailor who recalls how he was shipwrecked after his vessel encountered waves eight cubits (3.6 to 4.4 meters) high during a voyage to the king's mines, located in a foreign land. All the crew except for him are killed, and after being cast on to the "island of the ka," he meets a huge bearded serpent 30 cubits (13.5 to 16.5 meters) long. It addresses the sailor, telling him that it is the surviving member of a family of seventy-five serpents who lived on the island before a "star fell, and they [the serpents] went up in flames through it."[37]

Although the island in question probably lay off the east coast of Africa, the manner in which its serpentine inhabitants were engulfed in flames by a falling "star" suggests, once again, that it is an abstract memory of either a comet or meteorite strike, perhaps even the Carolina Bays impact event, which most likely affected not only the American continent, but also large parts of the ancient world.

Since the 1980s scientists have been investigating a "charcoal-rich layer" found in geological layers around the world corresponding to a date of approximately 10,800 BCE. This date, as we have seen, corresponds with the onset of the Valders readvance in North America and the Younger Dryas event in Europe. Almost certainly this charcoal-rich layer was laid down in the wake of the proposed Carolina Bays impact event by fire ash and burned debris rising into the upper atmosphere. Here it would have contributed to a prolonged period of darkness before raining back down to Earth and forming this thick, oily black layer, which is between 1.5 centimeters and thirteen centimeters in thickness. It has been found now in France, the Netherlands, Germany, Belgium, Great Britain, White Russia, India, South Africa, Australia, and, more significantly, Egypt.[38] Known as the Usselo horizon, after the site in the Netherlands where it was originally identified by Dutch geologist and mineralogist Johan "Han" Kloosterman (see the preface), this stunning discovery will hopefully now provide the impetus for the scientific community to begin looking for further evidence of this impact event in other parts of the world.

So having established that Plato may well have described the island of Cuba when he wrote about the main island of Atlantis, we now find that he pinpointed pretty accurately the time frame in which the low-lying regions of the Bahamas and Caribbean were twice drowned, initially, most probably, by a super-tsunami triggered by an impact event and later by ice meltwater flowing at a fast rate into the Gulf of Mexico. How he managed to achieve this incredible feat might never be known. Yet there is no doubt that Plato somehow got it right. Yet even so we still have one major dilemma to resolve.

If the myths and legends surrounding the inundation of the Bahamas and Caribbean derive originally from eyewitness accounts, it would imply that these archipelagos must have been occupied at the time of the Valders readvance, circa 10,900 BCE. Yet such a conclusion goes against everything that the archaeologists tell us about the earliest inhabitants of these islands. In their opinion the first Paleo-

American Indian peoples to reach the Greater Antilles arrived circa 6000–5000 BCE. According to them, no archaeological evidence exists to even hint at a prior occupation of these island groups.

It is a strange dilemma that now becomes critical to this debate. If the archaeologists are right, then there never were any Atlanteans, just a series of beautiful, tropical islands, some of them with navigable rivers, that played no role whatsoever in the rise of civilization in the Americas. As we shall see next (and also in the epilogue), outside the constraints of archaeological opinion, there is compelling evidence to show that the sunken regions of the Bahamas and Caribbean were indeed occupied during some earlier epoch, and so may well hold important clues concerning the historical reality of lost Atlantis.

Part Five
EMERGENCE

23

SUNKEN SECRETS

It was the summer of 1993 and the hurricane season had still to make itself felt on the sun-drenched Bahamian island. Daily, huge motor cruisers, going between Florida and the more popular resorts in the archipelago, drew into Bimini's busy marina. Many people came specifically to follow in the footsteps of the island's most famous resident, the American writer Ernest Hemingway. He lived here periodically between 1931 and 1937, spending much of his time big-game fishing. Bimini's main nightspot, the Compleat Angler, was a shrine to the island's celebrated hero, its walls adorned with black-and-white pictures of the "old man of the sea" standing proud next to strung-up marlin or sailfish.

Yet behind the lazy facade of fishing exploits, rum punches, and laid-back islanders, something else stirred on the island. From her base on North Bimini (there are in fact two adjacent main islands—North Island and South Island), Bahamian historian Donnie Fields readied herself for another day of field exploration along its slim coastline. At the time she was a key member of a dedicated team of volunteers, headed by Californian archaeologist William "Bill" Donato and united under the banner Project Alta. Every year the group came to the island in search of indisputable proof that Bimini was a surviving fragment of lost Atlantis.

PREHISTORIC FOOTPRINTS

Fields—who through her frequent visits to the island became almost the guardian of Bimini's lost heritage—decided to examine a remote area of beach for evidence of ancient occupation. Having cut her way through thick, inhospitable undergrowth, she stepped down onto the hot sand and saw before her something of immense value to our understanding of Bahamian prehistory.

On exposed mud rock, leading right to the water's edge, were human footprints. Investigating further, she uncovered no fewer than twenty-four individual impressions belonging to three separate individuals, probably a family unit consisting of a father, mother, and child.[1]

The direction of the footprints was quite clear. They led directly out into the channel that lay between the two main islands. It meant that those who had walked this path before the mud hardened did so when the sea level was much lower and the islands still formed part of a single landmass.

Realizing the significance of her discovery, Fields made casts of several of the footprints and submitted them for scientific analysis. Those who saw them proposed that the shape and depth of one of the sets implied that they belonged to a person 1.63 meters in height.[2] Furthermore, it was considered that "the casts also evidence the toes in relation to a high arch often associated with Cro-Magnon humans and some Amerindian peoples."[3]

Fields showed photographs of the casts to marine geologist John Gifford of the University of Miami, who had previously contested evidence that the Great Bahama Bank had been occupied before its final submergence. Yet he had no hesitation in accepting the footprints as genuine and proposed that they were perhaps seven thousand years old.[4] Such an admission was truly astonishing. That an academic of Gifford's caliber should have conceded that the footprints were this old meant that they were probably much older still.

In making such an assessment, Gifford had gone completely against conventional archaeological opinion concerning the prehistory of the Bahamas. This contends that the archipelago was unoccupied before the Lucayan American Indians arrived circa 600–700 BCE. Furthermore, as we have already established, the Great Bahama Bank, on which the Bimini Islands are situated, disappeared for the most part between 8000 and 3000 BCE,[5] even though, as we saw in chapter 22, the initial inundation of low-lying regions probably began during the Valders readvance, circa 10,900–9600 BCE. Gifford's proposed age of the footprints is based purely on his understanding of Caribbean archaeology, which asserts that the earliest inhabitants arrived in the Greater Antilles sometime around 6000–5000 BCE. It is, however, possible that the human footprints found on North Bimini were made by people who occupied the Great Bahama Bank when the western Atlantic seaboard was devastated by a comet impact sometime around thirteen thousand years ago.

So who were these unknown individuals, walking across an open mudflat in the northern part of the Bahamian landmass thousands of years before the Lucayans reached the islands? Were they ancestors of the Yuchi tribe of Oklahoma, who believed they inhabited the former Bahamian landmass before it was torn apart "by fires and clouds of different colors," causing it to sink beneath the waves?[6] Were they the ancestors of Mesoamerican populations, such as the Quiché-Maya and the Cakchiquel, who left their mythical homeland in the east during a period of darkness? Were they related to the People of the Serpent, who arrived on the mainland by boat out of the east, after the Great Serpent had fallen to Earth, causing devastation and floods?

These were all tantalizing questions, although in isolation the prehistoric footprints discovered by Donnie Fields in 1993 were not enough. More hard evidence would be required if the members of Project Alta were going to demonstrate that the Great Bahama Bank had formerly been occupied by a prehistoric race connected with Plato's Atlantis. Yet their quest was by no means a new one. Indeed, the very reason why the team began visiting Bimini in the first place is a fascinating, though highly unusual, story that cannot be ignored.

THE SLEEPING PROPHET

It begins in September 1926, when Bimini's lazy world was rudely interrupted by one of the Bahamas' fiercest foes—the tropical hurricane. It wreaked havoc across the island, tearing down trees, razing homes, and destroying commercial property. Victims included the Bimini Bay Rod and Gun Club as well as Hotel Bimini, both owned by an American millionaire who had invested heavily in the island.

Shortly before the disaster struck, this unnamed millionaire had been introduced to a very remarkable man from Hopkinsville, Kentucky, who ran a rather unorthodox medical practice in Virginia Beach, Virginia. It was said that he could prescribe treatments for illnesses and problems to patients simply by laying down on a couch, allowing himself to fall into a trancelike sleep, and pronouncing the solution vocally while in an unconsciousness state. It was for this reason that he quickly became known as the Sleeping Prophet.

This gifted individual, whose name was Edgar Cayce (1877–1945), had demonstrated already the potential of his strange psychic talents. He had helped to restore the sight of one of the millionaire's business associates, who suffered blindness following an automobile accident. Suitably impressed, the millionaire and his business circle had offered Cayce the finances he required to build a hospital at Virginia Beach. This they would provide in exchange for psychic information relating to potential mineral deposits and oilfields in the states of Kentucky and Florida.[7] The collaboration worked well, and eventually Cayce was asked to switch his attentions to Bimini in the hope that he might be able to detect untapped sources of oil and gold and to substantiate local rumors and stories concerning the presence on the island of Spanish treasure.

Cayce's first psychic session in connection with Bimini took place in his office at Virginia Beach just a month before the hurricane struck. It confirmed that the island did indeed contain "gold, bullion, silver, and . . . plateware."[8] More pertinently, he spoke of Bimini as being "the highest portion left above the waves of once a great continent."[9]

In the wake of the hurricane, the millionaire needed desperately to recreate his offshore empire. So Cayce was asked to accompany him and his business associates to Bimini for a three-day visit. He accepted, and the journey finally took place in February 1927. Upon his arrival in Bimini (incidentally, the only visit he would ever make to the island), Cayce was taken out to one of the sites he had earlier pinpointed in his psychic readings. Here he lay down and promptly provided four further channeled messages. These confirmed that they had arrived at the correct spot. Yet after the party failed to find anything of significance, Cayce came under increasing pressure to explain what was going on.

In response, the Sleeping Prophet produced even more readings. These suggested that no treasure would be found, "not because of the information being incorrect," but because it came from "a universal and infinite source" that had been channeled through a "carnal or material plane," in other words Cayce and his business associates.[10] "Hence we know sin lies at the door, and in that information as has been given respecting same, that *the house must be set in order*" (current author's emphasis) before anything at all could be found,[11] the moral of the story being that his psychic abilities could not be exploited in such an apparently selfish manner.

The psychic's unconscious mind now offered the Bimini businessmen other, more spiritually sound enterprises that would enable them to profit from the island's natural resources. These included the construction of a resort city, the reclamation of submerged land, and the utilization of wave power to create a hydroelectric plant as an unlimited source of free energy.[12] None of these proposals was ever realized.

THE SLIME OF AGES

Cayce did not take part in any further psychic questing on Bimini. Yet having become interested in the island's unknown past, his channelings began to focus on its role as the remnant of a sunken continent. Over a period of seventeen years, from 1927 until 1944, the lost world of

Atlantis became a familiar theme in Cayce's psychic dialogues (although his first readings on the subject were given as early as 1924).[13] He would make more than eight hundred references to the lost continent,[14] which his unconscious mind saw in terms of an enormous ocean-bound land-mass that stretched from the Bahamas and Caribbean across to the West Coast of Africa.

On a number of occasions during his later life, Cayce alluded to Bimini in connection with Atlantis's central island, which in his read-ings he referred to under the name of Poseidia. On December 19, 1933, for example, while speaking of three locations where the records per-taining to the arts and sciences of the Atlantean civilization were hid-den prior to its destruction, he revealed that one of them would be found "in the sunken portion of Atlantis, or Poseidia, where a portion of the temples may yet be discovered, under the slime of ages of sea water—near what is known as Bimini, off the coast of Florida."[15]

Whether the person to whom the reading was being directed was familiar with Cayce's earlier business interests in Bimini is question-able. What does seem clear, however, is that his extraordinary talents, in respect to both his diagnosis of medical ailments and his vision of the world's early history, provided him with a huge following toward the end of his life. It led eventually to the formation of the Edgar Cayce Foundation, a worldwide organization dedicated to the preservation and final confirmation of Cayce's psychic readings.

PROPHECIES OF POSEIDIA

It was in 1940 that Edgar Cayce delivered what is arguably his most important prophecy on Atlantis's imminent reemergence. Although Bimini is not referred to directly in this all-important reading, Cayce claimed, "Poseidia [i.e., the sunken lands off the islands of the Bahamas and Caribbean] will be among the first portions of Atlantis to rise again. Expect it, in sixty-eight and sixty-nine; not so far away!"[16]

It was this profound statement that was to initiate a number of well-coordinated research expeditions to the Bahamas in the years that followed. Invariably, these would be organized by members of the Association for Research and Enlightenment (ARE), the research division of the Edgar Cayce Foundation, often under the leadership of Edgar Cayce's son, Hugh Lynn Cayce.[17]

With the approach of 1968—the much-anticipated first year of discovery—the ARE stepped up its surveillance of the waters around Bimini. More expeditions were mounted and flyovers made. From 1965 through to 1968, the organization's interests in the Bahamas were handled by geologist William Hutton, who, for some reason, liked to refer to himself in official ARE publications simply as "the Geologist."[18] Intriguingly enough, nothing that might help confirm the presence of a former Atlantean civilization was discovered on any of these expeditions, dampening hopes that Cayce's prediction concerning the reemergence of a "portion" of Poseidia would be fulfilled during the allotted time frame of "sixty-eight and sixty-nine."

THE TEMPLE SITE

It was at this point that fate stepped in and took a hand in affairs. On a regular flight between Miami and Nassau during the summer of 1968, Captain Robert Brush and his copilot, Trigg Adams, found themselves north of Andros, the largest island in the archipelago. As they made visual contact with the tiny islet known as Pine Cay, the two men noticed a well-defined rectangular structure in the waters below. It was identified as the foundations of a building, the eastern end of which had been sectioned off about a quarter of the way along its length by an interior wall.[19]

In all their previous flights over these sun-kissed isles, the two pilots—both of whom were members of the ARE[20]—had never seen anything like this before. Brush in particular realized that they had discovered something of possible archaeological significance.

Upon their return to Miami, Brush and Adams excitedly related

news of the discovery to two friends, both of whom were also followers of Edgar Cayce. They were J. Manson Valentine, a zoologist and
research associate at Honolulu's Bishop Museum, as well as the honor-
ary curator of the Museum of Science at Miami, and Dimitri Rebikoff,
a noted French oceanographer and underwater surveyor. So impressed
were they by what Brush and Adams had to say that plans were made
immediately to hire a boat and dive onto the site, which they succeeded
in doing during the second half of August 1968.

Valentine and Rebikoff determined that the underwater feature was
approximately thirty-four by twenty meters in size, oriented perfectly
east–west, and marked out by a thick bed of dark seagrass. Underneath
these marine flowering plants, a familiar sight in the shallow waters
of the Bahamas, were perfectly laid limestone blocks about a meter in
thickness.[21]

Satisfied that the ruin was indeed the remnant of a lost civilization,
Valentine and Rebikoff made the decision to join forces with Brush and
Adams to form the Marine Archaeology Research Society in order to
search for further evidence of anomalous underwater features.[22] More
significantly, Valentine and Rebikoff agreed, somewhat prematurely, to
promote the Andros site as firm evidence of Atlantis's reemergence during the all-important year of 1968.

In a press release dispatched from Miami on August 23, 1968,
Valentine boldly announced that "an ancient temple" had been located
in the Bahamian waters.[23] Its "walls are sloping. I dug into the sand
and managed to feel about another three feet [one meter] down. It is
obviously much deeper, but we will not know how much until we exca-
vate. The material is a kind of masonry and it is definitely man-made."[24]
He ended the statement by saying that he hoped the "temple" might be
"part of Atlantis, the ancient lost continent, which, legend has it, vanished beneath the sea after a mighty cataclysm centuries ago."[25]

Not everyone shared Valentine and Rebikoff's view that the Andros
"temple" site constituted proof of Atlantis's reemergence. In the late
1970s, David Zink, professor of English at the U.S. Air Force Academy

in Colorado, investigated the structure with a diving team as part of his annual Project Poseidia expeditions on Bimini.[26] He determined it to be constructed not, as was first imagined, of enormous limestone blocks, but of piles of loose rock. Indeed, Zink stated in his book *The Stones of Atlantis,* originally published in 1978, that a reporter named John Keasler of the *Miami News* interviewed an Andros islander named Reuben Russell, who claimed to have helped build the structure as a sponge pen for a Nassau gentleman sometime in the 1930s.[27]

Despite these revelations, Zink remained unconvinced of the "temple" site's modern construction. He pointed out that its great distance from the shoreline seemed to argue against its use as a sponge pen. Furthermore, the fact that it was located in just one meter of water would have made if difficult for local fishing boats to approach the structure.[28] Moreover, there is no hard evidence to suppose that the statement made by Russell even related to the same structure as the one found by Brush and Adams.

Anthropologist R. Cedric Leonard in his book *Quest for Atlantis,* published in 1979, makes some interesting observations about the site, which he visited with a party of friends on June 3, 1970. According to him, "The local inhabitants, for at least the last three generations, believed this ruin to be the remains of a pen for storing conch shells and sponges: there are many such pens scattered about the area, but none of them are built of stone. Such pens are built of wood, much smaller, of light construction, and in deeper water so that boats may easily pass over. Moreover, they are not laid out in perfectly straight lines having 90° corners."[29]

The jury is still out as to the true identity of the Andros "temple" site. Yet the publicity that inevitably surrounded its discovery swiftly drew others to begin their own search of the Great Bahama Bank for sites of archaeological interest, particularly in the shallows off Andros. At little more than a meter or so in depth, its waters are ideal for aerial surveillance, and very quickly new underwater features were coming to light.

It was Robert Brush who discovered what is arguably one of the most enigmatic structures to be identified in the waters off Andros. On a flight a little west of its southern coastline, he spotted what appeared to be a huge dark ring around ninety meters in diameter and a meter or so in width. Within it were two further concentric circles of approximately the same thickness. This inexplicable feature lay in just half a meter of water and only twenty meters out from the shoreline. On-site investigations revealed that the largely fragmentary rings were defined by a "three-tiered" layer of stone covered by a layer of seagrass.[30]

In the late 1970s, film footage of this new Andros site was featured in an unbroadcast television documentary titled *A Special Report: Atlantis in the Bahamas,* put together by producers Douglas Kenyon and Thomas Miller and director Cecilia Gonzalez. The footage taken from the air appeared to support the conclusion regarding its artificial construction. This much was true. However, meticulous, on-site investigations of the Andros ring feature by Gregory Little and his wife, Lora Little, in 2003, showed conclusively that it was nothing more than a low-walled sponge pen built by local fishermen (see the epilogue).

DIVING TALES

During the early 1970s, the search for Atlantis in the Bahamas drew the attention of various internationally renowned authors whose popular books have featured this subject (often with little concern for notes and references or primary sources of information). Among the most prolific writers in this field were Charles Berlitz, Brad Steiger, and Alan Landsburg, the last of whom focused on Andros in his own quest to find evidence of a lost civilization. With an enthusiasm that matched, and possibly even outshone, his contemporaries, Landsburg obtained interviews with local divers who claimed to have found no fewer than fourteen artificial structures in its coastal waters.[31]

His quite staggering findings are outlined in a book, cowritten with his wife, Sally, and published in 1974, titled *In Search of Ancient*

Mysteries. Apparently, these structures, once again in just a meter of so of water, were said to possess walls of "big blocks of beautifully square-cut [lime]stone, tightly fitted together," and up to 1.3 meters thick.[32] Some of the sites were fairly close together, while others were as much as eight kilometers apart.[33] The largest known structure was allegedly eighty-one meters long, twenty-seven meters wide, and divided into three separate rooms or compartments.[34]

An "underwater explorer" interviewed by Alan Landsburg insisted that, upon digging close to the base of one of the structures, he had come across "buried pottery and ceramic figures."[35] Apparently, the figurines were tested using the process known as thermoluminescence, which can determine the age of ceramics. The results provided a date of manufacture in the region of 5000–3000 BCE.[36] Unfortunately, the Landsburgs failed to record the current whereabouts of these important artifacts.

THE ROAD TO NOWHERE

Then on September 2, 1968, just days after the ill-conceived press release concerning the discovery of the Andros "temple," Valentine and his diving colleagues were taken out to a location some eight hundred meters beyond Paradise Point on Bimini's North Island. Here a local guide named Bonefish Sam showed them an underwater structure that has become known to the world as the Bimini Road (see fig. 23.1).

This enigmatic feature, more than 638 meters in length, is made up of a double row of enormous regular-shaped blocks that are almost totally immersed in the sand. Some are as much as four square meters with smooth, pillowlike upper surfaces. Extending beyond this section of the road is a mosaic of much smaller rectangular stones, many up to two meters square, that curve gracefully to make a ninety-degree turn in the direction of the nearby beach. The stones' placement gives the whole structure the appearance of a letter *J*. After this point, the causeway continues in a fragmentary form for another 110 meters before it

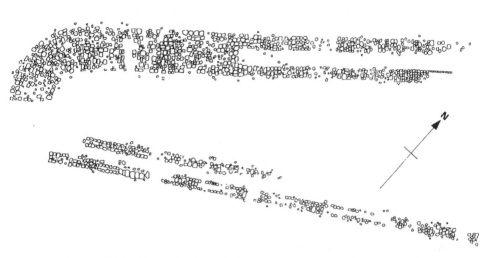

98 metres   126 metres   155 metres

Figure 23.1. Ground plan of the stone causeway known as the Bimini Road, located close to the Bahamian island of North Bimini (after David Zink). Is this feature simply a formation of local beach rock or does it represent the work of human hands?

peters out and becomes lost beneath the shifting sands. Although the road appears at first to run parallel with the local coastline, it is in fact fourteen degrees askew, being oriented approximately southwest.

The thickness of the blocks in the parallel rows varies, although for the most part each one has a depth of between sixty and ninety centimeters.[37] Some blocks are placed on top of others, but the majority rest on the bedrock. Generally, stones are parted by gaps of between ten and fifteen centimeters, although some are as much as sixty-seven to seventy-eight centimeters distance from each other.[38]

Having become convinced that the road structure was of artificial construction, Valentine announced his conclusions in the summer 1969 issue of *Muse News,* the journal of the Miami Museum of Science.[39] Like his press release of the previous summer concerning the Andros "temple" site, this news piece prompted a fierce reaction, particularly from marine geologists such as John Gifford, who was at the time a geology student preparing for his master's thesis at the University of Miami. Under the sponsorship of the National Geographic Society, Gifford, in the company of several well-qualified colleagues, including John E. Hall, an associate professor of archaeology at Miami, investigated the road site in December 1969.[40]

Unanimously they concluded that the structure was simply "Pleistocene beach rock," a well-known feature on Bahamian shorelines. This is formed over a long period of time, often several thousand years, by the accumulation on the sea bottom of aquatic debris, most commonly crushed seashells, or "shell-hash." The mixture cements together to form a coarse-grained limestone that, through the destructive actions of storms, marine life, and wave erosion, often cracks and fractures to produce individual blocks placed in such a manner as to resemble an artificial causeway.

Further condemnation of the road structure came from Wyman Harrison, a geologist with Environmental Research Associates Inc. Along with two colleagues, R. J. Byrne and M. P. Lynch, he investigated the site in 1971. In an important article published subsequently in the magazine *Nature,* Harrison outlined his own reasons for concluding that the feature was indeed beach rock.

Harrison's arguments against the road's artificial manufacture can be summarized as follows:

1. The formation is composed of "coarse-grained limestone lying on a stratum of denser limestone of finer grain." The stone blocks are therefore still in situ, and so could not have been removed from elsewhere.
2. An "examination of the opposing faces of the lifted and unmoved pieces indicates an exact correspondence of bedding planes and surface morphology," implying that the characteristic features present in one block are more or less identical to those directly facing it, once again proving that they remain in situ.

3. "At no place are blocks found to rest on a similar set beneath," showing that they have not been stacked in courses that would, of course, have added weight to the idea that the road was of artificial construction.

4. The formation is composed of "shell-hash cemented by a blocky calcite" of a type common to the area and formed when the land was still subaerial, that is, above sea level.[41]

Despite such criticisms, supporters of the road structure have attempted to highlight geological anomalies that in their opinion are indicative of its artificial construction.

The points in favor of the road's artificial construction can be summarized as follows:

1. Harrison's conclusion that the formation was composed only of beach rock left in situ should be questioned in the knowledge that the road stones are in fact made of three different types of rock.[42] These include bioclastic limestone, oolitic limestone, and the much harder substance called micrite.[43] Even though these rock types are indigenous to the area, they could never have formed together, side by side, suggesting that at least some of the blocks originated at different locations and were removed to their present site in antiquity.

2. The geologist's claim that the characteristic features present in one block are more or less identical in pattern to those directly facing it is based on just a few samples taken from rocks using hand tools alone.[44] Although it is openly accepted that some of the blocks were obviously "neighbors" when in situ, the presence of rock types from other strata completely disproves this theory. Furthermore, John Parks, a geologist who accompanied David Zink's Poseidia expeditions during the 1970s, examined rock samples from several different stones, some of them neighbors, and found that their composition varied from stone to stone.

For example, "One sample was dominated by aragonite crystals, another by sparry calcite. This implied that adjacent stones were formed in different chemical environments."[45]

3. Harrison's claim that at no place were blocks found to rest on similar blocks is also questionable. Although double or multiple layering is indeed rare, on the road's southern leg—the so-called long arm of the *J*—many stones in the middle of the ninety-degree curve are more than one course in height.[46] Furthermore, some have flat stones—occasionally with sharply defined angles, others of a different composition—wedged beneath them. More important, several examples have small stone legs beneath their corners.[47]

PERSONAL EXAMINATION OF THE ROAD

I was able to view the Bimini Road in the company of Donnie Fields, Bill Donato, and other members of the Project Alta team for the first time in June 1998. An hour or so of snorkeling over the underwater feature was simply not enough for me to make a reliable assessment of what I was witnessing in the shallow waters off Paradise Point. The pillowlike surfaces of the stones were unquestionably caused by water erosion when the stone blocks lay at low-tide mark thousands of years ago. Moreover, their regular shape seemed overly accentuated by the sand and seagrass that fills the gaps between each stone. Sadly, on that occasion, I saw nothing that might prove that the geologists had gotten it wrong.

However, in 2006 I returned to Bimini, where, along with Bill Donato and Greg and Lora Little (see the epilogue), I reexplored the Bimini Road and was witness to the discovery of a new road-like structure off Paradise Point. It is made of the same type of beach rock and continues in a straight line for a distance of around two hundred meters. Yet unlike the Bimini Road, which runs almost parallel to the beach, this new feature juts out at a ninety-degree angle. This makes it clear it is not the remnants of an ancient shoreline, the often-cited explanation for the Bimini Road, which is located just to the southwest of here. This new structure is known today as the Paradise Point Pier, which is actually a very apt description. It does look like it was created as a jetty, pier, or quay using local beach rock, a known practice among the coastal Maya of the Yucatán peninsula and also among certain maritime cultures of the Mediterranean. The existence of the Paradise Point Pier and other similar structures off Andros Island (see the epilogue) and also off the Cay Sal Bank, close to the north coast of Cuba (see chapter 24), argues strongly that these structures are not simply natural features without any importance to archaeology. What is more there is clear evidence of human activity close to both the Bimini Road and the Paradise Point Pier over a prolonged period of time.

ANCIENT ARTIFACTS OR SHIP'S BALLAST?

A number of curious stone artifacts have been found in the shallow waters off Paradise Point. One is a cut-and-dressed piece of masonry picked up in 1975 by David Zink close to the road's fragmentary southern arm, known to Bimini researchers as Rebikoff's Pier.[48] Originally the stone would have been thirty-two square centimeters square, with a thickness of just eight centimeters. It appears to be made from a conglomerate containing a mixture of chert and limestone not native to the Bahamas.[49] On two of its edges are clearly defined tongues that run along their entire length, while on a third edge is a long straight groove that would fit nicely into either of its "male" counterparts.[50]

Its origin, or how it came to be here, remains obscure.

Many more examples of worked stones have been located in the proximity of the road. They include several pieces of granite and marble, neither rock being indigenous to the region.[51] A large chunk of marble, weighing between ninety and 135 kilograms, was found, for instance, in 1975 close to the road by Gary Varney, a dowser and member of Zink's Poseidia diving team. Upon examination it was considered to resemble a stylized feline head, although this interpretation is open to question.[52]

One of the most baffling finds to be made in the vicinity of the Bimini Road was retrieved from its southern arm in June 1995 by local diver Bill Keefe, the owner, with his wife, Nowdla, of the Bimini Undersea Adventures Shop. It is an intriguing example of cut-and-dressed masonry, measuring fifty-six by forty-seven centimeters across its upper surface with a thickness of just eleven centimeters. It weighs twenty-five kilograms and has smooth edges that seem to have been eroded by the actions of the sea.

After Nowdla Keefe had cleansed off its encrustation, this clearly worked stone was found to be made from black "fine grained granite" of a type quarried only in Vermont, New Hampshire, Washington State, and Italy.[53] More important, it possessed a "sophisticated joining feature" in the form of a deep triangular groove, or notch, cut into the edge of one of its surfaces.[54] Few would argue that the Keefe Stone is not the product of a culture known to have occupied the Bahamas. Moreover, no one can deny that it is a dressed stone that shows clear evidence of tool marks and long-term erosion. Yet exactly how old is it? Is it really a building block belonging to some hitherto unknown culture, or is it simply discarded ship's ballast?

For long journeys empty trading vessels would be weighted down with quarry stones, either placed loose in the hold or bolted to the hull. When the ship reached port the ballast would be removed and left on a quayside. Here it would remain until required by a vessel that had been emptied of its cargo and needed to be stabilized for its return journey. If a ship laden with ballast was wrecked, as frequently occurred in the treacherous shallows of the Bahamas, its masonry would be dislodged across the ocean floor. In time, tropical hurricanes and tidal movement would scatter these pieces far and wide, leading any underwater explorers who came across them to conclude perhaps that they had discovered the remnants of a lost civilization.

If, as local tradition asserts, the Bimini Road was once considered a hazard to local shipping, it is conceivable that trading vessels were occasionally wrecked here, thus explaining the various loose pieces of masonry found in its vicinity. On the other hand, the uniqueness of some of these finds, such as the tongue-and-groove stone found by Zink and the black stone retrieved by Bill Keefe, does suggest that there could be other, more intriguing explanations for their presence in these waters.

When visiting Bimini in June 1998, I found the Keefe Stone lying in a shed filled with diving tanks and weight belts. It is just about maneuverable, so Bill Donato and I carried it on to the quayside for closer inspection. Since Nowdla Keefe had removed almost all of its encrustation, it was difficult to estimate how long it might have lain in the water before discovery. The shallow, triangular groove was certainly interesting, but what drew my attention most was its sheer blackness. It was not a form of granite I recognized, and in my opinion it more resembled hornblende schist. All I can conclude is that it seems unlikely that this stone began its life as discarded masonry destined for the cargo hold of a colonial vessel.

Several other artifacts of purported human manufacture have also turned up on the seabed close to the road. They include a number of large hexagonal slabs around a meter in diameter yet only a few centimeters deep,[55] as well as much larger stones identified as fallen monoliths. The first of these was discovered during one of Zink's Poseidia expeditions in the 1970s. A second example was found by Bill Donato on Rebikoff's Pier during the early 1970s.[56] It tapers toward one end and may well have stood erect, like the monoliths so familiar to the prehistoric world.[57] A third example was found north of the road by Donnie Fields. Nearby was a tight ring of large stones with a diameter of around three meters.

Are these really evidence of a lost civilization, or are they simply the product of yearning desires of those who need desperately to confirm the validity of Edgar Cayce's spiritual prophecies? Perhaps the former solution is correct, although before anyone is going to take these claims seriously more detailed reports, drawings, and photographs of discoveries will need to be submitted and acknowledged by scientific institutions.

THE MYSTERY OF MOSELLE SHOAL

Over the years there have been repeated claims of ruined Atlantean temples awaiting discovery off the coast of Bimini. Even though these reports have always proved groundless, the most frequently mentioned location in connection with them is Moselle Shoal, a reef with a north–south alignment located some five kilometers north of Bimini. Its entire length is strewn with shipwrecks and discarded ship's ballast, including cut, dressed, and drilled granite and marble blocks often regarded as evidence of lost civilizations.

There is, however, more than simply scattered masonry in the waters around Moselle Shoal. On a surveillance flight south of the reef during the mid-1970s, J. Manson Valentine, in the company of long-time friend and colleague Jim Richardson, identified a cluster of possible archaeological features in between five and nine meters of water. They included "an area criss-crossed by an intricate grid-work of straight and curved lines," as well as "an extremely complex underwater system of squares, rectangles, and divided circles."[58] In the same vicinity was a cluster of "cell-like units, the whole forming an artefact fully a hundred yards [i.e., 91.5 meters] long, shaped roughly like a foot of many toes." This, he calculated, "pointed at Bimini's northern cape."[59]

Jacques Mayol, the famous world-record-holding freestyle diver, investigated the site on behalf of Valentine. He took a series of quite remarkable photographs, which upon development showed the precise regularity of these cell-like structures. According to Valentine, they were "delineated by straight, dark lines as uniform as the rulings on a tennis court."[60] Hexagonal markings and depressions in the sand were also identified, where the "cells," which averaged around four meters across, appeared to be most numerous.[61]

The whole complex apparently conveyed to Valentine and his colleagues a mathematical symmetry that led them to conclude that "this astonishing artefact was the work of highly sophisticated men, probably at some time in the remote past."[62] Judging by the resulting photographs, the team did indeed discover a site of potential archaeological interest constructed by a culture of graceful sophistication.

Whether these strange subsurface features related to the Bimini Road, its supposed fallen monoliths, the retrieved pieces of masonry, or the various underwater features off Andros is now impossible to determine. Time and time again, anomalies identified in the shallow waters of the Great Bahama Bank are all too easily dismissed as the delusions of gullible believers in the mysteries of Atlantis.

This is a sad situation. What seems inescapable, however, is the part that has been played by Edgar Cayce. Whether his predictions concerning the reemergence of Atlantis were real or imaginary is now irrelevant, for over the past seventy-five years they have gained so much attention that they have now taken on a life of their own.

As fate would have it, strange underwater structures were indeed found in the waters off Andros and Bimini during the summer of 1968, the first of the two designated years of discovery according to Cayce's crucial 1940 reading. Even though these enigmatic features were brought to the public's attention by existing members of the Edgar Cayce Foundation, this entire sequence of events shows the sheer power of prediction, whatever the historical validity of the structures involved.

Cayce became embroiled in the greater mysteries of Bimini following his participation in a bizarre psychic quest to find buried treasure on the island. The exact story behind this misadventure may never be known. Did his channeled readings allude to Atlantis simply to impress the businessmen who promised him financial help for his proposed hospital in Virginia Beach? Could they have learned of local legends suggesting that Bimini was once part of a sunken landmass?

Interestingly enough, tantalizing evidence does exist to suggest that an age-old tradition regarding the breakup of the Great Bahama Bank was preserved on Bimini until fairly recently. When in the Compleat Angler during my visit to the island in June 1998, I was reading items pinned to a notice board when I was drawn to a clipping from the *Miami Herald* dated Sunday, June 17, 1990. It was a story about the island's proposed associations with lost Atlantis. After reviewing the case for the Bimini Road and highlighting the meditational activities of Cayce's latter-day followers, the article went on to quote one of Bimini's elderly fishing guides, a colorful figure named "Bonefish" Ben Francis. Upon being questioned as to whether he believed the island once formed part of lost Atlantis, he had apparently replied, "I heard stories from the old people when I was a little boy that the [Bahamian] islands were once all one mass."[63]

Since Ben Francis must have been well past the age of retirement when he was interviewed by the *Miami Herald,* he would seem to have been recalling childhood memories from the 1920s or 1930s, the time frame in which Cayce announced for the first time that Bimini was a remaining "portion" of lost Atlantis.

Is it possible that Cayce's pronouncements concerning Atlantis's imminent reemergence influenced local lore, or could it be that the businessmen who financed Cayce's trip to Bimini were blatantly aware of an age-old tradition among the islanders that spoke of the Bahamas as once being "all one mass"? Did they then look toward Kentucky's Sleeping Prophet for confirmation of these stories, which might have been construed as evidence that Bimini was a surviving fragment of lost Atlantis? If this was so, then in some strange way they would appear to have gotten it right.

So far, Andros, Bimini, and Moselle Shoal have offered up sunken secrets. Yet this was just the beginning. As the 1970s got under way, those who sought to locate the "mother lode" or nerve center of the Bahamas' antediluvian world were about to be rewarded.

24

OUT OF THE BLUE

Following his slightly premature announcement of an Atlantean "temple" being found off Andros Island in August 1968, J. Manson Valentine adopted a more scientific approach to his archaeological exploration of the Bahamas. Along with close friend Jim Richardson, he familiarized himself with all the natural and artificial features one might expect to find in Bahamian waters and began to make a series of important aerial surveys over every part of the former landmass. Where possible, the diver Jacques Mayol would trail behind in a motor cruiser listening for instructions from the circling light aircraft. It was a combination that would repeatedly pay dividends (see fig. 24.1 on page 386).

Valentine and Richardson initially concentrated their efforts on the fifty-kilometer stretch between Beach Keys and South Riding Rocks, on the northern edge of the Great Bahama Bank.[1] Here they were able to make out several "straight divisions" in outline, as well as "a right angle and triangle," none of which had any obvious explanation.[2] One and a half kilometers farther south, just north of the island of Orange Key, they were able to trace "an assemblage of abutting rectangles on a grand scale, dimly but positively delineated."[3]

Another anomalous feature located close to Bimini's North Island was "a strangely formed 'arrow' marked out in the sea grass" with a northwest axis, "its shaft attached to a U-shaped base, causing the

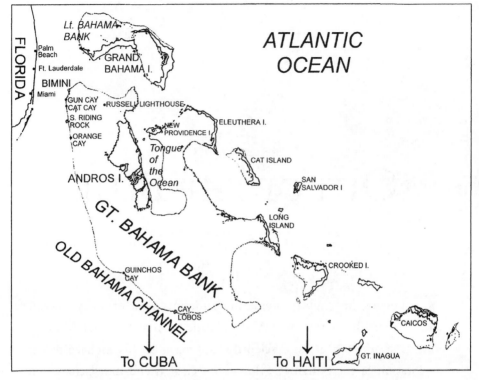

Figure 24.1. Extent of the Great Bahama Bank and other submerged land platforms of the Bahamas, highlighting sites mentioned in this work.

whole design to resemble a gigantic spur."[4] Upon closer inspection it was found to be thirty-three meters long and constructed of large stone blocks. A similar structure of almost identical design, although much larger in size, was identified by Valentine and Richardson on the banks of Joulter's Key, some forty-eight kilometers to the east.[5]

More peculiar was a site located one hundred kilometers east-southeast of Bimini. It consisted of two "very conspicuous" parallel tracks that ran for "nearly seven miles [eleven kilometers]" in the direction of an islet named Russell Light House.[6] These linear features converged on an enormous star-shaped enclosure, completely devoid of vegetation, focused on "three polygonal holes."[7] Mayol dived onto the site and found that the main hole was stopped up by a loose pile of gigantic stones.[8]

IN SEARCH OF THE MOTHER LODE

The true purpose of Valentine's surveillance of the Bahamas was to discover the heart and soul of what he took to be Edgar Cayce's Poseidia. It was with such thoughts in mind that he and Richardson made a highly important flight along the leeward (western) edge of the Great Bahama Bank on September 29, 1972.

This low-level journey by light aircraft took them south to a point where the great sea shelf drops sharply down to the Old Bahama Channel, a deep waterway that forms the division between the former Bahamian landmass and Cuba, situated to the south. Turning to a southeasterly heading, they remained at a height of seven hundred meters and followed the edge of the shallow bank until they could see below them the tiny island of Cay Guinchos.

In the shallows, Valentine and Richardson could make out "the most striking assemblage of biserial lines yet seen . . . the total effect being not unlike that produced by terracing since the avenues are more or less parallel."[9] Clearly enthralled by what they were observing, Valentine speculated that "perhaps this rich site will turn out to be some sort of ancient, ceremonial center."[10]

The flight continued southeastward for between fifty-five and sixty-five kilometers until Valentine and Richardson reached another tiny islet named Cay Lobos, also on the very edge of the Old Bahama Channel. Having spotted its lighthouse below, the two men knew they were now within twenty kilometers of Cuba, a realization that must have unnerved them slightly. Since Fidel Castro's Communist regime forbade any unauthorized American aircraft from entering Cuban airspace, they were now risking life and limb in their efforts to discover underwater features. Yet, having already flouted U.S. federal laws by venturing this close to Cuba, there was no going back, so they continued to scan the shallows for further evidence of ancient occupation.

What they witnessed next was what Valentine felt he would find in this section of the Great Bahama Bank, something he referred to as the "mother lode," the shining gem of the sunken landmass. For, according to him, the two men now perceived "algal growth patterns of such obviously planned regularity that it is quite apparent they could not have been created by random proliferation of the flora."[11] These linear features lay on the absolute edge of the sea cliff, facing out across the Old Bahama Channel toward a corresponding shallow reef in front of the island of Cayo Romano, located on the northern coast of Cuba.[12]

Continuing along the line of the sea cliff, Valentine and Richardson noticed even more distinctive features. Valentine described them as "an enormous, patterned field of dark algae enclosing a pale trapezoid at one end . . . margined by a dense border . . . undulating on the 'land' side but absolutely straight along the drop-off on the outside."[13] There seemed every likelihood that what they could see were walls. Farther away, they could make out "many shadowy, rectangular forms and more straight lines."[14]

As they neared Diamond Point, close to the southwest corner of the Great Bahama Bank, the two men now identified a whole series of straight lines intersecting "at right, obtuse and acute angles."[15] It was a view that later prompted Valentine to picture the setting as "an architect's plan for an exceedingly complex urban development."[16] Indeed, Valentine imagined that he and Richardson might even have been gazing at the remnants of an "antediluvian city."[17] For some while the two men circled over what was conceived to be the mother lode, taking photographs and calculating coordinates.

There are no easy explanations for such well-defined underwater features. Having flown low over the Bahamas in search of potential archaeological anomalies, I can confirm that, after just a few hours of flight time, natural features become easily recognizable. For kilometer after kilometer there may be nothing but shifting sands or vast areas of dark marine growth. Any linear or curvilinear feature, generally highlighted by dark seagrass, instantly draws your attention and looks completely out of place in the midst of the sparkling blue waters.

THE CUBAN CONNECTION

What exactly did Valentine and Richardson discover on that eventful day in September 1972? What were these regular features etched out in the shallows of the former Bahamian landmass? Were they simply anomalies of nature, or did they represent the remnants of a veritable metropolis, once occupied by a human population that thrived at the southernmost edge of the Great Bahama Bank? If this was indeed the case, its positioning, so close to the outlying islands on Cuba's northern coast, implied that the Bahamian mother lode was some kind of staging post that linked these two similarly sized landmasses.

Interestingly enough, it was Valentine himself who first proposed a prehistoric connection between the Great Bahama Bank and Cuba. In an article written in 1976 for *The Explorers Journal* he pointed out, "Both coasts run a parallel course, strongly suggesting contact at one time, an assumption that is well borne out by the fact that there are many endemic faunal elements common to both Cuba and the Bahamas, animals whose presence in both regions cannot easily be explained by transportation, especially in view of the fact that they have never spread to the neighbouring mainland."[18]

Valentine correctly surmised that the relationship between the two landmasses was originally a geological one, in that previously they had been linked together like conjoined twins, back to back, before being split apart by rift faulting in some past geological age.[19]

More pertinently, it has long been considered that the shallow waters north of Cuba might hold important clues concerning the Great Bahama Bank's strange antediluvian world. As early as the 1950s light-aircraft pilots reported seeing what they described as underwater "stone-work" that was "well within Cuban waters."[20]

Similar sightings "north of Cuba" of an alleged "submerged building complex covering over ten acres" might even have convinced the Cuban government that a veritable city awaited discovery in its vigorously defended waters.[21] There are, for instance, unconfirmed reports that this "building complex" was explored with the assistance of Soviet submarines.[22] As unlikely as this story might seem, it is a fact that following the publication of Russian academic Nikolai Zhirov's authoritative work *Atlantis—Atlantology: Basic Problems* in 1970, the Soviet Union embraced his findings and actively sought evidence for the existence of Atlantis in different parts of the Atlantic Ocean.[23]

Among those who felt they had glimpsed the remains of a lost citadel in Cuban waters was Leicester Hemingway, brother of the writer Ernest Hemingway. During a flight into the country, Leicester noticed, beyond its northern coast, "an expanse of stone ruins, several acres in area and apparently white, as if they were marble."[24] The exact location of these underwater features remains unclear. If they were not on the southern extremity of the Great Bahama Bank, they are likely to have been in the vicinity of one of the many islets and cays that mark the position of Cay Sal Bank. This is an enormous three-sided sea shelf more than one hundred kilometers in length and width, situated approximately seventy kilometers north of Cuba.

THE CASE FOR CAY SAL

As mentioned in chapter 7, Cay Sal Bank was drowned rapidly following the rise in sea level that accompanied the termination of the Ice Age. Yet professional diver Herb Sawinski noted curious features of possible archaeological interest here. A former chairman of the Museum of Discovery and Science at Fort Lauderdale, Florida, he spent many years exploring underwater caves and blue holes throughout the Bahamas. Blue holes are formed when the ceilings of large underwater caves collapse, revealing the caverns below; their locations are discerned from above by the dark-blue water found in the caves. Among the discoveries made by Sawinski were two further Bimini Road–like features, one off Anguilla Island and the other off the main island of Cay Sal; a pair of enormous cut-and-dressed blocks located inside a sea cave known as the Quarry; and evidence, both here and in another cave at Raspberry Reef, of quarry marks. Since these caverns have been underwater for several thousand years, the possibility that they might have been hewn out, or at least enhanced, by human hands is most baffling.

In a letter to Bill Donato, Sawinski described the following additional anomalies he found:

1. An underwater causeway of large pillowlike stones, similar to the Bimini Road, running in a southeasterly direction from a position some twenty meters out from the largest of the Anguilla islands, located in the southeast corner of the Cay Sal Bank. The blocks are regularly four meters square and weigh as much as several tons apiece. They run for a distance of around one hundred meters toward a smaller cay before disappearing beneath the sand. Significantly, the causeway is oriented at ninety degrees to the nearby coast, invalidating the idea, asserted by marine geologists, that formations of beach rock only ever run parallel to the shoreline. According to Sawinski, caves close to the Anguilla Road have also produced various inexplicable artifacts, including conch-shell firestones, pottery shards, and bones of unknown origin.

2. A similar stone causeway located off the main island of Cay Sal that, according to Sawinski, is "not as distinctive as those off Bimini and Anguilla." Once again, it is at an angle of ninety degrees to the nearby shoreline and runs for only a short distance before making a right-angle turn. It then continues for a distance of approximately one and a half kilometers before coming to an abrupt halt in front of a sheer drop-off that plunges to a depth of 480 meters. Another breakaway wall-like structure departs from the main feature and continues in a south-southeasterly direction toward a small cay. Under the guidance of Sawinski, this particular structure was investigated in the early 1980s by Charles Berlitz and his wife, Lin. Photographs of the site appeared subsequently in Berlitz's best-selling book

Atlantis—The Lost Continent Revealed, published in 1984.

3. At a cay referred to by Sawinski as "the Quarry" are several underwater caves, one of which contains "two large cut stones about 5 × 5 × 8 [feet, i.e., 1.5 × 1.5 × 2.4 meters], one lying on top of the other." Apparently, the walls of the cave are remarkably "smooth and straight," implying that it started its life as a quarry. Sawinski also points out that "you'll know you're in the right area, when you find a large, ancient anchor lying across the blocks."

4. A cave located at what Sawinski refers to as "Raspberry Reef" has interior walls that he concludes are "hewn and sculptured," suggesting that it began life as a quarry.[25]

PERSONAL VISIT TO THE BANK

In June 1998 I was able to visit Cay Sal Bank with Project Alta, who, with funding from the Edgar Cayce Foundation, hired an ex–U.S. Navy research vessel, the *Ocean Window,* for this express purpose. During a three-day trip out from our base in Bimini, we were able to inspect the stone causeway off Anguilla Island. The whole operation was conducted with almost military precision, with various divers being designated a specific area to investigate and photograph. I swam the entire length of the "road" two or three times and can confirm that it does indeed resemble both the Bimini Road and Paradise Point Pier. What is more, just like the Paradise Point Pier, the example off Anguilla Island definitely juts out at right angles from the shoreline. All I can say is that whatever action was responsible for this structure was also responsible for both the Bimini Road and Paradise Point Pier (and see the epilogue for the discovery in 2003 of another similar feature off the coast of Nicholls Town, Andros Island, which is known today as the Andros Platform).

I was also assigned to examine various sea caves off Anguilla Island. I found no evidence of prehistoric occupation, although one of the other divers found what he took to be a conch-shell firestone of probable Lucayan origin. On land, Bill Donato found evidence of more recent occupation in the form of a makeshift camp and other discarded rubbish. Quite clearly, the island had become a temporary haven for Cuban refugees fleeing Castro's Communist regime. Whether these individuals made it to Florida or were rounded up by the Cuban authorities and taken back to the mainland, we shall never know.

The only point I can add is that Cay Sal Bank, and Anguilla Island in particular, has one of the most eerie atmospheres I have ever encountered on my travels. This rather subjective opinion was not helped by the fact that, while exploring the underwater shoreline in the company of another member of the team, we were pursued by a particularly ferocious barracuda more than a meter long. For several minutes it pinned us against the razor-sharp reef, baring its teeth. It was an experience I do not wish to repeat!

THE ATLANTEAN RACE

By the end of 1974 Valentine had compiled a dossier on some thirty sites of potential archaeological interest located in shallow waters on the Great Bahama Bank. At his untimely death (caused through complications following a spider bite) on September 2, 1994—coincidentally, the twenty-sixth anniversary of the discovery of the Bimini Road—his dossier was bulging with files on no fewer than sixty sites, most of which warranted further investigation.[26]

Many of these features will perhaps turn out to be natural in origin—flights of fancy on the part of those who discovered them. Nevertheless, it would be foolhardy to dismiss all such claims in this manner. If it could be ascertained that just one of them was of artificial construction, it would open the way for serious debate on the possibility that a previously unknown culture once occupied the Great Bahama Bank. It would demonstrate also that this culture reached a level of sophistication comparable to that of the Neolithic peoples of Europe and the Near East in the wake of the last Ice Age. Low circular and linear walls or enclosures imply domestic functions, such as the containment of animals, the cultivation of domesticated plants, or the foundations of buildings. On the other hand, some of the structures might have served more religious functions, similar to the stone buildings and monuments of Göbekli Tepe in southeast Anatolia, which date to circa 9500–8000 BCE.

What we can also say is that the proposed archaeological anomalies on the Cay Sal Bank, as well as the widespread placement of unidentified features on the very edge of the Great Bahama Bank, hint strongly at ancient contact between this hypothetical ancient population and nearby Cuba. Is it therefore simply coincidence that Cuba fits all the criteria for having been Plato's Atlantis? If a high culture of this order did once exist, then it must have extended across from Cuba to the former Bahamian landmass. As we shall see, tangible evidence of antediluvian contact between Cuba and the submerged regions of the Bahamas does exist.

GUARDIANS OF THE DEEP

At 170 kilometers in length, Andros is the largest of the Bahamas group. It is in fact composed of two main islands divided by a channel that cuts through the center of the landmass. Unbelievably enough, with its pine-covered valleys and freshwater lakes, the topography of Andros more resembles a Swiss Alpine landscape than it does a tropical island. Its virtually inaccessible lakes also conceal entrances to blue holes that plunge downward for depths of up to 135 meters before linking with a mazelike network of passageways and caverns that extend for kilometer after kilometer and often exit far out to sea. Many contain stalagmites and stalactites, showing that at various points in their history, most probably during periods of glaciation, these caves were above the water line. Their true age is conjectural, although one estimate places a date of forty thousand to fifty thousand years ago for their original formation by the actions of the sea.[27]

The wildlife that inhabits the blue holes and caverns of the Bahamas might as well be from another planet. Strange blind fish, unique species of giant crustaceans, and other rare mollusks survive in almost total darkness. The Seminole American Indians, who reached Andros from Florida in the nineteenth century, firmly believed that the blue holes were the home of an altogether more bizarre occupant—a sea beast known as the lusca, described either as half octopus and half shark, or half snake and half squid.[28] With a tentacled head and bulbous body, it could grow to more than seventy meters in length and was said to gorge on those unlucky enough to be sucked into the whirlpools, known as the "breath of the lusca," that mark the entrance to blue holes. Disturbingly, this chthulhoid creature, like something out of an H. P. Lovecraft horror story, is no myth, either.

There are several well-attested cases of giant "scuttles," Bahamian for octopus, attacking fishing boats off the coast of Andros.[29] More disturbingly, in 1896 a giant carcass of an unknown species of cephalopod was washed up on the beach of Anastasia Island, off Florida. One of its damaged tentacles was ten meters in length.[30] Tests conducted in 1957 on samples taken from the "Florida monster," as it became known, revealed that it was indeed an unknown species of octopus. During the 1970s or 1980s part of a badly decayed tentacle five meters long was washed up on a beach near Small Hope Bay Lodge on Andros. Tissue samples extracted from the remains produced similar results to that of the "Florida monster."[31]

It was these same blue holes off Andros that Herb Sawinski was exploring in 1963 when he entered a previously uncharted cavern beyond the island's eastern shoreline. Deep inside, his flashlight picked out something that seemed totally inconceivable. Despite the fact that the cave was flooded permanently, the walls bore several carved petroglyphs of geometric forms, concentric rings, and stickmen, similar to those executed by cave artists in other parts of the Bahamas and Caribbean.[32] Yet how was this possible, as archaeologists consider that Andros was uninhabited prior to circa 600–700 CE? So what was this decoration doing in a cave submerged beneath seven and a half meters of water? The petroglyphs in particular must have been done by a culture comparable with the Guayabo Blanco, who occupied Cuba between circa 5000 BCE and 250 CE. This therefore implied that the cave artists who painted these petroglyphs must have inhabited Andros before the waters rose up to reclaim the island's low-lying areas sometime around 5000–3000 BCE.

Sawinski kindly sent me a copy of the black-and-white photograph he took of the underwater petroglyphs. Although it is difficult to make out individual designs, it is clear that they do resemble the Guayabo Blanco cave art found on Cuba. More difficult to explain are the stickmen, for, as we have already noted, these are considered by archaeologists to date to a much later period, suggesting that they were executed by Lucayan artists. Yet this seems impossible, unless we take into account minor drops in sea level that occurred between 2700–2000 BCE and 1500–600 BCE.

That the Lucayans utilized partially submerged caves for burials is not in doubt. Skeletal remains have been found in caverns off Andros in particular, while in the imaginatively named Stargate Blue Hole, divers found a virtually intact Lucayan canoe. However, these items could have been placed in easily accessible caves and blue holes by swimmers. It does not imply that the waters rose up to reclaim them after the burials had taken place.

If nothing else, such discoveries show how strongly the Lucayans, like the later Seminole American Indians from Florida, revered the blue holes and caverns of Andros as otherworldly entrances guarded by sea beasts, such as the tentacled lusca.

ROBERT PALMER'S UNDERWORLD

More difficult to explain is the evidence of human activity found in the blue holes and caverns on Grand Bahama, an island at the northern end of the archipelago, which once formed part of the Great Bahama Bank's smaller, northerly placed neighbor, the Little Bahama Bank.

Robert Palmer was a British diver of great renown who, before his tragic death in 1997, enthusiastically explored the cave systems of the Bahamas. He also wrote a book on the subject, titled *The Blue Holes of the Bahamas,* published in 1985. Palmer is a prime example of someone who was not restrained by orthodox opinion. Had he known that archaeologists consider the Bahamas to have been uninhabited prior to circa 600–700 CE, Palmer might not have told us, "Man moved into the Bahamas *before* the seas ceased rising, barely 5,000 years ago."[33] (author's emphasis) This statement was made not by consulting archaeological books but through his own knowledge and experience of the region.

Among the many discoveries Palmer made during his dives in and around Grand Bahama was a "communal grave mound" inside the so-called Skylight Room, a high-domed hall that forms part of the island's Lucayan Caverns. These consist of a whole series of winding passages and caves that extend for at least ten kilometers beneath the island. The mound was in fact a large conelike structure made up of loose boulders positioned in an enormous chamber, which Palmer believed had once contained an underground lake.[34] Indeed, he speculated that the mound, or stone cairn, may have been built so that it stood within the chamber's darkened waters, like some kind of primeval mound of creation emerging from the watery void.[35]

More significant is the fact that directly above the position of the mound was a circular skylight. Even though the roof of the cavern is permanently underwater, the setting, according to Palmer, is spectacular: "When the sun is overhead, a single shaft of light pierces the darkness, lancing down through the clear water to illuminate the top of the mound. The individuals buried here must have been great indeed to warrant such a monument. Who they were, we shall never know."[36]

And indeed we won't, for when the location of the mound became more widely known, less scrupulous cave divers pulled it apart looking for souvenirs.[37] Mercifully, Palmer and his colleagues managed to retrieve a few loose bones, including part of a human skull and a shin-bone, which were sent to the Smithsonian Institution for examination. From the "flatness" of the skull, it was concluded that it had belonged to a Lucayan American Indian.[38]

I have a problem with this explanation, since it makes no sense of the evidence available. As with the decorated cave discovered off Andros by Sawinski, the Skylight Room among the Lucayan Caverns on Grand Bahama must have been underwater for at least five thousand years, and possibly even longer. The communal burial mound and overhead sky-light can only have been constructed by an unknown culture that long antedated the arrival in the Bahamas of the Lucayan American Indians. More significantly, there seems to be a direct relationship between the design of the Skylight Room and the many Cuban caverns that also have circular skylights. These, as we have seen, enabled shafts of sun-light to pick out specific petroglyphs or areas of the cave at the time of the equinoxes, like the zenith tubes of the Olmec civilization. If this comparison is valid, it provides evidence of contact between those responsible for the decorated caves of Cuba and the unknown individu-als buried in the communal grave mound inside the Skylight Room on Grand Bahama. Since the Cuban cave art—particularly that in Punta del Este's Cueva #1—could date to as early as circa 5000 BCE, it sug-gests that the culture responsible for the grave mound and cave art of the Bahamas might also have thrived during this same age, and, con-ceivably, even earlier still.

Elsewhere on Grand Bahama another underwater cavern has pro-duced evidence of early human occupation. At the eastern end of the island, by Sweetings Cay, is an underwater complex of passages and caves known as the Zodiac Caverns, each bearing the name of one of the twelve astrological signs. They are accessed via various entrances located beneath the island's lakes. It was deep inside the narrowing of one such entrance, leading into Gemini, that in 1982 one of Palmer's colleagues, Rob Parker, came across a "scattered area of bones."[39] At first it was assumed that they might have been washed into the cave entrance by an exceptionally high tide. However, this seemed improbable as the cave was "well below water when man first arrived in the area."[40] A second theory suggested the bones might be "the remains of some animal from the far past of the cave," that is, when it was still above sea level.[41] Yet subsequent analysis of the remains has shown them to be human, with one piece being part of a cheekbone.[42] For them to have come to rest so deep inside an underwater cave strongly indicates that they date from a time frame before the cave system's final inundation around five thousand years ago.

MEL FISHER'S LAST MESSAGE—A FINAL CLUE?

Donnie Fields's prehistoric footprints on Bimini prove that there was human occupation on the Great Bahama Bank prior to the submergence of its low-lying regions. More important, the evidence of a human presence in underwater caves on Andros and Grand Bahama and the accumulation of linear and curvilinear features on the southwestern edge of the former Bahamian landmass all suggest that this antediluvian race was related directly to the earliest inhabitants of Cuba.

Is it possible that the prehistoric race of Cuba, as well as the displaced peoples of the former Bahamian landmasses, evolved into the mound-building cultures of Cuba, Florida, and the Mississippi Valley? Were they also the ancestors of Mesoamerican peoples such as the Quiché, the Cakchiquels, and the People of the Serpent of Mayan tradition? Were their descendants the Yuchi tribe of Oklahoma, who as the legendary Shawano, the Eagle-Serpent People, functioned as a ruling elite among the American Indian mound builders? Were the ancestors of these people the true Atlanteans, the real inhabitants of Plato's ill-fated Atlantic island?

I think the answer is yes. Whereas Cuba might have been Atlantis's shining jewel, its flagship, so to speak, the former Bahamian and Caribbean landmasses, especially the Great Bahama Bank and Cuba's Bay of Batabanó, can be seen as Plato's sunken kingdom, the archipelagos as a whole constituting Atlantis's island empire.

There seems every indication that the shallows of the Great Bahama Bank, as well as the other submerged regions of the Bahamas and Caribbean, hold important clues regarding the genesis of American civilization. More than this, they may well provide us with proof positive of an organized island culture that achieved a settled, Neolithic lifestyle before its expansion was rudely curtailed in the aftermath of the proposed Carolina Bays comet impact of circa 10,800 BCE.

Those who were not drowned in the earthquakes and tsunamis that would have accompanied this event were displaced initially onto the American mainland, preserving the memory of the fiery snake, or "ole moon," that had fallen to Earth, causing mass devastation and floods. Later migrations to and from the Greater and Lesser Antilles, the "homeland," helped diffuse the lingering memory of this terrifying catastrophe that had brought to a close a previous world age of humankind. It was these stories that were conveyed to Phoenician and Carthaginian voyagers, who carried them back to the ancient world. Here they came to the attention of a Greek philosopher named Plato, who went on to create the myth of Atlantis. In the opinion of the author, no other scenario fits the evidence.

This is not to say that we now have proof that Plato's magnificent Atlantean city existed only in the mind of its maker. It could yet lurk beneath the "slime of ages" that covers the edge of the Great Bahama Bank, where J. Manson Valentine and Jim Richardson detected their "mother lode" in September 1972. Alternatively, it could await discovery within the murky waters of Cuba's Bay of Batabanó, which may well have been the role model for Plato's Atlantean plain. On the other hand, the city of Atlantis could appear out of the blue in an altogether different part of the Caribbean.

During the writing of this book I learned that world-renowned treasure salvor Mel Fisher was confident that he had at last located the city of Atlantis. He would not reveal where it had been found and made it clear to close friends that he would only ever divulge his findings when the government of the country in question was on better terms with the United States.

Fisher was the celebrated discoverer, following a twenty-year search that ended in 1985, of the Spanish treasure galleon *Nuestra Señora de Atocha,* which sank off the Florida Keys after hitting storms on a journey from Havana to Spain in September 1622. This man was arguably one of the greatest treasure hunters ever, so learning that he believed he had found Atlantis was not to be taken lightly.

Through the cooperation of his daughter Taffi, I was able to speak with Fisher by telephone on several occasions during the second half of 1998. He confirmed the rumors about his great discovery and told me that the underwater site in question had been detected initially through satellite imagery and later verified by sonar scans. He was sure that what he had found matched exactly Plato's description of the Atlantean city. In a later conversation Fisher let slip certain facts that led me to conclude that the site in question consisted of a whole series of submerged structures located in the Caribbean Sea, not that far from Cuban waters.

Exactly what Fisher had really discovered may never be known, as it is possible he took the secret with him to the grave, for sadly he died, at the age of seventy-six, on December 19, 1998. We must therefore keep on searching in the hope that one day the world will have the final answers to history's greatest enigma.

THE NEW QUEST
FOR ATLANTIS

O n May 14, 2001, Reuters of London reported that deep-sea structures, thought to be ruins of a "lost city," had been discovered in deep water off the west coast of Cuba. Aboard a Cuban research vessel named the *Ulises,* Canada-based salving company ADC Communications had used satellite-integrated ocean-bottom positioning systems, echo sounders, and high-precision side-scan double-frequency sonar to explore the site, located beneath the Gulf of Guanahacabibes in the Yucatán Channel.

"What we see in our high-resolution sonar images," Paulina Zelitsky, the Russian-born president of ADC Communications, told Reuters, "are limitless, rolling, white sand plains and, in the middle of this beautiful white sand, there are clear man-made large-size architectural designs. It looks like when you fly over an urban development in a plane and you see highways, tunnels and buildings."[1] She further added that the anomalies represented "symmetrical architecture" spread across a several-mile area and picked out on the sonar printouts in lighter and darker shades.

The site itself was situated close to the edge of an underwater platform known as the Cuban Shelf. This falls off sharply in a series of steps that drop down to a depth of several thousand meters. It was on one of these shelves, in around six hundred to seven hundred meters of water, that the structures were located. Nearby, apparently, was an "extinct volcano, geological faults and a river bed," this last fact implying that the land shelf, which rose to a height of around forty meters, had once been above water.

The Reuters report ended by saying that a joint investigation involving the Cuban Academy of Sciences and the National Geographic Society was now being planned. A remote robot video camera and a one-man submersible craft would be dispatched to the dark depths of the Yucatán Channel to explore more closely this extensive series of ruins.

INSTANT CONFIRMATION

I became aware of this extraordinary discovery a day or so after the Reuters release surfaced online, and clearly I was ecstatic! In the first edition of *Atlantis in the Caribbean,* published just a year earlier under the title *Gateway to Atlantis,* I had argued that Plato's story of Atlantis was based on the memory of a cataclysm, a comet impact, that had devastated the Bahamian and Caribbean archipelagos around the beginning of the Younger Dryas mini–Ice Age. I had proposed also that Plato's "Atlantic island," the shining jewel of his Atlantean island empire, was based on knowledge of Cuba, the largest island of the Greater Antilles.

Now the discovery of underwater ruins off the west coast of Cuba was adding credence to my theories, something that did not go unnoticed by my contemporaries. There was suddenly great praise for my work. I was asked to speak at a prestigious conference held annually in the Canary Islands and hosted by legendary Norwegian explorer and writer Thor Heyerdahl. Indeed, he was looking forward to meeting me, apparently. Yet due to prior commitments I was unable to attend this event, so I never got to meet Heyerdahl. Sadly, he departed this world the following year at the ripe old age of eighty-eight.

EXCLUSIVITY DEALS

What I did manage to do was make contact with Paulina Zelitsky and her partner, Paul Weinzweig. On several occasions I spoke to them in Cuba, attempting to better understand their discoveries. I sent them a copy of *Gateway to Atlantis,* which they eagerly digested, concluding, to me at least, that they had found Atlantis itself. They confirmed also that they were gathering together a scientific team to further investigate the site and that very shortly a Remote Operated Underwater Vehicle (ROV) would be used to take a closer look at the extensive ruins.

I kept my literary agent informed on developments, hoping there might be a book in this for me—a sequel perhaps to *Gateway to Atlantis.* However, this was not what the literary agent had in mind. Knowing that National Geographic had offered Zelitsky and Weinzweig a six-figure exclusivity deal on the discoveries, he went to Random House, one of the largest publishers in the world, and got them interested in the project. One of their top commissioning editors then went out to Cuba with my literary agent to meet the ADC executives and discuss their own exclusivity deal. Once again a six-figure deal was put on the table. Random House would publish a book on the discoveries that, although credited to Paulina Zelitsky and Paul Weinzweig, would in fact have been ghost written by me. All this, it must be pointed out, was being discussed based on the meager, yet quite tantalizing, sonar images being touted by ADC Communications as visible evidence of the apparent ruins lying in nearly seven hundred meters of water.

After the initial flurry of media interest in these discoveries, and with Random House's and National Geographic's exclusivity deals still on the table, everything went quiet for a few weeks. All parties knew that nothing more could be done, and no deal agreed to, until ADC had dispatched its ROV to inspect the ruins and gain the necessary video footage to show the world what was really going on down there.

THE VIDEO FOOTAGE ARRIVES

The day my literary agent rang to say he was now in possession of the all-important video footage I was at Highclere in Hampshire, England. This is the stately home of the Earls of Carnarvon, familiar to TV viewers as the setting for *Downton Abbey*. I was there researching a new book on the mysteries of Tutankhamun and had just finished talking to the current Lord Carnarvon when the call came through. As a result, the journey back to my home in Essex was now diverted via my agent's home in West London. Here, in the company of my ex-wife, Sue, we sat down to watch the twenty minutes or so of raw footage showing exactly what awaited discovery at the bottom of the Yucatán Channel. (For a brief view of the footage, go to the link provided in the Notes.[2])

What I witnessed that fateful night in July 2001 was utterly puzzling and even a little eerie. In complete silence, and amid a constant stream of white "snow" that flowed past the camera eye of the ROV (actually organic debris being swept along the bottom of the Yucatán Channel by powerful currents and illuminated by the ROV's low-light camera), I could clearly make out the presence of gigantic stone blocks. Some appeared fairly regular, with right-angled sides and well-defined corners. In size they ranged from three to five meters in length, and from two to three meters in width and height, with weights reaching in excess of several tons a piece. Another stone block was almost pyramidical in shape, while still others were more rounded in appearance. Some of the stones were quite clearly lodged on top of others in a haphazard manner.

I looked closely for any carved relief or tool marks on the faces of the blocks, but saw none. Afterward, the videotape was played again, and it was at this point that I had to admit something to myself. No matter what this unique footage showed, whether the remains of lost Atlantis or a huge pile of natural rock, it was of frustratingly poor quality. No way was this going to help explain what awaited discovery in the Gulf of Guanahacabibes. Much clearer video footage, obtained using the proposed one-man submersible craft, would be needed before any meaningful decisions could be made. I would later find out that both National Geographic and Random House shared this same opinion, forcing them both to withdraw their exclusivity deals and, eventually, lose all interest in the project.

That was the end of the road for this extraordinary saga. Without the necessary funding to pursue their investigation of what they now firmly believed was Plato's lost city of Atlantis, ADC Communications went back to doing what they do best—treasure salving. This is what they had been doing when the "lost city" was first detected, strangely enough around the same time that *Gateway to Atlantis* had been published the previous year.

ROWS OF MEGASTRUCTURES

What exactly ADC Communications discovered in Cuba's Gulf of Guanahacabibes might now never be known. What is not in doubt, however, is that they did find something. That "something" was spread out across an area of several kilometers and bore a clear rectilinear ground plan consisting of rows of megastructures divided by "streets." Yet was this evidence of a lost civilization or something else altogether? Perhaps these features were nothing more than prefabricated debris dumped into the ocean by Soviet vessels operating out of Cuban waters at the height of the Cold War. This remains a distinct possibility.

An even greater problem with the ADC discovery is the incredible depth of the supposed ruins, located on a sea ledge between six hundred and seven hundred meters below sea level. Even at the height of the last Ice Age, some twenty thousand years ago, when great volumes of water were locked up in the ice sheets that covered much of the Northern Hemisphere, the sea level was never any more than around 120 meters lower than it is today. This means that the structures situated on the Cuban Shelf can never have seen the light of day, not under any normal circumstances at least.

EXTREME GEOLOGY

The only way these underwater features can ever have been above sea level is if they had been plunged to their current depth through an extremely violent geological process involving the sudden shifting or movement of underlying tectonic plates. In this manner one plate is pushed upward at the same time that another bucking up against it is suddenly thrust downward. Strangely enough there *is* evidence of just such an upward thrust "belt" that curves around the entire length of Cuba from its extreme eastern end, along its northern coastline, right across to the Cuban Shelf in the Gulf of Guanahacabibes. The only problem is that the actions of this thrust, caused through a collision between an arc of volcanic islands and the so-called Bahamas Platform, which once formed the southern extreme of the North American plate, are thought to have occurred during the Cretaceous period, some one hundred million years ago.

Very little is known, or even properly understood, about the creation of the Cuban Shelf on which the structures observed by the ADC team are located. Yet very clearly only an act of terrifying proportions could have plunged an entire lost city down to six hundred or seven hundred meters below sea level in one terrible "day and night" of "earthquakes and floods," to quote the words of Plato regarding the destruction of Atlantis.

Despite having proposed Cuba as a vestige of Plato's former Atlantic island, I am quite prepared to dismiss the discoveries made by ADC Communications as either misinterpretations of natural landforms existing on the Cuban Shelf or Soviet waste from the modern era. Nothing here helps my case for Atlantis being a memory of what took place in the Bahamas and Caribbean at the end of the last Ice Age. What is more, there is far better evidence coming to light of archaeological ruins existing at underwater locations in this region of the world, and at the forefront of this research are two remarkable people—Greg and Lora Little.

PRESSING QUESTIONS

Greg Little is a criminal psychologist and the creator of a large number of highly successful prisoner rehabilitation programs in use today across the United States and beyond, even into Europe. His wife, Lora Little, is a professional psychotherapist. Both share a deep interest in the life and work of the renowned psychic Edgar Cayce and spend their spare time working together as a team exploring the mysteries of the past.

In 2001 they picked up a copy of *Gateway to Atlantis,* which they both felt raised pressing questions regarding the alleged artificial nature of underwater features lying in shallow waters off various Bahamian islands. They knew also that the ARE, which partly exists to study the life readings of Edgar Cayce, had over the years funded various expeditions to the Bahamas in an attempt to explore some of these underwater structures. Yet despite these well-meaning and highly resourceful trips, which, for the most part, concentrated their efforts on the islands of Bimini, very few questions had ever been answered.

This frustrated the Littles, who felt that more could be done to better investigate these potential archaeological sites, which seemed to cluster in three areas: off the coasts of North and South Bimini; off Andros, the largest of the Bahamian islands; and farther south, off Cay Sal Bank, with its cluster of tiny islets close to Cuban waters. It was also around this same time that the Littles came to hear of ADC Communications' apparent discovery of its "ruined city" off the west coast of Cuba. Aware of my own theories proposing that Atlantis was based on a memory of Cuba and the former Bahamian landmass and that Cuba was the most likely site of the Seven Caves, the point of emergence of the first peoples in Mesoamerican mythological tradition, the Littles now began their own investigations into this important subject.

In early 2003 they took a trip to Bimini, familiarized themselves with the *J*-shaped structure known as the Bimini Road, and then hired a light aircraft to take them to Andros. Here, in February and March of that year, they were able to inspect a weird *e*-shaped feature off the island's northwest coast known as Rebikoff's "*e*," due to its resemblance to this letter, and also the huge triple circle, thought to be composed of large stones, spotted from the air by commercial pilots Robert Brush and Trigg Adams in 1968 (see chapter 23). Both turned out to be natural features marked out by dark seagrass. The Littles also inspected one of the roadlike features at Cay Sal Bank (described in chapter 24), concluding that, along with the Bimini Road, it might be an artificial breakwater made from available beach rock.

THE ANDROS PLATFORM

Just before leaving Andros in March 2003 the Littles met someone who pointed out the location of a vast underwater feature off the coast of Nicholls Town in the northeast corner of the island. This turned out to be a vast mosaic of enormous stone blocks that are generally square in shape, with the largest between seven and a half and nine meters in size. Each one has straight edges and well-defined angles, suggesting that this underwater feature is artificial and thus of human construction.

The entire structure has the appearance of a huge, multitiered platform, over the top of which, close to its northern end, is what appears to be an access ramp composed of smaller blocks. The whole thing runs parallel to the beach for a distance of approximately 450 meters and has a width of around forty-five meters. In the Littles' opinion, it most likely acted as a breakwater or platform for unloading cargo. Quite possibly it is the product of an unknown maritime culture, perhaps even the Phoenicians, who are known to have constructed similar breakwaters in the Mediterranean.[3]

Based on the presence around the island's coastline of much earlier shorelines, it is estimated that the Andros Platform, the name given to this underwater feature, would have been above sea level around four thousand years ago. If so, then perhaps the Bimini Road, as well as the "road" feature at Cay Sal Bank and the Paradise Point Pier off North Bimini, could all have been constructed by the same maritime culture responsible for the Andros Platform.

Although this hardly amounts to the existence of an Atlantean civilization that might have thrived in the Bahamas and Caribbean when the proposed comet impact occurred at the beginning of the Younger Dryas mini–Ice Age, circa 10,800 BCE, it does strengthen the theory that an ocean-going Mediterranean culture could have reached the Bahamas as early as 2000 BCE. If correct, it supports the idea that these ancient voyagers might well have picked up stories from indigenous peoples of a terrifying cataclysm that broke up the Bahamian landmass during some former age. These, of course, would have been the same stories told to the earliest Spanish explorers to reach the Caribbean in the wake of Columbus's celebrated journey to the New World in 1492.

A number of other potential archaeological features are now under investigation in the Bahamas. They include a line of three rectangular "building foundations" located on an underwater shelf at a depth of thirty meters some distance to the west of Bimini.[4] Their positioning above a former shoreline as much as twelve thousand years old means they could represent buildings that have long since fallen into a state of ruin. Greg and Lora Little have explored these curious structures on various occasions. Yet the currents here are so strong it is difficult to remain underwater for any length of time. This makes a thorough investigation of the site exceedingly difficult.

Should it be confirmed that these mysterious underwater features are indeed artificial in nature it would go a long way to providing vital evidence for the existence of an indigenous culture on the Bahamian landmass when the comet impact took place, circa 10,800 BCE. If this is correct, then there is a chance they could have been caught in the blast before being drowned by rising sea levels in the aftermath of this catastrophic event.

BROWN'S RUINS

By far the most impressive, and arguably the most significant, structure to come to light in Bahamian waters in recent times is what has become known as Brown's Ruins, named in honor of its finders, Eslie and Krista Brown. For many years they owned a dive shop on North Bimini, and have worked closely with Greg and Lora Little during their investigation of the underwater features found in the mostly shallow waters around North and South Bimini.

Yet in 2011 the Browns made their own, quite remarkable discovery, which has since been investigated by them in the company of the Littles. It is a vast underwater structure located around fifty kilometers south of Bimini, somewhere beyond the tiny islands of North Cat Cay and South Cat Cay, close to the western edge of the Great Bahama Bank.[5] It takes the form of a seamount that lies in around 6 meters of water and consists of thousands of stone blocks spread out in a huge teardrop shape across an area estimated to be 160 meters by 40 meters in size. Many of the blocks are rectilinear in shape and regularly 2.5 meters in length, 1 meter in width, and 0.6 meters in depth, with a weight of around three to four tons a piece. There are also a number of columnar blocks present at the site, as well as smaller stones resembling cubes and triangles.

At the northern edge of this veritable strewn field of rock debris is a clear layer of much larger stone slabs. Together these have the appearance of a raised platform, like those seen at the summits of pyramids in Central and South America. So might Brown's Ruins have once been a raised, open-air temple structure? It is an exciting prospect, which should not be dismissed as far-fetched. Yet if this is correct, how old is it?

Brown's Ruins sits on an ancient shoreline that was submerged by rising waters around six thousand years ago. This, however, does not tell us how old it might be. It simply provides us with a *terminus ante quem,* the very latest date that construction could have taken place at the site. Indeed, Brown's Ruins could have existed at an infinitely earlier age, arguably even at the time of the Younger Dryas impact event, as we shall see.

THE BLUESCHIST DEBATE

Stone samples examined by two scientific laboratories in the United States have revealed that the stone blocks making up Brown's Ruins are of a type of metamorphic rock known as blueschist. This only forms under extremely high pressure at a depth of thirty-five kilometers beneath the Earth's surface. Once formed it can be thrust upward by violent geological processes involving the movement of tectonic plates. The blueschist at Brown's Ruins has a distinct blue-purple hue, due to the presence of the mineral glaucophane. It also contains a degree of quartz, while some stones at the site have been found to contain small traces of the semiprecious mineral opal.

It is important to make clear here that there are no sources of blue-schist in the Bahamas. *None whatsoever.* What this means is that the stone blocks forming Brown's Ruins have to have come from somewhere outside of the Bahamas. The blueschist was thus brought to its present location not through the actions of nature, but through human pro-cesses. More important, its original source must have been some consid-erable distance away, although from where exactly remains a matter of debate at this time.

Although blueschist does not occur naturally in the Bahamas, it *is* found in the Greater Antilles, with the nearest sources being the Blue Mountains of Jamaica and the mountains of central and eastern Cuba (it can be found also in Hispaniola). Conversely, no known exploitation of these natural resources of blueschist can be traced. All that is known is that blueschist celts, or axes, have been found in Jamaica. These are thought to be associated with a rare source of blueschist on Union Hill, which separates the east and west branches of the Morant River in the southwest corner of the island. However, the material used to make these celts, which belonged to the early Neolithic inhabitants of the island, derives not from any exposed outcrop, but from river pebbles.

OCEAN-GOING RACE

Elsewhere in the world, blueschist has been used as a building material for thousands of years. For instance, it was employed by the Minoans of Crete in the construction of walls and buildings, circa 1600 BCE. The main sources of this blueschist are thought to have been quarries in either mainland Greece or Asia Minor (modern Turkey).

Greg and Lora Little are presently of the opinion that the origin of the blueschist making up Brown's Ruins might well have been the Mediterranean. This is because its composition better matches the sources found in Greece and Asia Minor than it does those found in the Greater Antilles. They point out that Plato spoke of the Atlantean civilization as an ocean-going race that reached as far as the Mediterranean in its pursuit of conquest. It might therefore have established colonies in Europe, southwest Asia, and even Egypt that were able to exploit the same sources of blueschist later mined by the Minoans of Crete.

These are bold assertions. Yet as the Bahamas are only thought to have been occupied for the first time circa 600–700 CE, we have no real idea who was responsible for the creation of Brown's Ruins. (The Littles have discounted the possibility that the stone blocks could have been ship's ballast dumped at the site due to the sheer volume of material making up the strewn field.)

The source of the blueschist could well have been either Greece or Asia Minor, although equally there remains a chance that it derives from a currently unidentified outcrop in the Greater Antilles. Since I have proposed that the seat of the Atlantean island empire was Cuba, perhaps we might one day find a previously unrecorded blueschist quarry deep within its interior.

That Brown's Ruins, or the Blue Temple as I like to call it, is the vestige of an advanced culture that thrived on the former Bahamian landmass during some distant epoch remains a distinct possibility. The site might even provide us with the best physical evidence yet for the existence of an Atlantean civilization of the type alluded to by Plato in the *Timaeus* and *Critias,* written circa 350 BCE.

THE FATE OF BROWN'S RUINS

Yet if this is correct what exactly happened to Brown's Ruins? Why are its stone blocks scattered over such a vast area? It is the underwater feature's teardroplike appearance that perhaps provides the key. With its blunt, rounded end facing north, it looks very much as if something of immense power has hit it from this direction, creating the long tail of debris that trails away toward the south. This violent action seems confirmed in the knowledge that the structure's raised platform, made up of enormous stone slabs, is located at the northern end of the teardrop.

It doesn't take a genius to work out that the most likely mechanism behind this catastrophic destruction was a powerful tsunami,[6] perhaps even a super-tsunami of the sort proposed in connection with the Younger Dryas impact event (see chapter 22). If fragments of the comet did strike the Atlantic Ocean east of Florida and north of the Bahamas, then it would have produced violent tsunamis of exactly the type that might have been behind the devastation seen in connection with Brown's Ruins.

Research into Brown's Ruins continues. Due, however, to changes in Bahamian law regarding the issuing of permits for the underwater exploration of archaeological sites, it has not been possible to conduct any further investigations there in recent years. It could take five to ten more before this unfortunate political situation changes and work might be allowed to continue. This is a terrible shame, as sitting beneath the Bahamian waters could be a building structure, arguably even an open-air temple, that was decimated by a super-tsunami triggered by the Younger Dryas impact event of circa 10,800 BCE. What is more, it is located in precisely the area identified in this book as the location of the former Atlantean landmass that was drowned, as Plato was at pains to point out, following one terrible "day and night" of "earthquakes and floods."

What all this shows is that we no longer have to look toward the Mediterranean for answers to the enigma of Plato's Atlantis. Nor do we have to assume that Plato got his dates wrong when he proposed that his lost island empire had been destroyed in around 9600 BCE (give or take a millennium or two). What is more, we now have tentative physical evidence for the existence of an Atlantean culture in exactly the region indicated by Plato, as well as a likely mechanism behind its destruction. Accepting these facts can only lead to the discovery of even further clues regarding the final fate of the Atlantean civilization and its impact on the proto-Neolithic societies that emerged at the end of the Younger Dryas cold spell, circa 9600 BCE.

I speak here of Göbekli Tepe in southeast Turkey, Gunung Padang in Java, and the gradual rise of our own civilization worldwide. So for all those who, like Greg and Lora Little, might wish to take up the gauntlet and begin their own investigations into the mysteries of Atlantis, this must now be your unwavering goal.

NOTES

Abbreviations: cf.= carried from; fn.= footnote; npn.= no page number; pl.= plate.

1. THE OLD PRIEST SPEAKS

1. The chronology and reigns of all Egyptian kings are taken from Gardiner, *Egypt of the Pharaohs.*
2. Herodotus, *History of Herodotus,* bk. 2, chap. 177. For a further discussion on Solon's visit to Egypt, see Freeman, *Work and Life of Solon,* 155–57, 179–85; and Forsyth, *Atlantis: The Making of Myth,* 37–40.
3. Plato, *Timaeus,* 22b. The English translation of the *Timaeus* used in the text is that of Cornford, *Plato's Cosmology,* chosen for its concise English and standard referencing system.
4. Ibid.
5. Ibid., 22c.
6. Ibid., 22e.
7. Ibid., 23b.
8. Ibid., 23b–23c.
9. Plutarch, *Lives,* s.v. "Solon," 69.
10. Plato, *Timaeus,* 23c.
11. Ibid., 23e–24a.
12. Ibid., 24e.
13. Ibid.
14. Ibid.
15. Ibid.
16. Camp, *Lost Continents,* 28.

17. See, for example, Allen, *Atlantis: The Andes Solution,* 9–10, 15; and Zapp and Erikson, *Atlantis in America,* 142–43.

18. Plato, *Timaeus,* 24e.

19. Pseudo-Aristotle, *De Mundo,* 3, 392b.

20. Camp, *Lost Continents,* 293.

21. Pseudo-Aristotle, *De Mundo,* 3, 392b.

22. Ibid.

23. Aelian, *Historical Miscellany,* III, xviii.

24. Ibid.

25. Ibid.

26. Ibid.

27. Ibid.

28. Ibid.

29. Ibid.

30. Strabo, *Geography of Strabo,* vol. I, iv, 6.

31. Ibid.

32. Plato, *Timaeus,* 24e.

33. Ibid., 25a.

34. Ibid.

35. Ibid., 25a–25b.

36. Ibid., 23e.

37. Ibid.

38. Plato, *Laws,* 656E–657A.

39. Gardiner, *Royal Canon of Turin,* pl. 1, c. 2; pl. ll, 1–9.

40. Ibid. The characters here are damaged, so the exact figure is unclear.

41. Ammianus Marcellinus, *Roman History of Ammianus Marcellinus,* bk. 22, chap. xvi, v. 21.

42. Ibid., bk. 22, chap. xvi, v. 22.

43. Plato, *Timaeus,* 24d.

44. Ibid., 25b.

45. Ibid., 25c.

46. Ibid., 25b–25c.

47. Ibid., 25c–25d.

2. EGYPTIAN HERITAGE

1. Plutarch, *Lives,* s.v. "Solon," 69.

2. Ibid., 72.

3. Ibid., 69–70.

4. Herodotus, *History of Herodotus,* bk. 2, chaps. 169–71 and 175.

5. Ibid., 2.177.

6. Plutarch, *Isis and Osiris,* 354d–e.

7. Ammianus Marcellinus, *Roman History of Ammianus Marcellinus,* bk. 22, ch. xvi, v. 22.

8. See, for example, Gamboa, *History of the Incas,* 25. He, however, makes different calculations based on events in the Bible and his own knowledge of the life of Solon.

9. Griffiths, "Atlantis and Egypt," 11–12.

10. For a full account of the dating of the Thera eruption, see Phillips, *Act of God,* 227–32.

11. Ibid., 214.

12. Ibid., 217.

13. Ibid., 217–18, 220–22.

14. Griffiths, *Atlantis and Egypt,* 12; Galanopoulos and Bacon, *Atlantis: The Truth behind the Legend,* 96.

15. See, for example, Luce, *End of Atlantis;* Galanopoulos and Bacon, *Atlantis: The Truth behind the Legend;* and Mavor, *Voyage to Atlantis.*

16. Galanopoulos and Bacon, *Atlantis: The Truth behind the Legend,* 38, 170.

17. Ibid., 132–34.

18. Griffiths, *Atlantis and Egypt,* 20.

19. Plato, *Timaeus,* 24e.

20. Bramwell, *Lost Atlantis,* 137.

21. Galanopoulos and Bacon, *Atlantis: The Truth behind the Legend,* 96–97.

22. Zangger, *Flood from Heaven,* 109.

23. See Zangger, *Flood from Heaven,* for a full account of the author's view that Troy was Atlantis.

24. Fears, "Historical Perspective," 131.

25. Plato, *Timaeus,* 25d.

26. Ashe, *Land to the West,* 135.

27. Pseudo-Scylax, *Periplus,* 112; English translation from Nordenskiöld, *Periplus,* 8.

28. Ibid.

29. Aristotle, *Meteorologica,* bk. II, i, 354a.

30. Avienus, *Ora Maritima,* bk. II, 114–32. Translation from the Latin original by Ann Deagon.

31. Ibid., II, 405–15.

32. *New Encyclopedia Britannica,* vol. 10, s.v. "Sargasso Sea," 452.

33. Columbus, *Life of the Admiral Christopher Columbus,* 69.

34. Ibid., 69–70.

35. Ibid.

36. Babcock, *Legendary Islands of the Atlantic,* 29.

37. Columbus, *Life of the Admiral Christopher Columbus,* 70.

38. Craton, *History of the Bahamas,* 43–44.

39. Hosea, "Atlantis: A Statement of the 'Atlantic' Theory," 198.

40. *New Encyclopedia Britannica,* vol. 10, s.v. "Sargasso Sea," 452.

41. Ashe, *Land to the West,* 139.

42. Plato, *Timaeus,* 25d.

43. Ashe, *Land to the West,* 170–72.

44. Ibid., 172.

45. Kurlansky, *Cod,* 29.

46. See Koudriavtsev, *Atlantis: Ice Age Civilization.*

47. Cahill, *New England's Ancient Mysteries,* 14.

48. Ibid.

49. Ibid., 15.

50. Ibid.

51. Ibid.

52. Ibid.

53. Cahill, *New England's Ancient Mysteries,* 9–10; and Reader's Digest, *World's Last Mysteries,* 55.

54. Fell, *America BC,* 95, 160–61).

55. See McGlone et al., *Ancient American Inscriptions.*

56. See, for example, Ashe, *Land to the West,* 139.

57. Zhirov, *Atlantis—Atlantology,* 179–85.

58. O'Brien and O'Brien, *Shining Ones,* 438–41.

59. Ibid., 436–38.

60. Ibid., 439.

61. Ibid.

62. Ibid., 441.

63. Ibid.

64. Ibid.

65. Edmund Marriage, nephew of Christian and Barbara Joy O'Brien, personal conversations with author, May 1998.

66. Babcock, *Legendary Islands of the Atlantic,* 78; cf., Brown, *Guide to Madeira,* 148.

3. THE ATLANTICUS

1. Camp, *Lost Continents,* 210; and Chambers, *History and Motives of Literary Forgeries,* 11.
2. Chambers, *History and Motives of Literary Forgeries,* 11.
3. Ashe, *Atlantis: Lost Lands, Ancient Wisdom,* 26.
4. Proclus, *Commentaries of Proclus on the* Timaeus, vol. 1, 168.
5. Ibid., 169.
6. Plato, *Critias,* 108e. The English translation of the *Critias* employed in this book is that of A. E. Taylor from his *Plato: Timaeus and Critias.*
7. Ibid.
8. Ibid., 108e–109a.
9. Ibid., 112e.
10. Ibid., 113a–113b.
11. Ibid., 113b.
12. Ibid.
13. Ibid., 113ca.
14. Ibid.
15. Ibid., 113d.
16. Ibid., 113e.
17. Ibid.
18. Ibid.
19. Ibid., 114a.
20. Ibid.
21. Ibid.
22. Lemprière, *Classical Dictionary,* s.v. "Neptunus," 391–92.
23. Ibid.
24. Plato, *Critias,* 114b.
25. Ibid.
26. Lemprière, *Classical Dictionary,* s.v. "Gades," 243–44.
27. See Schulten, Tartessos.
28. Plato, *Critias,* 114ca.
29. Plato, *Timaeus,* 25a.
30. Ibid., 24e.

31. Plato, *Critias*, 114d–114e.

32. Ibid., 114e.

33. Ibid., 116ca.

34. Ibid., 114e.

35. Zhirov, *Atlantis—Atlantology*, 46–47.

36. Plato, *Critias*, 114e.

37. Donato, "Re-examination of the Atlantis Theory," 46.

38. Newby, *Warrior Pharaohs*, 77.

39. Reeves and Wilkinson, *Complete Valley of the Kings*, 77.

40. Plato, *Critias*, 115a–115b.

41. Vaughan and Geissler, *New Oxford Book of Food Plants*, 22; and Corner, *Natural History of Palms*, 290–91.

42. Heyerdahl, *Early Man and the Ocean*, 218–19.

43. Ibid.

44. Ibid., 219.

45. Kelly and Dachille, *Target: Earth*, 253.

46. Plato, *Critias*, 115b–115ca.

47. Ibid., 115d–116a.

48. Ibid., 116ca.

49. Ibid.

50. Ibid.

51. Ibid., 116e.

52. Ibid., 117a.

53. Ibid., 117b.

54. Ibid., 117b–117c.

55. Ibid., 117c–117d.

56. Ibid., 118d–118e.

57. Ibid., 117e.

4. THE VIEW OVER ATLANTIS

1. Plato, *Critias*, 117e–118a.

2. Ibid., 118a.

3. Ibid., 118b.

4. Ibid., 118c–118d.

5. Ibid., 119c.

6. Ibid., 119d.

7. Ibid., 119e.

8. Ibid., 120a.

9. Ibid., 120b.

10. Ibid.

11. Thucydides, *History of the Peloponnesian War,* 1, 4.

12. Camp, *Lost Continents,* 187–88.

13. See, for example, Mavor, *Voyage to Atlantis,* pl. 23b.

14. Lemprière, *Classical Dictionary,* s.v. "Neptunus," 391–92.

15. Camp, *Lost Continents,* 188.

16. Ibid.

17. Plato, *Critias,* 12lb–121c.

18. Babcock, *Legendary Islands of the Atlantic,* 3.

19. Forsyth, *Atlantis: The Making of Myth,* 172–73.

20. Ibid., 172.

21. Ibid., 175–76.

22. Ibid., 169–76.

23. Camp, *Lost Continents,* 188–89.

24. Ibid., 231.

25. Herodotus, *History of Herodotus,* bk. 1, chap. 98.

26. Plato, *Critias,* 118a–118b.

27. Ibid.

28. Ibid., 113d.

29. Ibid., 117e.

30. Plato, *Critias,* 108e–109a, as translated in Donnelly, *Atlantis: The Antediluvian World,* 11–12.

5. ISLES OF THE BLEST

1. Strabo, *Geography of Strabo,* vol. II, iii, 6.

2. See, for example, Proclus, *Commentaries of Proclus on the* Timaeus, vol. 1, 64. The author records views and opinions for and against Atlantis as debated during the third century CE by the philosophers of the Platonic Academy at Alexandria.

3. Zhirov, *Atlantis—Atlantology,* 60.

4. Harden, "Phoenicians on the West Coast of Africa," 142.

5. Ibid., 174.

6. Ibid.

7. Ibid., 142.

8. Ibid., 176.

9. Ibid.

10. Ibid.

11. Ibid.

12. Ibid.

13. Ibid.

14. Ibid.

15. Ibid.

16. Ibid.

17. Ibid.

18. Ibid., 177.

19. Ibid., 145–46.

20. Ibid., 141–50.

21. Ibid., 176.

22. Ibid.

23. Ibid.

24. Ibid. 144.

25. Pseudo-Scylax, *Periplus,* 112; English translation from Nordenskiöld, *Periplus,* 8.

26. Ibid.

27. Ibid.

28. Pseudo-Aristotle, *On Marvellous Things Heard,* 84; cf. Camp, *Lost Civilizations,* 294.

29. Ibid.

30. Ibid.

31. Ibid.

32. Pliny, *Natural History,* bk. VI, chap. xxxvii. Please note that all references from Pliny's *Natural History* cite the book number first and then the chapter number. For a breakdown of which of the, in all, 37 books of Pliny's *Natural History* are contained in individual volumes of the ten-volume series utilized in this current work see the entry for Pliny in the Bibliography.

33. Gordon, *Before Columbus,* 39.

34. Pseudo-Aristotle, "On Marvellous Things Heard," 84, 135–36.

35. Ibid., 136.

36. Ibid.

37. Ibid.

38. Diodorus Siculus, *Library*, vol. III, 53.

39. Ibid.

40. Ibid.

41. Ibid., 54.

42. Ibid.

43. Ibid.

44. Herodotus, *History of Herodotus*, bk. 4, chap. 184.

45. Ibid.

46. Diodorus Siculus, *Library*, vol. III, 54.

47. Ibid.

48. Ibid.

49. Ibid., 55.

50. Ibid.

51. Ibid.

52. Ibid.

53. Ibid., 56.

54. Ibid., 54.

55. Ibid., 60.

56. Ibid.

57. Ibid.

58. Hellanicus of Lesbos, *Atlantis*, in James, *Sunken Kingdom*, 289.

59. Lemprière, *Classical Dictionary*, s.v. "Pleiades," 484–85.

60. Keyser, "From Myth to Map," 152.

61. Ibid., 149.

62. Hellanicus of Lesbos, *Atlantis*.

63. Pliny, *Natural History*, bk. IV, chapt. xiii.

64. Keyser, "From Myth to Map," 162.

65. Diodorus Siculus, *Library*, vol. V, 19.

66. Ibid.

67. Ibid.

68. Ibid.

69. Pseudo-Aristotle, "On Marvellous Things Heard", 84.

70. Diodorus Siculus, *Library*, vol. V, 20.

71. Ibid.

72. Ibid.

73. Harden, *Phoenicians*, 178.

74. Plutarch, "Life of Sertorius," in *Lives*, 399–400.

75. Ibid., 400.

76. Ibid.

77. Ibid.

78. Ibid., 399–400.

79. Harden, "Phoenicians on the West Coast of Africa," 141, n. 3, after an account by a Swede named Podolyn in 1778, who took possession of the coins in Madrid. Podolyn's story is quoted in full in Hennig, *Terrae incognitae.*

80. Lemprière, *Classical Dictionary,* s.v. "Elysium," 219–20.

81. Ibid.

82. Ibid.

83. Thomson, *History of Ancient Geography,* 41, n. 1.

84. Gordon, *Before Columbus,* 39.

6. FORTY DAYS' SAIL

1. Pliny, *Natural History,* bk. II, chap. xcii.

2. Ibid., bk. IV, chap. xxii. For a translation of the name Cassiterides, see Wilson, *Lost Lyonesse,* 16.

3. Pliny, *Natural History,* bk. IV, chap. xxii.

4. Lemprière, *Classical Dictionary,* s.v. "*Fortunatae Insulae,*" 241.

5. Pliny, *Natural History,* bk. VI, chap. xxxvi.

6. Ibid., bk. VI, chap. xxxvi.

7. Keyser, "From Myth to Map," 168 (map).

8. Galvão, *Discoveries of the World,* 11, 26.

9. Babcock, *Legendary Islands of the Atlantic,* 1.

10. Cortésao, *Nautical Chart of 1424,* 48.

11. Ibid., 97.

12. Ibid., 48, n. 1.

13. Lemprière, *Classical Dictionary,* s.v. "Hesperia," 273.

14. Ibid., s.v. "Hesperus," 274.

15. Hesiod, *Theogony,* vv. 214–16, 518.

16. Apollodorus, *Library,* vol. II, v. 11.

17. Honorius of Autun, in Ashe, *Land to the West,* 139.

18. Ashe, *Land to the West,* 137.

19. Columbus, *Life of the Admiral Christopher Columbus,* 57.

20. Pliny, *Natural History,* bk. VI, chap. xxxvi.

21. Galvão, *Discoveries of the World,* 4.

22. Pliny, *Natural History,* bk. VI, chap. xxxvi. English trans., Ann Deagon.

23. Pliny, *Natural History,* bk. VI, chap. xxxvi.

24. Columbus, *Life of the Admiral Christopher Columbus,* 68.

25. Ibid., 120, 126.

26. Lemprière, *Classical Dictionary,* s.v. "Solinus, Julius," 574.

27. Official case document dated December 31, 1536, in Nash, *America: The True History,* 159–60.

28. Solinus, *Polyhistor: De memoralibus mundi,* fol. vi(r).

7. CLUES TO CATASTROPHE

1. Ashe, *Atlantis: Lost Lands, Ancient Wisdom,* 16.

2. Proclus, *Commentaries of Proclus on the* Timaeus, vol. 1, 64.

3. Ibid.

4. Ibid., 86.

5. Ibid., 64.

6. James, *Sunken Kingdom,* 172–73.

7. Proclus, *Commentaries of Proclus on the* Timaeus, vol. 1, 64.

8. Ibid.

9. See Taylor's "Introduction" in Proclus, *Commentaries of Proclus on the* Timaeus; cf. Plato, *Timaeus,* 37–40. See also Cornford, *Plato's Cosmology,* 75–93, 120–34.

10. See Taylor's "Introduction" in Proclus, *Commentaries of Proclus on the* Timaeus; cf. Plato, *Timaeus,* 37–40. See also Cornford, *Plato's Cosmology,* 75–93, 120–34.

11. Bramwell, *Lost Atlantis,* 64; Camp, *Lost Continents,* 18.

12. Proclus, *Commentaries of Proclus on the* Timaeus, vol. 1, 148.

13. Ibid., 80–81.

14. Diodorus Siculus, *Library,* vol. II, 47, 2.

15. Ibid., 47, 3.

16. Proclus, *Commentaries of Proclus on the* Timaeus, vol. 1, 148.

17. Homer, *Odyssey,* vii, 24.

18. Plutarch, *Face of the Moon,* ch. 26, 941a–941c. I have chosen to use the Loeb translation and have included in brackets alternative renditions for the two key words. Other English translations vary considerably, changing the emphasis or meaning of this passage.

19. Keyser, "From Myth to Map," 163.

20. Ashe, *Land to the West,* 180–81.

21. Plutarch, *Face of the Moon*, ch. 26, 941a.

22. Ibid., ch. 26, 941a, fn. a.

23. Ibid., ch. 26, 941b.

24. For the Pillars of Hercules earlier ascribed to Briareus see Aelian, *Various History* bk. v, chap. 3, and to Cronus, see Frazer, ed., Apollodorus, *Library,* vol. 1, bk. 2, ch. 5 n. 35: "According to Eustathius . . . the pillars [of Hercules] were formerly named the Pillars of Cronus, and afterwards the Pillars of Briareus."

25. Irwin, *Fair Gods and Stone Faces,* 241.

26. Ashe, *Land to the West,* 191.

27. Ibid.

28. These titles were Ashe et al., *Quest for America,* 42–45, which also featured contributions from major writers such as Thor Heyerdahl and J. V. Luce; and Ashe, *Atlantis: Lost Lands, Ancient Wisdom,* 26–27, published as part of Thames and Hudson's Art and Enlightenment series in 1992.

29. Gaffarel, *Histoire de la découverte de l'Amerique,* vol. 1, 18.

30. Ibid., 19.

31. Frazer, *Folk-lore in the Old Testament,* vol. 1, 281.

32. Cruxent and Rouse, "Early Man in the West Indies," 51.

33. Ibid.

34. Hine and Steinmetz, "Cay Sal Bank, Bahamas," 157; and Wilber, Milliman, and Halley, "Accumulation of Bank-Top Sediment," 973.

35. Hine and Steinmetz, "Cay Sal Bank, Bahamas," 157.

36. Ibid.

37. Hine and Steinmetz, "Cay Sal Bank, Bahamas," 157; and Wilber, Milliman, and Halley, "Accumulation of Bank-Top Sediment," 973.

38. Clarke, "Examination of the Legend of Atlantis," 29.

39. Plato, *Timaeus,* 25a, in Clarke, "Examination of the Legend of Atlantis," 24.

40. Clarke, "Examination of the Legend of Atlantis," 24.

41. Spedicato, "Apollo Objects, Atlantis, and Other Tales."

42. Ashe, *Atlantis: Lost lands, Ancient Wisdom,* 27.

43. Proclus, *Commentaries of Proclus on the* Timaeus, vol. 1, 151.

44. Aelian, *Historical Miscellany,* III, xviii.

8. DEALING IN DRUGS

1. James and Thorpe, *Ancient Inventions,* 350.

2. Balabanova, Parsche, and Pirsig, "First Identification of Drugs," 358.

3. *Equinox,* "Mystery of the Cocaine Mummies."

4. Balabanova, Parsche, and Pirsig, "First Identification of Drugs," 358.

5. Galvão, *Discoveries of the World,* 87.

6. James and Thorpe, *Ancient Inventions,* 340.

7. Jacobs, "Toke Like an Egyptian," 36.

8. Jacobs, "Toke Like an Egyptian," 36; Balabanova, Parsche, and Pirsig, "First Identification of Drugs," 358; and "Research Verifies Use of Hashish."

9. Jacobs, "Toke Like an Egyptian," 36.

10. *Equinox,* "Mystery of the Cocaine Mummies."

11. *Equinox,* "Mystery of the Cocaine Mummies"; "Research Verifies Use of Hashish."

12. Ibid.

13. *Equinox,* "Mystery of the Cocaine Mummies," after the work of Rosalie David, Manchester Museum.

14. Ibid.

15. Przeworski, "Notes d'archeologie Syrienne et Hittite," 133–45.

16. Ibid., 142.

17. Ibid., 140.

18. Ibid., 136.

19. Ibid., 134–35.

20. Ibid.

21. Ibid., 137.

22. Ibid.,137, n. 2.

23. Ibid., 133.

24. Ibid., 140.

25. Ibid.

26. Gordon, *Before Columbus,* 142.

27. Ibid., 142, n. 127.

28. Ibid., 142.

29. Ibid.

30. Przeworski, "Notes d'archeologie Syrienne et Hittite," 138–39.

31. James and Thorpe, *Ancient Inventions,* 349.

32. Ibid., 348.

33. Van Sertima, *They Came Before Columbus,* 213–22.

34. Ibid., 215.

35. Ibid.

36. Ibid., 214.

37. Ibid., 216.

38. Ibid.

39. Ibid., 216–17.

40. Ibid., 213.

41. Ibid.

42. Ibid.

43. Ibid., 214, after G. Binger, *Du Niger au Golfe de Guinée,* vol. 2, Paris, 1892, 364. For more on smoking known to the Moors and the origin of the word tobacco see Weiner, *Africa and the Discovery of America,* vol. 2, 122–26.

44. Van Sertima, *They Came Before Columbus,* 216.

45. Ibid., 9, 12.

46. Ibid., 10.

47. Jaime Ferrer, letter to Christopher Columbus, August 5, 1495, in Thacher, *Christopher Columbus,* vol. 2, 368–69.

48. Ibid., 369.

9. OLMECS AND ELEPHANTS

1. O'Connor, "Earliest Royal Boat Graves," 3–7.

2. Ibid.

3. Herodotus, *History of Herodotus,* bk. 4, chap. 43.

4. Ibid.

5. Ibid.

6. Harden, "Phoenicians on the West Coast of Africa," 146.

7. See Lichtheim, *Ancient Egyptian Literature,* "The Tale of the Shipwrecked Sailor," 211–15, lines 1–185.

8. Ibid., line 25.

9. Ibid., line 29.

10. Kaster, *Wings of the Falcon,* 63; and Gordon, *Before Columbus,* 58.

11. Lichtheim, *Ancient Egyptian Literature,* "The Tale of the Shipwrecked Sailor," line 98.

12. Ibid., line 130.

13. Ibid., lines 148–54.

14. Gordon, *Before Columbus,* 63.

15. Houlihan, *Animal World of the Pharaohs,* 199.

16. Smith, *Elephants and Ethnologists,* 22–23; pl. 2, opp. p. 20; pl. 4, opp. p. 23.

17. Soustelle, *Olmecs,* 44.

18. Ibid., 21.

19. Ibid., 9–10, 15.

20. Stirling, "Discovering the New World's Oldest Dated Work of Man," 183–218.

21. Irwin, *Fair Gods and Stone Faces,* 141, 157.

22. Ibid.

23. Soustelle, *Olmecs,* 9.

24. Gordon, *Before Columbus,* 21–25.

25. Jairazbhoy, *Ancient Egyptians and Chinese,* 20.

26. Ibid.

27. Drucker, Heizer, and Squier, "Radiocarbon Dates, 72–73.

28. Soustelle, *Olmecs,* 47, 49.

29. Jairazbhoy, *Ancient Egyptians and Chinese,*12–13.

30. Ibid., 16.

31. Van Sertima, *They Came Before Columbus,* 146–7.

32. Jairazbhoy, *Ancient Egyptians and Chinese,* 16. See also Soustelle, *Olmecs,* 5.

33. Gilmore and McElroy, *Across Before Columbus?* 299.

34. Ibid., 300.

35. Ibid.

36. McGlone et al., *Ancient American Inscriptions,* 21, 24.

37. Campbell and Abadie, *Mystic Image,* vol. 2, 145–47.

38. Fritze, *Legend and Lore of the Americas,* s.v. "Jomon/Valdivia Trans-Pacific Contacts (3000 BC)," 141–42. See also Pearson, "Migration from Japan to Ecuador," 85–86.

39. See Meggers, "Jomon-Valdivia Similarities," 11–19.

40. Guthrie, "Human Lymphocite Antigens."

41. See, for example, Irwin, *Fair Gods and Stone Faces,* 68, 70–71, regarding the reliefs known as the "dancers" at Monte Alban.

42. See, for example, Gordon, *Before Columbus,* 21–35; and Irwin, *Fair Gods and Stone Faces,* 175–88.

43. Vaillant, "Bearded Mystery," 243–52.

44. Ibid., 250.

45. Stirling, "Great Stone Faces," 326–27. See also Irwin, *Fair Gods and Stone Faces,* 144.

46. Irwin, *Fair Gods and Stone Faces,* 146–54.

47. Ibid., 153.

48. Ibid., 151, 156.

49. Ibid., 156–57.

10. THE MUREX MERCHANTS

1. Wright, *Biblical Archaeology,* 187.

2. Ward, "Ancient Lebanon," 18.

3. Ibid., 18–19.

4. See Sanchoniathon's *Theology of the Phoenicians,* in Cory, *Cory's Ancient Fragments,* 9.

5. Ibid., 7, 14.

6. Bunbury, *History of Ancient Geography,* 14, n. 9.

7. Herodotus, *History of Herodotus,* bk. 4, chap. 196.

8. Ibid., 4.42.

9. Ibid.

10. Pliny, *Natural History,* bk. VI, chap. xxxvi.

11. Babcock, *Legendary Islands of the Atlantic,* 1.

12. Harden, *Phoenicians,* 176.

13. Bunbury, *History of Ancient Geography,* 86.

14. Strabo, *Geography of Strabo,* vol. III, v. 11.

15. Gordon, *Before Columbus,* 125.

16. Ibid., 124–25.

17. Harden, *Phoenicians,* 104.

18. Gordon, *Before Columbus,* 125.

19. Ibid.

20. Ibid.

21. Cyrus Gordon, personal communication to John L. Sorenson, September 1995. See Sorenson and Raish, *Pre-Columbian Contact,* vol. 1, entry G-165, 375–76.

22. 2 Samuel 5:11; 1 Chronicles 14:1. All Bible references and quotations from the authorized and revised edition of 1611, Oxford University Press, 1905.

23. 1 Kings 5:1, 9:10; 2 Chronicles 2:3.

24. Picard and Picard, *Life and Death of Carthage,* 287.

25. Cahill, *New England's Ancient Mysteries,* 8.

26. Ibid.

27. Ibid.

28. Ibid., 9.

29. Ibid.
30. Ibid.

11. SHIPWRECKS AND SAILORS

1. Marx, *Search for Sunken Treasure,* 33.
2. Ibid.
3. Ibid.
4. Ibid.
5. Ibid., 34.
6. Ibid.
7. Fell, *America BC,* rev. 1989 ed., 320.
8. Marx, *Search for Sunken Treasure,* 34–35.
9. Ibid.
10. Fingerhut, *Explorers of Pre-Columbian America,* 20.
11. Ibid.
12. Ibid.
13. Marx, *Search for Sunken Treasure,* 34.
14. Eccott, "Comalcalco: Maya Innovation or Old World Intervention?" 9; and Steede, "Comalcalco: An Early Classic Maya Site," 35–36.
15. Steede, "Mexico's Pyramidal Comalcalco," 16.
16. Ibid.
17. Fell, "Alphabetic Libyan Mason's Marks," 224–30.
18. McGlone et al., *Ancient American Inscriptions,* 313–14.
19. Ibid.
20. Eccott, "Comalcalco—The 'Roman Mason Marks.'"
21. Steede, "Mexico's Pyramidal Comalcalco," 16.
22. Eccott, "Comalcalco: A Case for Early Pre-Columbian Contact and Influence," 21–29; and Eccott, "Comalcalco—The 'Roman Mason Marks.'"
23. Eccott, "Comalcalco: A Case for Early Pre-Columbian Contact and Influences," 21–29.
24. Prescott, *History of the Conquest of Mexico,* vol. 1, 228; and Steede, "Comalcalco: An Early Classic Maya Site," 35.
25. Eccott, "Before Columbus," 18–19; and Heine-Geldern, "Ein Römischer Fund," 117–19.
26. Irwin, *Fair Gods and Stone Faces,* 258.

27. Fell, *America BC,* rev. 1989 ed. 318; and Sorenson and Raish, *Pre-Columbian Contact,* vol. 2, entry M-143, 106.

12. ATLANTIC VOYAGERS

1. Miller and Taube, *Gods and Symbols,* s.v. "Tobacco," 169.
2. Ibid.
3. Ibid., s.v. "Schellhas Gods," 146–47.
4. For Iberic-Celtic dating in America see Fell and Whittall, "Proposed Correlation of North American and European Culture Sequences," in Fell, *America BC,* rear inside board.
5. Whishaw, *Atlantis in Andalucia,* 44, 46, 71, 76, 173.
6. Ibid., 6, 71.
7. Ibid., 6, 33, 76.
8. Strabo, *Geography of Strabo,* vol. III, i, 6.
9. Whishaw, *Atlantis in Andalucia,* 150.
10. James and Thorpe, *Ancient Inventions,* 340.
11. Ibid., 340–41.
12. Colin McKeown of the British Museum, personal communication with author, February 1999.
13. Irwin, *Fair Gods and Stone Faces,* 286.
14. Ibid.
15. Ibid., 286.
16. Bankes, *Peru before Pizarro,* 138.
17. Ibid.
18. Burger, *Chavín and the Origins of Andean Civilization,* 16.
19. Ibid., 70.
20. Ibid., 181.
21. Ibid., 165. Here the date cited for the late Initial Period at Chavín de Huántar is circa 1000 BCE. In this current work the date has been increased to circa 1200 BCE to conform with more recent dating estimates.
22. Ibid., 129.
23. Ibid., 168.
24. Ibid., 180.
25. Ibid., 129.
26. Ibid .
27. Ibid., 117.

28. Ibid.

29. Irwin, *Fair Gods and Stone Faces,* 287.

30. Mortimer, *Peru: History of Coca,* 228.

31. Plato, *Critias,* 114b.

32. Ibid.

33. Pliny, *Natural History,* bk. IV, chap. xxii.

34. Odelain and Séguineau, *Dictionary of Proper Names,* s.v. "Geder," 134.

35. Ibid., s.v. "Gedor," 134.

36. Bérard, "L'Atlantide de Platon," 193–205. See also Forsyth, *Atlantis: The Making of Myth,* 100.

37. Pseudo-Scylax, *Periplus,* 112; English translation from Nordenskiöld, *Periplus,* 8.

38. Diodorus Siculus, *Library,* vol. III, 54.

39. Bramwell, *Lost Atlantis,* 110, after the work of Felix Berlioux.

13. THE RETURN TO PARADISE

1. Columbus, *Life of the Admiral Christopher Columbus,* 46–7.

2. Cortésao, *Nautical Chart of 1424,* 59, after Jean Nicholas Buache (1741–1825). The original word *Antillia* in Buache's legend has been substituted with the preferred *Atulliae* proposed by Konrad Kretschmer in 1897.

3. Ibid., 59–60, after Heinrich Wuttke, who in 1870 proposed that the key word was in fact *A(r)cules;* Crone, The Origin of the Name Antillia," 260–62; and Crone, "Pizigano Chart," 278–79.

4. Cortésao, *Nautical Chart of 1424,* 60; and Crone, "Pizigano Chart," 278–79.

5. Cortésao, *Nautical Chart of 1424,* 59.

6. Babcock, *Legendary Islands of the Atlantic,* 70.

7. Ibid.

8. Babcock, *Legendary Islands of the Atlantic,* 169.

9. Cortésao, *Nautical Chart of 1424,* 109.

10. Ibid., 85.

11. Ibid., 78.

12. Benincasa map, 1482, in Ravenstein, *Martin Behaim,* map 2.

13. Cortésao, *Nautical Chart of 1424,* 67.

14. Ibid., 74.

15. Ibid., 68, table III: "The Antilia Group of Islands in Fifteenth Century Cartography."

16. Bradford, *Christopher Columbus,* 45–46.

17. Babcock, *Legendary Islands of the Atlantic,* 70, 151.

18. Ravenstein, *Martin Behaim,* 46.

19. Cortésao, *Nautical Chart of 1424,* 94.

20. Babcock, *Legendary Islands of the Atlantic,* 146.

21. Ibid.

22. Ibid., 145.

23. Whishaw, *Atlantis in Andalucia,* 91.

24. Ibid.

25. Ibid., 92–93.

26. Ibid., 93, cf. Fray Angel Ortega, *Historia de la Rabida.*

27. Babcock, *Legendary Islands of the Atlantic,* 145.

28. Ravenstein, *Martin Behaim,* 77.

29. Cortésao, *Nautical Chart of 1424,* 70.

30. Galvão, *Discoveries of the World,* 26.

31. Ibid.

32. Ibid.

33. Bradford, *Christopher Columbus,* 71.

34. Deacon, *Madoc and the Discovery of America,* 7–8.

35. Columbus, *Life of the Admiral Christopher Columbus,* 50.

36. Pseudo-Aristotle, *On Marvellous Things Heard,* 84.

37. Columbus, *Life of the Admiral Christopher Columbus,* 50.

38. Ibid., 50–51.

39. Cortésao, *Nautical Chart of 1424,* 70.

40. Babcock, *Legendary Islands of the Atlantic,* 78; and Johnson, *Phantom Islands of the Atlantic,* 112.

41. Johnson, *Phantom Islands of the Atlantic,* 112.

42. Ravenstein, *Martin Behaim,* 46.

43. Cortésao, *Nautical Chart of 1424,* 2–3.

44. Ibid., 110.

45. Babcock, *Legendary Islands of the Atlantic,* 153–55, 162.

46. Camp, *Lost Continents,* 21–22.

47. Hapgood, *Maps of the Ancient Sea Kings,* 61.

48. Ibid., 61–62.

49. Bradford, *Christopher Columbus,* 125–26; and Columbus, *Life of the Admiral Christopher Columbus,* 82.

50. Bradford, *Christopher Columbus,* 126.

51. Ibid., 129.

52. Bradford, *Christopher Columbus,* 131; and Columbus, *Life of the Admiral Christopher Columbus,* 86.

53. Strode, *Pageant of Cuba,* 43.

54. Ibid., 45.

55. Ibid., 48.

56. Ibid., 43, 48.

57. Ibid., 49.

58. Ibid., 54.

59. Babcock, *Legendary Islands of the Atlantic,* 75.

60. Ibid., 74.

61. vonHagen, *Golden Man,* 55, 125.

62. Wilson, *World Atlas of Treasure,* 163.

63. vonHagen, *Golden Man,* 90.

64. For a full account of the expedition, see Raleigh, *Discoverie of Guiana.*

65. vonHagen, *Golden Man,* 82–90.

66. Cortésao, *Nautical Chart of 1424,* 88.

67. Babcock, *Legendary Islands of the Atlantic,* 69.

68. Ibid.

69. Cortésao, *Nautical Chart of 1424,* 106.

14. THE EXALTED ONE

1. Thacher, *Christopher Columbus,* vol. 1, 295.

2. Cortésao, *Nautical Chart of 1424,* 94.

3. Ibid., 73.

4. Columbus, *Life of the Admiral Christopher Columbus,* 51.

5. Ibid., 57.

6. Williams, *Madoc,* 39–40.

7. Nordenskiöld, *Periplus,* 54.

8. Ibid.

9. Cortésao, *Nautical Chart of 1424,* 81.

10. Ibid., 73.

11. Thacher, *Christopher Columbus,* vol. 1, 290.

12. Castle, *Proceedings against the Templars,* 15.

13. Ibid.

14. Ibid., 37.

15. Burman, *Supremely Abominable Crimes,* 816.

16. Berry, *Encyclopaedia heraldica,* vol. 1, s.v. "Knighthood," npn.

17. Berry, *Encyclopaedia heraldica,* vol. 1, s.v. "Knighthood," npn.; and Robert Bryden, an expert on the Knights Templar, personal communication with author, March 1999.

18. See, for example, Gardner, *Bloodline of the Holy Grail,* 400.

19. Columbus, *Life of the Admiral Christopher Columbus,* 39–40.

20. Ravenstein, *Martin Behaim,* 29–30.

21. Ibid., 30.

22. See ibid., 30–31, for a full appraisal of Martin Behaim's conferred knighthood.

23. Ibid., 29.

24. Ibid.

25. Babcock, *Legendary Islands of the Atlantic,* 7; and Moore, *Penguin Encyclopedia of Places,* s.v. "Azores," 68–69.

26. Babcock, *Legendary Islands of the Atlantic,* 168.

27. Ashe, *Land to the West,* 138; Cortésao, *Nautical Chart of 1424,* 40.

28. Babcock, *Legendary Islands of the Atlantic,* 7.

29. Cortésao, *Nautical Chart of 1424,* 40.

30. Babcock, *Legendary Islands of the Atlantic,* 7.

31. Cortésao, *Nautical Chart of 1424,* 48.

32. Babcock, *Legendary Islands of the Atlantic,* 146.

33. Ibid., 47.

34. Ibid., 147.

35. Nordenskiöld, *Periplus,* 15.

36. Babcock, *Legendary Islands of the Atlantic,* 148.

37. Ibid., 149.

38. Odelain and Séguineau, *Dictionary of Proper Names,* s.v. "Attalia," 46–47.

39. Hosea, "Atlantis: A Statement of the 'Atlantic' Theory," 199.

40. Ibid., 199–200.

41. Clifford Wright, professor of South Asian Studies at the School of Oriental and African Studies, London, personal communication with author, April 1999.

42. Ibid.

43. Herodotus, *History of Herodotus,* bk. 5, chap. 58.

44. Odelain and Séguineau, *Dictionary of Proper Names,* s.v. "Athaliah," 46. Confirmed by Jo Ann Hackett, professor of biblical Hebrew at Harvard University, March 1999.

45. Jo Ann Hackett, professor of biblical Hebrew at Harvard University, personal communication with author, March 1999.

46. Harris, *Grammar of Phoenician Language*, s.v. "Atla," 136.

47. Jo Ann Hackett, professor of biblical Hebrew at Harvard University, personal communication with author, March 1999.

48. *Cassell Pocket English Dictionary*, s.v. "Elevated," 261.

49. Ibid., s.v. "Elevate," 261.

50. Lemprière, *Classical Dictionary*, s.v. "Atlas," 92.

51. Homer, *Odyssey*, vol. I, 52–4.

52. Hesiod, *Theogony*, 517–19.

53. Galvão, *Discoveries of the World*, 5.

54. Bunbury, *History of Ancient Geography*, 74, 86.

55. Ibid., 7.

56. For the linguistic root of *Elysium* see Thomson, *History of Ancient Geography*, 41, 41 n. 1.

57. Homer, *Iliad*, xiv, 201.

58. Nordenskiöld, *Periplus*, 161.

59. Hosea, "Atlantis: A Statement of the 'Atlantic' Theory," 200.

60. Hosea, "Atlantis: A Statement of the 'Atlantic' Theory," 200–201, cf. Brasseur de Bourbourg, *Histoire des nations civilisées*.

15. FAIR GODS FROM AFAR

1. Galvão, *Discoveries of the World*, 51.

2. Prescott, *History of the Conquest of Mexico*, vol. 1, 188.

3. Davies, *Aztecs*, 254.

4. Sahagún, *Florentine Codex, Book 12: The Conquest of Mexico*, 44.

5. Davies, *Aztecs*, 255.

6. Sahagún, *General History*, bk. 12, 44.

7. Cortés, *Letters from Mexico*, 85–86; and Carrasco, *Quetzalcoatl and the Irony of Empire*, 201–2.

8. Cortés, *Conquest of Mexico*, 96–99.

9. See, for example, Miller and Taube, *Gods and Symbols*, s.v. "Quetzalcoatl," 141–42; and Mackenzie, *Myths of Pre-Columbian America*, 260.

10. Brasseur de Bourbourg, *Histoire des nations civilisées*, vol. 1, 151.

11. Prescott, *History of the Conquest of Mexico*, vol. 1 52.

12. Davies, *Aztecs*, 258.

13. See, for example, Quetzalcoatl atop a pyramid in the Codex Telleriano-Remensis, sixteenth century, Aztec, in Miller and Taube, *Gods and Symbols,* s.v. "Quetzalcoatl," 141–42; and Spence, *Myths of Mexico and Peru,* 80.

14. Spence, *Myths of Mexico and Peru,* 81; and Carrasco, *Quetzalcoatl and the Irony of Empire,* 56–58.

15. Brasseur de Bourbourg, *Histoire des nations civilisées,* vol. 1, 109.

16. Prescott, *History of the Conquest of Mexico,* vol. 1, 62.

17. Spence, *Myths of Mexico and Peru,* 65.

18. Ibid.

19. Spence, *Myths of Mexico and Peru,* 65.; and Prescott, *History of the Conquest of Mexico,* vol. 1, 52.

20. Spence, *Myths of Mexico and Peru,* 65.

21. Burland and Forman, *Feathered Serpent and Smoking Mirror,* 115–16; Miller and Taube, *Gods and Symbols,* s.v. "Quetzalcoatl," 142.

22. All accounts of omens taken from Prescott, *History of the Conquest of Mexico,* vol. 1, 258–59.

23. Ibid., 259.

24. Ibid., 259–60, n. 11.

25. Burland and Forman, *Feathered Serpent and Smoking Mirror,* 110.

26. Prescott, *History of the Conquest of Mexico,* vol. 1, 344.

27. See Carrasco, *Quetzalcoatl and the Irony of Empire,* 200–204.

28. Prescott, *History of the Conquest of Mexico,* vol. 1, 292.

29. Ibid., 261.

30. Ibid., 533.

16. PEOPLE OF THE SERPENT

1. Miller and Taube, *Gods and Symbols,* s.v. "Creation Accounts," 68–71.

2. Brasseur de Bourbourg, *Histoire des nations civilizes,* vol. 1, 110.

3. Brasseur de Bourbourg, *Histoire des nations civilizes,* vol. 1, 111.

4. Irwin, *Fair Gods and Stone Faces,* 62.

5. Miller and Taube, *Gods and Symbols,* s.v. "Quetzalcoatl," 141–42.

6. Mackenzie, *Myths of Pre-Columbian America,* 257.

7. Tedlock, *Popol Vuh,* 21.

8. Ibid., 145.

9. Ibid., s.v. "Sovereign Plumed Serpent," 356.

10. Ibid., 192.

11. Ibid., 149, s.v. "Serpents *Kumatz*," 355.

12. Thompson, *People of the Serpent,* 79.

13. Stacy-Judd, *Atlantis—Mother of Empires,* 101, 285–86.

14. Brasseur de Bourbourg, *Histoire des nations civilizes,* vol. 1, 77.

15. Ibid., 77–79.

16. Stacy-Judd, *Atlantis—Mother of Empires,* 285–86.

17. Brasseur de Bourbourg, *Histoire des nations civilizes,* vol. 1, 77.

18. Ibid., 79.

19. Ibid., 80.

20. Stacy-Judd, *Atlantis—Mother of Empires,* 286–8.

21. Brasseur de Bourbourg, *Histoire des nations civilizes,* vol. 1, 110.

22. Ibid.

23. Gilbert and Cotterell, *Mayan Prophecies,* 118.

24. Ibid., 122.

25. Love, *Paris Codex,* 95.

26. Ibid.

27. Thompson, *People of the Serpent,* 21, 77.

28. Ibid., 77.

29. Ibid.

30. Ibid., 78.

31. Ibid., 78–79.

32. Ibid.

33. Brasseur de Bourbourg, *Histoire des nations civilizes,* vol. 1, 108.

34. Ibid.

35. Spence, *Myths of Mexico and Peru,* 233.

36. Miller and Taube, *Gods and Symbols,* s.v. "Aztlan," 42.

37. Spence, *Myths of Mexico and Peru,* 11.

38. Durán, *Historia de las indias,* 415.

39. Davies, *Aztec Empire,* 17.

40. Ibid.

41. Davies, *Aztecs,* 6.

42. Ibid.

43. Davies, *Aztec Empire,* 17; and Van Zantwijk, *Aztec Arrangement,* 54.

44. Davies, *Aztecs,* 7.

45. Toor, *Treasury of Mexican Folkways,* 457. Many thanks to my colleague Richard Ward for coming across this valuable reference.

46. Ibid.

47. Prescott, *History of the Conquest of Mexico,* Vol. 1, 10–11, fn.

48. Brotherston, *Painted Books from Mexico,* 48.

49. Prescott, *History of the Conquest of Mexico,* vol. 1, 10.

50. Ibid., 10, fn.

51. Mackenzie, *Myths of Pre-Columbian America,* 87, cf. Brasseur de Bourbourg, *Histoire des nations civilizes,* vol. 1

52. Tedlock, *Popol Vuh,* 148.

53. Davies, *Aztecs,* 8–9, cf. Diego Durán, *Historia de las indias,* ii, 26.

54. Tedlock, *Popol Vuh,* 152.

55. Ibid., 158.

56. Ibid., 159.

57. Ibid., 161–62.

58. Ibid., 160.

59. Ibid., 179.

60. Ibid.

61. Ibid., 296.

62. Ibid., 149–52.

63. Chonay and Goetz, *Title of the Lords of Totonicapán,* 170.

64. Merezhkovsky, *Secret of the West,* "Annals of the Cakchiquels," 127.

65. Recinos and Goetz, *Annals of the Cakchiquels,* 43.

66. Chonay and Goetz, *Title of the Lords of Totonicapan,* 170.

67. Ibid.

68. Ibid.

69. Ibid.,180, 182.

70. Ibid., 170.

71. Recinos and Goetz, *Annals of the Cakchiquels,* 48.

72. Tedlock, *Popol Vuh,* 158.

73. Ibid., 301.

74. Recinos and Goetz, *Annals of the Cakchiquels,* 55.

75. Cruxent and Rouse, "Early Man in the West Indies," 51.

76. Irwin, *Fair Gods and Stone Faces,* 53.

77. Ibid.

78. Brasseur de Bourbourg, *Histoire des nations civilizes,* vol. 1, 151, 155.

79. Miller and Taube, *Gods and Symbols,* s.v. "Chicomoztoc," 60.

80. Ibid., s.v. "Mountains," 119–21.

81. Stacy-Judd, *Atlantis—Mother of Empires,* 296–97.

82. Brasseur de Bourbourg, *Histoire des nations civilizes,* vol. 1, 68.

83. Brasseur de Bourbourg, *Histoire des nations civilizes,* vol. 1, 108.

84. Fallon, *Guide to Cuba,* 231.

85. Ibid.

86. Ibid.

17. THE OLD, OLD RED LAND

1. Steward, *Handbook of South American Indians,* vol. IV, 23–24.

2. Cruxent and Rouse, "Early Man in the West Indies," 52.

3. Keegan, *Bahamian Archaeology,* 13, 28–29.

4. Irwin, *Fair Gods and Stone Faces,* 98.

5. Brasseur de Bourbourg, *Histoire des nations civilisées,* vol. 1, 68.

6. Brinton, "Archaeology of Cuba," 231–34.

7. Ibid., 232.

8. Ibid.

9. Hill, *Cuba and Puerto Rico,* 249.

10. Brinton, "Archaeology of Cuba," 232.

11. For the earliest dates for the Mississippi Valley mound-building culture, see Kennedy, *Hidden Cities,* 12, 279–80.

12. Brinton, "Archaeology of Cuba," 232.

13. Ibid., 233.

14. Ibid.

15. Ibid.

16. Harlow, "Hard Rock."

17. Riverend, *Brief History of Cuba,* 18.

18. Ibid.

19. Ibid.

20. Tabío and Rey, *Prehistoria de Cuba,* 230.

21. Cruxent and Rouse, "Early Man in the West Indies," 47.

22. Ibid.

23. Ibid., 47–48.

24. Moure and de la Calle, *Arqueologia aborigen de Cuba,* 78.

25. Ibid.

26. Ibid.

27. Jimenez, *Cuevas y pictografías,* 69.

28. Hadingham, *Early Man and the Cosmos,* 177.

29. Miller and Taube, *Gods and Symbols,* 28, s.v. "Caves," 56.

30. Crampsey, *Puerto Rico,* 29.

31. Ibid.

32. Ibid.

33. Miller and Taube, *Gods and Symbols,* s.v. "Directions," 77–8.

34. Braghine, *Shadow of Atlantis,* 253.

35. Hill, *Cuba and Puerto Rico,* 77.

36. Ibid.

37. A. J. Reedman, head of the British Geological Survey International, the overseas division of the British Geological Survey, personal communication with author, May 1999.

38. Information supplied by the North Prairie Wildlife Center/U.S. Geological Survey in June 1999.

39. Ibid.

40. Morison, *Christopher Columbus, Mariner,* 119.

41. Ibid.

42. Ibid.

43. Strode, *Pageant of Cuba,* 36.

44. Ibid.

45. Durán, *Historia de las indias,* 415.

46. In Merezhkovsky, *Secret of the West,* "Annals of the Cakchiquels," 127.

47. Ibid.

48. Mackenzie, *Myths of Pre-Columbian America,* 87.

18. HISPANIOLA VERSUS CUBA

1. Clarke, "Examination of the Legend of Atlantis," 24.

2. Spedicato, "Apollo Objects, Atlantis, and Other Tales."

3. Ibid.

4. Ibid.

5. Ibid.

6. Ibid.

7. Ibid.

8. Ibid.

9. Plato, *Critias,* 113c.

10. Keegan, *Bahamian Archaeology,* 88.

11. Ibid., 89.

12. Ibid.

13. Ibid.
14. Ibid., 10.
15. Joyce, *Central American and West Indian Mythology,* 181.
16. Hill, *Cuba and Puerto Rico,* 12, 52.
17. Plato, *Critias,* 118a.
18. Moure and de la Calle, *Arqueologia aborigen de Cuba,* 16.
19. Ibid., 107.
20. Ibid., 106.
21. Mellaart, *Çatal Hüyük,* 170.
22. Plato, *Critias,* 119e.
23. Hill, *Cuba and Puerto Rico,* 108

19. THE OLE MOON BROKE

1. Tabío and Rey, *Prehistoria de Cuba,* 51.
2. Gaffarel, *Histoire de la découverte de l'Amerique,* vol. 1, 18.
3. Ibid., 19.
4. Frazer, *Folk-lore in the Old Testament,* vol. 1, 281.
5. Peter Martyr d'Anghiera, *De Orbe Novo,* vol. II, 254.
6. Wilkins, *Secret Cities of Old South America,* 112.
7. Thompson, *People of the Serpent,* 77.
8. Mahan, *Secret,* 5. I would like to thank Bill Donato for drawing my attention to this important work.
9. Ibid.
10. Ibid., 30.
11. Ibid.
12. See, for example, Hine and Steinmetz, "Cay Sal Bank, Bahamas," 157.
13. Keegan, *Bahamian Archaeology,* 13, 28–9.

20. RATTLING OF THE PLEIADES

1. Thompson, *People of the Serpent,* 79.
2. Gilbert and Cotterell, *Mayan Prophecies,* 118.
3. Hadingham, *Early Man and the Cosmos,* 156.
4. Ibid., 154–55.
5. Ibid., 145–47.

6. Clube and Napier, *Cosmic Serpent,* 263.

7. Ibid., 263.

8. Braghine, *Shadow of Atlantis,* 252–53.

9. Certainly, this was the conclusion of Allan and Delair. See their book *When the Earth Nearly Died,* p. 317.

10. Zerries, "Primitive South America," 246.

11. Ibid.

12. Ibid., 243.

13. Haliburton, *History of Man,* 17.

14. Ibid., 13.

15. Ginzberg, *Legends of the Jews,* vol. 1, 162.

16. Haliburton, 13 fn.

17. Ibid., 13–14.

18. Plato, *Timaeus,* 22b–22ca.

19. Ibid., 22d.

20. Ibid., 22ca.

21. Clube and Napier, *Cosmic Serpent,* 108.

22. Ibid.

23. Mahan, *Secret,* 30.

24. Tedlock, *Popol Vuh,* 161–62.

25. Kelso de Montigny, "Gigantic Meteorite," 229–38.

26. Kelso de Montigny, "Redating the Past," 185–87.

27. Kelso de Montigny, "Gigantic Meteorite," 229.

28. Ibid., 230.

29. Ibid., 233.

30. Ibid.

31. Ibid., 233–34.

32. Ibid., 234.

33. Ibid., 235.

34. Ibid., 235–37.

35. Ibid., 237.

36. Ibid.

37. Ibid.

38. Alan H. Kelso de Montigny, personal communication with author, December 1998 and June 1999.

39. See introduction by Peter Tompkins, in Muck, *Secret of Atlantis,* viii.

21. COSMIC PINBALL

1. Goodrick-Clarke, *Occult Roots of Nazism,* 174; and Sklar, *Gods and Beasts,* 74.

2. Bellamy, *Moons, Myths, and Man,* 61–62.

3. Ibid., 266.

4. Muck, *Secret of Atlantis,* 152–53.

5. Ibid., 153.

6. Ibid.

7. Ibid., 152.

8. Ibid., 154.

9. Ibid.

10. Melton and Schriever, "Carolina 'Bays,'" 52–66. See also Melton, "Origin of the Carolina 'Bays,'" 151–54.

11. Melton and Schriever, "Carolina 'Bays,'" 59.

12. Ibid., 55–56.

13. Ibid., 55.

14. Muldrow, "Comet that Struck the Carolinas," 87.

15. Prouty, "Carolina Bays and Their Origin," 167–222.

16. Ibid., 178.

17. Ibid., 179.

18. Ibid.

19. Ibid.

20. Savage, *Mysterious Carolina Bays,* 7.

21. Ibid.

22. Prouty, "Carolina Bays and Their Origin," 214.

23. Ibid., 174.

24. Savage, *Mysterious Carolina Bays,* 7.

25. Ibid., 27–28.

26. Nininger, "When the Sky Rains Stone and Iron," 16, 29; and Wylie, "On the Formation of Meteorite Craters," 211–14.

27. Johnson, "Supposed Meteorite Scars," 461.

28. Muldrow, "Comet that Struck the Carolinas," 83–89.

29. Ibid., 88.

30. Prouty, "Carolina Bays and Their Origin," 167–224. See also McCampbell, "Meteorites and the 'Carolina Bays,'" 388–92, for a review of the air-shock wave theory.

31. Prouty, "Carolina Bays and Their Origin," 221.

32. Ibid., 174, 222.

33. Olivier, "The Great Siberian Meteorite," 42–44.

34. Ibid., 43.

35. See Kobres, "Path of a Comet, 394–405.

36. Savage, *Mysterious Carolina Bays,* 96.

37. Carson and Hussey, "Oriented Lakes of Arctic Alaska," 417–39.

38. Kelly, "Origin of the Carolina Bays," 204.

39. Plafker, "Oriented Lakes and Lineaments," 513–17.

40. Ibid., 503, 509.

41. Ibid., 516– 17.

42. Muck, *Secret of Atlantis,* 157.

43. Ibid., 164.

44. Ibid.

45. Ibid.

46. Ibid., 184.

47. Ibid., 167.

48. Eyton and Parkhurst, "Re-evaluation."

49. Ibid.

50. Ibid.

51. Ibid. See also Olivier, "Great Siberian Meteorite," 43.

52. Ibid.

53. Ibid.

54. Ibid.

55. Levy, *Comets: Creators and Destroyers,* 156.

56. Eyton and Parkhurst, "Re-evaluation."

57. Ibid.

58. Savage, *Mysterious Carolina Bays,* 23.

59. Hancock, Bauval, and Grigsby, *Mars Mystery,* 254–56, particularly after the work of Sir Fred Hoyle.

60. Ibid., 255.

61. Muck, *Secret of Atlantis,* 156.

62. See Donnelly, *Ragnarok.*

63. Braghine, *Shadow of Atlantis,* 256–57.

64. Ibid., 250.

65. Ibid., 252–53.

66. Muck, *Secret of Atlantis,* 169–70.

67. Ibid.

68. See Landa, "Relacion de las casas," 348.

69. Stacy-Judd, *Atlantis—Mother of Empires,* 102.

70. Mahan, *Secret,* 30.

71. Plato, *Timaeus,* 25c-25d.

72. Muck, *Secret of Atlantis,* 188.

73. Spedicato, "Apollo Objects, Atlantis, and Other Tales."

74. Hibben, *Lost Americans,* 170. For a full account of the Pleistocene fauna found in the Alaskan muck, see 91–98. For the reference to the suspected age of the glacial destruction in Alaska being "ten thousand years ago," see 91.

75. Ibid., 177–78.

76. Ibid., 177.

77. Ibid., 91, 97, 168.

78. See, for instance, Couto, "On Two Mounted Skeletons," 423–27.

79. Hibben, *Lost Americans,* 168.

22. END OF THE ICE AGE

1. Powell, "Mythologic Philosophy: 1. The Genesis of Philosophy," 799.

2. Ibid.

3. Donnelly, *Ragnarok,* 179.

4. Spedicato, "Apollo Objects, Atlantis, and Other Tales."

5. Ibid.

6. Ingram, Robinson, and Odum, "Clay Mineralogy," 1–10.

7. Ibid.

8. Muldrow, "Comet that Struck the Carolinas," 87.

9. Prouty, "Carolina Bays and Their Origin," 192.

10. Savage, *Mysterious Carolina Bays,* 78–79.

11. Ibid., 95.

12. Ibid.

13. Prouty, "Carolina Bays and Their Origin," 209.

14. Broecker, Ewing, and Heezen, "Evidence for an Abrupt Change," 434, n. 1.

15. Emiliani, "Paleoclimatological Analysis," 1083–88.

16. Ibid., 1083.

17. Ibid., 1086.

18. Wright, Patten, and Winter, "Two Pollen Diagrams," 1386.

19. Wright, "Glacial Fluctuations," 161–74.

20. Ibid., 168.
21. Emiliani, "Paleoclimatological Analysis," 1087.
22. Wright, "Glacial Fluctuations," 169.
23. Emiliani, "Paleoclimatological Analysis," 1086.
24. Ibid.
25. Wright, "Glacial Fluctuations," 169.
26. Emiliani, "Paleoclimatological Analysis," 1086.
27. Wright, "Glacial Fluctuations," 169, 173.
28. Ibid., 174.
29. Ibid., 162.
30. Plato, *Critias,* 108e.
31. Muck, *Secret of Atlantis,* 248.
32. Coe, *Breaking the Maya Code,* 275.
33. Reymond, *Mythical Origin of the Egyptian Temple,* 35, 113. For a full appraisal of the Edfu foundation texts, see Collins, *Gods of Eden,* 173–80.
34. Reymond, *Mythical Origin of the Egyptian Temple,* 108, 118.
35. Reymond, *Mythical Origin of the Egyptian Temple,* 119; and Jelinkova, "Shebtiw in the temple of Edfu," p. 41.
36. Reymond, *Mythical Origin of the Egyptian Temple,* 28–29, 142–43, 208.
37. Lichtheim, *Ancient Egyptian Literature,* vol. 1, "The Tale of the Shipwrecked Sailor," 211–15.
38. Kloosterman, "Usselo Horizon."

23. SUNKEN SECRETS

1. Joseph, "Project Alta," 2.
2. Ibid.
3. Ibid.
4. Ibid.
5. Wilber, Milliman, and Halley, "Accumulation of Bank-Top Sediment," 973.
6. Mahan, *Secret,* 30.
7. Hutton, *Coming Earth Changes,* 168–69.
8. Edgar Cayce reading, 996–1, August 14, 1926, in Hutton, *Coming Earth Changes,* 170.
9. Ibid.
10. Edgar Cayce reading, 996–8, February 1927, in Hutton, *Coming Earth Changes,* 171.

11. Ibid.

12. Edgar Cayce reading, 996–12, March 2, 1927, in Hutton, *Coming Earth Changes,* 173.

13. See introduction by Hugh Lynn Cayce, in Cayce, *Edgar Cayce on Atlantis.*

14. Cayce, *Atlantis—The Edgar Cayce Readings,* vol. 22, 1.

15. Edgar Cayce reading, 440–5, December 19, 1933, in Hutton, *Coming Earth Changes,* 183.

16. Edgar Cayce reading, 958–3, June 28, 1940, in Hutton, *Coming Earth Changes,* 174.

17. Cayce, Schwartzer, and Richards, *Mysteries of Atlantis Revisited,* 156–57.

18. Hutton, *Coming Earth Changes,* 176–77.

19. Berlitz, *Mysteries from Forgotten Worlds,* 92; Berlitz, *Mystery of Atlantis,* 2 plates, between pp. 96 and 97; Zink, *Stones of Atlantis,* 9–10; and Valentine, "Underwater Archaeology," 180.

20. Zink, *Stones of Atlantis,* 9.

21. Donato, "Re-examination of the Atlantis Theory," 128–29.

22. Cayce, Schwartzer, and Richards, *Mysteries of Atlantis Revisited,* 159.

23. Quotes based on statements originally made by J. Manson Valentine, from a teletype received by Robert Cummings, a Canadian broadcaster, as quoted in Steiger, *Atlantis Rising,* 147.

24. Ibid.

25. Ibid.

26. See Zink, *Stones of Atlantis.*

27. Ibid., 21.

28. Donato, "Re-examination of the Atlantis Theory," 129–30.

29. Leonard, *Quest for Atlantis,* 48–49.

30. Valentine, "Underwater Archaeology," 180.

31. Landsburg and Landsburg, *In Search of Ancient Mysteries,* 71.

32. Ibid., 72.

33. Ibid., 73.

34. Ibid.

35. Ibid.

36. Ibid., 74.

37. Harrison, "Atlantis Undiscovered," 287.

38. Zink, *Stones of Atlantis,* 47; and Steele, "Bimini Revealed," 142.

39. Valentine, J. Manson, "Archaeological Enigmas."

40. Gifford, "The Bimini 'Cyclopean' Complex," 189.

41. See, for example, Harrison, "Atlantis Undiscovered," 287–89. See also Shinn,"Atlantis: Bimini Hoax," 130–42, for further arguments against the road's artificial construction.

42. Bill Donato, personal communication with author, June 1998.

43. Bill Donato, personal communication with author, April 1998; and Valentine, "Underwater Archaeology," 176.

44. Bill Donato, personal communication with author, April 1998.

45. See Zink, *Stones of Atlantis,* 58.

46. Ibid.

47. See Cayce, Schwartzer, and Richards, *Mysteries of Atlantis Revisited,* 163; Donato, "Bimini and the Atlantis Controversy," 9; and Valentine,"Underwater Archaeology," 177.

48. Zink, *Stones of Atlantis,* 60.

49. Ibid., 62.

50. Zink, *Stones of Atlantis,* 60; Steele, "Bimini Revealed," 143; and Donato, "Re-examination of the Atlantis Theory," 135.

51. Donato, "Bimini and the Atlantis Controversy," 9.

52. Zink, *Stones of Atlantis,* 62–63.

53. Joseph, "Project Alta," 7. See also Donato, "Project Alta: Parts 2 and 3," 3.

54. Donato, "What You Did Not See," 6.

55. Donato, "Bimini and the Atlantis Controversy," 9.

56. Donato, "Architecture of Atlantis," 29.

57. Ibid.

58. Valentine, "Underwater Archaeology," 182.

59. Ibid., 183.

60. Ibid.

61. Ibid.

62. Ibid.

63. Clipping from *Miami Herald,* June 17, 1990, 41 (headline and author not provided).

24. OUT OF THE BLUE

1. Valentine, "Underwater Archaeology," 178.

2. Ibid.

3. Ibid.

4. Ibid., 179–80.

5. Ibid., 180.

6. Ibid., 182.

7. Ibid.

8. Ibid.

9. Ibid., 181.

10. Ibid.

11. Ibid., 182.

12. Ibid.

13. Ibid.

14. Ibid.

15. Ibid.

16. Ibid.

17. Ibid.

18. Ibid., 181.

19. Hill, *Cuba and Puerto Rico,* 381–83.

20. Berlitz, *Atlantis—The Lost Continent Revealed,* 81.

21. Berlitz, *Mystery of Atlantis,* 178.

22. Ibid.

23. See, for example, Collins, "Soviet Oceanographers," 36–37, for a review of the discoveries made in 1979 by the Soviet survey ship *Vitias,* under the directorship of Andrei Aksenov, deputy director of the Soviet Academy's Institute of Oceanography.

24. Berlitz, *Atlantis—The Lost Continent Revealed,* 81.

25. Herb Sawinski, letter to Bill Donato, May 21, 1998.

26. Vanda Osman and Bill Donato, personal communication with author, December 1997, based on earlier conversations with J. Manson Valentine's widow, Anna.

27. Palmer, *Blue Holes of the Bahamas,* 78, 141.

28. Bright, *There Are Giants in the Sea,* 137; and Palmer, *Blue Holes of the Bahamas,* 73.

29. Rose Blanchard, who worked at the Forfar Field Station on Andros from 1975 to 1979, e-mail communication with author, December 8, 1998; and Bright, *There Are Giants in the Sea,* 137.

30. Bright, *There Are Giants in the Sea,* 131, 133, after Professor Addison Verrill.

31. Rose Blanchard, who worked at the Forfar Field Station on Andros from 1975 to 1979, e-mail communication with author, December 8, 1998.

32. Herb Sawinski, personal communication with author, various occasions, 1998 and 1999. Also Sawinski, e-mail communication with author, February 2, 1999.

33. Palmer, *Blue Holes of the Bahamas,* 20.

34. Ibid.

35. Ibid.

36. Ibid.

37. Ibid., 87.

38. Ibid.

39. Ibid., 90.

40. Ibid.

41. Ibid.

42. Ibid.

EPILOGUE. THE NEW QUEST FOR ATLANTIS

1. Reuters, "Looking for Lost Riches." Additional information was gained directly from Paulina Zelitsky and Paul Weinzweig, personal conversations with author, May 17–29, 2001.

2. See History Channel, "Paulina Zelitsky Discovers Symmetrical Structures."

3. Little and Little, *A.R.E.'s Search for Atlantis.* For the section on the Andros Platform, see 144–72, and see 206–11 on the possible function of the structure.

4. Little, "A.R.E.'s Search for Atlantis—2007 Summary."

5. For accounts, images, and videos of Brown's Ruins, see Little, "2011 Great Bahama Bank Expedition Report"; Little and Little, "Search For Atlantis Project: 2012"; and Collins, "Has an Atlantean Temple Been Discovered."

6. The idea that the teardroplike shape of Brown's Ruins indicates that the site suffered the impact of a tsunami was first suggested to the current author by Marty Thibeaux in an e-mail on September 5, 2013.

BIBLIOGRAPHY

Dates: If two dates are shown, the first given is the original year of publication and the second is the edition consulted by the author.

Abbreviations: npp. = no place of publication; nd. = no date; OUP = Oxford University Press, Oxford; *ESOP* = Epigraphic Society Occasional Publications/ Papers; *ZAS* = Zeitschrift for Agyptische Sprache, Leipzig.

Aelian. *Historical Miscellany.* Edited and English translation by N. G. Wilson. Cambridge, Mass., and London: Harvard University Press, 1997.

Aelian. *Various History: The Fifth Book.* See Stanley, *Claudius Aelianus His Various History,* 1665, 122–32.

Allan, D. S., and J. B. Delair. *When the Earth Nearly Died.* Bath, England: Gateway Books, 1995.

Allen, Jim M. *Atlantis: The Andes Solution.* Moreton-in-Marsh, Gloucestershire, England: The Windrush Press, 1998.

Ammianus Marcellinus. The Roman History of Ammianus Marcellinus. Translated by C. D. Yonge. London: Henry G. Bohn, 1862.

Apollodorus. *The Library.* Translated by Sir James George Frazer. 2 vols. London and Cambridge, Mass.: William Heinemann/Harvard University Press, 1921.

Aristotle. *Meteorologica.* English translation by H. D. P. Lee. London and Cambridge, Mass.: William Heinemann/Harvard University Press, 1962.

Pseudo-Aristotle. *De Mundo.* E. S. Forster, trans. See Ross, *Works of Aristotle.*

———. *On Marvellous Things Heard.* W. S. Hett, trans. In Camp, *Lost Continents,* 294.

Ashe, Geoffrey. *Atlantis: Lost Lands, Ancient Wisdom.* London: Thames and Hudson, 1992.

————. *Land to the West: St. Brendan's Voyage to America.* London: Collins, 1962.

Ashe, Geoffrey, Thor Heyerdahl, Helge Ingstad, J. V. Luce, Betty J. Meggers, and Brigitta L. Wallace, *The Quest for America.* London: Pall Mall Press, 1971.

Avieni. *Ora Maritima.* Adolf Schulten, ed. Apud Librarium/A. Bosch, Barcinone and Apud Weidmannos, Berolini, 1922.

Avienus, Rufus Festus, see Avieni

Babcock, William H. *Legenday Islands of the Atlantic: A Study in Medieval Geography.* New York: American Geographical Society, New York, 1922.

Balabanova, Svetlana, Franz Parsche, and Wolfgang Pirsig. "First Identification of Drugs in Egyptian Mummies." *Naturwissenschaften* 79 (1992): 358.

Banks, Rev. J. *The Works of Hesiod, Callimachus, and Theognis.* London: Geo. Bell and Sons, London, 1909.

Bankes, George. *Peru before Pizarro,* Oxford, England: Phaidon, 1977.

Bellamy, H. S. *Moons, Myths and Man: A Reinterpretation.* 1936, Reprint, London: Faber and Faber, 1949.

Bérard, Victor. "L'Atlantide de Platon." *Annales de géographie,* 38, no. 213 (May 15, 1929): 193–205.

Berlitz, Charles. *Atlantis—The Lost Continent Revealed.* London and Basingstoke, Hampshire, England: Macmillan, 1984.

————. *Mysteries from Forgotten Worlds—Rediscovered Lost Civilizations.* London: Souvenir Press, 1972.

————. *The Mystery of Atlantis.* 1969. Reprint, St. Albans, Hertsfordshire, England: Panther, Frogmore, 1977.

Berry, William. *Encyclopaedia heraldica.* 3 vols. London: Sherwood, Gilbert and Piper, 1837.

Binger, G. *Du Niger au Golfe de Guinée.* Vol. 2. Paris: Hachette, 1892.

Björck, Svante, Bernd Kromer, Sigfus Johnsen, Ole Bennike, Dan Hammarlund, Geoffrey Lemdahl, Goran Possnert, et al. "Synchronized Terrestrial-Atmospheric Deglacial Records Around the North Atlantic," *Science* 274 (November 15, 1996): 1, 155–60.

Bradford, Ernle, *Christopher Columbus.* London: Michael Joseph, 1973.

Braghine, Col. A. *The Shadow of Atlantis.* 1940. Reprint, Kempton, Ill.: Adventures Unlimited Press, 1997.

Bramwell, James. *Lost Atlantis.* London: Cobden-Sanderson, 1937.

Brasseur de Bourbourg, l'Abbe. *Histoire des nations civilisées du Mexique et de l'Amerique-centrale, durant les siecles antérieurs a Christophe Colomb.* Vol. 1. Paris: Libraire de la Societe de Geographie, 1857.

Bright, Michael. *There are Giants in the Sea*. London: Robson Books/Guild Publishing, 1989.

Brinton, Daniel G. "The Archaeology of Cuba," *American Archaeologist* 2, no. 10 (1898): 231–34.

———. *The Myths of the New World: A Treatise on the Symbolism and Mythology of the Red Race of America*. New York: Leypoldt and Holt, 1868.

Broecker, Wallace S., Maurice Ewing, and Bruce C. Heezen. "Evidence for an Abrupt Change in Climate Close to 11,000 Years Ago." *American Journal of Science* 258 (June 1960): 429–48.

Brotherston, Gordon. *Painted Books from Mexico*. London: British Museum Press, 1995.

Brown, A. Samler. *Guide to Madeira and the Canary Islands (with Notes on the Azores)*. 5th ed. London: Sampson Low and Marston, 1898.

Bunbury, Edward Herbert. *A History of Ancient Geography*. 1883. 2 vols. 2nd ed., New York: Dover, 1959.

Burger, Richard L. *Chavín and the Origins of Andean Civilization*. 1992. Reprint, London: Thames and Hudson, 1995.

Burland, Cottie, and Werner Forman. *Feathered Serpent and Smoking Mirror*. London: Orbis Publishing, 1975.

Burman, Edward. *Supremely Abominable Crimes: The Trial of the Knights Templar*. London: Allison and Busby, 1994.

Bury, Rev. R. G. *Plato: Timaeus, Critias, Cleitophon, Menexenus, Epistles.*, London and New York: Loeb/William Heinemann and G. P. Putnam, 1929.

Cahill, Robert Ellis. *New England's Ancient Mysteries*. Salem, Mass.: Old Saltbox Publishing House, 1993.

Camp, L. Sprague de. *Lost Continents: The Atlantis Theme in History, Science, and Literature*. 1954. Reprint, New York: Dover Publications, 1970.

Campbell, Joseph, and M. J. Abadie. *The Mythic Image*. 2 vols. Princeton, N.J.: Princeton University Press, 1974.

Carrasco, David. *Quetzalcoatl and the Irony of Empire: Myths and Prophecies in the Aztec Tradition*. 1982. Reprint, Chicago and London: University of Chicago Press, 1984.

Carson, Charles E., and Keith M. Hussey. "The Oriented Lakes of Arctic Alaska." *Journal of Geology* 70 (1962): 417–39.

Cassell Pocket English Dictionary. 1891. Reprint, London: Cassell, 1995.

Castle, Brother E. J. *The Proceedings against the Templars in France and England for Heresy, etc. AD 1307–11*. Taken from the official documents of the period, privately published (and in the possession of Templar expert Robert Bryden of Edinburgh), circa 1900.

Cayce, Edgar. *Atlantis—The Edgar Cayce Readings*. Vol. 22. Virginia Beach, Va.: A.R.E., 1987.

Cayce, Edgar Evans. *Edgar Cayce on Atlantis*. Edited by Hugh Lynn Cayce. 1968. Reprint, London: Howard Baker, 1969.

Cayce, Edgar Evans, Gail Cayce Schwartzer, and Douglas G. Richards. *Mysteries of Atlantis Revisited*. San Francisco: Harper and Row, 1988.

Chambers, Edmund Kerchever. *The History and Motives of Literary Forgeries*, 1891. Reprint, npp.: Folcroft Library, 1975.

Chonay, Dionisio José, and Delia Goetz, trans. *Title of the Lords of Totonicapan*. In *The Annals of the Cakchiquels/Title of the Lords of Totonicapán*, translated by Dionisio José Chonay, Delia Goetz, and Adrián Recinos. 2 books in 1 vol. Norman, Okla.: University of Oklahoma Press, 1953.

Chonay, Dionisio José, Delia Goetz, and Adrián Recinos, trans. *The Annals of the Cakchiquels/Title of the Lords of Totonicapán*. 2 books in 1 vol. University of Oklahoma Press, Norman, Oklahoma, 1953.

Clarke, Hyde. "Examination of the Legend of Atlantis in Reference to Protohistoric Communication with America." June 1885. Reprint, London: Longmans, Green and Co., 1886.

Clube, Victor, and Bill Napier. *The Cosmic Serpent*. London: Faber and Faber, 1982.

Coe, Michael D. *Breaking the Maya Code*. London: Thames and Hudson, 1992.

Collins, Andrew. *Gods of Eden: Egypt's Lost Legacy and the Genesis of Civilization*. London: Headline, 1998.

———. "Has an Atlantean Temple Been Discovered in the Bahamas?" AndrewCollins.com. www.andrewcollins.com/page/news/browns.htm (accessed February 18, 2016).

———. "Soviet Oceanographers Stir Up Atlantis Myth." *Strange Phenomena* 1, no. 1 (1979): 36–37.

Columbus, Ferdinand. *The Life of the Admiral Christopher Columbus by his Son Ferdinand*. Translated and annotated by Benjamin Keen. London: The Folio Society, 1960.

"Comet That Launched Noah's Ark," *Times* (London) April 22, 1996.

Corner, E. J. H. *The Natural History of Palms*. London: Weidenfeld and Nicolson, 1966.

Cornford, Francis Macdonald. *Plato's Cosmology: The Timaeus of Plato Translated with a Running Commentary.* New York and London: Kegan Paul, Trench, Trubner/Harcourt, Brace, 1937.

Cortés, Hernán. *Letters from Mexico.* Edited and translated by Anthony Pagden. New Haven, Conn., and London: Yale University Press, 1986.

Cortésao, Armando. *The Nautical Chart of 1424 and the Early Discovery and Cartographical Representation of America: A Study of the History of Early Navigation and Cartography.* Coimbra, Portugal: University of Coimbra, 1954.

Cory, Isaac Preston. *Cory's Ancient Fragments.* 1832. Reprint, Minneapolis, Minn.: Wizards Bookshelf, 1975.

Couto, Carlos de Paula. "On Two Mounted Skeletons of *Megalocnus rodens.*" *Journal of Mammalogy* 37, no. 3 (August 1956): 423–27.

Crampsey, Robert A. *Puerto Rico,* Newton Abbot, Devon, England: David and Charles, 1973.

Craton, Michael. *A History of the Bahamas.* 1962. Reprint, London: Collins, 1968.

Crone, G. R. "The Origin of the Name Antillia." *Geographical Journal,* March 1938, 260–66.

———. "The Pizigano Chart and the 'Pillars of Hercules.'" *Geographical Journal,* April–June 1947, 278–79.

Cruxent, Jose M., and Irving Rouse. "Early Man in the West Indies." *Scientific American* 221 (1969): 42–52.

d'Anghiera, Peter Martyr. *De Orbe Novo: The Eight Decades of Peter Martyr D'Anghera,* 2 vols. Translated by Francis Augustus MacNutt. New York, N.Y.: G. P. Putnam's Sons, 1912.

Davies, Nigel. *The Aztecs.* 1973. Reprint, London: Abacus, 1977.

———. *The Aztec Empire: The Toltec Resurgence.* Norman, Okla.: University of Oklahoma Press, 1987.

Davis, Henry. *The Works of Plato.* Vol. 2, *The Republic, Timaeus and Critias.* London: Henry G. Bohn, 1849.

Deacon, Richard. *Madoc and the Discovery of America.* London: Frederick Muller, 1967.

Diodorus Siculus. Library of History (*Bibliotheca Historica*). Translated by C. H. Oldfather. 10 vols. London and Cambridge, Mass.: William Heinemann/Harvard University Press, 1935.

Donato, William M. "The Architecture of Atlantis: A General Survey." *Atlantis Organisation Journal* no. 15 (December 1996): 28–31.

———. "Bimini and the Atlantis Controversy." *Ancient American* 1, no. 3 (November/December 1993): 4–13.

———."Project Alta: Parts 2 and 3, and the Television Productions." *Atlantis Organisation Journal* no. 14 (November 1995): 1–7.

———. "A Re-examination of the Atlantis Theory," Master's thesis, California State University, Fullerton, 1979.

———. "What You Did Not See (or Hear) on Arthur C. Clarke's *Mysterious Universe*." *Ancient American,* no. 14 (1996): 4–7.

Donnelly, Ignatius. *Atlantis: The Antediluvian World*. 1882. Reprint, New York and London: Harper, 1902.

———.*Ragnarok: The Age of Fire and Gravel*. 1883. Reprint, London: Sampson Low, Marston, Searle and Rivington, 1888.

Drucker, Philip, Robert F. Heizer, and Robert J. Squier. "Radiocarbon Dates from La Venta, Tabasco." *Science* 126 (July 12, 1957): 72–73.

Durán, Diego. *Historia de las indias de Nueva España e Islas de Tierra Firme*. Translated by Doris Heyden. In *The Flayed God: The Mesoamerican Mythological Tradition,* by Roberta H. Markman and Peter T. Markman. San Francisco: Harper, 1992.

Eccott, David. "Before Columbus (the Calixtlahuaca Roman Head)." *Quest for Knowledge* 1, no. 5 (Autumn 1997): 18–19.

———. "Comalcalco: A Case for Early Pre-Columbian Contact and Influence." *Chronology and Catastrophism Review* 1 (1999): 21–29.

———. "Comalcalco: Maya Innovation or Old World Intervention?" *Ancient American* 3, no. 24 (July–August 1998): 8–16.

———."Comalcalco—The 'Roman Mason Marks': A Closer Look." Unpublished paper, 1999.

Emiliani, Cesare, Stefan Gartner, Barbara Lidz, Koneta Eldridge, Dwight K. Elvey, Ting Chang Huang, Jerry J. Stipp, and Mary F. Swanson. "Paleoclimatological Analysis of Late Quaternary Cores from the Northeastern Gulf of Mexico." *Science* 189 (September 26, 1975): 1083–88.

Eyton, J. Ronald, and Judith I. Parkhurst. "A Re-evaluation of the Extra Terrestrial Origin of the Carolina Bays." Department of Geography Paper no. 9, University of Illinois, Urbana Champaign, April l975.

Fallon, Stephen. *Guide to Cuba*. 1995. Reprint, Chalfont St. Peter, Buckinghamshire, England, and Old Saybrook, Conn.: Bradt/Globe Pequot Press, 1996.

Fears, J. Rufus, "The Historical Perspective: Atlantis and the Minoan Thalassocracy—A Study in Modern Mythopoeism." In *Atlantis: Fact or Fiction?* Edited by Edwin S. Ramage, 103–36. London and Bloomington, Ind.: Indiana University Press, 1978.

Fell, Barry. "Alphabetic Libyan Mason's Marks on Mochica Adobe Bricks." *ESOP* 20 (1991): 224–30.

———. *America BC: Ancient Settlers in the New World.* 1976. New York: Quadrangle/The New York Times Book Co., 1977. Revised edition, New York: Pocket Books, 1989.

Fell, Barry, and James P. Whittall. "Proposed Correlation of North American and European Culture Sequences." In *America BC: Ancient Settlers in the New World* by Barry Fell, rear inside board. 1976. New York: Quadrangle/The New York Times Book Co., 1977. Revised edition, New York: Pocket Books, 1989.

Fingerhut, Eugene R. *Explorers of Pre-Columbian America: The Diffusionist Inventionist Controversy.* Claremont, Calif.: California State University, Los Angeles/Regina Books, 1994.

Flem-Ath, Rand, and Rose Flem-Ath. *When the Sky Fell: In Search of Atlantis.* London: Weidenfeld and Nicolson, 1995.

Forsyth, Phyllis Young. *Atlantis: The Making of Myth.* Montreal and London: McGillQueen's University Press/Croom Helm, 1980.

Frazer, James George. *Folk-lore in the Old Testament.* 3 vols. London: Macmillan, 1919.

Freeman, Kathleen. *The Work and Life of Solon.* London: University of Wales Press, 1926.

Fritze, Ronald H. *Legend and Lore of the Americas before 1492.* 1988. Reprint, Santa Barbara, Calif., and Denver, Colo.: ABC-CLIO/Oxford, 1993.

Gaffarel, Paul, *Histoire de la découverte de l'Amerique depuis les origines jusqu'a la mort de Christophe Coolomb.* 2 vols. Paris: Societe Bourguignonne de Geographie et Histoire, 1892.

Galanopoulos, A. G., and E. Bacon. Atlantis: The Truth behind the Legend. London: Nelson, 1969.

Galvão, António. *The Discoveries of the World from Their First Originall unto to the Yeere of Our Lord 1555.* See Raleigh, *Discoverie of Guiana.*

Gamboa, Pedro Sarmiento de, *History of the Incas, and Captain Baltasar de Ocampo: The Execution of the Inca Tupac Amaru.* Translated by Sir Clements Markham. N.p.: Hakluyt Society, 1907.

Gardiner, Alan H. *Egypt of the Pharaohs.* 1961. Reprint, OUP, 1964.

———. *The Royal Canon of Turin.* 1959. Reprint, OUP, 1987.

Gardner, Laurence. *Bloodline of the Holy Grail.* London: Element Books, 1996.

Gifford, John A. "The Bimini 'Cyclopean' Complex." *International Journal of Nautical Archaeology and Underwater Exploration* 2 (1973): 189.

Gilbert, Adrian, and Maurice Cotterell. *The Mayan Prophecies.* Shaftesbury, Dorset, England: Element Books, 1995.

Gilmore, Donald Y., and Linda S. McElroy, eds. *Across Before Columbus? Evidence for Transoceanic Contact with the Americas prior to 1492.* Edgecomb, Maine: NEARA Publications, 1998.

Ginzberg, L. *The Legends of the Jews.* Vol. 1. Philadelphia, Pa.: The Jewish Publication Society of America, 1909.

Goodrick-Clarke, Nicholas. *The Occult Roots of Nazism.* 1985. Reprint, New York and London: I. B. Tauris, 1992.

Gordon, Cyrus H. *Before Columbus: Links between the Old World and Ancient America.* 1971. Reprint, London: Turnstone Press, 1972.

Green, Peter. *Alexander to Actium: The Hellenistic Age.* London: Thames and Hudson, 1993.

Griffiths, J. Gwyn. "Atlantis and Egypt." In *Atlantis and Egypt with Other Selected Essays,* 3–30. Cardiff: University of Wales Press, 1991.

Guthrie, James L. "Human Lymphocite Antigens: Apparent AfroAsiatic, South Asian and European HLAs in Indigenous American Populations." Unpublished draft, February 1998.

Hadingham, Evan. *Early Man and the Cosmos.* London: William Heinemann, 1983.

Haliburton, R. G. *The History of Man Derived from a Companion of the Customs and Superstitions of Nations: The Festivals of the Dead.* Halifax, Nova Scotia, Canada: T. Chamberlain, 1863.

Hancock, Graham, Robert Bauval, and John Grigsby. *The Mars Mystery.* London: Michael Joseph, 1998.

Hapgood, Charles. *Maps of the Ancient Sea Kings.* 1966. London: Turnstone Books, 1979.

Harden, Donald. *The Phoenicians.* London: Thames and Hudson, 1962.

———. "The Phoenicians on the West Coast of Africa." *Antiquity* XXII (1948): 141–50.

Harlow, George. "Hard Rock: A Mineralogist Explores the Origins of Mesoamerican Jade." Unpublished paper. New York: Department of Mineral Sciences at the American Museum of Natural History, nd., circa 1998

Harris, Zellig. *A Grammar of Phoenician Language.* New Haven, Conn.: American Oriental Society, 1936.

Harrison, W. "Atlantis Undiscovered—Bimini, Bahamas." *Nature* 230 (April 2, 1971): 287–89.

Hastings, James, ed., *Encyclopaedia of Religion and Ethics*. 13 vols. 1915. Reprint, Edinburgh: T. and T. Clark, 1930.

Heine-Geldern, Robert. "Ein Römischer Fund aus dem Vorkolumbischen Mexiko." *Anzeiger der Osterreichischen Akademie der Wissenschaften* 16 (1961): 117–19.

Hellanicus of Lesbos. *Atlantis*. In *The Sunken Kingdom: The Atlantis Mystery Solved* by Peter James. 1995. Reprint, London: Pimlico, 1996.

Hennig, R. *Terrae incognitae*. Leiden, the Netherlands, 1936.

Herodotus. *The History of Herodotus*. 2 vols (vol. 1: bks. 1-4; vol. 2: bks. 5–9). 1910. London and New York: J. M. Dent/E. P. Dutton, 1940.

Hesiod, *Theogony*. See Banks, *Works of Hesiod, Callimachus, and Theognis*.

Heyerdahl, Thor. *Early Man and the Ocean*. London: George Allen and Unwin, 1978.

Hibben, Frank C. *The Lost Americans*. New York: Thomas Y. Crowell, 1946.

Hill, Robert T. *Cuba and Puerto Rico with the Other Islands of the West Indies*. London: T. Fisher Unwin, 1898.

Hine, Albert C., and John C. Steinmetz. "Cay Sal Bank, Bahamas—A Partially Drowned Carbonate Platform." *Marine Geology* 59 (1984): 135–64.

Hitching, Francis. *The Mysterious World—An Atlas of the Unexplained*. 1978. Reprint, New York: Holt, Rinehart and Winston, 1979.

Homer. *The Iliad*. English translation by A. T. Murray. 2 vols. 1925. Reprint, Cambridge, Mass., and London: Harvard University Press/William Heinemann, 1967.

———. *The Odyssey*. English translation by A. T. Murray. 2 vols. 1919. Reprint, Cambridge, Mass., and London: Harvard University Press/William Heinemann, 1984.

Hosea, L. M. "Atlantis: A Statement of the 'Atlantic' Theory Respecting Aboriginal Civilization." *Cincinnati Quarterly Journal of Science* II, no. 3 (July 1875): 193–211.

Houlihan, Patrick F. *The Animal World of the Pharaohs*. London: Thames and Hudson, 1996.

Hutton, William. *Coming Earth Changes—the Latest Evidence*. 1996. Reprint, Virginia Beach, Va.: ARE Press, 1997.

Ingram, Roy L., Maryanne Robinson, and Howard T. Odum. "Clay Mineralogy of Some Carolina Bay Sediments." *Southeastern Geology* 1 (1959): 1–10.

Irwin, Constance. *Fair Gods and Stone Faces: Ancient Seafarers and the New World's Most Intriguing Riddle*. 1963. Reprint, London: W. H. Allen, 1964.

Jacobs, William. "Toke Like an Egyptian." *Fortean Times,* December 1998, 34–38.

Jairazbhoy, R. A. *Ancient Egyptians and Chinese in America.* London: George Prior Associated Publishers, 1974.

James, Peter. *The Sunken Kingdom: The Atlantis Mystery Solved.* 1995. Reprint, London: Pimlico, 1996.

James, Peter, and Nick Thorpe. *Ancient Inventions.* 1994. Reprint, London: Michael O'Mara Books, 1996.

Jelinkova, E. A. E., "The Shebtiw in the Temple of Edfu." *ZAS,* no. 87 (1962): 41–54.

Jimenez, A. Nuñez. *Cuevas y pictografías.* Havana, Cuba: Estudios Espeleologicos y Arquelogicos, 1964.

Johnson, Donald S. *Phantom Islands of the Atlantic.* 1994. Reprint, London: Souvenir Press, 1997.

Johnson, Douglas W. "Supposed Meteorite Scars of South Carolina," *Science* 79 (1934): 461.

Joseph, Frank. "Project Alta: Search and Discovery in the Bahamas." *Ancient American* 3, no. 23 (April/May 1998): 2–7.

Joyce, Thomas A. *Central American and West Indian Archaeology.* London: Philip Lee Warner, 1916.

Kaster, Joseph, trans and ed. *Wings of the Falcon: Life and Thought in Ancient Egypt.* New York: Holt, Rinehart, and Winston, 1968.

Keegan, William F. *Bahamian Archaeology: Life in the Bahamas and Turks and Caicos before Columbus.* Nassau, Bahamas: Media Publishing, 1997.

Kelly, Allan O. "The Origin of the Carolina Bays and the Oriented Lakes of Alaska." *Popular Astronomy* 59 (1951): 199–205.

Kelly, Allan O., and Frank Dachille. *Target: Earth—The Role of Large Meteors in Earth Science.* Carlsbad, Calif.: Target: Earth, 1953.

Kelso de Montigny, Alan H. "Did a Gigantic Meteorite, i.e., an Asteroid, Fall into the Caribbean, and Thus Create the Lesser Antilles about 6000 Years Ago?" *International Anthropological and Linguistic Review* 1, no. 4 (1954): 229–38.

———. "Redating the Past." *International Anthropological and Linguistic Review* 1, no. 2–3 (1954): 185–87.

Kennedy, Roger G. *Hidden Cities—The Discovery and Loss of Ancient North American Civilization,* London and New York: Penguin, 1994.

Keyser, Paul T. "From Myth to Map: The Blessed Isles in the First Century BC." *Ancient World* 24, pt. 2 (1993): 149–68.

Kloosterman, Johan B. "The Usselo Horizon, a Worldwide Charcoal-Rich Layer of Alleröd Age." Unpublished paper, 1999.

Kobres, R. "The Path of a Comet and Phaeton's Ride." *World and I* 10 (February 1995): 394–405.

Koudriavtsev, Viatscheslav. *Atlantis: Ice Age Civilization.* Moscow: Institute of Metahistory, 1997.

Krickeberg, W., W. Muller, H. Trimborn, and O. Zerries. *Pre-Columbian American Religions.* London: Weidenfeld and Nicolson, 1968.

Kurlansky, Mark. *Cod: A Biography of the Fish That Changed the World.* 1997. Reprint, London: Jonathan Cape, 1998.

Landa, Diego de. "Relacion de las casas de Yucatán." In *Mysteries of the Mexican Pyramids* by Peter Tompkins. 1976. Reprint, London: Thames and Hudson, 1987.

Landsburg, Alan, and Sally Landsburg. *In Search of Ancient Mysteries.* London: Corgi, 1974.

Las Casas, Bartolome. *History of the Indies.* Translated by Andrée Collard. New York and London: Torchbook/Harper and Row, 1971.

Lawton, Ian, and Chris Ogilvie-Herald. *Giza: The Truth.* London: Virgin, 1999.

Lemprière, J. *A Classical Dictionary.* London: Routledge, 1919.

Leonard, R. Cedric. *Quest for Atlantis.* New York: Manor Books, 1979.

Levy, David H. *Comets: Creators and Destroyers.* New York: Touchstone/Simon and Schuster, 1998.

Lichtheim, Miriam. *Ancient Egyptian Literature.* Vol. 1. *The Old and Middle Kingdoms.* 1973. Reprint, Berkeley, Los Angeles, London: University of California Press, 1975.

Little, Dr. Gregory L. "The A.R.E.'s Search For Atlantis—2007 Summary: Part Two of Three: Discoveries at Bimini: Columns, Marble Building Ruins, and Possible Building Foundations in 100-Feet of Water." *Alternative Perceptions Magazine* 115 (August 2007).

———. "2011 Great Bahama Bank Expedition Report." AP Magazine. http:// apmagazine.info/index.php?option=com_content&view=article&id=191 (accessed February 19, 2016).

Little, Gregory L., and Lora Little. "Search For Atlantis Project: 2012." AP Magazine. www.apmagazine.info/index.php?option=com_content&view =article&id=317 (accessed February 19, 2016).

Little, Gregory L., and Lora H. Little. *The A.R.E.'s Search for Atlantis: The*

Ongoing Search for Edgar Cayce's Atlantis in the Bahamas. Memphis, Tenn.: Eagle Wing Books, 2003.

Lizana, Bernardo de. *Devocionario de Nuestra Señora de Izamal y conquista espiritual de Yucatánci.* Valladolid, Spain: Gerónimo Morillo, 1633.

Love, Bruce. *The Paris Codex: Handbook for a Maya Priest.* Austin, Texas: University of Texas Press, 1994.

Luce, J. V. *The End of Atlantis: New Light on an Old Legend.* 1969. Reprint, np.: Thames and Hudson/Book Club Associates, 1973.

Mahan, Joseph B. *The Secret—America in World History before Columbus.* Columbus, Ga.: privately published, 1983.

Markman, Roberta H., and Peter T. Markman. *The Flayed God: The Mesoamerican Mythological Tradition.* San Francisco: Harper, 1992.

Marx, Robert F. *The Search for Sunken Treasure.* Toronto, Ont.: Key Porter Books, 1996.

Mavor, James W. *Voyage to Atlantis.* London: Souvenir Press, 1969.

McCampbell, John. "Meteorites and the 'Carolina Bays.'" *Popular Astronomy* 53 (1944): 338–92.

McGlone, William R., Phillip M. Leonard, James L. Guthrie, Rollin W. Gillespie, and James P. Whittall Jr. *Ancient American Inscriptions: Plow Marks or History?* Sutton, Mass.: Early Sites Research Society, 1993.

Mackenzie, Donald A. *Myths of Pre-Columbian America.* London: Gresham, nd., circa 1924.

Meggers, Betty J. "Jomon-Valdivia Similarities: Convergence or Contact?" In *Across Before Columbus? Evidence for Transoceanic Contact with the Americas prior to 1492,* edited by Donald Y. Gilmore and Linda S. McElroy, 11–19. Edgecomb, Maine: NEARA Publications, 1998.

Mellaart, James. *Çatal Hüyük—A Neolithic Town in Anatolia.* London: Thames and Hudson, 1967.

Melton, F. A. "The Origin of the Carolina 'Bays.'" *Discovery,* June 1934, 151–54.

Melton, F. A., and W. Schriever. "The Carolina 'Bays'—Are They Meteorite Scars?" *Journal of Geology* 41 (1933): 52–66.

Merezhkovsky, Dimitri. *The Secret of the West.* 1933. Reprint, London: Jonathan Cape, 1936.

Miller, Mary, and Karl Taube. *The Gods and Symbols of Ancient Mexico and the Maya.* 1993. London: Thames and Hudson, 1997.

Moore, W. G. *The Penguin Encyclopedia of Places.* 1971. Harmondsworth, Middlesex, England: Penguin, 1978.

Morison, Samuel Eliot. *Christopher Columbus, Mariner.* 1942. Reprint, London: Meridian/Penguin, 1983.

Mortimer, William Golden, *Peru: History of Coca, "the Divine Plant of the Incas."* New York: J. H. Vail and Company, 1901.

Moure, Ramón Dacal, and Manuel Rivero de la Calle. *Arqueologia aborigen de Cuba.* Havana, Cuba: Gente Nueva, 1986.

Muck, Otto. *The Secret of Atlantis.* 1976. Reprint, London: Collins, 1978.

Muldrow, Edna. "The Comet That Struck the Carolinas." *Harper's,* pt. 168, 1933, 83–89.

Muller, C. *Geographi Graeci minores.* 3 vols. Paris, 1855–61.

Muller, J. G. *Geschichte der Amerikanischen Urreligionen.* Basel, Switzerland: Schweighauferischen Berlagsbuchhandlung, 1855.

Nash, William Giles. *America: The True History of its Discovery.* London: Grant Richards, 1926.

New Encyclopedia Britannica. Vol. 10. Chicago, Ill.: University of Chicago, 1993.

Newby, P. H. *Warrior Pharaohs: The Rise and Fall of the Egyptian Empire.* London: Faber and Faber, 1980.

Nininger, H. H. "When the Sky Rains Stone and Iron." *Literary Digest* 117 (March 17, 1934): 16, 29.

Nordenskiöld, A. E. *Periplus: An Essay on the Early History of Charts and Sailing-Directions.* 1897. Reprint, New York: Burt Franklin, nd.

O'Brien, Christian, and Barbara Joy O'Brien. *The Shining Ones.* Kemble, Cirencester, Gloucestershire, England: Dianthus Publishing, 1997.

O'Connor, David. "The Earliest Royal Boat Graves." *Egyptian Archaeology* 6 (1995): 3–7.

Odelain, O., and R. Séguineau. *Dictionary of Proper Names and Places in the Bible.* 1966. Reprint, London: Robert Hale, 1991.

Olivier, Chas. P. "The Great Siberian Meteorite: An Account of the Most Remarkable Astronomical Event of the Twentieth Century, from Official Records." *Scientific American,* July 1928, 42–44.

Ovid. *Tristia and Ex Ponto.* Translated by Arthur Leslie Wheeler. London: William Heinemann, 1924. Reprint, Cambridge, Mass.: Harvard University Press, 1965.

Palmer, Robert. *The Blue Holes of the Bahamas.* London: Jonathan Cape, 1985.

Pearson, Richard. "Migration from Japan to Ecuador: The Japanese Evidence." *American Anthropology* 70 (1968): 85–86.

Phillips, Graham. *Act of God: Moses, Tutankhamun and the Myth of Atlantis.* London: Sidgwick and Jackson, 1998.

Picard, Gilbert Charles, and Colette Picard. *The Life and Death of Carthage.* Sidgwick and Jackson, 1968.

Plafker, George. "Oriented Lakes and Lineaments in Northern Bolivia." *Bulletin of the Geological Society of America.* 75 (1964): 503–22.

Plato. *Critias.* See Taylor, *Plato: Timaeus and Critias.*

Plato. *The Laws.* Translated by Trevor J. Saunders. 1970. Reprint, Harmondsworth, Middlesex, England: Penguin, 1984.

Plato. *Timaeus.* See Cornford, *Plato's Cosmology,* and Davis, *Works of Plato.*

Pliny. *Natural History,* 10 vols. (vol. I: books 1–2; vol. II: books 3–7; vol. 3: books 8–11; vol. IV: books 12–16; vol. V: books 17–19; vol. VI: books 20–23; vol. VII: books 24–27; vol. VIII: books 28–32; vol. IX: books 33–35; vol. X: 36–37). Vols. 1–5, and 9 translated by H. Rackham, vols. 6–8 translated by W. H. S. Jones, and vol. 10 translated by D. E. Eichholz. Cambridge, Mass./London: William Heinemann, 1949–54.

Plutarch. *The Face of the Moon.* See Plutarch, *Plutarch's Moralia.*

———. *Isis and Osiris.* See Plutarch, *Plutarch's Moralia.*

———. *Lives,* trans. John and William Landhorne, William Tegg, London, 1865

———. *Plutarch's Moralia,* Translated by H. Cherniss and W. C. Helmbold. London: William Heinemann, 1957.

Popol Vuh. See Tedlock, *Popol Vuh.*

Powell, Major J. W. "Mythologic Philosophy: 1. The Genesis of Philosophy." *Popular Science Monthly,* October 1879, 795–808.

Prado, A. *The World of Ancient Spain.* Geneva, Switzerland: Minerva, Genéve, 1976.

Prescott, William H. *History of the Conquest of Mexico.* 2 vols. New and revised edition, London: George Routledge and Sons, 1843.

Proclus. *The Commentaries of Proclus on the* Timaeus *of Plato.* Translated by Thomas Taylor. 2 vols. London: Privately printed, 1820.

Prouty, W. F. "Carolina Bays and Their Origin." *Bulletin of the Geological Society of America* 63 (February 1952): 167–222.

Przeworski, Stefan. "Notes d'archeologie Syrienne et Hittite." *Syria* 11 (1930): 133–45.

Raleigh, Sir Walter. *The Discoverie of Guiana,* and António Galvão, *The Discoveries of the World from Their First Originall unto the Yeere of Our Lord 1555.* 2 books in 1 vol. 1601, Reprint, Bibliotheca Americana/The World Publishing Company, Cleveland, Ohio, 1966.

Ramage, Edwin S., ed. *Atlantis: Fact or Fiction?* London and Bloomington, Ind.: Indiana University Press, 1978.

Ravenstein, E. G. *Martin Behaim: His Life and His Globe.* London: George Philip, 1908.

Reader's Digest. *The World's Last Mysteries.* London, New York, Montreal, Sydney, Cape Town: Reader's Digest Association, 1977.

Recinos, Adrián, and Delia Goetz, trans. *The Annals of the Cakchiquels.* In *The Annals of the Cakchiquels/Title of the Lords of Totonicapán,* translated by Dionisio José Chonay, Delia Goetz, and Adrián Recinos. 2 books in 1 vol. Norman, Okla.: University of Oklahoma Press, 1953.

Reeves, Nicholas, and Richard H. Wilkinson. *The Complete Valley of the Kings.* London: Thames and Hudson, 1996.

"Research Verifies Use of Hashish, Cocaine, Nicotine in Prehistoric Cultures." *Sociology of Drugs,* March 1993.

Reuters. "Looking for Lost Riches in Cuba's Seas: Underwater Surveyors Say They May Have Found Sunken City." May 14, 2001.

Reymond, E. A. E. *The Mythical Origin of the Egyptian Temple.* Npp.: Manchester University Press, 1969.

Riverend, Julio le. *Brief History of Cuba.* Havana, Cuba: Instituto Cubano del Libro, 1997.

Ross, W. D. *The Works of Aristotle.* vol. 3. 1931. Reprint, Oxford, England: OUP, 1963.

Roux, Georges. *Ancient Iraq.* 1966. Reprint, London: Penguin, 1980.

Sahagún, Fray Bernardino de. *Florentine Codex, Book 12: The Conquest of Mexico.* Translated and edited by A. J. O. Anderson and C. E. Dibble. Santa Fe, N.M.: The School of American Research and the University of Utah, 1955.

Sanchoniathon *The Theology of the Phoenicians.* See Cory, *Cory's Ancient Fragments.*

Savage, H., Jr. *The Mysterious Carolina Bays.* Columbia, S.C., University of South Carolina Press, 1982.

Schulten, Adolf. *Tartessos, ein Beitrag zur ältesten Geschichte des Westerns.* Hamburg, Germany: L. Friederichsen, 1922.

Shinn, E. A. "Atlantis: Bimini Hoax." *Sea Frontiers* 24, no. 3 (May–June 1978): 130–42.

Sklar, Dusty. *Gods and Beasts: The Nazis and the Occult.* New York: Thomas Y. Crowell, 1977.

Smith, G. Elliot. *Elephants and Ethnologists.* London and New York: Kegan Paul, Trench, Trubner / E. P. Dutton, 1924.

Solinus, Caius Julius. *Polyhistor: De memoralibus mundi.* Venice: 1498.

Sorenson, John L., and Martin H. Raish. *Pre-Columbian Contact with the Americas across the Oceans: An Annotated Bibliography.* 2 vols. 1996. Provo, Utah: Research Press, 1996.

Soustelle, Jacques. *The Olmecs: The Oldest Civilization in Mexico.* 1979. Reprint, Norman, Okla.: University of Oklahoma Press, 1985.

Spedicato, Emilio. "Apollo Objects, Atlantis and Other Tales: A Catastrophical Scenario for Discontinuities in Human History." 1st revised ed., *NEARA* (Journal of New England Antiquities Research Association) 26 (1991): 1–14. Also published in *Kadath* 84 (1995): 29–55. All references taken from the fifth section of the revised edition, titled "An Interpretation of the Plutonic Story of Atlantis."

Spence, Lewis. *Atlantis in America.* London: Ernest Benn, 1925.

———. *The Myths of Mexico and Peru.* 1913. Reprint, London: George G. Harrap, 1920.

Stacy-Judd, Robert B. *Atlantis—Mother of Empires.* 1939. Reprint, Santa Monica, Calif.: De Vorss and Co., 1973.

Stanley, Thomas, trans. *Claudius Aelianus His Various History.* London: Thomas Dring, 1665.

Steede, Neil. "Comalcalco: An Early Classic Maya Site." In *Across Before Columbus? Evidence for Transoceanic Contact with the Americas prior to 1492,* edited by Donald Y. Gilmore and Linda S. McElroy, 35–40. Edgecomb, Maine: NEARA Publications, 1998.

———. "Mexico's Pyramidal Comalcalco—A Thousand Years Older Than Suspected." *Ancient American* 4, no. 26 (January–February 1999): 16.

Steele, John. "Bimini Revealed." In *The Mysterious World—An Atlas of the Unexplained,* by Francis Hitching, 141–43. 1978. Reprint, New York: Holt, Rinehart and Winston, 1979.

Steiger, Brad. *Atlantis Rising.* 1973. Reprint, London: Sphere, 1977.

Steward, J. H., ed. *Handbook of South American Indians.* Vol. IV, *The Circum-Caribbean Tribes,* New York: Cooper Square Publishers, 1963.

Stirling, Matthew W. "Discovering the New World's Oldest Dated Work of Man." *National Geographic Magazine* 76 (August 1939): 183–218.

———. "Great Stone Faces of the Mexican Jungle." *National Geographic Magazine* 78, no. 3 (September 1940): 309–34.

Strabo. *The Geography of Strabo.* English translation by Horace Leonard Jones. 8 vols. Vol. I, 1917; vol. II, 1923, London: William Heinemann; Reprints, vol. I, 1949; vol. II, 1988, Cambridge, Mass.: Harvard University Press.

Strode, Hudson. *The Pageant of Cuba.* Jarrolds, London, 1935

Tabío, Ernesto E., and Estrella Rey. *Prehistoria de Cuba, Historia.* Havana, Cuba, Editorial de Ciencias Sociales, 1985.

Taylor, A. E. *Plato: Timaeus and Critias.* London: Methuen, 1929.

Tedlock, Dennis, trans. *Popol Vuh: The Mayan Book of the Dawn of Life,* 1985. New York: Touchstone/Simon and Schuster, 1996.

Thacher, John Boyd. *Christopher Columbus: His Life, His Work, His Remains.* 3 vols. 1903. New York: AMS Press/Kraus Reprint Corp. 1967.

Thomson, J. Oliver. *History of Ancient Geography.* Cambridge, Mass.: Cambridge University Press, 1948.

Thompson, Edward Herbert. *People of the Serpent: Life and Adventure among the Maya.* London: G. P. Putnam's Sons, 1932.

Thucydides. *The History of the Peloponnesian War.* Translated by Richard Crawley. 1910. Reprint, London: J. M. Dent, 1957.

Tompkins, Peter. *Mysteries of the Mexican Pyramids.* 1976. Reprint, London: Thames and Hudson, 1987.

Toor, Francis. *A Treasury of Mexican Folkways.* New York: Crown, 1947.

Vaillant, George C. "A Bearded Mystery." *Natural History.* 31 (May–June 1931): 243–52.

Valentine, J. Manson. "Archaeological Enigmas of Florida and the Western Bahamas." *Muse News* (Miami Museum of Science), June 1969.

———. "Underwater Archaeology in the Bahamas." *Explorers Journal,* December 1976, 176–83.

Van Sertima, Ivan. *They Came Before Columbus.* New York: Random House, 1976.

Van Zantwijk, R. *The Aztec Arrangement: The Social History of Pre-Spanish Mexico.* Norman, Okla.: University of Oklahoma Press, 1984.

Vaughan, J., and C. A. Geissler. *The New Oxford Book of Food Plants.* Oxford, England: OUP, 1997.

vonHagen, Victor W. *The Golden Man: The Quest for El Dorado.* Farnborough, Hants, Hampshire, England: Saxon House/BCA, 1974.

Ward, William A. "Ancient Lebanon." In *Cultural Resources in Lebanon.* Beirut, Lebanon: Beirut College for Women, 1969.

Weiner, Leo. *Africa and the Discovery of America.* vol. 2. Philadelphia, Pa.: Innes and Sons, 1922.

Whishaw, E. M. *Atlantis in Andalucia: A Study of Folk Memory*. London: Rider, 1929.

Wilber, R. Jude, John D. Milliman, and Robert B. Halley. "Accumulation of Bank-Top Sediment on the Western Slope of Great Bahama Bank: Rapid Progradation of a Carbonate Megabank." *Geology* 18 (October 1990): 970–74.

Wilkins, Harold T. *Secret Cities of Old South America: Atlantis Unveiled*. London: Rider and Co., 1952.

Williams, Gwyn A. *Madoc: The Making of a Myth*. Fakenham, Norfolk, England: Eyre Methuen, 1979.

Wilson, Beckles. *Lost Lyonesse: Evidence, Records and Traditions of England's Atlantis*. 1902. Reprint, London: AdCo Associates, 1986.

Wilson, Derek. *The World Atlas of Treasure*. London: Pan Books/BCA, 1981.

Wright, G. Ernest. *Biblical Archaeology*. Philadelphia, Pa., and London: Westminster Press/Gerald Duckworth, 1957.

Wright, Herbert E., Jr. "Glacial Fluctuations, Sea-Level Changes, and Catastrophic Floods." In *Atlantis: Fact or Fiction?* Edited by Edwin S. Ramage, 161–74. London and Bloomington, Ind.: Indiana University Press, 1978.

Wright, Herbert E., Jr., Harvey L. Patten, and Thomas C. Winter. "Two Pollen Diagrams from Southeastern Minnesota: Problems in the Regional Late-Glacial and Postglacial Vegetational History." *Geological Society of America Bulletin* 74 (1963) 1,371–95 and plates.

Wylie, C. C. "On the Formation of Meteorite Craters." *Popular Astronomy* 41 (1933): 211–14.

Zangger, Eberhard. *The Flood from Heaven: Deciphering the Atlantis Legend*. London: Sidgwick and Jackson/Book Club Associates, 1992.

Zapp, Ivar, and George Erikson. *Atlantis in America: Navigators of the Ancient World*. Kempton, Ill.: Adventures Unlimited Press, 1998.

Zerries, Otto. "Primitive South America and the West Indies." In *Pre-Columbian American Religions,* W. Krickeberg, W. Muller, H. Trimborn, and O. Zerries. London: Weidenfeld and Nicolson, 1968.

Zhirov, N. F. *Atlantis—Atlantology: Basic Problems*. Moscow: Progress Publishers, 1970.

Zink, David. *The Stones of Atlantis*. Scarborough, Ont.: Prentice-Hall, 1978.

TV DOCUMENTARIES AND VIDEOS

Equinox. "Mystery of the Cocaine Mummies." BBC, Channel 4, 1996.

History Channel. "Paulina Zelitsky Discovers Symmetrical Structures 2200 Feet on Ocean Floor near Cuba." www.youtube.com/watch?v=x3EBGB3O3XI (accessed February 21, 2016).

Kenyon, Douglas, and Thomas Miller, producers; Cecila Gonzalez, director. "A Special Report: Atlantis in the Bahamas." Unbroadcast television documentary, circa late 1970s.

INDEX

Numbers in *italics* preceded by *pl.* indicate plate numbers.

ABOUT THE AUTHOR

Andrew Collins is a writer and historian living in the United Kingdom. He is the author of more than a dozen books that challenge the way we perceive the past. Among them are *From the Ashes of Angels* (1996), which establishes that the Watchers of the Book of Enoch and the Anunnaki of the Sumerian texts were a powerful elite that catalyzed the Neolithic revolution in the Near East at the end of the last Ice Age; *Gods of Eden* (1998), which demonstrates the greater antiquity of Egyptian civilization, and *Tutankhamun: The Exodus Conspiracy* (coauthored with Chris Ogilvie Herald, 2002), which reveals the truth behind the discovery of Tutankhamun's famous tomb; *The Cygnus Mystery* (1999), which shows that the constellation of Cygnus has been universally venerated as the place of first creation and the entrance to the sky world since Paleolithic times; and *LightQuest* (2012), which demonstrates that many UFOs are most likely plasma constructs that display sentience, clear intelligence, and interactive qualities.

In 2008 Andrew and colleague Nigel Skinner Simpson discovered a previously unrecorded cave complex beneath the pyramids of Giza, which has brought him worldwide acclaim. It is a story told in his book *Beneath the Pyramids* (2009). Andrew is also the author of *Göbekli Tepe: Genesis of the Gods* (2014), which reveals the role played by Göbekli Tepe in the origins of civilization and the rise of myths and legends regarding the Watchers of the Book of Enoch, the Anunnaki of Mesopotamian mythology, and the Garden of Eden of the book of Genesis.

For more information on Andrew Collins, go to **www.andrewcollins.com.**

BOOKS OF RELATED INTEREST

Gobekli Tepe: Genesis of the Gods
The Temple of the Watchers and the Discovery of Eden
by Andrew Collins
Introduction by Graham Hancock

From the Ashes of Angels
The Forbidden Legacy of a Fallen Race
by Andrew Collins

Atlantis beneath the Ice
The Fate of the Lost Continent
by Rand Flem-Ath and Rose Flem-Ath
Afterword by John Anthony West

Our Dolphin Ancestors
Keepers of Lost Knowledge and Healing Wisdom
by Frank Joseph

Atlantis and the Coming Ice Age
The Lost Civilization—A Mirror of Our World
by Frank Joseph

Advanced Civilizations of Prehistoric America
The Lost Kingdoms of the Adena, Hopewell,
Mississippians, and Anasazi
by Frank Joseph

Lost Knowledge of the Ancients
A Graham Hancock Reader
Edited by Glenn Kreisberg

Forbidden History
Prehistoric Technologies, Extraterrestrial Intervention,
and the Suppressed Origins of Civilization
Edited by J. Douglas Kenyon

INNER TRADITIONS • BEAR & COMPANY
P.O. Box 388 • Rochester, VT 05767 • 1-800-246-8648
www.InnerTraditions.com

Or contact your local bookseller